RUSSIA'S HERO CITIES

RUSSIA'S HERO CITIES

FROM POSTWAR RUINS TO
SOVIET HEROARCHY

―❦―

IVO MIJNSSEN

INDIANA UNIVERSITY PRESS

This book is a publication of

Indiana University Press
Office of Scholarly Publishing
Herman B Wells Library 350
1320 East 10th Street
Bloomington, Indiana 47405 USA

iupress.org

© 2021 by Ivo Mijnssen

All rights reserved
No part of this book may be reproduced or utilized in any form or by any means, electronic or mechanical, including photocopying and recording, or by any information storage and retrieval system, without permission in writing from the publisher. The paper used in this publication meets the minimum requirements of the American National Standard for Information Sciences—Permanence of Paper for Printed Library Materials, ANSI Z39.48-1992.

Manufactured in the United States of America

Cataloging information is available from the Library of Congress.

ISBN 978-0-253-05620-7 (hardback)
ISBN 978-0-253-05622-1 (paperback)
ISBN 978-0-253-05621-4 (ebook)

First Printing 2021

For Jessy

CONTENTS

Acknowledgments   ix

Note on Transliteration   xiii

The Hero Cities   xv

Short Description of Hero Cities   xvii

1. Heroism across Generations   1
2. Creating an Idealized Past: The Soviet Heroarchy from Stalin to Brezhnev   14
3. Victory Square: The Place of Memory in Tula   58
4. Great Expectations: A Worthy Life   98
5. Novorossiysk as a Monumental Ensemble: Little Land and the Ideal of War   141
6. Brezhnev's Beloved Novorossiysk: Wartime Glory and Window to the World   186
7. Impossible Continuity   230

Appendix: Archives and Interviews   263

Bibliography   267

Index   295

ACKNOWLEDGMENTS

THIS BOOK'S GENESIS BEGAN IN May 2009, not far from Saint Petersburg. That the Hero City of Leningrad's past continues to shape the identity of the "Northern Capital" is obvious to all visitors who pass the neoclassicist columns on the highway from the airport and the war monument on the outskirts of town—not to speak of the imperial palaces.

But on that warm spring day, the traces of the Great Patriotic War, as Russians still call World War II, presented themselves in a different form: on a battlefield called Nevskiy Pyatachok, just about fifty miles from downtown. German and Soviet forces fought over this tiny but strategically significant bridgehead for a year and a half. Tens of thousands were killed.

When I approached it in 2009, I first noticed the pompous Soviet memorial next to the street. When we got out of the car, we walked past mass graves full of names, followed by newer graves with room for more names. Then, and without warning, we found ourselves in the middle of the battlefield, superficially grown over with grass. Right underneath, we saw trenches and remnants of field kitchens, but also boots, gas masks, and so many bones. The river Neva, immediately behind, still runs rusty brown because of all the metal in it.

I realized how close to the surface the war remains in contemporary Russia—both literally and figuratively. The political level is more obvious, the towering significance of war memory a key to understanding Putin's rule. Other aspects remain harder to discover, hidden in shame, unknown to the younger generation, shrouded in the secrecy of closed archives.

For a Swiss citizen whose country has been spared from the twentieth century's wars, the experience on Nevskiy Pyatachok was a physical reminder of their horror. And for someone like me, a historian of Eastern Europe, who had mostly approached the past through books, it felt like an impulse—to find out more about the Great Patriotic War's legacy, to go closer and to places that are perhaps lesser known. I chose the Hero Cities and the provincial centers of Tula and Novorossiysk.

In both cities, I not only found people who taught me a lot but also true allies, to whom I am very thankful. If I had not met Dima and Masha in a rather odd international youth camp at Lake Seliger in 2010, I do not think I would have ever even traveled to Tula. But they and their families hosted me and made sure I also experienced some of the more agreeable aspects of suburban Russian life.

Memorial, a crucial organization for anybody who is interested in Russia's difficult history provided me with amazing support—especially activist Pavel Ponarin and Memorial's honorary chair, Sergey Shcheglov. The journalist Irina Paramonova showed herself to be one of the best experts on the city's politics, and Natal'ya Spiridenko of the Levada Center Tula helped me identify additional respondents.

Novorossiysk's cultural life would doubtlessly be much poorer without the untiring local historian Sergey Novikov, who also read my chapters on the city and made sure I corrected some errors. Tamara Yurina wrote the most meticulously researched book on the battle, and she always answered all my detailed questions. Lyudmila Rostovtseva and Denis Konyukhov provided invaluable assistance in finding interviewees.

I am deeply grateful to the archivists and librarians in Tula, Novorossiysk, and Krasnodar. They do amazing work, with very little financial assistance, in rundown buildings, and for low wages. Even if this meant that I sometimes had to pay to use electricity and that regulations tended to be complicated and bureaucratic, they helped me where they could.

In the Moscow archives, I spent an unforgettable time in Galina Mikhailovna Tokareva's kingdom, the Komsomol archives—often with cookies and tea. In the Russian capital, I was also able to take advantage of advice and materials provided by Alexander Vatlin, Viktor Dönninghaus, and Ivan Kurilla. The drive out to the monument of the Panfilovtsy with Il'ya Andronov on a snowy winter day remains vivid in my memory. I appreciated the opportunity to work at Deutsches Historisches Institut Moskau thanks to a stipend from the institution.

I could not have conducted the research that went into this book without generous financial support from various institutions. The Basel Graduate School of History provided me with a yearlong research grant, which allowed me to get the project started. The Gerda Henkel Stiftung generously supported me between 2012 and 2015.

Along the way, I continued to be amazed by the passion of my colleagues and their love for their research. Polly Jones organized an archival research trip to Moscow, which not only acquainted me with the intricacies of working in these odd institutions but also introduced me to some wonderful people, among whom I would like to mention Vicky Davis in particular. She ended up writing a highly recommendable book about Novorossiysk.

As a visiting scholar at the Center for Russian, East European, and Eurasian Studies at Stanford University, I felt well taken care of by the staff and colleagues there, particularly Robert Crews, Norman Naimark, and the librarians at the Hoover Institution. I think back fondly to the long discussions and the Soviet film club I participated in with Markian Dobczansky, Anna Whittington, and Orysia Kulick.

The initial manuscript largely took shape in Basel and Zurich. At times, this felt like an endless process, and it was my colleagues in Basel who kept me company—during lunches at our shared office and over beers after work. Ever since we first worked together, almost fifteen years ago, Philipp Casula has been an intellectual inspiration and an attentive reader. Boris Belge organized a memorable conference on Brezhnevian "hyperstability" before he joined the team in Basel.

Many of them read parts or the entire manuscript—also during our retreats in Swiss mountain towns, when everybody wanted to enjoy the outdoors and nevertheless worked hard. Thanks to Anne Hasselmann, Jörn Happel, and Bianca Hönig for their extensive feedback and to Lenka Fehrenbach, Carla Cordin, Sandrine Mayoraz, Nadine Freiermuth-Samardzic, Alexis Hofmeister, and Martin Jesske for the for the collegiality they showed over many years. Nina Miric helped to polish the manuscript.

I am deeply grateful for my mentors and advisers who accompanied me on my academic journey. Abbot Gleason, who passed away too early, first sparked my interest in Soviet history at Brown; Heiko Haumann kept it alive in Basel. Frithjof Benjamin Schenk and Amir Weiner were the most uncomplicated dissertation advisers one could wish for. I fondly remember meeting Benjamin for the first time in Munich, where he agreed without any hesitation to take me on as a PhD candidate. Amir traveled all the way from California to Basel to take part in my defense and advised me on the American publication process, which can seem daunting at times.

Both of them understood that my decision to leave academia for a position at the newspaper *Neue Zürcher Zeitung* meant that the publication of this book would take a bit more time than planned. Peter Rásonyi, my boss at NZZ, was always very supportive, even if it meant that he had to grant me extended leaves to finish it. Andreas Rüesch, one of my kindred spirits at the paper, has read the conclusion and let me share in his Russia expertise. Last but not least, my favorite graphic designer at the paper, Anja Lemcke, agreed to draw a wonderful map for the book.

Jennika Baines, my editor at IUP, has guided me through the twists and turns of the publication process with clear demands and deadlines, which never hid her profound curiosity and enthusiasm. In the last phase, Sophia Hebert, Darja Malcolm-Clarke, and Megan Schindele were extremely competent and helpful sources of support. I am also grateful for the feedback of the two anonymous reviewers.

Finally, I could not have gotten through this without my friends and family, my neighbors at Bertastrasse in Zurich, who listened to me talk about Hero Cities for many hours. Steff Renner was a willing travel partner who joined me on adventures in Moscow and Krasnodar. I am grateful to my parents, Dani and Pete, for asking the right questions, reading parts of the manuscript, and making sure I knew they were confident in my path. My brother Remo and his family were the best distraction I could wish for.

My most important partner in this venture—aside from the four-legged Penny and Deliah, who spent hours snoring next to me or sitting on my lap—has been my wife, Jessy. You have put up with a life partner who was gone for months to do his research, sometimes distracted and stressed because of it, but you never questioned my decision to pursue it. I am thankful for your support, without which this would have been an extremely lonely path. This book is dedicated to you.

Vienna, September 2020

NOTE ON TRANSLITERATION

IN THE INTEREST OF READABILITY and intuitiveness, I apply the BGN/PCGN transliteration system. It does not contain any special characters but nevertheless allows for precision, including the use of soft and hard signs. The only exception is that I do not add a *Y* to the letter *E* at the beginning of a word or when it comes after vowels. In the reference notes, I use the following abbreviations when citing Russian archival material: f. for collection (*fond*), op. for inventory (*opis'*), d. for file or folder (*delo*), l. (*list*) for page and ll. (*listy*) for pages. Abbreviations for archival names are explained in the appendix.

Figure 0.1 Map showing the thirteen Hero Cities within the borders of the former Soviet Union. © Anja Lemcke

SHORT DESCRIPTION OF HERO CITIES

LENINGRAD

Besieged between September 1941 and January 1944, the population of Leningrad endured famine, cold, and relentless bombardment. On May 1, 1945, Joseph Stalin ordered a salute for four Hero Cities: Leningrad, Stalingrad, Sevastopol', and Odessa. In the following years, he purged Leningrad's leadership, jealous of its uniquely elevated symbolic status. Leningrad, called Saint Petersburg again today, was reintegrated into the Soviet canon of heroic places.

STALINGRAD/VOLGOGRAD

Soviet leaders already called the site of the most horrifying battle in World War II a Hero City during the conflict. It officially received the title in 1945. The completely destroyed city, renamed Volgograd in 1961, would become a symbol for reconstruction after the war as well as an industrial center. The memorial ensemble for the battle on Mamayev Kurgan today remains the most important war monument in the country.

SEVASTOPOL'

The battle for Sevastopol' lasted for more than eight months before the city fell on July 4, 1942. Even before it was named a Hero City on May 1, 1945, the Crimean port had become a symbol of dogged resistance against overwhelming enemy forces. Soviet propaganda often connected its sacrifice to the Crimean War in the 1850s. When Russia annexed the peninsula in 2014, Vladimir Putin used this tradition of military feats as one of the justifications.

ODESSA

The battle for Odessa began on August 8, 1941, and lasted more than two months before the evacuation of the remaining Soviet defenders and a significant part of the civilian population succeeded. Under Romanian and German occupation, tens of thousands of Jews were murdered, before the Red Army retook the city in 1944. It was recognized as a Hero City on May 1, 1945, after which it was rebuilt and became an important economic and tourism center.

MOSCOW

The Soviet capital was only elevated into the first tier of the Soviet heroarchy on May 8, 1965, twenty years after the end of the war. Before the rule of Leonid Brezhnev, Moscow's role had been somewhat controversial, as it stood for the first phase of the war, during which the USSR sustained catastrophic losses—not least because of the leadership's blunders. After 1965, however, Moscow became the most prominent Hero City.

BREST FORTRESS

The fortress on the 1939 border between Belarus and Poland was among the first places the Germans attacked during Operation Barbarossa on June 22, 1941. Some defenders held out for weeks, even though the front was already hundreds of miles to the east. Brest Fortress received the Gold Star on the eve of Victory Day in 1965. It subsequently became one of the most important centers of Soviet tourism and patriotic rituals.

KIEV

During the rapid German advance in the summer of 1941, the Soviet armies in the Ukrainian capital were encircled. When they surrendered on September 26, hundreds of thousands became prisoners of war, which meant certain death for many. The catastrophic defeat and the civil war–like conditions that persisted even after the war in Ukraine meant that Kiev was only recognized as a Hero City in 1965.

NOVOROSSIYSK

Novorossiysk's claim to heroism was based on its ability to withstand the German onslaught in the Caucasus and its service as one of the bridgeheads for the counteroffensive in 1943. Among the veterans of these battles was

Brezhnev, whose deep emotional connection and patronage guaranteed that Novorossiysk became a Hero City in 1973. For the same reason, the port city benefited greatly from large investment programs for housing and urban infrastructure.

KERCH'

The second Hero City in Crimea received its honorary title at the same time as Novorossiysk, on September 14, 1973. During the war, Kerch' changed hands multiple times between 1941 and 1944, being occupied for almost two years. Two Soviet landing operations to retake the city failed, at a loss of tens of thousands of lives. In 2018, four years after the annexation of Crimea, Russia built a strategically significant bridge from Kerch' to the mainland.

MINSK

The capital of Belarus received the Gold Star on June 26, 1974. Local historians attribute the long wait to its controversial wartime role: the city had fallen in the first days of the invasion and remained under German control for three years. During this time, some political groups and portions of the population collaborated with the Nazis. Minsk became a Hero City in recognition of its role as a center of partisan activity. In Belarus, the war cult remains a tenet of national ideology.

TULA

The last city awarded during the Brezhnev era, Tula became a Hero City on December 7, 1976. It has always stood in the shadow of Moscow, which is only two hundred kilometers away. Tula, however, was the first city in the autumn of 1941 to withstand the German tank armies on their seemingly unstoppable advance toward the capital. For the past three hundred years, Tula has been a crucial center of the defense industry.

SMOLENSK

Located on the main road to Moscow, Smolensk fell to the Wehrmacht on July 31, 1941. Three hundred thousand Soviet troops were encircled and taken prisoner in one of the most devastating early battles of the war. The Red Army retook the city only in July 1943, again under great loss. It became a Hero City on May 6, 1985.

MURMANSK

From June to October 1941, German and Finnish troops laid siege to the only Soviet port in the northern coast not to freeze in winter. They failed to take the city. Together with Smolensk, Murmansk was the only Soviet Hero City to receive the honorary title after Brezhnev's death, in May 1985. Three years later, the title was officially discontinued.

RUSSIA'S HERO CITIES

ONE

Heroism across Generations

AT DAWN ON SEPTEMBER 11, 1966, twenty-five hundred Soviet youngsters board buses to play at war. Twenty-five years have passed since the Red Army defended Moscow against the onslaught of the German Wehrmacht during the Great Patriotic War. Now, the members of the youth organization Komsomol gather for the finals of the All-Union Tours to the Sites of Revolutionary, Military, and Labor Glory (*Vsesoyuznyy Pokhod po Mestam Revolyutsyonnoy, Boevoy i Trudovoy Slavy*)—to show themselves as worthy successors of the wartime heroes and to pay tribute.

The young men and women, all of whom have won regional military-patriotic tournaments, fan out along the former front lines outside the capital. They compete in teams, conducting reconnaissance, clearing imaginary minefields, and destroying bridges. The general staff of the games makes sure the past feels as present as possible; during the maneuvers, draftees receive their enlisting orders directly from veterans of the war, and the organizers consistently appeal to youths' patriotic duty to the Union of Soviet Socialist Republics (USSR). They must be ready "to defend the achievements of [the] October [Revolution] at each frontier and at all times."[1]

Later in the day, commemorative rituals distance the present from the war while symbolically bridging the quarter century that has passed. Participants in the games end their missions by laying wreaths at monuments before they return to Moscow, where one hundred thousand peers welcome them. They collectively take an oath: "Here, on Red Square, in front of the Kremlin's holy walls, we, the grandchildren of those who stormed the Winter Palace, the children of those who took the Reichstag, swear with all of our hearts to be true to the cause of Lenin and the Party!"[2]

In order to heighten the symbolic power of the oath, the central square of the Soviet Union has been transformed into a festive commemorative landscape. World War II–era tanks, *Katyusha* missiles, and air defense guns create a sense of military readiness.[3] Posters with the slogans "Glory to the Hero City of Moscow!" and "Greetings to the Hero Defenders of Moscow!" adorn the State Department Store. The oath takes place in front of the eternal flame, symbolizing the "fire of Leninism ... the fire of struggle, the fire of revolution" lit by the representatives of the Hero Cities.[4]

This description of a highly significant commemorative event in 1966 gives the reader an idea of how carefully arranged Soviet ritualized space was. Red Square lay at its center, and Moscow was the primus inter pares among the main symbols of Soviet resistance during the war: the Hero Cities, eponymous with the longest, bloodiest, and costliest battles. Contemporary publications called them the "mighty bastions that rose in the path of the enemy's hordes."[5]

During the tenure of Leonid Il'ich Brezhnev (1964–82), these cities received the highest Soviet awards in recognition of their feats. Moscow, Leningrad, Stalingrad, Sevastopol', Odessa, Brest Fortress, and Kiev—joined by Novorossiysk, Kerch', Minsk, Tula, Smolensk, and Murmansk in the 1970s and 1980s—came to embody the heroism of the Soviet people.

Forming an exclusive club of quasi-sacred cities, they were the protagonists of the Soviet war cult, which reached its climax after 1965 and which continues to inspire reverence in contemporary Russia.[6] A unique and highly significant cultural phenomenon, Hero Cities received special salutes on holidays, hosted commemorative events, and were featured in thousands of books and on such items of everyday consumption as matchboxes and postcards. *Russia's Hero Cities* describes their position in Soviet society and indicates the presence of the past in their inhabitants' lives.

A SOCIALIST CONTRACT BORN OF TRAUMA

The memory of the Great Patriotic War (1941–45) continued to occupy a towering position even decades after its end because the conflict had wreaked havoc on the Soviet Union. An estimated twenty-seven million people—the number remains contentious—had died in the Soviet Union when the confrontation with Nazi Germany ended on May 9, 1945. This abstract statistic hides a sea of suffering in a country engulfed by total war, waged by a murderously racist German occupier. Most of the victims were civilians, while millions of soldiers in both armies died on the front lines, often underfed and poorly supplied. The war devastated wide swaths of the Soviet Union and left its economy in shambles. According to official estimates, the battling armies had destroyed 1,710 cities; 70,000 villages; 32,000 industrial enterprises; and 65,000 kilometers of railway. Overall damage was estimated at 2.6 trillion rubles in prewar currency.[7]

Yet the Soviet Union emerged victorious—a superpower that would come to control all of Eastern Europe and exert its influence over large parts of the world during the Cold War. According to Amir Weiner, the Great Patriotic War came to represent the "Armageddon of the Revolution" that had proved the superiority of socialism over capitalism once and for all.[8] The war cult was inextricably linked with heroism, even though the Stalinist regime, brought to the brink of collapse by the German onslaught, had an ambiguous relationship with commemoration. Only under Brezhnev, in the wake of the twentieth anniversary of victory in 1965, did a canonized and idealized official war memory emerge.[9]

It put an end to the intellectual and political struggles raised within the debates on the human costs of the war and the mistakes of the leadership in the 1950s.[10] The Soviet ideological apparatus, which severely curtailed freedom of speech and independent academic research, drew the limits of official discourse even more tightly.[11] Chapter 2 deals with the social and political mechanisms by which this process took place. Jan Assmann's assertion that any society needs collective memories to gain clarity about its values applies to the Soviet Union to an extraordinary degree.[12] The state was the main actor in the politics of history, and history was its central legitimizing force.[13]

During Brezhnev's tenure, war memory transformed from a societal trauma into an ideology of integration due, at least in part, to the general secretary's personality. Brezhnev's war experience had shaped him profoundly, both physically and mentally. He had witnessed the humiliation of retreat as a party cadre in Ukraine, had been seriously wounded in the battle for Novorossiysk in 1943, and had been cherished as a war hero during the victory parade in Moscow in 1945.[14]

The horrors of the war and the Stalinist terror, however, had made him determined to avoid a repetition of this kind of large-scale violence—even though he remained stuck in the past values and events that had formed his worldview. His eighteen-year rule was the most humane in Soviet history, relying on a system that provided considerable stability, a comparatively decent standard of living, and ideological innovation. Only in the second half of his rule would the reluctance to change and the growing formalism degenerate into the stagnation many observers uncritically associate with Brezhnev.[15]

Official war memory provided a compelling narrative that turned suffering into heroism in the service of state-sponsored values. Through collective intergenerational sacrifice and discipline under the leadership of the Communist Party, the story went, the Soviet people had transcended death and destruction to build a thriving socialist society.

The promise of this "socialist contract" (to quote Christine Varga-Harris) between the population and the state—growing welfare against sacrifice for the greater good as defined by the party—was enticing in the 1960s.[16] The Soviet population enjoyed unprecedented economic opportunities, limited personal freedom, and curtailed levels of repression. Many Soviet ideologues rightly feared that materialism and consumerism could threaten socialist convictions, while individualism would displace collectivism. Ideological innovations were necessary: the leadership thus bolstered socialism with official war memory and anchored state-sponsored demands in a widely revered, heroic past that virtually everyone could relate to through personal experience or family history.

Moreover, official war memory served as a tool to overcome a simmering generational conflict.[17] Soviet citizens born after the war grew up in a society that had little in common with the horrors of the 1930s and 1940s. They were nevertheless surrounded by their legacy—its scars tangible in city landscapes and parents' biographies, war memory told and retold in schools, lessons taught in elaborate commemorations at monuments and former battlefields.[18] This presence, as well as its appropriation by the postwar generation, is a significant focus of *Russia's Hero Cities*.

During the first half of the Brezhnev era, the new socialist contract fueled ideological and social dynamism. This was particularly evident in Hero Cities, which included the economic and political centers of Moscow and Leningrad, republican capitals such as Kiev and Minsk, and many strategic industrial cities. All experienced significant immigration and turbulent growth in the postwar years; more than one hundred million Soviet citizens moved from the countryside to cities between 1956 and 1989.[19]

Soviet propaganda cast Hero Cities as exemplars, meant to be emulated by the entire nation. Their inhabitants were expected to live up to the feats of their forefathers, through discipline and loyalty. In particular, numerous campaigns targeted younger city dwellers, highlighting "transgenerational unity." In return, the cities received an elevated status and an attractive local identity—well anchored in a socialist-patriotic framework.

The symbolic privilege Hero Cities enjoyed in the Soviet Union had a strong impact on their political and economic situations. The highly ritualized, politically correct interactions associated with official war memory formed the nexus within which power relations were negotiated. Alexei Yurchak and Victor Dönninghaus have singled out the crucial importance of ritual politics during the Brezhnev era.[20] But their mechanisms and concrete consequences remain poorly understood.

In Hero Cities, both regional and central authorities used their position in the Soviet hierarchy of heroes—the "heroarchy"—to articulate demands and gain advantages.[21] Award ceremonies and anniversaries of the war provided the background against which cities asked for and often received investments. Conversely, they had to meet additional production obligations, with factory brigades shouldering the norms of fallen heroes. This connection of heroism, emulation, and socioeconomic issues had a long tradition in the Soviet Union, dating back to Stalinism.

This study, then, provides a unique approach to resource allocation and mobilization in a nonmarket economy, complementing the few comparable studies, such as Blair A. Ruble's *Leningrad*. Hero Cities' wartime roles and the labor feats of the postwar urban collective were the yardsticks used to measure obligation and entitlement; they grew in importance throughout the Brezhnev era, as socialist slogans became stale and economic stagnation replaced the dynamism of the 1960s in the second half of the following decade. Diminished resources also curtailed the state's ability to uphold its end of the socialist contract, resulting in a growing imbalance between popular expectations and their fulfillment.

TWO LATECOMERS: TULA AND NOVOROSSIYSK

In the book's second part, the focus shifts to case studies on the creation of official war memory in two provincial Hero Cities: Tula and Novorossiysk. Both moved to the top of the Soviet heroarchy during the Brezhnev era. Tula, Hero City since 1976, is located less than two hundred kilometers from the capital. The Black Sea port of Novorossiysk, the southernmost Hero City, received the award in 1973.

Two turning points in the war are associated with these cities. The successful defense of Tula stopped the Wehrmacht's main tank force on its advance to Moscow in 1941, saving the capital. Novorossiysk's dogged resistance in 1942 barred the Germans from controlling the Black Sea coast and tied down forces they would have needed desperately in Stalingrad, nine hundred kilometers to the northeast.

Novorossiysk's and Tula's strategic significance was not limited to the Great Patriotic War. Tula had produced a significant part of the empire's weapons since the eighteenth century, earning it the title of "shield and arsenal of the Russian state."[22] Its agricultural hinterland supplied Moscow. Novorossiysk's location made it the "key to the Caucasus."[23] After the war, its port became a hub for exports, transforming the city into one of the Soviet Union's most international.

As the last city to receive the title under Brezhnev, in 1976, Tula had to apply repeatedly until it was recognized, overcoming great skepticism about whether it was worthy of the honor. Novorossiysk, on the other hand, was Brezhnev's Hero City; the general secretary had fought there on the beachhead of Malaya Zemlya and been wounded. "I almost died multiple times in Novorossiysk," he would tell his confidant Viktor Golikov later on, and he did everything to promote the city on the national stage.[24] Novorossiysk became part and parcel of the increasingly bizarre personality cult that developed around his wartime heroism in later years.

Named in the mid-1970s, these latecomers did not quite enjoy the reverence and prominence of Stalingrad, Leningrad, Sevastopol', and Odessa, which had become Hero Cities in 1945. The fact that the battles in Tula and Novorossiysk were not as significant has further contributed to them being largely overlooked by Western historiography.[25] The notable exception is Vicky Davis's excellent monograph on commemorative culture in Novorossiysk.

Davis conducted research in the city for many years, assembling an impressive body of interviews that *Russia's Hero Cities* cannot match.[26] Instead, this study uses interviews as one component in a collage of sources, including in-depth research in local and national archives.[27] Moreover, the focus extends beyond commemoration and its political appropriation to a conceptual analysis of Hero Cities, their economic functions, and their transformation over time.

As products of the Brezhnev era, however, the Hero Cities provide invaluable insights into the social and political dynamics of the late Soviet Union; they were distinct from other peripheral cities exactly because of their elevated symbolic status.

Still, the extent to which they were recognized and rewarded varied. It depended not only on the skill of local leaders in using their symbolic capital but also on their positions in the Soviet Union's clientelist networks. Public interaction followed clearly circumscribed rules. Once the award was received, a visit by Leonid Brezhnev elevated the Hero City on the national stage. It was a carefully crafted ritual, aimed at strengthening the bonds among him, the regional leadership, and the "people."

This bond was most often articulated through the notion of "worthiness" (*dostoinstvo*). The center in Moscow, local elites, and the population each interpreted the term for their own purposes—to claim additional labor obligations but also better housing, supplies, and services, which were deemed essential to a worthy life. The socialist contract included sacrifice, patriotism, and military service on the one hand and the paternalist state's obligation to provide decent living conditions for the Soviet population on the other.[28]

The balance among these contradictory demands was determined through personal, behind-the-scenes connections. Nothing demonstrates this better than the fact that Novorossiysk received funds to build thousands of new apartments—a privilege that was unheard of elsewhere and that resulted significantly from Brezhnev's personal affection for the city.

The Hero Cities illustrate that a simple state-society dichotomy does not suffice to describe the multifaceted processes at play.[29] Studying Tula and Novorossiysk also contributes to a better understanding of relations between the center and the periphery. The cities are suitable subjects for a much-needed investigation into the lives of average Soviet citizens under Brezhnev—all the more because our image of the Soviet Union is often skewed toward the capitals: the overwhelming majority of historiography focuses on Moscow and Leningrad, cities whose inhabitants were better supplied and better paid than most of their compatriots.[30] Tula and Novorossiysk were more representative of the many midsize industrial towns that experienced growing pains, which were as common in the postwar era as they had been during the rapid industrialization of the 1930s.

THE SMOOTH SURFACE OF OFFICIAL MEMORY

The bestowal of Hero City status not only facilitated solutions to economic and social challenges but also changed urban space: new monuments were constructed, streets renamed, tourist routes established, and apartment blocks built in honor of war heroes. These elements followed and made visible a memorial cultural topography that was intimately tied to the political and societal needs of the Soviet system—a tradition in city construction that the Brezhnev era had inherited from Stalinism.[31] The construction histories and opening ceremonies of the memorials on Tula's Victory Square and Novorossiysk's Malaya Zemlya serve as red threads to track the transformative power of official war memory.

Monuments communicated values and political goals.[32] The smooth surface of Tula's and Novorossiysk's memorial landscapes neatly followed official war memory and embodied the story of heroism and intergenerational continuity.

As the war monuments replaced Stalin in central squares and complemented Lenin statues, they literally and figuratively filled the void left by de-Stalinization. They visibly stabilized a dislocated urban space, and at the same time, they glorified the military and paid tribute to victory.[33] The monuments marked the central squares with an idealized and heroic official memory—often concealing traces of the war. They created across many cities a homogenous memorial landscape, which contained the same elements everywhere, such as eternal flames, obelisks, military gear from the war, and stylized statues of soldiers and workers. Unlike other spaces in downtown areas expressly built for military parades, war monuments formed part of citizens' everyday lives. They were places to pay tribute to the fallen and to celebrate life.

Many of the migrants who moved to the booming provincial centers in the 1950s had little knowledge of local events and relied heavily on official media for their grasp of wartime events. This lack of knowledge made the idealized retelling easier. Still, there were not only top-down interventions into urban space but also developments from the bottom up. The physical transformation of the eerie battlefields into thoroughly ritualized spaces in Hero Cities lasted decades, and the postwar generation followed the development critically.[34]

This book attempts to access popular reception through interviews with Novorossians and Tulyaki who grew up in the cities in the 1960s and 1970s. Although respondents largely reproduced and accepted heroic discourse, their experiences of urban transformation, as well as familial and regional memories, also revealed ambiguities, taboos, and contradictions.

Respondents talked about their personal interpretations of official and unofficial rituals and the unwritten rules they followed in commemorating the war. Family memories complement Soviet and post-Soviet historiography, illuminating some "blank spots" as well as providing regional knowledge[35] and information on everyday life—both at the time they were experienced and in their retelling.[36] These two levels of narration need to be distinguished analytically. Another factor is Marianne Hirsch's "postmemories"—memories that were passed down through families and the media.[37] Their secondhand nature does not make them less valuable; they are good indicators of the narratives that have maintained themselves in the regions over the passing decades. The rich tapestry of sources used here contributes to a nuanced picture—particularly since it makes use of the available academic literature to check the veracity of many statements.

For the researcher, a Swiss historian who is clearly an outsider in Tula's and Novorossiysk's milieus, these interviews presented a considerable challenge.[38]

The twenty-seven men and women of the postwar generation who agreed to talk about their youth and their city met me with a lot of goodwill but also some confusion and distrust. Follow-up interviews, personal recommendations, and the services of local civil society organizations helped in overcoming inhibitions, as did a consistently expressed interest in respondents' family histories, which some told for the first time.

Others claimed they would not be able to tell me anything interesting, and I noticed a tendency to avoid saying anything bad about their cities in front of a stranger.[39] They reverted to a kind of official position.[40] Some mistook the open questions of a narrative interview for ignorance, leading various respondents to explain the Soviet Union in general rather than talk about their personal lives. I therefore started later interviews with more concrete questions.[41] Most respondents liked to discuss the topic of the Hero Cities, since the perceived indifference of Western societies to the eastern experience in World War II is an often-heard grievance in today's Russia.

Ultimately, *Russia's Hero Cities* explains how their honorary status shaped these towns, their inhabitants, and the Soviet Union—both during the Brezhnev era and beyond. Indeed, the lasting impact of official war memory is among the most puzzling phenomena in contemporary Russia. While the Soviet war cult declined after Brezhnev's death in 1982 and disappeared during the collapse of the Soviet Union, it has reemerged in the last two decades as a central element of societal integration under Vladimir Putin. The last part of the book describes the conditions that accompanied this transformation of official war memory—in post-Soviet Russia at large and in Novorossiysk and Tula in particular.

To what extent does war memory both reflect and shape societal change and political outlooks? While many of the values associated with the war cult remained, new aspects—religious, personal, and economic—have transformed its role. In the midst of manifold changes and crises, official war memory and Hero Cities remain highly significant, representing and to an extent fulfilling a wish for continuity and stability.

NOTES

1. *Rossiyskiy Gosudarstvennyy Arkhiv Sotsial'no-Politicheskoy Istorii* (RGASPI), f. M-1, op. 38, d. 39, l. 131; d. 41, ll. 81–86. (All translations from Russian are mine.)

2. RGASPI, d. 39, l. 158.

3. RGASPI, d. 41, ll. 143–44.
4. RGASPI, d. 39, ll. 136, 158.
5. Kutuzov et al., *Goroda-Geroi Velikoy Otechestvennoy Voyny*, 6.
6. Andreev and Bordyugov, "Prostranstvo Pamyati," 124.
7. Kolesnikov and Rozhkov: *Ordena i Medali SSSR*, 17–18. On the postwar period, see also Zubkova and Ragsdale: *Russia after the War*. These numbers are not uncontested. Peter Almquist calculated total economic losses from the war at 4,734 billion rubles—or 893 billion dollars—in 1940 prices. Almquist, *Red Forge*, 192.
8. "The war was universally perceived as the Armageddon of the Revolution, the ultimate clash dreaded yet expected by the first generation to live in a socialist society, the event that would either vindicate or bring down the system." Weiner, *Making Sense of War*, 17.
9. "The term official memory refers to those dominant or hegemonic narratives that underpin and help to organize the remembrance and commemoration of war at the level of the nation-state." Ashplant, Dawson, and Roper, *Politics of War Memory and Commemoration*, 22.
10. T. G. Ashplant and his coauthors emphasize that attempts at shaping cultural memory are marked by intellectual and political struggles as a rule. Ashplant, Dawson, and Roper, *Politics of War Memory and Commemoration*, 10.
11. Building on Michel Foucault, Swiss historian Philipp Sarasin writes that discourses entail both words and deeds. They encompass, build on, and represent themselves as practice and "a compact materiality with its own, describable rules ... guiding the societal construction of things." The notion of discourse used here goes beyond speeches and publications to include social practices. Only the contextualization of words and deeds within a framework of values and perceptions endows them with meaning. Sarasin, *Geschichtswissenschaft und Diskursanalyse*, 34.
12. Jan Assmann divides collective memory into two ideal types for analytical purposes: *communicative memory* (Kommunikatives Gedächtnis) and *cultural memory* (Kulturelles Gedächtnis). The first term describes oral memories that break off after three or four generations. Recollections that are conveyed through media, on the other hand—books, monuments, or movies—are part of cultural memory, "a collective term for all the knowledge that guides actions and experiences within a society's specific framework of interaction, and which is used repeatedly from generation to generation." Assmann, "Kollektives Gedächtnis und kulturelle Identität," 9.
13. They were "judgments, dictated by the Party's wisdom," writes Hösler. Joachim Hösler: *Die sowjetische Geschichtswissenschaft 1953 bis 1991*, 29.
14. For Brezhnev's biography, see Schattenberg, *Leonid Breschnew*.
15. For recent examples, see Crump, *Brezhnev and the Decline of the Soviet Union*, and Vanyukov, *Epokha Zastoya*. Conversely, a strand of revisionist

historiography tries to provide a more nuanced description of the epoch that the author of this book also identifies with. See Bacon and Sandle, *Brezhnev Reconsidered*; Belge and Deuerlein, *Goldenes Zeitalter der Stagnation?*; and, most recently, Fainberg and Kalinovsky, *Reconsidering Stagnation in the Brezhnev Era*.

16. Varga-Harris, "Forging Citizenship on the Home Front," 104.

17. Rituals were a crucial tool in this process, according to Christel Lane: "Ritual activity occurs in a social context where there is ambiguity or conflict about social relations, and it is performed to resolve or disguise them." *Rites of Rulers*, 11.

18. Astrid Erll includes in memory media not only sources such as books but also rituals and monuments. "Medium des kollektiven Gedächtnisses," 11.

19. Still, in 1970, only nine cities had a population of more than one million. French, *Plans, Pragmatism and People*, 70, 74.

20. Dönninghaus and Savin, "Leonid Brezhnev," 179–94. Yurchak highlights the formalized and immutable nature of "authoritative discourse" under Brezhnev, which followed an established formula that became increasingly void in his later years. *Everything Was Forever*, 32.

21. Günther, *Der sozialistische Übermensch*, 158.

22. Garbuzov, "Tula's Military Feat," 12.

23. Shiyan, *Novorossiysk*, 31.

24. Podyma, "Viktor Golikov."

25. In contrast, there are numerous books on the war's battles and commemoration in the "original" Hero Cities. See Ganzenmüller, *Das belagerte Leningrad*; Kirschenbaum: *Legacy of the Siege of Leningrad*. On Stalingrad, see Arnold, *Stalingrad im sowjetischen Gedächtnis*. On Sevastopol' and Odessa, see Qualls, *From Ruins to Reconstruction*. On Odessa, see King, *Odessa*.

26. Davis interviewed 124 Novorossians and 10 respondents from the rest of the country. Additionally, she relies on memoirs and local newspapers. *Myth Making in the Soviet Union*, 7. Aside from pseudonyms and socioeconomic classification, Davis provides little information about her respondents. I conducted 15 interviews in Tula in May 2012 and April 2013, of which I analyzed 10 in detail. In Novorossiysk, I interviewed 12 respondents in 2013 and selected 10 for further analysis. The interviews are not representative of the population at large but feature a variety of backgrounds and perspectives: among the sample criteria were different social and professional backgrounds and a mix between those who had occupied active positions within the Komsomol and the Communist Party and those who kept their distance. I secured the support of the Levada Center and the NGO Memorial in finding respondents from a working-class background, which had proved difficult. In Novorossiysk, I paid them 600 rubles per interview. Most interviews were conducted in respondents' homes, and all of them in Russian.

27. It uses archival materials and Soviet publications to track the construction history as well as the ritual usage of these places. Among these sources are files from regional party organizations and from Moscow, where the Russian Soviet Federative Socialist Republic's Council of Ministers had the final say on most financial and artistic decisions. The most important sources on official and unofficial usages of these places are Komsomol files, regional newspapers, and interviews.

28. Varga-Harris: *Stories of House and Home*, 18–19.

29. This simplified view is also evident in the only comprehensive study of the Brezhnevian war cult, by Nina Tumarkin: *The Living and the Dead*.

30. This lack of attention extends to publications on Soviet provinces at large, which remain understudied, especially for the second half of the Soviet period. See Malte Rolf's overview and his discussion on the importance of regional case studies for an understanding of the Soviet Union: *Das sowjetische Massenfest*, 30–31.

31. See, for instance, the description of Stalinist city planning in Nizhnyy Novgorod by Heather DeHaan: *Stalinist City Planning*, 14–17.

32. Burkhardt, "Der Trifels und die nationalsozialistische Erinnerungskultur," 241.

33. "War memorials are the churches of the Soviet military build-up." Ignatieff, "Soviet War Memorials," 161.

34. Massey argues that the dominant image of any place will be a matter of contestation and will change over time. Massey, *Space, Place and Gender*, 120–21.

35. Although archival materials and official publications provide a lot of background information, they are nevertheless marked by authoritative discourse, exhibiting striking overlap and often containing identical formulations. To a certain extent, interviews can compensate for this one-sidedness of official sources. Oksana Sarkisova and Olga Shevchenko argue that a regional perspective helps in overcoming the dichotomy between public and private, which often leads to oversimplifications. The "middle range," as they call it, makes it possible to pick up on both the stories of individuals and state-sponsored discourses. Sarkisova and Shevchenko, "'They Came, Shot Everyone,'" 100.

36. Haumann, "Die Verarbeitung von Gewalt," 385–87.

37. Hirsch, *Family Frames*.

38. The researcher must be aware that in oral history, he generates the source in cooperation with the respondent, and it is important to problematize the conditions of this interaction. Stephan, "Erinnertes Leben."

39. Respondents' interest in presenting themselves in a certain light and the researcher's interest and questions determine the story told. Schäfer and Völter, "Subjekt-Positionen," 168–71.

40. Viktor Zaslavsky, who conducted the first independent opinion polls in the USSR, struggled with respondents' perceptions that he was asking "official" questions. In these cases, they provided generic answers. Zaslavsky, *In geschlossener Gesellschaft*, 45. When I noticed such tendencies, I tried to steer respondents away by asking questions about their actions at specific moments.

41. The narrative interview opens with a general question and only asks for specific dates, events, and topics in the second part. Rosenthal: *Erlebte und erzählte Lebensgeschichte*, 189. This strategy was not unproblematic. Specifically, I replaced the question "Please tell me about life in your city under Brezhnev" with "Do you remember where you were and what you were doing when Novorossiysk was awarded Hero City status?"

TWO

Creating an Idealized Past
The Soviet Heroarchy from Stalin to Brezhnev

THE TERM *HERO CITY* FIRST appeared in 1934.[1] Nikolay Bukharin, editor of the newspaper *Izvestiya* at that time, wrote an article about the anniversary of the Seventh All-Russian Congress of Soviets, Workers, Peasants, Cossacks, and Red Army Deputies in December 1919. He described the deprivations in Leningrad, the host city of the congress: It had already suffered from famine during the First World War. Now it was at the center of the Civil War between Communists and the approaching counterrevolutionary White Armies but was also torn apart by the terror accompanying the expropriation of the city's former upper class.

Bukharin, however, drew a picture of unity, where, in spite of all difficulties, "the heroic working class of the Proletarian capital unanimously supported its iron vanguard."[2] The climax of the congress, as Bukharin described it, was the demand of an "old machinist" to award this "Hero City" the honorary Red Banner.[3]

This heroization of cities may seem surprising. It appears to be a uniquely socialist practice—mostly found in the Soviet Union. Among other states of the Eastern Bloc, only Yugoslavia had Hero Cities.[4] There are individual examples of the name being attributed to places, such as Warsaw, but it was not done consistently.[5] Other countries have regularly awarded orders to military units and individuals, but the decoration of geographic entities is unusual save for a few exceptions.[6] However, the notion that cities were the main obstacles for an invader also drew from prerevolutionary traditions: the fight of Moscow's inhabitants against the Poles in 1612 and the burning of the city in the Patriotic War against Napoleon in 1812 occupied an important place in tsarist mythology. That war's centenary in 1912 was celebrated with great pomp.[7] The inhabitants of Smolensk received a large monument for their resistance in 1812. Sevastopol' was another member of the imperial pantheon for its role in the Crimean War.[8]

For the most part, Soviet discourse stressed instances of socialist heroism in the broadest sense. The early articles on Leningrad emphasized its defense in the Civil War. In a piece titled "Fortress City," Aleksandr Makhanov, secretary of the Leningrad City Committee (*Gorkom*) in charge of propaganda and agitation during the war, lauded the workers' contribution: "The city of Lenin never knew defeat, never gave the enemy an inch (*pyad'*) of its territory. This is a fortress city, a Hero City, a city of victors.... Comrade Stalin personally led the defense of Piter during this period, unified the forces and the will of Piter's proletariat, lit the flame of belief in victory and assured the turnaround at the front."[9]

The fortress, manned by a selfless population under capable leadership, would remain one of the central signifiers for Hero Cities. Equally important was the emphasis on the unity of workers and soldiers.

While Soviet sources described Leningrad primarily as Lenin's city, the emphasis on Stalin's achievements as commander of the defense connected it directly to Lenin's successor. In 1937, a second Hero City that was even more closely linked to him appeared: Tsaritsyn, which was renamed Stalingrad in 1925 in an early manifestation of a personality cult that would soon grow beyond all proportion. Although Tsaritsyn had been the first Soviet city to officially receive an award—the Honorary Red Banner in May 1919—it was only referred to as a Hero City eighteen years later.

The atmosphere of the 1937 Stalinist purges is tangible in the *Izvestiya* article about the opening of a museum focused on the defense of Tsaritsyn in the Civil War. The author consistently highlights Stalin's decisive role in the defense. At the same time, special correspondent P. Petrov emphasized the internal enemies Stalin had to fight before he could organize an effective defense, including Leo Trotsky, who would be assassinated by a Soviet agent in 1940.[10]

Already in the 1930s, then, Hero Cities had become important symbols for official Soviet memory. Their status was intimately tied to the Stalinist personality cult, which endowed them with political significance. In his book on the "socialist Übermensch," Hans Günther traces the influence of hero myths on Stalinist culture and beyond. According to Günther, Maksim Gor'kiy was heavily influenced by Friedrich Nietzsche. The Soviet writer posited the hero and, concomitantly, the New Soviet Man as a counter-model to petty bourgeois attitudes (*meshchanstvo*).[11]

Soviet heroes enjoyed material privileges. Carriers of the title "Hero of the Soviet Union"—established on April 16, 1934, and first awarded four days later to a group of pilots—were highest in the "heroarchy" of the USSR.[12]

By *heroarchy*, a term that originated from the nineteenth-century historian Thomas Carlyle, Günther means a bureaucratic, hierarchical system of awards with concomitant premiums and privileges.[13] Members of the pantheon did not pay income tax and received a monthly pension, free urban public transport, and one free long-distance trip per year.[14]

This connection between feats in the name of socialism and individual reward had been one of the fundamental driving forces of Soviet society since its inception. Stephen Kotkin describes it in relation to the Bolshevik identity that formed in Magnitogorsk, E. Thomas Ewing sees it at the heart of the Soviet educational system, and for David Brandenberger the emulation of heroes was one of the key aspects of Stalinist patriotic discourse.[15] Characters like Stakhanov came to embody the Labor Hero; Pavlik Morozov was the epitome of a party faithful.[16]

Stalinist heroes were not conceived of as independent actors—they remained in a role subservient to the state and the leader. The Hero City symbolized a direct connection between the most advanced, most patriotic, and most heroic parts of the Soviet people and their leader, Joseph Stalin. As Katerina Clark points out, "Soviet society's leaders became 'fathers' (with Stalin as the patriarch); the national heroes, model 'sons'; the state, a 'family' or 'tribe.' The new root metaphor for society provided the state with a single set of symbols for enhancing its increasingly hierarchical structure by endowing it with a spurious organicity."[17]

In Hero Cities, this societal metaphor was transposed from individuals to a model urban collective—dedicated, loyal, and hierarchical. Individual feats served as examples for the entire Soviet Union; Erwin Oberländer sees this hero-and-leader cult as an inherent part of "Soviet patriotism." Understanding that class struggle did not suffice to craft lasting loyalty toward the Soviet state, Stalinist leaders began to connect "socialist values" with more "concrete" patriotic elements in 1934. The goal was to strengthen the emotional connection between people and party state.[18]

Even though this patriotism contained nationalist elements, David Brandenberger sets "National Bolshevism" apart from Russian nationalism. "National Bolshevism . . . describes a peculiar form of Marxist-Leninist etatism that fused the pursuit of communist ideals with more statist ambitions reminiscent of tsarist 'Great Power' (*velikoderzhavnye*) traditions."[19] National Bolshevism purported the people and state to be one. Resorting back to long-established notions of the Russian people's superior qualities, it envisioned a kind of messianic mission for the Soviet Union. Extraordinary people—heroes—were needed to advance this mission.[20]

The Soviet hero, then, was the vanguard—more dedicated, more patriotic, and more capable than the average citizen. He had to fight constant struggles in a society that was presented as a battlefield for the future communist utopia. In the extreme polarization of the 1930s—with forced industrialization, purges, preparation for war against bourgeois and fascist "enemies"—heroes and leaders could reduce complexity to a simple *us* versus *them* scheme. In the Great Patriotic War, the most extreme and bloody form of polarization became reality.

COLLECTIVE FEATS AND IMPREGNABLE FORTRESSES

Wartime conditions cast a new light on the Hero Cities of Leningrad and Stalingrad. On August 23, 1941, two weeks before the siege of Leningrad began, Soviet writer Dem'yan Bednyy published a poem for the Hero City in *Pravda*. "Lenin's city" may be under attack, Bednyy wrote, but "all of our military strength, Moscow, all cities, and the entire Soviet people are with you." The enemies would "either perish or surrender," and the "fascists will be smashed at your granite threshold" (*granitnyy tvoy porog*).[21]

During the brutal blockade, which claimed the lives of one million inhabitants, the Soviet press consistently upheld the second capital's heroic image.[22] Even though the enemy may be "pitiless," wrote an *Izvestiya* correspondent on September 14, 1941, the "cradle of the Proletarian revolution," "the warrior-city, the Hero City enters a relentless and fearless fight."[23]

Descriptions of suffering and death were admissible only in the form of metaphors in Leningrad and, subsequently, also in other Hero Cities: they were always presented as military fortresses whose entire population fought selflessly and heroically. When the siege was broken in January 1943, *Izvestiya* wrote: "The blockade tormented the Hero City, proud, courageous and impregnable (*gordyy, muzhestvennyy, stoykiy*) Leningrad for many months. But the city lived, resisted, held its ground, tenaciously and patiently, hardened into stone (*okamanevshiy*) by hatred toward the enemy, animated by a will of steel. Leningrad stood fast, courageously enduring deprivation and sorrow."[24]

When the city was completely liberated on January 28, 1944, *Pravda* did not report casualty numbers, merely stating that Leningrad had sustained "severe wounds," thereby again referring to an abstract collective body that did not contain individuals.[25] The official war memory could not allow the notion that millions of civilian victims had died in vain.

Similarly abstract was the depiction of Stalingrad once the battle for it had begun in the early fall of 1942. *Pravda* called it a "Hero City, warrior city, city of our beautiful traditions and of the Bolshevist will of steel" in its editorial. The anonymous author drew parallels to the Civil War and emphasized the connection to Stalin, whose "mighty will" had assured victory in 1918 and would do so again in 1942.[26] The description seamlessly integrated into an established discourse.

As the battle turned savage, the language of the war correspondents, such as Boris Polevoy, another winner of the Stalin Prize, became more emotional while remaining within the heroic framework. On October 12, 1942, he described roads littered with shattered glass and ripped open by constant explosions: "Before my eyes lies the city of barricades, the city of soldiers, the Hero City (*gorod-barrikada, gorod boets, gorod-geroy*)." In spite of the raging battles, Polevoy wrote, "the city stands valiantly and unshaken (*muzhestvennyy i nepokolebimyy*). They can destroy it, but they can never take it."[27]

Echoing the writer Ilya Ehrenburg, Polevoy called on Soviet soldiers to kill the Germans and not let them cross the Volga. Stalingrad was no longer just a Hero City; it was a "city of rage (*gorod gneva*)." At the same time, "the heroic love of Soviet people for the city of Stalin" formed "the wall, strong and insurmountable, against which one German division and corps after another crashes."[28] People and city discursively became one, and the city was anthropomorphized at the same time that people were objectified, becoming a "wall."

This description was far removed from the actual fighting on the ground. The Red Army only managed to hold on to the western bank of the Volga by a thread and fought the Wehrmacht in bombed-out houses and sewers. The soldiers called it a "rat's war."[29] Moreover, the Soviet intelligence service People's Commissariat for Internal Affairs (NKVD) executed hundreds of its own soldiers.[30] Many civilians who had not managed to escape before the battle got stuck between the lines, subjected to brutal Luftwaffe bombardments that claimed the lives of tens of thousands. Total losses in the battle are loosely estimated at 1.8 million soldiers and civilians.[31]

Stalinist publications idealized the fighting in Hero Cities because they had to live up to a reality that was prescribed by ideology. In the first book published on Hero Cities in 1943, N. Gessen explains that they are fundamentally different from Western European cities: while the latter were often given up to the Wehrmacht without a defense to protect the civilian population, "the Soviet city becomes a fortress when a mass of Soviet patriots defends it."[32] Under conditions of total war, every civilian became a patriot, a fighter, and a hero. This depiction of a unified collective concealed the ruthlessness of the leadership, which completely disregarded the needs of the population in the name of defense.

Thirty years later, Aleksandr Kolesnik would take this notion further in his book on people's militias in the Hero Cities (*narodnoe opolchenie*). These units, levied en masse in the first year of the war, were poorly armed and suffered heavy casualties. Kolesnik, however, recast them as the embodiment of the people as well as of the unity of military and civilian forces. According to him, the Red Army was the fundamental force that destroyed fascism, the people's "military vanguard." Nonetheless, he maintained, victory was only possible because of the unity of front and rear.[33]

Kolesnik described the Red Army as a military formation of a "new sort," filled by the "living force" of the masses and firmly founded on them. Soviet citizens defended their homeland (*rodina*) not in the interests of their masters or the bourgeoisie but for the most just cause imaginable—the "defense of the socialist fatherland."[34] This collective was undefeatable: "The failures of the Red Army in the beginning of the war did not destroy the Soviet people's will to resist. Quite the contrary: the Soviet people, carrying within themselves the deepest patriotism, which united ardent love for the homeland, reverence for its revolutionary and national traditions, devotion (*predannost'*) to the socialist order and the cause of the great Party of Communists, committed heroic feats and made sacrifices in the name of the freedom and independence of their *own* fatherland."[35]

From this viewpoint, victory was inevitable because of objective historical criteria, namely the lack of class antagonism in the USSR. The simplistic emphasis on equality hides the strict hierarchies of Stalin's dictatorial rule.

The unity of the Soviet people and their patriotism are thus the two elements that transformed Soviet cities into heroic collectives.[36] Mass death, hunger, and starvation are recast as "mass heroism," committed in the name of shared values.[37] Vagueness was therefore both inevitable and desired because it avoided critical questions arising from the cities' war histories. Sabine Arnold explains that *Hero City* "meant the people in the city, without having to determine whether the inhabitants, the defenders or only the members of the city committee of the CPSU were meant."[38] Thus, all actors could claim inclusion in the heroic collective—which in turn could be used as an example to emulate in a variety of societal contexts.

The notion of a unified collective was particularly hard to maintain in those Hero Cities that were under occupation. The population struggled for survival and often had to make difficult choices between collaboration and repression in the case of resistance. According to official war memory, their inhabitants either fought or died but never sought an arrangement with the occupiers.[39]

A case in point is Sevastopol', which was described as a Hero City during the war. The duration of its defense against the German onslaught lay at the center of the narrative: the Crimean city was besieged for 250 days before it fell in July 1942—not least because of Soviet strategic blunders in the second year of the war. In April, *Izvestiya* wrote that the "sea fortress (*morskaya krepost'*), the Hero City Sevastopol' was, is and always will be Soviet."[40] The author compared Sevastopol's defense to the battle for the city in the Crimean War in 1854, drawing a parallel to heroic events in Russia's prerevolutionary past.[41] In the first years of World War II, these historical links were frequently used to raise patriotic dedication—even if there existed a tension between Soviet and pre-Soviet heroes throughout Stalin's rule.[42]

The occupation by German and Romanian troops lasted almost two years and was accompanied by numerous acts of violence against civilians and by the extinction of the city's Jewish population. As the Red Army was approaching in April 1944, however, Sevastopol' regained its mythical significance. Stalin Prize winner Leonid Sobolev sees it appear in the mist and gazes upon "Sevastopol'—immortal city of valor, fidelity, and glory, knight of the Black Sea, Russian fortress" (*Sevastopol'—bessmertnyy gorod muzhestva, vernosti i slavy, ryzar' Chernogo Morya, russkaya krepost'*). The city was an example to emulate for the soldiers fighting against Nazi Germany—"the heroism of its defenders raised new heroes."[43]

Sobolev's article is the first to connect various Hero Cities; he mentions that many of those soldiers who had defended Stalingrad were now about to liberate Sevastopol'. Moreover, he links it with Odessa, the fourth city to join the ranks of heroes: "The shared fate (*pereklichka*) of Hero Cities in the great war of our people is full of significance. Two days ago I was still in Odessa, which had just been liberated, today I see the second Hero City—Sevastopol'."[44]

RESURRECTION AND SERVICE TO THE STATE

The signifier *Hero City*, then, served as a rallying cry during the war—and as a description of a mythic past after liberation. The cities' canonization was closely linked to pronouncements from Stalin. His famous order of November 7, 1942, was the point of departure; it included the four Hero Cities—Leningrad, Stalingrad, Sevastopol', and Odessa—as well as Moscow and Tula, which would be added to their ranks only decades later.[45] Their "heroic defenders... showed exemplary and dedicated valor, iron discipline, steadfastness and the ability for victory."[46] One month after the order, the Presidium of the Supreme Soviet, responsible for all awards and orders, issued medals to the defenders, the first of their kind.[47]

Even more important was Stalin's order 20 of May 1, 1945, in which he announced impending victory and ordered twenty artillery salutes to be fired in the sixteen Republican capitals[48]—as well as in the four Hero Cities.[49] The values they stood for—valor, fidelity, steadfastness, discipline, and self-sacrifice—were those that society was called upon to emulate regularly.[50] The combination of Hero Cities and the political centers of the resurgent, territorially enlarged Soviet Union illustrates that the focus had already shifted to postwar challenges. This shift changed the role of Hero Cities, which had become important symbols of reconstruction.

All of them were, however, completely ruined. By the time Sevastopol' was liberated, only 3,000 out of 110,000 people remained.[51] The "return to life" was presented as a resurrection from the dead, which meant not only physical reconstruction but also the preservation of the fallen heroes' memory. Karl Qualls writes in his study of Sevastopol' that "reborn cities became new symbols of progress and economic strength."[52] This symbolism fit neatly into conceptions of Stalinist heroes. Katerina Clark points out that such heroes often sacrifice their lives but are resurrected metaphorically because their comrades continue the cause in their name.[53] The urban collective was expected to pick up the "banner" of their fallen wartime compatriots. The Soviet values discursively linked with heroism were increasingly transferred to the economic realm.[54]

This tendency is evident in articles about Stalingrad and Leningrad. Stalingrad, which had been completely destroyed like Sevastopol', was in the process of "resurrection," Ivan Zimenkov wrote in *Izvestiya*, just over half a year after its liberation. In 1943, it was already producing industrial goods for the front again.[55] A year later, triumphant reports spoke of the reopening of huge factories and the construction of new housing for forty-two thousand people. This reconstruction, wrote *Izvestiya*, was a "new bright page in the annals (*letopis'*) of the Hero City."[56]

The direct link to Stalin heightened the city's value. When the dictator received the exclusive Order of Victory on July 30, 1944, "inexpressible emotion and joy took hold of the Hero City's workers, which carries the name of the great leader . . . of the Soviet people." In response, the workers swore to contribute everything they could to the "growing industry of the Hero City."[57]

The Soviet press also celebrated the resurrection of Leningrad, even though the city would take many more years to be rebuilt. The celebration, as Steve Maddox has pointed out, boosted morale—in Leningrad and elsewhere in the USSR.[58] "The Leningrader is full of energy," wrote a jubilant *Pravda*. "The great city—the warrior-city, the Hero City is alive."[59] On the first anniversary of its liberation, Leningrad was awarded the Order of Lenin. Petr Popkov, head of the Leningrad City Executive Committee (Gorispolkom), received the award and thanked Stalin, "the organizer and inspirer (*vdokhnovitel'*) of the Soviet people's great victories."[60]

Popkov finished his speech with an oath: "We swear to the Party, the government and the entire Soviet people that the Leningraders will also work selflessly to help the front in the future." The USSR's head of state, Mikhail Kalinin, echoed this pledge, when he expressed confidence that Leningrad would show itself "worthy" of this high award through "selfless labor."[61] Labor as the unit in which "worthiness" was measured appeared consistently in Soviet discourse into the Brezhnev era.

Hero Cities were thus presented not only as promising a brighter future but also as intimately tied to Stalin. This connection was important to the regime, which had been brought to the brink of collapse. The Stalinist leadership was thus walking a fine line in commemorating the war. On the one hand, it needed heroes because the population revered their sacrifice and the places where the bloodiest and longest battles had taken place. Stalinist discourse used this deep respect to strengthen popular identification with the state and the leader.[62]

On the other hand, the war had exposed Stalin's weaknesses. He had not heeded the warnings of the impending German onslaught in the summer of 1941 and thus lost a third of the country. The generalissimo's blunders called his wisdom into question. Once the tide had turned after the Battle of Stalingrad in February 1943, it took another two years to defeat the Germans. Stalin needed an idealized version of this war, and so Soviet losses, almost consistently higher than German ones, were systematically kept secret. In 1946, Stalin arbitrarily put the number of Soviet citizens killed during the war at seven million.[63] The figure would remain a dogmatic truth for a decade.

Equally worrisome for the Kremlin, wartime heroism had been just as much the result of individual initiative and creativity as of top-down control. Weakened central leadership had created islands of independence within the horror—a "breath of fresh air," in the words of Boris Pasternak.[64] For Stalin, this independence signified a potential challenge to his authority; as Catherina Merridale has shown, the wartime generation grew accustomed to the relative freedom of life on the front lines.[65] In his novel *Life and Fate*, the great writer Vasily Grossman monumentalized independent heroes—including the fictional tank commander Pyotr Novikov, who, to save his men, delays Stalin's order to attack but still wins the battle.

Moreover, the experience of fighting in Western Europe had profoundly shaped many veterans. "What the army of many millions had seen abroad inevitably made them think about life in their own country and led them to certain conclusions that did not suit the system at all," argues Russian historian Elena Senyavskaya.[66] Veterans felt they had earned a better life. Amir Weiner develops this notion further: "Whereas the front did not breed Western-style democrats, it did produce an assertive Soviet individual who held tight to his (and it was mostly his and not her) newly earned-in-blood right to define his identity and status based on his wartime exploits."[67]

Their experiences produced powerful new social bonds and a confident identity—not necessarily dissident but also not easily instrumentalized for political purposes. The first two years after the war were thus comparatively pluralistic as far as war memory was concerned. May 9, or Victory Day, was celebrated as an official holiday, and writers and journalists related personal experiences in the Soviet press. In cities, first and foremost Leningrad, commissions extended campaigns to collect materials about the war and instituted museums. Jewish intellectuals documented the history of the Holocaust. In villages and neighborhoods, modest monuments were built for fallen soldiers and victims of the war—often without state funds.[68]

Regional memories stood alongside an official memory that the leadership of the Communist Party of the Soviet Union (CPSU) propagated. Heroism stood at the center of both. As every family had suffered losses, the war carried intense personal significance for Soviet citizens. No systematic war cult emerged yet, however; the omnipresent ruins and the millions of war wounded who roamed the city streets, the famine in many regions, and the profound economic depression created an unsuitable background for any attempt at idealizing the war.[69] Many veterans were reluctant to share their memories—which were too traumatic to be articulated.[70] According to Catherine Merridale, their coping strategy was to "bury and ignore the past."[71]

As the party reconsolidated political power, Stalin began to purge popular military leaders and centralize war memory. Georgiy Zhukov, the supreme commander of the Red Army, was removed from his post in June 1946 and transferred to the remote Odessa Military District. Victory Day ceased to be a state holiday in 1947. The hardliner Andrey Zhdanov introduced a strict control of literature and the arts (*Zhdanovshchina*). Official discourse suppressed any notion of exceptional suffering that would "elevate" a city like Leningrad above the Soviet people.[72] Even if Bernd Bonwetsch's claim that Stalin was "the only historian" is exaggerated, the Soviet leader's retelling of the war became the dominant narrative.[73]

The Stalinist state had an inordinate amount of power to shape public perceptions of the war. It used its propaganda machine and often its means of repression to marginalize and silence competing narratives. On September 10, 1947, it dealt a devastating blow to the war heroes, withdrawing all pensions and privileges from carriers of awards and medals. The Stalinist press presented this subjugation as an initiative from the people: "Reconstruction of the economy, which was destroyed during the war, did not only require intensive labor by all Soviet people but also the use of colossal financial means. The manifold wishes by carriers of orders and medals of the USSR, to use the state means that were employed for their benefit for economic reconstruction instead attest to their huge patriotism and their dedication to overcoming the aftereffects of the war as quickly as possible."[74]

Even if one does not doubt popular dedication to reconstruction, the claim that veterans voluntarily relinquished the modest privileges that helped them survive appears cynical in light of their often-destitute living conditions. To be fair, the Soviet Party state had few options in the postwar years. Public admission of postwar desolation, however, would have called the heroic surface of the community of victors into question. In order to defend its claim to rule, the Stalinist leadership had to present the sacrifices it demanded from the population as voluntary; heroes had to serve the state.[75]

THE MEANING OF VICTORY

After Stalin died in 1953, many taboos resurfaced. The dictator had formed the center of the Soviet political system and of official discourse. His death led to far-reaching realignments; the Stalinist model of rule was no longer an option for the new leadership. The unrest and bloody uprisings that erupted in both the Soviet Union and the Eastern Bloc showed that de-Stalinization and a relaxation of repression could lead to the collapse of the entire socialist system. The new Soviet leader Nikita Khrushchev walked a thin political line between de-Stalinization, reform, and new mechanisms of control.

On the one hand, the Khrushchev era was marked by a return to the "Leninist core" of socialist ideology and a distancing from Stalin's personality cult.[76] Utopia reappeared in Khrushchev's speeches, including his promise at the Twenty-Second Party Congress in 1961 that the current generation would live under communism by 1980. The partial opening of the country to outside influences and the ambition to measure the quality of life in comparison to Western living standards, however, created contradictions. As Polly Jones has pointed out, the term "Thaw" for the era is correct only insofar as it captures "the fragility, the potential for reversal (or 'freeze') which each tentative forward step carried."[77] De-Stalinization "wounded the Soviet ideological consensus" but also forced the leadership to fill the discursive vacuum at its center.[78]

The de-Stalinization of war memory was a particularly sensitive issue. In his famous Secret Speech in 1956, Khrushchev blamed his predecessor for numerous crimes and errors. He refuted the notion that Stalin's "genius" had won the war. Instead, he criticized the generalissimo's inadequate reaction to reports of the impending German attack and the subsequent "nervousness and hysteria which Stalin demonstrated while interfering with actual military operations." Khrushchev also accused him of having weakened the Red Army by purging leading officers between 1937 and 1941.[79]

Compared to Stalinist depictions that gave the leader little to no blame, Khrushchev's version was shockingly critical.[80] He assigned direct responsibility for the loss of millions of soldiers and large swaths of Soviet territory to Stalin, by connecting the purges to the disasters of the first war months.[81] In the leader's stead, Khrushchev created a new hero: "The main credit for the victorious ending of the war belongs to our Communist Party, to the armed forces of the Soviet Union, and to the tens of millions of Soviet people uplifted by the Party."[82] Unlike Stalin's depiction of the Soviet people as "screws and bolts" in the great machine of the state, in Khrushchev's vision, they became the victors—led by the CPSU.[83]

If de-Stalinization had dislocated official discourse, the victory of the "entire people" (*vsenarodnyy*) became a powerful symbol to fill the gap—provided it was interpreted within a communist framework and applied to the present—thus motivating society to emulate the same values.[84] The victorious collective provided new opportunities for identification. "After 1953, the 'Great Patriotic War' became the key symbol of . . . national identity," writes Catriona Kelly.[85]

De-Stalinized official war memory was anything but uncontested. Khrushchev's conclusions about the personality cult were only released to a select party public. Officially, the Central Committee resolved on June 30, 1956, that the Stalin cult did not affect the development of socialism in a decisive way. By 1957, revisionist forces who demanded further de-Stalinization and antirevisionists who wanted to put the leader back on his pedestal were gridlocked, with Khrushchev hesitating to join either side.[86] This competition created a surprisingly liberal intellectual atmosphere:[87] Russian historian Sergey Kudryashov considers the period between 1957 and 1967 "the most productive" for research on the war.[88]

Khrushchev's new general line thus left ample room for interpretation. While the leadership agreed on elevating the role of the party in Stalin's stead, the new direction created contradictions; after all, Stalin had headed the CPSU, and many of the party's current leaders had been complicit in his crimes. Moreover, if the status of the Red Army rose as well, would this not detract from the achievements of the party?

The contentious discussions were also evident in the editors' collective for the official six-volume *History of the Great Patriotic War of the Soviet Union*

1941–1945⁸⁹ and the one-volume *Short History*, published in 1965 and aimed at a broad audience.⁹⁰ The Central Committee had commissioned these publications from the Institute for Marxism-Leninism (subsequently the main body responsible for canonizing official war memory). Its director, Petr Pospelov, had also prepared the Secret Speech.

Numerous files in the Party Archive in Moscow (RGANI) show that between 1962 and 1964, Pospelov had to defend himself repeatedly against former members of his collective who accused him of being too soft on Stalin. Pospelov won the day by arguing that the focus needed to be on "the heroic efforts and victories of the Soviet people and its armed forces" rather than on Stalin's role.⁹¹ Heroism was the lowest common denominator.

Not least, it was Marshall Georgiy Zhukov who tried to capitalize on this consensus to advance veterans' interests and the public profile of war memory. Zhukov, back from his exile and serving as minister of defense since 1955, played an important political role after Stalin's death, as Khrushchev's ally against his rivals. In letters to the Central Committee in 1955 and 1956, he demanded that Heroes of the Soviet Union receive a pension: "The Soviet people will greet the reintroduction of this remuneration (*voznagrazhdenie*) with great satisfaction (*udovletvorenie*)—as an expression of the Communist Party's attention and concern toward those who served in the military to defend the Soviet homeland. This will [also] fulfill an important function in the education of Soviet youth."⁹²

Zhukov succeeded in his second attempt. On May 9, 1956, pensions were reintroduced. His attempts at heightening the Hero Cities' status also met with positive results. He remarked that "not a single significant monument in the country" had been built since the end of the war. Zhukov advocated memorial construction at the "places of extraordinary battles of the past war, which the Soviet people consider holy."⁹³

Komsomol first secretary Aleksandr Shelepin echoed Zhukov's words when he wrote to the Central Committee in 1956, saying that the USSR's "monument propaganda" was totally insufficient.⁹⁴ Zhukov argued that monuments would serve as symbols for the education of the people, "youth in particular," and as "worthy" places for excursions and delegations to visit.⁹⁵ He demanded they be constructed in Moscow, Stalingrad, Sevastopol', and Odessa—"which have won immortal glory with the people." Zhukov announced that the Ministry of Defense and the Ministry of Culture SSSR would launch a design competition.⁹⁶ This started the process for the construction of a monument in Moscow—a process that would last until 1993.⁹⁷ In the other three cities, planning and construction also took years. In Volgograd, the monumental ensemble opened in 1967.⁹⁸

Nonetheless, the design competition marked the first high-level political decision to build a unified memorial landscape in the Hero Cities. By the mid-1960s, a veritable boom in monument construction set in, which would mark the entire Brezhnev era.[99] Hero Cities benefited significantly from the additional symbolic and financial capital linked to this construction.

A NEW PANTHEON

The cities grew increasingly prominent—and collected new awards. Leningrad received a second Order of Lenin in 1957, and Kiev acquired it twice—in 1954 and 1961. After 1961, Kiev was referred to as a Hero City.[100] Battle sites in the western Soviet Union experienced a revaluation, possibly because Khrushchev had his power base in Ukraine. Moreover, the first months of the war no longer represented the kind of taboo they had under Stalin. Some of his mistakes were actively discussed.

The authors collective under Petr Pospelov wrote that Zhukov had wanted to retreat from Kiev to a better defensive position in July 1941. "Stalin was against this and ordered that Kiev be held," leading to the encirclement of hundreds of thousands of Soviet soldiers. The fact that the authors did not publish exact numbers once more points to the boundaries of "Thaw"-era liberties.[101]

The heroes of the war's first day also finally received recognition. The Wehrmacht had attacked the fortress of Brest early in the morning on June 22, 1941. Outnumbered, unprepared, and outgunned, its defenders held out for a month, even though the front had already moved hundreds of miles to the east. According to official war memory, the Soviet soldiers fought "to the last cartridge, to the last sigh (*vzdokh*)."[102]

While the dedication of the fortress's defender is no doubt highly remarkable, the context of the battle was anything but heroic: the German Army handed over the city of Brest, which had been part of Poland before the war, to the Red Army on September 21, 1939, as part of the secret additional protocol of the Molotov-Ribbentrop Pact. The two armies even held a joint parade in the Belarusian city. Because of the Soviet Union's territorial expansion, its western borders remained poorly fortified in 1941, allowing the Wehrmacht's rapid advancement.

Moreover, not all defenders had fought "to the last sigh": four hundred surrendered and were taken prisoner by the Germans. Many of them died, but some also served in German-sponsored paramilitary units in the occupied territories.[103] Elena Senyavskaya writes that Stalinist war memory tried to "forget" the defenders of Brest Fortress because they symbolized Stalin's mistakes.[104]

Under Khrushchev, they became the embodiment of the Soviet people's dedication to defend the homeland—while Moscow's prewar collaboration with Berlin remained a taboo.

Not least, it was the journalist Sergey Smirnov who contributed significantly to public awareness of Brest Fortress's fate. In 1957, he published *Brestskaya Krepost'* (Brest Fortress), for which he won the Lenin Prize in 1965, and in 1963, he published *Rasskazy o Neizvestnykh Geroyakh* (Stories of Untold Heroes).[105] As a veteran, he enjoyed the societal status that allowed him to back his claim of telling the "truth" about the war. Because of his fame as a writer and as host of the television show *Podvig*, he also reached a large audience.

Smirnov claimed that the history of the war remained largely unwritten—in spite of numerous publications: "The martyr's (*muchenicheskaya*) epic of besieged Leningrad still awaits its historians and writers. And the great city on the Volga, where the fiercest battle in the history of humankind raged for such a long time! ... Or destroyed Sevastopol'; Voronezh, divided in two by the front line, or famous 'Malaya Zemlya' (*Little Earth*) near Novorossiysk!"[106]

He skillfully mixed the official canon of war memory with a demand to open it. This coincided with the promotion of local history under Khrushchev, albeit embedded within a patriotic canon of values.[107] By claiming, moreover, that the histories of the battles of Leningrad and Stalingrad were unknown, he implicitly criticized their idealization. Finally, he maintained that the heroism of Voronezh and Novorossiysk, along with that of Kerch', deserved to be put on the same level as that of the existing Hero Cities.

Smirnov devotes an entire chapter to the defense of the Adzhimushkay Quarry near the town of Kerch' on Crimea. He calls this episode, which was covered up by Stalinist propaganda, one of the many "blank spots" of the war.[108] Smirnov describes the battles that resulted in the fall of Sevastopol' and the chaotic evacuation of the peninsula in the summer of 1942.[109] A garrison stayed behind to cover the retreat across the Kerch's strait. It was forced into the Adzhimushkay Quarry, where a century of mining had created an intricate network of tunnels.

Civilians and stragglers from the Red Army soon joined the garrison, which ultimately numbered more than ten thousand. The tunnels were almost impossible to supply, lacking water and food. Still, Smirnov emphasizes that the "subterranean garrison felt their kinship with their military brothers of the Hero City" and continued its resistance. Because the Wehrmacht had cordoned off the quarry, attempts at escape were doomed.

While highlighting its heroism, Sergey Smirnov does not deny the tragic end of the story: "when it had become impossible to stay underground," the commanders led the troops into the "last fight . . . in which the majority (*bol'shaya chast'*) of people fell, and the rest were taken prisoner."[110] In Brezhnev-era accounts, many of the troops break through the enemy blockade, and the quarry becomes a partisan base in the fall of 1943.[111] Smirnov mentions no partisans, but their insertion is telling. Heroic stories need redemption, and resistance against the Wehrmacht had to be constant—if not during the war itself, then at least in official war memory.

Partially because of Smirnov's efforts, Brest was named Hero Fortress on May 8, 1965, and Kerch' a Hero City on September 14, 1973, on the thirtieth anniversary of its liberation. Well-placed individuals such as Zhukov and Smirnov, then, could exert considerable influence on official war memory.

By the mid-1960s, these actors had the ear of the Soviet Union's political leadership. The celebrations of the twentieth anniversary of victory on May 9, 1965, marked a caesura. Official war memory moved to the center of power, and a prodigious military parade took place on Red Square in Moscow. Henceforth, Victory Day would become the most important holiday in the Soviet Union, matched only by the anniversary of the October Revolution and May Day.

On May 8, 1965, First Secretary Leonid Brezhnev had codified and standardized the status of Hero Cities. The "family" grew with the inclusion of Moscow and the "Hero Fortress" Brest. Volgograd, Sevastopol', Odessa, and Brest Fortress were awarded the Gold Star medal and the Order of Lenin. Leningrad, Moscow, and Kiev received the Gold Star medal—in addition to the Order of Lenin, which they had received previously.[112]

The Presidium of the Supreme Soviet USSR's decree number 26 stipulated that all cities that had shown "mass heroism" in the defense of the homeland during the Great Patriotic War were eligible.[113] This vague wording was typical for the highest Soviet awards. The title "Hero of the Soviet Union" was given for "individual or collective merits before the state, related to committing a heroic deed," and "linked to events that caught the attention of the whole world in their time."[114] Conversely, awards such as the Order of Glory necessitated concrete feats: fulfilling one's mission in a burning tank, killing ten to fifty enemy soldiers, or destroying one to three tanks with a hand grenade.[115]

Considering the exclusivity of the highest awards, the notion of the Soviet Union as a heroarchy can be applied to both individuals and places. The hierarchy in awards was based on tsarist precedent: in imperial Russia, the Order of Saint Andrew was the most prestigious, followed by the Order of Saint George and lower commendations.[116] Hero Cities were at the top; most of them had received a lower award before. Minsk received the Order of Lenin in 1966 before becoming a Hero City in 1974. Smolensk (1966) and Murmansk (1982) received the Order of the Patriotic War before their elevation to Hero City status in 1985.

The awards had both economic and political relevance. The leadership and the population of Hero Cities hoped for and often received benefits analogous to those of individual carriers of awards. Moreover, all cities that would attain hero status were important economic and strategic centers, both during and after the war. By the 1960s, they accounted for the majority of Soviet industrial output.

Three Hero Cities—Moscow, Kiev, and Minsk—were Republican capitals. With the exception of Novorossiysk and Brest Fortress, the remaining were Oblast' centers. There is thus a clear connection between a city's significance and its likelihood of receiving the Hero City award. The exact causality—whether they received the award because of their political and economic clout or whether this influence was the result of the award—varied; the former variant was more common.

Hero Cities regularly sent delegations to official occasions, and on Victory Day, they received special salutes. The high award also usually meant that the general secretary would visit and attach the Gold Star and the Order of Lenin to the city banner. The "representatives of the workers"—the local or regional party leadership—received the award and a certificate of merit (*gramota*). The Gorispolkom was responsible for their safekeeping.[117] In cases where the elevation was controversial (such as in Minsk), Brezhnev signaled displeasure by delaying the visit.[118]

The vagueness of the criteria for Hero Cities also meant that the leadership had some leeway in selecting new "family members." During the Brezhnev era, the historical value attributed to a battle or a city depended to an extent on its connection to leading figures. Considering the preeminent symbolical status of war commemoration for the legitimacy of the Soviet system, awards also contributed to the "sacralization" and ritualization of power. "Awarding orders, medals, etc. was an essential (*neot"emlemoy*) part of the emerging system of Soviet rituals, which fulfilled the demand for the heroization of everyday life after the war... and served as a means of encouragement and of differentiation," write Dönninghaus and Savin.[119] The elevation to hero status of a city linked with the war history of individual members of the elite increased their prestige within the ruling circles.

MAKING PEACE WITH STALIN

Hero Cities featured prominently in Brezhnev's speech to a select group of military and political leaders at the Kremlin on May 8, 1965. He proclaimed that "huge Nazi forces were wiped out under the walls of the Hero Cities."[120] Announcing Brest's new status as a Hero Fortress, Brezhnev said that the "selfless struggle of the heroes is the living embodiment of the lofty moral staunchness and patriotism of Soviet people. Honour and glory to them, comrades!"[121]

Brezhnev fused elements from Stalinist and Khrushchevian official memory, keeping closer to the former. He mentioned no repressions and no Hitler-Stalin Pact, only emphasizing the "treacherous attack" that interrupted "the peaceful labour of our people."[122] He claimed that "reactionary circles in the West" had first rearmed Germany and then tried to pacify Hitler by sacrificing Czechoslovakia as part of the Munich Agreement of 1938—"the most disgraceful manifestation of the imperialists' treacherous plot."[123]

Because the first period of the war "took place under conditions that were unfavourable for us and favourable for the enemy," said Brezhnev, "the Soviet people had to drink from the bitter cup of defeat and failure."[124] They nevertheless kept faith, inspired by Leninist ideas. "In the grave situation the Party and the Soviet people made a tremendous, truly heroic effort to strengthen the army and recast the economy on war lines, to convert the country into one big armed camp. The State Committee for Defence headed by Stalin, General Secretary of the CPSU (B) was organized to supervise everything calculated to defeat the enemy."[125]

Brezhnev, like his predecessor, called the party and the Soviet people the main protagonists of victory. His explicit reference to Stalin was sensational, however. He only mentioned the generalissimo once, but this was a clear signal to the revisionists that de-Stalinization was no longer a political priority.

Brezhnev mentioning Stalin did not amount to a full-scale rehabilitation, as some have claimed.[126] More accurate is Jonathan Brunstedt's assessment that the reference was only "mild" and that Brezhnev actually won the struggle against the more rabid neo-Stalinists around Central Committee secretary Aleksandr Shelepin: "Brezhnev and his supporters in the Politburo ... had no desire to elevate Stalin over and above what was necessary to merely recover the mythology of the war as a powerful ideological pillar."[127] Brezhnev stopped short of endowing Stalin with the supreme role he had enjoyed in wartime accounts: he was no longer the "soul" or the "inspiration" (*vdokhnovitel'*) of victory. The party now firmly occupied that position.

The Soviet intelligence services closely monitored the response to Brezhnev's praise of Stalin. Vladimir Semichastnyy, head of the KGB, filed a report about reactions in the military, noting that older officers believed there had been enough talk about Stalin's errors. One of them added that Khrushchev had hurt the prestige of the Red Army with de-Stalinization.[128] Semichastnyy admits that individual servicemen had expressed their "hostile attitude (*nedobrozhelatel'noe otnoshenie*) toward mentioning the names of comrades I. V. Stalin and G. K. Zhukov."[129] A colonel said, "Stalin and Zhukov annihilated so many people. Was it good to mention their names in a speech like this?"[130] A certain L. Pashkin went even further in his criticism, extending it—perhaps dangerously—to the Communist Party itself. "We say: Party, Party! . . . But where was the Party when Stalin annihilated the Party's best sons?"[131]

The reactions show that the conflict over the price of the war and Stalin's role continued to simmer. Jörg Ganzenmüller aptly observed that Brezhnev de-escalated it with an *Umarmungsstrategie* (strategy of embracement): he simply named everyone—soldiers, workers, generals, and Stalin—as members of the victorious collective and thereby neutralized competition.[132] "Embracing" was a fitting metaphor for Brezhnev's leadership style: he secured elite support by emphasizing consensus and the "stability of cadres"—in contrast to Stalin's terror and Khrushchev's unpredictability.[133]

Brezhnev managed to reestablish public consensus on the interpretation of the war. Commemoration was "staged from above and below," even according to Boris Dubin's highly critical assessment.[134] The Kremlin both included and repressed. Research was put under party control. By 1968 at the very latest, historians with a critical stance had been silenced, driven to emigration or even suicide.[135] Moreover, the Ministry of Defense's Main Political Directorate, under Central Committee member General Aleksey Epishev, established a special commission that vetted manuscripts before the censorship body Glavlit screened them.[136] Official war memory thus had the full support of two key ideological institutions: the military and the Institute for Marxism-Leninism. Additionally, the power of the state-controlled printing press stood behind it: Bernd Bonwetsch estimates that twenty thousand books about the war were published between 1965 and 1987, with a print run of one billion.[137]

TRANSGENERATIONAL UNITY

This recentralization was justified by the need to maintain the younger generation's reverence for the heroes of the Great Patriotic War. Participants of the October 1964 Central Committee Plenum deplored the "de-heroization" (*degeroizatsiya*) of the war, which amounted to calling the Soviet people's "heroic traditions" into question. Lamenting the "disorienting" effect of critical novels and history books, Epishev demanded steps against their "harmful and wrong effect on the education of our youth": re-heroization could strengthen young Soviets' will to defend their homeland.[138]

Those in charge of youth work did have reasons to worry: Komsomol membership had dropped drastically after the war, while disengagement from official youth programs had grown.[139] The children of the forties had an ambivalent relationship to the state that had always claimed to protect them but that asked for inhuman sacrifice during the war—not least because they were expected to show heroic behavior.[140]

The post-Stalinist leadership reacted with a reideologization and a limited opening to the outside world, embodied most of all by the World Youth Festival in Moscow (1957). This opening, however, fostered fears that Soviet youth would fall prey to Western influences—a view that Hilary Pilkington calls "paradigmatic" of the time.[141] Phenomena like the evolution of the *Stilyagi* counterculture led to campaigns by the official youth organization Komsomol against "hooliganism" or "parasitism" (*tuneyadstvo*).[142] At the same time, Gleb Tsipursky has shown that the leadership under Khrushchev was very serious and partially successful in its attempts to define a socialist mode of cultural consumption by providing some autonomy to youngsters. The emphasis on "socialist fun" was reversed under Brezhnev, with 1968 as a turning point.[143]

In the same year, Oleg Zinchenko, an official in the Political Department of the Red Army who worked with the Komsomol, connected the "disorientation" of youth with harmful influences from abroad. According to him, "the ruling circles of imperialist states" were increasingly employing "ideological diversion" against Soviet youth to subvert the country's unity.[144] The work of youth organizations was thus "aimed at the defense of revolutionary theory's purity, at the fight against depraved (*rastlennoy*) bourgeois ideology and morality."[145] Its goal was to strengthen communist convictions, Soviet patriotism, proletarian internationalism, and military capability.[146] Zinchenko emphasized the importance of conveying Soviet historical traditions across generations—with war memory as a keystone.[147]

Brezhnev echoed this appeal to young people's patriotism in his 1965 speech. The postwar generation had not experienced the Great Patriotic War, but it would nevertheless fight and sacrifice for Soviet values, claimed the leader of the USSR:

> Fortunately, the new generation of Soviet people has not had to experience the hardships of a world war. Those who are twenty today have never heard the wail of air raid alarms, bomb bursts and artillery bombardments. But the boys and girls of our country take inspiration in the same ideas for which their fathers and elder brothers fought in the past war. If need be, the Soviet youth will live up to the fighting traditions of the heroes of the Great Patriotic War. The Soviet youth will not spare their strength or flinch in the face of

any sacrifice in defending their Motherland and the gains of the October Revolution, in the name of the victory of communism.[148]

For Brezhnev, the twentieth anniversary was the moment when the Soviet people remembered "the dauntless sons and daughters of our people who fell in battle for the liberty and independence of our country, for the triumph of a just cause. May their deeds be an example for future generations!"[149]

Through official war memory, then, Brezhnev conveyed the desired socialist values—patriotism, selflessness, staunchness, and discipline—to the society of the mid-1960s. The regime saw official memory as a template for Soviet identity. Judging by the opportunities for identification and the positive portrayal of an event that was still extremely significant for virtually everyone, this template enjoyed considerable public support. The transgenerational reverence and hegemonic status it enjoyed made war memory a well-chosen topic to bolster the ideological foundations of the system.[150]

Brezhnev also chose the right date: Victory Day, May 9. Nina Tumarkin writes that it was "the only real, official holiday... *both* the tool of propagandists touting its triumphs and a memorial day for millions of relatives and friends of the war dead."[151] For all its clichés, adds Lisa Kirschenbaum, official war memory under Brezhnev "managed to communicate a sense, however diluted, of unredemptive loss."[152] He could not go back behind publicly disclosed figures such as Khrushchev's 1959 declaration about twenty million war dead.[153] Tragedy played a role in Brezhnev's 1965 speech:

> Our people's victory was no easy one. Such a cruel war as that fought by the Soviet Union has never fallen to the lot of any other people. The war claimed the lives of over 20 million Soviet people. It left tens of millions of orphans, widows, and invalids. An ocean of human suffering and sorrow is hidden behind these figures! There is hardly a family in our country in which the war has not left its tragic imprint. Human sacrifices were our greatest loss. We shall never forget a single drop of the blood that has been spilled by Soviet people for our country, for its liberty and happiness![154]

The war was presented as a "people's war," in which the entire population had made sacrifices for victory. At the same time, this devastating event was turned into an "optimistic tragedy" that, for all its loss and pain, had created the foundation of the Soviet Union's current power and the peaceful life of its citizens.[155] As a result, Brezhnev argued, the USSR had become a force for peace in the world.

Basing the fight for peace on a war is highly contradictory. However, the destruction and loss that Soviet society had suffered led to a widely shared notion among the population that there simply must never be another war. Brezhnev's own war experience, which had left him physically impaired and possibly traumatized, instilled in him a deep fear of armed conflict.[156] His past motivated him to pursue a policy of easing international tension (détente), which he regularly justified in public by referring to the horrors of the Great Patriotic War.[157]

However, the need for peace was not the only conclusion the Soviet Union drew from the war. Commemoration also conveyed a vague sense of threat—for propagandistic reasons, but possibly also because the society had never confronted its trauma and was thus susceptible to the notion that the USSR's enemies were waiting for an opportunity to attack and annihilate it. Official war memory drew a direct line of continuity between past and present. The Manichean worldview also legitimized high military expenditures and, according to Ellen Jones, inculcated the vast majority of citizens with a high level of respect for military institutions and service.[158]

In his speech, Brezhnev draws analogies between Nazism and current threats: "Comrades, the lessons of the Second World War show, above all, that the peoples must be vigilant with respect to the aggressive designs of imperialism."[159] The Vietnam War was a good illustration, according to the Soviet leader: "After fascism was defeated, a new imperialist striking force emerged with the United States at its head.... The US imperialists had evidently learned nothing from the fate of the German-fascist claimants to world domination."[160] He added: "We make no secret of it that a large portion of our national budget is spent on fortifying the fighting efficiency of our Armed Forces. The Soviet people know perfectly well that these expenditures are necessary and put the full weight of their support behind the measures taken by the Party and Government to strengthen the defence potential of our country."[161]

Official war commemoration provided a justification for the political line pursued by the Communist Party abroad and domestically. Depending on the international political climate, it could serve as a legitimation for both détente and the invasions in Czechoslovakia (1968) and Afghanistan (1979).

Not least, official war memory lessened the tension between ethnic Russian and multinational Soviet identity blueprints, which Yitzhak Brudny, David Brandenberger, and Jonathan Brunstedt have discussed at length.[162] Ideologists had to subsume both communism, which was essentially internationalist, and national love for the homeland.[163] Official war memory, although not entirely devoid of Russian nationalist overtones, provided the background for articulating this interethnic patriotism.[164] The First Secretary declared: "If there was a chief hero of the Great Patriotic War, that immortal hero was the entire close-knit family of the peoples of our country, welded together by indestructible bonds of fraternity."[165]

SITES OF REVOLUTIONARY, MILITARY, AND LABOR GLORY

To anchor official war memory and Soviet values in citizens'—and particularly the postwar generation's—everyday lives, the party's Ideological Commission established a canon of rituals. In January 1964, it initiated a campaign to promote nonreligious festivals and rites.[166] These rites not only helped stabilize the existing political order but also provided an emotional bond, a means for identifying with societal values and healing after crises. This latter point appears particularly important for Soviet war memory: experiences between 1941 and 1945 were too traumatic to confront in an unmediated fashion. Ritualization created the necessary distance to transform them into a transgenerational force of integration.[167]

At war memorials, youngsters would be initiated into the Komsomol and would swear to be good citizens. On Victory Day and the anniversaries of the October Revolution or the liberation of individual towns, workers would gather at monuments and collectively pledge to fulfill and exceed their production norms.[168] There, youth would also receive their passports or enlisting orders for the Red Army. Official war memory was thereby connected to other tenets of Soviet ideology, such as the revolution and labor.

The centerpiece of these rituals of patriotic education was the all-Union Tours (*Pokhod*) to the Sites of Revolutionary, Military, and Labor Glory.[169] The *buro* of the Komsomol's Central Committee instituted the first large-scale excursions to "places of military glory of the Soviet people" on May 25, 1965, a mere two weeks after the twentieth anniversary of Victory Day.

The initiators in Moscow established special staffs under the leadership of high-ranking retired officers on all administrative levels.[170] Within them, Komsomol activists collaborated with the military; the Volunteer Society for Cooperation with the Army, Aviation, and Fleet (*Dobrovol'noe Obshchestvo Sodeystviya Armii, Aviatsii i Floty*—DOSAAF); and the educational organization Knowledge (*Znanie*) to organize hundreds of thousands of excursions, rituals, reading sessions, and movie nights. In its invitation to all Komsomol members in 1965, the Central Staff wrote: "We invite you on an excursion. It lets you experience long hikes, and on your way you will experience our mighty rivers and our majestic mountain passes, you will steel your body and come to know the romanticism of scouting, you will get to know your home region better, the beauty of its nature, its heroic past."[171]

All these excursions had a historical or military theme, in most cases related to World War II: young people traveled to former battlefields, wrote down veterans' stories, put together documentations, and sometimes looked for the remains of soldiers missing in action. The physicality of "authentic" places or "sacred" items like banners or weapons did much to create a transcendental aura and a bond to the heroes of the past, whose "baton" the young generation was picking up. To encourage excellence, all excursions were organized as socialist competitions—another Stalinist technique. Youth groups competed to organize the best outing or museum, to sing the best song, or to write the best poem.

Most autumns between 1965 and 1987, winners of regional competitions would gather at the Convention of Winners (*Slet Pobediteley*). Nine out of twelve times, they were hosted by Hero Cities.[172] Three million young people participated in *pokhody* in 1965, and their number had multiplied to fifty-eight million by 1980.[173] They experienced a clearly structured memorial space—in small regional excursions, camping trips, and weeklong bus or boat tours through various cities. While short trips were ubiquitous, longer trips served as rewards for model workers and students—the Soviet "heroes" of the 1960s and 1970s.[174]

Pokhody were thus at once entwined in people's everyday lives and separated from them. Their mix of romanticism, competition, and patriotism had considerable appeal: it provided a respite from the cramped living conditions at home and a chance to explore the region and country and to meet peers from all corners of the Soviet Union. Because of official war memory's status, the excursions to places of *military* glory were more popular than those to places of *revolutionary* and *labor* glory, as numerous sources indicate. The former remained the predominant form—also as a consequence of the waning mobilizing power of socialist doctrine.[175]

The *pokhody* were part of patriotic tourism, for which Hero Cities were important destinations. *Sovety po Turizmu* (Tourism Councils) in the trade unions and the Komsomol's tourism departments collaborated to establish standardized routes. They conducted excursions intended to convey the values of official war memory to the young audience. Youngsters were to be kept engaged in their free time—following the notion of *turizm*, which was "meant to involve work, the enhancement of one's intellectual and physical capital, not leisure."[176] As active participants in ritualized activities, youngsters enacted the values through their own physical and intellectual performance.[177] At the same time, rituals provide space for idiosyncratic interpretation and adaptation, which helps to explain why some commemorative rituals survived the collapse of the USSR.[178]

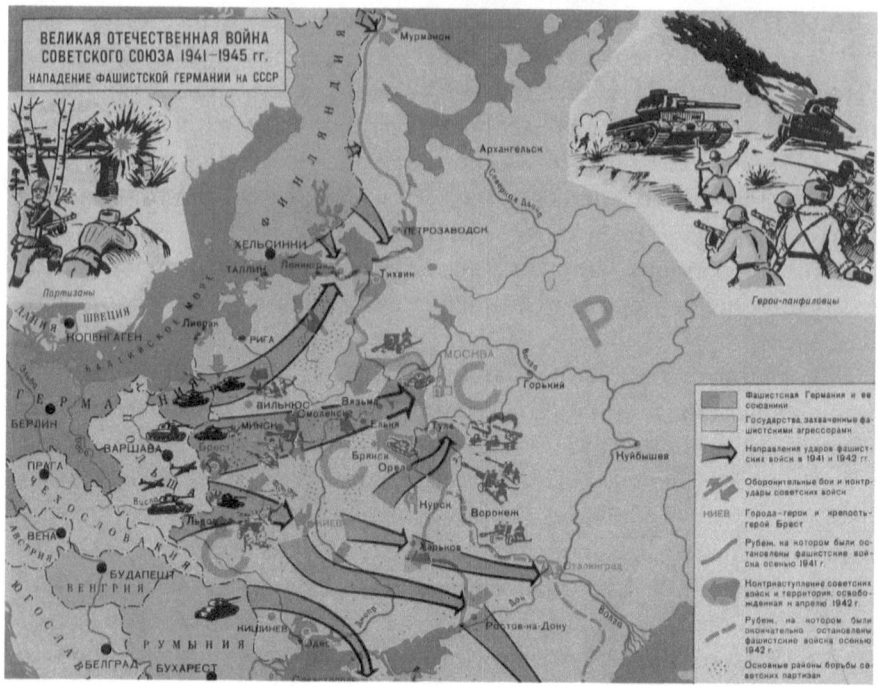

Figure 2.1. Map in atlas for fourth graders. No copyright, Soviet source

TEACHING AND GIFTING HERO CITIES

A curriculum that focused on the heroic past complemented its physical exploration in rituals. These elements combined in patriotic education (*patrioticheskoe vospitanie*), which referred back to pedagogical concepts established in the Stalinist era.[179] Maps and other forms of visual representation reinforced this spatial experience—and anchored it in schools and leisure activities. They created a "mental map" that highlighted wartime events as central aspects of Soviet identity.[180]

The map above (fig. 2.1) is from a fourth-grade atlas that was first published in 1970. It was used to teach ten-year-olds history in the second year of the beginner's course. Students thus had already received an overview and had begun discussing individual periods. The atlas is subdivided into thirteen maps that cover all of Russian and Soviet history from Kievan Rus' through the Patriotic War of 1812, continuing with the October Revolution and the Great Patriotic War.

The atlas was distributed all over the country. Its first edition contained 1,200,000 copies. For a revised version in 1988, more than twice as many books, 2,587,800, were printed. The price of twelve kopecks, low in spite of the good paper and the color prints used, also indicates that the atlas was intended for wide usage.

Unlike all other periods, the Great Patriotic War is featured on two atlas pages instead of one, which underlines its historical importance. The page above shows the first part of the war, and the second page (not shown) illustrates the advance on Berlin. Ominous gray arrows symbolize the German attack, which suffuses occupied countries with a light- to dark-gray hue.

The color coding may stand for the enforced conformity and the deadliness of the Nazi system, which contrasts with the vibrant orange and red of the Soviet territory. The arrows barrel into the USSR, but they are stopped along a consistent red front line from Murmansk to Stalingrad. Black, inhumane German tanks and planes clash with an army made up of Soviet people, depicted as tanks, rocket launchers, and howitzers manned by individual soldiers. Images in the top corners prioritize individual groups, the partisans and the *Panfilovtsy*.[181] Particularly around the anniversaries of important battles, teachers told students about the feats of these heroes, whose resistance against the invaders had saved the fatherland.[182]

Aside from these individual actors, the map highlights Hero Cities. The caption box on the right side assigns them a special red symbol (fifth from the top). Young readers were thus able to see at once that these cities formed the "bastions" of resistance along the German advance and constituted the backbones of the front line. As inhabitants of Hero Cities and as Soviet citizens, the postwar generation could identify with the feats of their forebears.

The map depicts a clash of good and evil by drawing clearly colored borderlines that disambiguate the civil war–like conditions and crimes committed by both sides in the "bloodlands."[183] It also conceals the chaos of the Soviet retreat and the reality of occupation: front lines are strong, and in areas conquered by the Wehrmacht, partisans (symbolized by red dots) continue to resist. Hero Cities hold this memorial space together.

The map also shows that even within this group, there was a primus inter pares: Moscow. When it became a Hero City in 1965, Moscow regained its position as the country's symbolic center. It is located in the middle of the map, the main goal of the German attack and Soviet defense efforts. Its letters are not only red but also capitalized, which elevates it further. A stylized image of the Kremlin identifies it as the seat of Soviet power.

The metaphor of the family and its patriarch is once more evident in this heroarchy. In Brezhnev's 1965 speech, Moscow is even explicitly anthropomorphized: "All of Moscow's mighty organism could feel the approaching danger." It was "the city" that "made a tremendous effort to contain the enemy at all costs, not to allow him to tread the streets and squares of the city that had been drenched in the blood of the heroes of three revolutions."[184]

Anthropomorphization creates an emotional bond to make an abstract entity more tangible and familiar. As a connector between the individual and the state, the Hero City thereby also personalizes the patriotic relationship to the country. Finally, the family allegory and Moscow's position in it point to a more patriarchal than egalitarian relationship among Hero Cities.

Other media reproduced this homogenized memorial landscape. Hero Cities featured not only in history books and tourist guides but also in consumer items. The historian Olga Martin explains that Soviet "consumers" were presented with a unified message in all aspects of life: "This is . . . a strategy for forming consciousness and cultural memory within a hermetically sealed system."[185] Items of everyday consumption satisfied the demand of a population that had profited from an increase in general welfare, which accelerated after the recurrent economic crises of the Khrushchev years were overcome. Patriotic tourism and consumer items celebrating the glorious past served the same kind of "rational" consumption that was meant to distinguish the Soviet Union from the "hedonistic" West.[186]

Matchboxes and pins are two especially interesting consumer categories. As relatively banal items, insists Evgeniy Dobrenko, they "not only reflect 'habits of consciousness' but also form part of the 'structures of everydayness.'"[187] The omnipresence of Hero Cities in such items reflected their towering presence in Soviet culture, linking the past and the present.

Many households were not connected to the gas or electricity grid for a long time, and so they needed matches for cooking and bathing. Matches were a symbolically charged item of last resort in times of crisis, and they were one of the most basic commodities Soviet citizens stocked up on when they feared trouble.[188] Because of their availability in every household, matchboxes were among the best places for "advertisement" by the government: images contained safety tips, production numbers, and patriotic themes.[189] They were produced and designed in specialized factories.

Hero City series were produced for numerous anniversaries, culminating on the thirtieth in 1975. Factories produced at least ten series, three on war monuments and two on Hero Cities. The pictures below (fig. 2.2) are from the second series.

CREATING AN IDEALIZED PAST 41

Figure 2.2. Matchbox images from 1975 depicting Hero Cities.
Courtesy of Viktor Martin, private collection

One can see from the lined and numbered paper that these matchbox images were carefully mounted into a special booklet. They are part of the personal collection of Viktor Martin and could also be bought independently.[190] Soviet enthusiasts founded a matchbox collectors' society in 1957 to share their hobby of *phillumeny* with others.[191] Whereas collectors had been considered petty bourgeois under Stalin, matchbox factories subsequently produced special series for them.

The link to war memory is already evident in the red framing of the images. To their left stands the Gold Star, underneath the numbers 1941–1945, symbolizing the war. The stylized images of famous monuments are encased in two wreaths, which signify mourning and commemoration. They converge in the Roman numerals XXX, which stand for the thirtieth anniversary of victory.

The drawings show six monuments. For Odessa, Minsk, Moscow, and Kiev, they are dedicated to the defenders or the "people" as a whole, while those in Sevastopol' and Novorossiysk commemorate Komsomol members and sailors of the Black Sea Fleet. The first group is abstract, generalizing loss and triumph and representing the vague but heroic collective.

The second group singles out a specific group for its contribution to the defense. Sevastopol's monument to the Komsomol members and its caption—"steadfastness, loyalty, courage" (*stoykost', vernost', muzhestvo*)—is a call to the postwar generation for emulation. "The best representatives of youth" were initiated into the Komsomol at the monument, which opened on October 29, 1963.[192] Here, as in many other places, the exemplary values Hero Cities embodied were combined with youths' obligation to show themselves "worthy" of their ancestors.

These images, then, both reflected *and* shaped the values associated with Hero Cities. Combined with tourist excursions, which followed predetermined routes featuring those monuments, they were supposed to influence ideas of space and define its symbolic dimension. In his book *Commemorative Badges of the Hero Cities*, Vladimir Goncharuk points out: "The memory of the war is immortalized in bronze, granite and marble obelisks and monuments. Today the millions of people who visit Hero Cities take an emblem with them without ceremony—a unique business card."[193]

Millions of these pins circulated to honor the Hero Cities and also to mark anniversaries, winners of socialist competitions, and sports events. The distribution of these commemorative badges began in the mid-1960s under the supervision of the Creative-Industrial Combine of the Artistic Fund of the Russian Federation, which was also responsible for the construction of most monuments.[194] The factory Pobeda in Moscow and Suvenir in Volgograd produced most of the pins.[195]

Unlike matchboxes, pins served purely as souvenirs, distinctions, and collectibles. As a widely available item of consumption, however, they also shaped the perception of the cities they depicted. Of particular interest is a collection of pins minted in honor of the Hero Cities in 1975 (fig. 2.3). They closely resemble the matchbox from the same year; they also show an iconic monument, feature the Gold Star, and display the name of the city on a ribbon.

The images, however, are more standardized than in other collections. Sevastopol' is the only Hero City whose emblem features a monument commemorating a prerevolutionary event, albeit one that also represents military glory: the Monument to the Scuttled Ships from the Crimean War. Novorossiysk also presents a symbol specific to the Navy, the Monument to the Unknown Sailor. For Kiev, the memorial "To the Liberators of Kiev" symbolizes the forcing of the Dnepr.[196] Brest is condensed into a fortress.

The other six cities' emblems are completely allegorical: three obelisks, the symbols unique to the Hero Cities, and two Rodina-Mat' statues that can be read as allegories for the homeland or for the victory goddess Nike.[197] Moscow,

Figure 2.3. Pins from 1975 showing ten Hero Cities.
Courtesy of Ivo Mijnssen, private collection

finally, stands for the war as a whole and for victory: instead of a structure specific to the city, only the years 1941–1945 are imprinted. Underneath, the name of the capital features much larger than those of the other cities, on a ribbon that stretches all the way across the pin. These visual clues reinforce Moscow's role as "patriarch" of the Hero Cities.

WAR AND POSTWAR GENERATIONS

Anchoring official war memory in everyday life nevertheless failed to conceal the profound disconnect in different Soviet cohorts' life experiences. While the war was a tangible memory for its veterans, it remained abstract for the postwar generation, whose identity was difficult to grasp for the aging men in power. The leadership around Brezhnev was rather homogenous. Born in the early twentieth century, many so-called *vydvizhentsy* had advanced their careers as a result of Stalinist purges. The war was a defining biographical experience. It did not equip them to deal with youngsters' lifeworlds in the 1960s and 1970s. This fifth Soviet generation, according to Yuriy Levada, was born between the mid-1940s and the late 1950s; the Brezhnev era constituted its formative years.[198]

The insecurity is at times tangible in official discourse: in a book on the history of Soviet youth, the historian Viktor Sorokin highlights the past's inclusive power and the notion of transgenerational heroism, which meant that youth had "picked up the baton of their forefathers." Nonetheless, he also admits to his own ignorance: "A new generation has made its appearance—the youth of the sixties. For these 18-year olds the battles of Stalingrad and Kursk, the liberation of Warsaw and Berlin are something in the history books. And that is not all—the development of the virgin lands, pioneer work on the Angara power project, are stories they hear from their elders.... Who are these boys and girls? Do they realize the price that was paid for their happiness today?"[199]

They did to an extent, as official war memory was present in their lives—through the stories told in public and by family members. Postwar devastation was nevertheless merely a childhood memory, if that. Still, as Vladimir Shlapentokh points out, the postwar generation was not immune to a feeling of fear, which lingered on decades after the Stalinist purges and the Great Patriotic War. "The fear was so pronounced that it passed from generation to generation. In effect, the post-Stalin leaders were able to reduce the scope of repressions while maintaining fear as a political instrument."[200] This fear also increased the impact of official war memory.

On a material level, the postwar generation had seen slow but steady improvements. Coming of age "at the zenith of Soviet socialism," it had benefited "from years of peaceful, evolutionary, organic development."[201] After the difficult years under Stalin, their families settled in more promising lives during the 1950s. This also meant a move into an apartment in one of the new housing projects of the Khrushchev and Brezhnev era. For many, this elevation was the most tangible embodiment of the "better life" Soviet leaders had promised.

The postwar generation was the most educated cohort in the USSR's history; higher education grew fourfold between the 1950s and the 1980s.[202] Upward social mobility was closely connected to educational opportunities, which many were able to take advantage of, at least in the booming 1960s. This was a rather unheroic cohort, which valued economic well-being at least as highly as ideological purity or sacrifice. "They focused their attention primarily upon professional advancement and the acquisition of a high standard of living. They generally did not openly express political opinions or actively participate in the activities of the Soviet government or the Communist Party beyond what was officially expected. Likewise, they did not openly break with the regime, as did their 'dissident' contemporaries."[203]

Although David Ruffley is right to stress the increased importance of materialism and careerism in the postwar generation, his analysis nevertheless falls short. First of all, active participation in "societal organizations" (*obshchestvennye organizatsii*), and often party membership, was a precondition for advancement. What is more, the increased penetration of citizens' everyday lives bolstered membership of societal organizations. This was particularly true for the postwar generation because they were the target audience of patriotic education campaigns and the many organizations founded to implement them.

Secondly, the emergence of official war memory in the mid-1960s coincided with an increase in living standards.[204] This created a significant amount of stability. Moreover, the two were presented and perceived as connected: the promise of a better life in exchange for patriotic service had already been central during the war.[205] Following Kotkin, one can understand the "empowering, if demanding" link between sacrifice and benefits as part and parcel of the Bolshevik social identity.[206]

Khrushchev aggressively propagated the notion of this "socialist contract." The fulfillment of the population's basic needs, first and foremost housing, (and, as Tsipursky points out, cultural needs[207]) became an important basis for the paternalistic system's legitimacy. This was all the more important because war and reconstruction had severely undermined the state's ability to fill these needs. Under Brezhnev, the contract was extended to broader areas of consumption. Still, the emphasis on service distinguished this model—at least theoretically—from Western notions of consumption.

The socialist contract was more complex than the purely economistic approach suggested by Linda Cook:[208] the population was not a passive receiver of state-sponsored privileges but an active player. During the 1920s and 1930s, proletarians had to work for the state; during the war years, soldiers had to fight. During the Brezhnev era, service became more ritualized and mediated for the postwar generation.

In return, they were able to confront the state as entitled citizens—an attitude Brezhnev himself encouraged, when he explained in 1970 that higher productivity required worthy living standards.[209] He prioritized "care for the individual" (*zabota o cheloveke*), which lay at the ideological foundation of Khrushchev's great housing projects. This changed the subject position of Soviet citizens, which Christine Varga-Harris observed in their petitions to the authorities. They "presented themselves as worthy individuals seeking the fulfillment of longstanding promises, while indicating a continuing investment into the radiant communist future that public discourse ardently associated with current housing construction."[210]

In addition, the Brezhnev era tolerated and even encouraged semilegal market activities as a coping and stabilizing strategy.[211] While the official system was able to provide its citizens with basic foodstuffs, education, health care, and housing, more exclusive goods were *defitsitnye* and thus only attainable through connections. To the postwar generation, consumer goods, which included Western items like jeans or music, were an inherent part of socialist welfare.

The socialist contract remains an ideal that was never wholly fulfilled by either side but that was handled pragmatically. Nevertheless, it is a useful instrument to analyze popular and state expectations and the discursive rules that guided the articulation of demands. Hero Cities, as examples for the rest of the country, are particularly interesting places to study it; the primary function of heroization was the mobilization of the urban population. In their research on awards, Bruno Frey and Jana Gallus distinguish between the confirmatory and discretionary award: the former is given for a clearly defined act, and the latter is vaguer and thus in keeping with the highest awards in the Soviet Union given to Hero Cities. Discretionary awards are supposed to appeal more strongly to intrinsic motivation, as they "leave the targeted performance sufficiently vague." Nonetheless, acceptance of the award infers a "special bond of loyalty."[212]

This is all the more important given that the problem of mobilizing the population became increasingly pressing throughout the Brezhnev era. Growth rates fell, and work discipline slackened in the 1960s. The fact that the CPSU abandoned the utopian future and settled Soviet society in "developed socialism" in 1967 was symptomatic:[213] the reformers around Prime Minister Aleksey Kosygin were acutely aware of the USSR's structural problems, even if such problems would only become obvious to the general population in the 1980s.

Attempts at adding dynamism to the economy through the introduction of limited market mechanisms all but ended in the wake of the suppression of the Prague Spring. After that, the Politburo majority favored employing "moral" instead of "material" incentives for the stimulation of the economy—a question the authorities wavered over throughout different eras.[214] Official war memory was thus increasingly connected to economic signifiers. Awards, but also the ever-increasing number of socialist competitions, were to act as stimulants.[215]

Avenues of upward social mobility narrowed for the postwar generation, and problems supplying the population multiplied, contributing to stagnation and to the slow but steady erosion of Brezhnev's success in the second half of the 1970s.[216] The discrepancy between official depictions of Soviet society and the direction of its development grew. Brezhnev's "strategy of embracement," which put stability above all, avoided controversial issues whenever possible; problems became more and more difficult to detect.[217]

Soviet "authoritative" discourse became "increasingly normalized, ubiquitous and predictable," especially in the second half of the Brezhnev era, according to Alexei Yurchak.[218] Lacking ideological innovation and unsure of where exactly the limits of the permissible lay, politicians and cultural figures preferred to copy and paste from the leadership's existing speeches and publications. Official discourse became a closed system, a self-reflexive, self-explanatory formation. "It became increasingly more important to participate in the reproduction of the *form* of these ritualized acts of authoritative discourse than to engage with their constative meanings."[219] However, Yurchak explicitly does *not* argue that this formalism was the same as passivity. Instead, the performative enactment of these rituals created space for the emergence of new meaning. Yurchak's approach, then, provides the basis to locate roots of social and discursive changes even in a seemingly "stagnant" epoch.

NOTES

1. This statement is based on a keyword search of the *Pravda Digital Archive*, which includes *Izvestiya*, *Pravda*, and *Literaturnaya Gazeta*.

2. Bukharin, "VII Vserossiyskiy i VII Vsesoyuznyy S"ezdy Sovetov," 3.

3. Petrograd was awarded this *pochetnoe revolyutsyonnoe Krasnoe Znamya* by decision of the congress. On December 5, 1919, it also received the Order of the Red Banner. Kolesnikov and Rozhkov, *Ordena i Medali SSSR*, 46.

4. Durdevich-Dukich, *Narodni Heroji Jugoslavije*.

5. Norman Davies cites a Polish history book from 1951 that referred to Warsaw as a Hero City. The Red Army's abandonment of the Warsaw rebels in 1944 was, however, hardly a cause for celebration. Soviet historiography was correspondingly hesitant to address it. Norman Davies, *Rising '44*, 522.

6. King George VI of Great Britain awarded the George Cross to Malta in April 1942 for its defense against German and Italian air raids. BBC, "Malta Gets George Cross for Bravery." Various Italian cities received the *Medaglia d'oro al valor militare* in recognition of partisan resistance during German occupation. Presidenza della Repubblica, "Onorificenze."

7. Schneider, "100 Jahre nach Napoleon," 45–66.

8. Plokhy, "City of Glory," 369–83.
9. Makhanov, "Gorod-Krepost'," 3.
10. Petrov, "Segodnya Otkrytie Muzeya Oborony Tsaritsyna im. Stalina," 2.
11. Günther, *Der sozialistische Übermensch*, 8–9.
12. Günther, *Der sozialistische Übermensch*, 158.
13. Carlyle defines *heroarchy* simply as "government of heroes," by which he means loyalty to revered men, upon which, in his opinion, all societal systems rested. Carlyle, *On Heroes*, 28–29.
14. Kolesnikov and Rozhkov, *Ordena i Medali SSSR*, 11.
15. Kotkin, *Magnetic Mountain*, 215; Ewing, *Teachers of Stalinism*, 270; Brandenberger, *National Bolshevism*, 29–45.
16. See Kelly, *Comrade Pavlik*.
17. Katerina Clark, *Soviet Novel*, 114.
18. Oberländer, *Sowjetpatriotismus und Geschichte*, 9.
19. Brandenberger, *National Bolshevism*, 6.
20. The completion of extraordinary feats is inherent in all definitions of a hero. See, for instance, Reemtsma, "Der Held, das Ich und das Wir," 3.
21. Bednyy, "Gorodu-Geroyu," 3.
22. For a Russian publication that analyzes the blockade critically, see Volkovskiy, *Blokada Leningrada v Dokumentakh Rassekrechennykh Arkhivov*.
23. "Muzhestvennye Zashchitniki Velikogo Goroda," 1.
24. "Slavnaya Pobeda pod Leningradom," 1.
25. "Velikaya Pobeda pod Leningradom," 1.
26. "Geroicheskiy Stalingrad," 1.
27. Polevoy, "Za Volgu-Matushku," 2.
28. Polevoy, "Stena Stalingrada," 2.
29. See the eyewitness accounts in Hellbeck, *Die Stalingrad Protokolle*; Beevor, *Stalingrad*.
30. In his book on Stalingrad, Jochen Hellbeck corrected earlier estimates that had assumed thousands of executions. Using archival research, Hellbeck arrives at the number 278. Hellbeck, *Die Stalingrad Protokolle*, 24.
31. Wette, *Stalingrad*, 15.
32. Gessen, *Goroda-Geroi*, 6. A similar publication published by the Moscow Komsomol maintains that "a city turns into a fortress when defended by the Soviet people." Moskovskiy Gorodskoy Komitet VLKSM, et al., *Goroda-Geroi Velikoy Otechestvennoy Voyny*, 2.
33. Kolesnik, *Narodnoe Opolchenie Gorodov-Geroev*, 348.
34. Kolesnik, *Narodnoe Opolchenie Gorodov-Geroev*, 15–18.
35. Kolesnik, *Narodnoe Opolchenie Gorodov-Geroev*, 24 (my emphasis).
36. Soviet historiography in general saw collectives rather than individuals as the decisive forces of history. Ganzenmüller, "Die siegreiche Rote Armee und ihre Führung," 17.

37. Sabine Behrenbeck writes that the hero risks and often sacrifices his life for the sake of the community. Behrenbeck, *Der Kult um die toten Helden*, 66.

38. Arnold, *Stalingrad im sowjetischen Gedächtnis*, 326.

39. As Jeffrey Jones shows in his study of Rostov-on-Don, the press openly described "grey areas" in the evaluation of collaboration in the first months after liberation, before a harder line took over. Jeffrey W. Jones, *Everyday Life and the 'Reconstruction' of Soviet Russia*, 150–51.

40. P. Ivanov, "Polgoda Oborony Sevastopolya," 3.

41. Plokhy, "City of Glory," 374.

42. Brandenberger, *National Bolshevism*, 66, 104, 234.

43. Sobolev, "Put' k Sevastopolyu," 3.

44. Sobolev, "Put' k Sevastopolyu," 3. An article in *Izvestiya* includes Odessa among the ranks of Hero Cities already on April 11, 1944: Ryl'skiy and Yanovskiy, "Salyut Gorodu-Geroyu!," 3.

45. In one article in 1941, Vsevolod Ivanov had already called Moscow a "Hero City . . . city of power and glory." However, this is the only mention before the city's official elevation in 1965. Vsevolod Ivanov, "Zhitel' Otchizny," 2.

46. Stalin, "Prikaz Narodnogo Komissara Oborony SSSR 7 Noyabrya 1942 Goda No 345," 130.

47. The recipients were soldiers and workers: 1.46 million in Leningrad; 29,500 in Odessa; 48,500 in Sevastopol'; and 754,000 in Stalingrad. Kolesnikov and Rozhkov, *Ordena i Medali SSSR*, 127, 135, 139, 143.

48. This included Petrozavodsk, which until 1956 was capital of the Karelo-Finnish Soviet Socialist Republic.

49. Stalin, "Prikaz Verkhovnogo Komanduyushchego No 20," 1.

50. Palmer, *Dictatorship of the Air*, 233.

51. Qualls, *From Ruins to Reconstruction*, 17.

52. Qualls, *From Ruins to Reconstruction*, 4. On Stalingrad's reconstruction, see also Arnold, *Stalingrad im sowjetischen Gedächtnis*, 233.

53. Katerina Clark, *Soviet Novel*, 49. Hans-Dieter Schmid observed similar moments in German history. Schmid, "Helden des Proletariats?," 135.

54. Weiner, *Making Sense of War*, 49.

55. Zimenkov, "Stalingrad Segodnya," 3.

56. "Trudovoy Den' Stalingrada," 3.

57. TASS, "Gorod-Geroy Privetstvuet Velikogo Vozhdya," 1.

58. Maddox, *Saving Stalin's Imperial City*, 77.

59. "Velikaya Pobeda pod Leningradom," 1.

60. "Orden Lenina," 2.

61. Quoted in "Orden Lenina," 2.

62. Günther, *Der sozialistische Übermensch*, 180. On popular acceptance of socialist heroes, see Satjukow and Gries, "Zur Konstruktion des 'sozialistischen Helden,'" 21, 33.

63. "Interv'yu Tov. I. V. Stalina s Korrespondentom 'Pravdy' Otnositel'no Rechi g. Cherchillya," 1. To an extent, the underreporting of casualties was linked to the lack of reliable statistics: commanders often kept silent about losses to cover up mistakes and receive additional supplies. By 1946, Stalin nevertheless must have known that his numbers were too low.

64. See Bonwetsch, "War as a 'Breathing Space,'" 138–53.

65. Merridale, *Ivan's War*.

66. Senyavskaya, *Psikhologiya Voyny v XX Veke*, 186–87.

67. Weiner, *Making Sense of War*, 367.

68. Konradova and Ryleva, "Helden und Opfer," 349–50. At the University of Basel, Anne Hasselmann wrote a dissertation called "Wie der Krieg ins Museum kam. Die Gestaltung der Erinnerung in den sowjetischen Museen Moskau, Minsk und Tscheljabinsk" on the evolution of war museums in the 1940s and 1950s. Mischa Gabowitsch has also published various papers on monument construction during the same era in the Soviet Union and Eastern Europe.

69. Beate Fieseler estimates that there were at least 2.5 million war wounded. Fieseler, "Arme Sieger," 208.

70. According to Senyavskaya, post-traumatic stress disorder (PTSD) was almost universal. Senyavskaya, *Psikhologiya Voyny v XX Veke*, 188.

71. Merridale, *Night of Stone*, 253.

72. In the so-called Leningrad Affair in 1949, the leadership of the city's Communist Party was liquidated, putting an end to official commemorations of the blockade. Steven Maddox, *Saving Stalin's Imperial City*, 191. Only in 1957 did Leningrad regain a prominent position—as part of a national heroarchy. Ganzenmüller, *Das belagerte Leningrad 1941–1944*, 336–43.

73. Bonwetsch, "Der 'Grosse Vaterländische Krieg' und seine Geschichte," 168.

74. Kolesnikov and Rozhkov, *Ordena i Medali SSSR*, 18. The privileges for carriers of awards would be reinstated only on September 6, 1967. Claims for benefits for broader strata were denied—for financial reasons. Prezidium Verkhovnogo Soveta SSSR: "Ukaz ot 6 Sentyabrya 1967 Goda."

75. The population also contributed "voluntarily" by buying bonds during and after the war. As part of monetary reform in December 1947, the state paid back one-third of them, which led to considerable dissatisfaction. Jeffrey W. Jones, *Everyday Life and the 'Reconstruction' of Soviet Russia*, 106.

76. See Furst, "Arrival of Spring?," 135–53. Oleg Kharkhordin has discussed this penetration of everyday lives on the level of the *kollektiv*, and Mark Smith has identified it in the housing campaigns of the Khrushchev era. Kharkhordin, *Collective and the Individual in Russia*; Mark Smith, *Property of Communists*.

77. Polly Jones, "Introduction," 14.

78. Political theorists Ernesto Laclau and Chantal Mouffe see discourses as unstable and only temporarily stabilized by key signifiers. Laclau and Mouffe, *Hegemony and Socialist Strategy*, 112.
79. Khrushchev, "Cult of the Individual—Part 3."
80. Stalin, *Über den Grossen Vaterländischen Krieg der Sowjetunion*, 6–7, 222.
81. Polly Jones also discusses the treatment of this link in the novels of Konstantin Simonov. Polly Jones, *Myth, Memory, Trauma*, 218.
82. Khrushchev, "Cult of the Individual—Part 4."
83. Stalin, "Vystuplenie na Prieme v Kremle v Chest' Uchastnikov Parada Pobedy," 232.
84. Jacob Torfing, following Laclau and Mouffe, defines *dislocation* as "the disruption of the symbolic order by events that cannot be represented or domesticated by that very order." Torfing, *New Theories of Discourse*, 53.
85. Kelly, "Retreat from Dogmatism," 263.
86. Hösler, *Die sowjetische Geschichtswissenschaft 1953 bis 1991*, 48–69.
87. Especially in literature. An example of a critical novel on the war during Khrushchev's tenure is Vladimir Dudintsev's *Not by Bread Alone*. Literature's contribution to de-Stalinization has been treated at length elsewhere; see, for instance, Polly Jones, *Myth, Memory, Trauma*.
88. Kudryashov, "Erinnerung und Erforschung des Krieges," 134. Joachim Hösler uses the years 1956 and 1966 as his start and end dates. Hösler, *Die sowjetische Geschichtswissenschaft 1953 bis 1991*, 3.
89. Pospelov et al., *Istoriya Velikoy Otechestvennoy Voyny Sovetskogo Soyuza 1941–1945*.
90. Its first edition had a circulation of seventy thousand. Pospelov et al., *Velikaya Otechestvennaya Voyna Sovetskogo Soyuza 1941–1945*.
91. Rossiyskiy Gosudarstvennyy Arkhiv Noveyshey Istorii (RGANI), f. 5, op. 55, d. 62, ll. 25–57.
92. Arkhiv Presidenta Rossiyskoy Federatsii (AP RF), f. 3, op. 53, d. 6, ll. 2–4, quoted in Zhukov, *Georgiy Zhukov*, 34, 103. He calculated the costs at less than one-twentieth of a percent of the Soviet state budget of 539.5 billion rubles in 1955. Rossiyskiy Gosudarstvennyy Arkhiv Ekonomiki (RGAE), f. 1562, op. 41, d. 113, l. 1, *ihistorian*, accessed September 7, 2018, http://ihistorian.livejournal.com/412544.html.
93. RGANI, f. 4, op. 16, d. 39, ll. 114–117, in Zhukov, *Georgiy Zhukov*, 35.
94. Hornsby, "Soviet Youth on the March," 421.
95. RGANI, f. 4, op. 16, d. 39, ll. 114–117, in Zhukov, *Georgiy Zhukov*, 35.
96. RGANI, f. 4, op. 16, d. 39, ll. 114–117, in Zhukov, *Georgiy Zhukov*, 36.
97. For a detailed description, see Tumarkin, "Story of a War Memorial," 125–46.

98. On the opening ceremony, see Arnold, *Stalingrad im sowjetischen Gedächtnis*, 316.

99. Voronov, *Sovetskaya Monumental'naya Skul'ptura 1960–1980*, 6. By 1991 there were more than seventy thousand monuments all over the Soviet Union.

100. The Order of Lenin did not automatically mean that a city was called "Hero City." Multiple places and institutions received the award without the concomitant status.

101. Pospelov et al., *Velikaya Otechestvennaya Voyna*, 90. The authors had controversial discussions about the number of soldiers that were encircled. Quoting Western sources, some estimated them at over 650,000, others at 452,000. RGANI, f. 5, op. 55, d. 123, l. 72. Pospelov and the others wrote somewhat vaguely that there were 677,085 men on this front, of which 150,541 made it out of encirclement. Of the rest, they write, some joined the partisans, and others were taken prisoner. Pospelov et al., *Velikaya Otechestvennaya Voyna*, 90.

102. Golikov, *Podvig Naroda*, 169.

103. On Brest Fortress, see Chiari and Maier, "Volkskrieg und Heldenstädte," 737–56; Gubarenko, "Die Brester Festung," 97–102.

104. Senyavskaya, *Psikhologiya Voyny v XX Veke*, 222.

105. Rumyantsev, "Smirnov Sergey Sergeevich."

106. Sergey Smirnov, *Rasskazy o Neizvestnykh Geroyakh*, 84–85.

107. At that point, an entire series of books was published all over the USSR, all of which had a similar format and title: *Our . . . Area* (fill in the Oblast' or Kray). See also Donavan, "'How Well Do You Know Your Krai?,'" 467.

108. Sergey Smirnov, *Rasskazy o Neizvestnykh Geroyakh*, 3, 116.

109. Sergey Smirnov, *Rasskazy o Neizvestnykh Geroyakh*, 87.

110. Sergey Smirnov, *Rasskazy o Neizvestnykh Geroyakh*, 115.

111. Golikov, *Podvig Naroda*, 161.

112. *Gosudarstvennyy Arkhiv Rossiyskoy Federatsii* (GARF), f. R-7523, op. 82, d. 216, ll. 78–82.

113. GARF, f. R-7523, op. 82, d. 216, ll. 78–82.

114. Kolesnikov and Rozhkov, *Ordena i Medali SSSR*, 25–26.

115. Kolesnikov and Rozhkov, *Ordena i Medali SSSR*, 86–87.

116. See Hurley, *Russian Orders, Decorations, and Medals Under the Monarchy*.

117. GARF, R-7523, op. 82, d. 216, ll. 78–82.

118. Brezhnev did not visit Minsk until 1978. Bohn, *Minsk*, 117. According to a guide in the Belarusian Great Patriotic War Museum, the award was controversial because of the widespread collaboration during three years of German occupation.

119. The most extreme case were undoubtedly Leonid Brezhnev's four Gold Star medals, all of which he received while in office. Dönninghaus and Savin, "Leonid Brezhnev," 180, 187.

120. Brezhnev, *Great Victory of the Soviet People*, 12. Brezhnev's work was released by Progress Publishers, the official Soviet printing house for propagating its ideology abroad.
121. Brezhnev, *Great Victory of the Soviet People*, 20–21.
122. Brezhnev, *Great Victory of the Soviet People*, 7.
123. Brezhnev, *Great Victory of the Soviet People*, 8. The 1948 brochure *Falsifiers of History*, which is considered the definite Stalinist account of the war, also combines the elevation of Stalin's wartime role with an attack against the West. As a result of the "imperialists'" goal of directing "Hitlerite aggression against the Soviet Union," the USSR had no choice but to sign the nonaggression pact with Germany in 1939. Sovetskoe Informatsyonnoe Buro, *Fal'sifikatory Istorii*, 31, 53. The Soviet Union only admitted to the existence of the secret protocol in 1989. S"ezd Narodnykh Deputatov SSSR, "Postanovlenie Snd SSSR," accessed September 24, 2018.
124. Brezhnev, *Great Victory of the Soviet People*, 9–10.
125. Brezhnev, *Great Victory of the Soviet People*, 10–11.
126. See, for instance, Dubin, "Litso Epokhi," 26.
127. Brunstedt, "Building a Pan-Soviet Past," 162.
128. RGANI, f. 5, op. 30, d. 462, l. 40. On Khrushchev's conflict with the army and waning support in later years, see Taubman, *Khrushchev: The Man and his Era*, 578–619.
129. RGANI, f. 5, op. 30, d. 462, l. 43.
130. RGANI, f. 5, op. 30, d. 462, l. 43.
131. RGANI, f. 5, op. 30, d. 462, l. 43.
132. Ganzenmüller, "Die siegreiche Rote Armee und ihre Führung," 24.
133. Schattenberg adds that he tried to appear to be a "Russian bear, prone to give friendly hugs" in his attempts to ease geopolitical tensions in the early 1970s. Schattenberg, *Leonid Breschnew*, 485, 613.
134. Dubin, "Litso Epokhi," 27. See also Klumbyte's and Sharafutdinova's conception of Brezhnev era power: Klumbyte and Sharafutdinova, "What Was Late Socialism?," 9.
135. Aleksandr Nekrich was the most prominent victim. His historical analysis of the war's initial months was published in 1965 but then was pulled from the libraries as "anti-Soviet." Excluded from the party, he emigrated to the United States in 1976. The head of the authors' collective of a new History of the CPSU, Yuriy Petrov, committed suicide after a reprimand. Bonwetsch describes an "atmosphere of intimidation." Bonwetsch, "Der 'Grosse Vaterländische Krieg,'" 175.
136. Lazarev, "Russian Literature on the War and Historical Truth," 35.
137. Bonwetsch, "Der 'Grosse Vaterländische Krieg,'" 176.
138. RGANI, f. 5, op. 33, d. 230, ll. 58, 60, 63. Klaus von See notes that societies tend to rely more strongly on heroes in times of transition. See "Held und Kollektiv," 4.

139. Furst, *Stalin's Last Generation*, 95.
140. Julie deGraffenried describes this as the conflict of two paradigms: "Sacrificing Childhood" versus "Happy Childhood." DeGraffenried, *Sacrificing Childhood*, 77.
141. Pilkington, *Russia's Youth and Its Culture*, 69.
142. Furst, "Arrival of Spring?," 144 See also Tromly, "Soviet Patriotism and Its Discontents."
143. Tsipursky, *Socialist Fun*, 9, 210.
144. Zinchenko, Oleg, A. Mamaev, and T. Khasmamedov, *Boevoy Otryad*, 58.
145. Zinchenko, Oleg, A. Mamaev, and T. Khasmamedov, *Boevoy Otryad*, 58.
146. Prokof'ev, *Voenno-Patrioticheskoe Vospitanie v Vysshey Shkole*, 5.
147. Zinchenko, Oleg, A. Mamaev, and T. Khasmamedov, *Boevoy Otryad*, 58, 96.
148. Brezhnev, *Great Victory of the Soviet People*, 52.
149. Brezhnev, *Great Victory of the Soviet People*, 6.
150. *Hegemony*, as Antonio Gramsci uses the term, means both eliminating competing forces and winning the consent of the population. It needs to be constantly organized and renewed by a repressive state and a strong propaganda machine. These propagandistic efforts, however, only succeed if the population receives them favorably. An issue like war memory is particularly suited for exploring the gray areas between a state-imposed discourse and grassroots initiatives. Gramsci, *Selections from the Prison Notebooks*, 12, 340–41.
151. Tumarkin, *Living and the Dead*, 37.
152. Kirschenbaum, "Nothing Is Forgotten," 73.
153. Khrushchev first mentioned the figure in a conversation with W. Averell Harriman, the former US ambassador to the Soviet Union. Thompson, *Conversation between N.S. Khrushchev and Governor Harriman*.
154. Brezhnev, *Great Victory of the Soviet People*, 16.
155. Vayl' and Genis, *60-e*, 89.
156. Zubok, *Failed Empire*, 185, 202.
157. Schattenberg believes this dedication to peace was heartfelt and sees Brezhnev's fear of failure as an important reason for his addiction to sleeping tablets in the mid-1970s. Schattenberg, *Leonid Breschnew*, 457.
158. Ellen Jones, *Red Army and Society*, 151.
159. Brezhnev, *Great Victory of the Soviet People*, 45.
160. Brezhnev, *Great Victory of the Soviet People*, 46, 48.
161. Brezhnev, *Great Victory of the Soviet People*, 52.
162. Yitzhak Brudny, *Reinventing Russia*, 6; Brandenberger, *National Bolshevism*, 6.
163. See Oberländer, *Sowjetpatriotismus und Geschichte*, 16–18.
164. Brunstedt even considers its expansion under Brezhnev as a response to the challenge of ethnic Russian nationalism. Brunstedt, "Soviet Myth of the Great Fatherland War," 155.

165. Brezhnev, *Great Victory of the Soviet People*, 29. The "Soviet people" (*Sovetskiy Narod*) were enshrined in the 1977 constitution.

166. Binns, "Changing Face of Power," 173. These rituals caused controversy. See Brudnyy, *Obryady Vchera i Segodnya*; Kampars and Zakovich, *Sovetskaya Grazhdanskaya Obryadnost'*.

167. Heiko Haumann points out that rituals have a healing function in a society that has suffered great violence. Haumann, "Die Verarbeitung von Gewalt im Stalinismus am Beispiel ausgewählter Selbstzeugnisse," 384.

168. Binns, "Changing Face of Power," 175–78.

169. The Komsomol began its programs for patriotic education in 1955, mobilizing youth for the restoration of wartime graves and monuments as well as organizing tourist trips to battle sites. However, there were no large-scale campaigns yet. Brunstedt, "Building a Pan-Soviet Past," 161. On the development of patriotic tourism, see Gorsuch, "'There's No Place Like Home.'"

170. Marshal Ivan Konev served as the first head of the Central Staff, replaced by Marshal Ivan Bagramyan after his death in 1973.

171. *Rossiyskiy Gosudarstvennyy Arkhiv Sotsial'no-Politicheskoy Istorii* (RGASPI), f. M-1, op. 47, d. 551, l. 4.

172. Usyskin, "Istoriya Turizma v Rossii."

173. Yuliya Melikhova: "VLKSM."

174. The organization of longer excursions remained a problem throughout the existence of the *pokhody*. In part, the problem was related to a lack of imagination. A report from Tula in 1966 complains that even single-day excursions were "boring." The best of them are "entertaining and educational," the worst a "drunken ramble" (*progulka s vypivkoy*). RGASPI, f. M-1, op. 38, d. 83, l. 7. In addition, for economic reasons, enterprises were reluctant to give their workers multiple days off.

175. Hans Günther notes that labor heroism was generally more difficult to convey than wartime heroism: "Für die Masse der Bevölkerung spiegelte der Arbeitsheld nur ihre eigene mühselige, stationäre Existenz wider." Günther, *Der sozialistische Übermensch*, 167.

176. Gorsuch and Koenker, introduction to *Turizm*, 3.

177. Wulf, "Performative Welten," 7, 18.

178. Kertzer writes about the "multivocality" of ritual symbols, "the variety of different meaning attached to the same symbol." Kertzer, *Ritual, Politics and Power*, 11. To analyze rituals, Wulf suggests describing them in detail and then exploring their meaning in view of the rituals' creators and the experiences of their participants. Wulf, "Performative Welten," 32–33.

179. *Vospitanie* refers to "character training, political education, and moral guidance that accompanied and informed academic instruction (*obuchenie*)." Ewing, *Teachers of Stalinism*, 192. On the evolution of Stalinist schools, see Holmes, *Kremlin and the Schoolhouse*.

180. Schenk, "Mental Maps," 495.

181. On the Panfilov myth, see Sokolow, "Von Mythen des Kriegs zu Mythen der Literatur," 715–17.

182. On the teaching of history during the postwar era, see Kelly, *Children's World*, 531.

183. Snyder, *Bloodlands*.

184. Brezhnev, *Great Victory of the Soviet People*, 13.

185. Olga Martin, email message to author, August 31, 2013.

186. Chernyshova, *Soviet Consumer Culture in the Brezhnev Era*, 160.

187. The first commemorative publications dedicated to Hero Cities appeared in 1944: a series of stamps featured Stalingrad, Leningrad, Sevastopol', and Odessa. Dobrenko, "Art of Social Navigation," 163.

188. O'Flynn, "Wanted: Matches."

189. "This barrage of indoctrination messages constitutes one grand national institutional commercial." Markham, "Is Advertising Important in the Soviet Economy?," 35.

190. Olga Martin, email message to author, August 31, 2013.

191. The 1957 Youth Festival in Moscow also marked the birthplace of the collectors' scene. Vikhlyaeva, "Znachki o Novorossiyske," 163, 167; Barmakov, "Ordena i Medali na Spichechnykh Etiketkakh."

192. Golikov, *Podvig Naroda*, 145.

193. Goncharuk, *Pamyatnye Znachki Gorodov-Geroev*, 5. This notion is reminiscent of Martina Löw's concept of "branding." Löw, *Soziologie der Städte*, 86.

194. Goncharuk, *Pamyatnye Znachki Gorodov-Geroev*, 5–6.

195. Vikhlyaeva, "Znachki o Novorossiyske," 163, 167.

196. The Red Army's crossing of the River Dnepr was the most important feat attributed to the Hero City of Kiev. See Golikov, *Podvig Naroda*, 129–32.

197. Only Hero Cities had the right to erect an obelisk with an image of the Order of Lenin, the Gold Star, and the words of the Presidium of the Supreme Soviet's decree. GARF, f. R-7523, op. 82, d. 217, ll. 78–82. Mother Russia and the victory goddess frequently merged in Soviet sculpture. Arnold, "Die Dankbarkeit der Heldenmasse," 100.

198. Levada, "'Rupture de Générations' en Russie," 24. According to Donna Bahry, generations are "fundamental guideposts" for understanding Soviet society. Bahry, "Politics, Generations, and Change in the USSR," 61. On the delineation of generations, see Mannheim, *Essays on the Sociology of Knowledge*, 297.

199. Sorokin, *They March Ahead*, 53.

200. Shlapentokh, *Normal Totalitarian Society*, 98.

201. Raleigh, *Russia's Sputnik Generation*, 5.

202. Bacon, "Reconsidering Brezhnev," 17.

203. Ruffley, *Children of Victory*, 5.

204. Dietmar Neutatz also emphasizes the integrative effects of improved living standards in the 1960s and early 1970s. Neutatz, "Identifikation und Sinnstiftung," 58. Chernyshova claims that a "consumer revolution" took place during the Brezhnev era. Chernyshova, *Soviet Consumer Culture in the Brezhnev Era*, 1.
205. Varga-Harris, "Forging Citizenship on the Home Front," 104.
206. Kotkin, *Magnetic Mountain*, 223.
207. Tsipursky, *Socialist Fun*, 186.
208. According to her, the simple equation was loyalty against social welfare. Cook, *Soviet Social Contract and Why it Failed*, 1.
209. Schattenberg, *Leonid Breschnew*, 350.
210. Varga-Harris, *Stories of House and Home*, 19.
211. Millar, "Little Deal," 695.
212. Frey and Gallus, "Awards Are a Special Kind of Signal," 4, 9.
213. Plaggenborg, *Experiment Moderne*, 100.
214. On reform discussions under Khrushchev and Brezhnev, see Breslauer, *Khrushchev and Brezhnev as Leaders*, 141–255. On the social costs of reform, see Zaslavsky, *In geschlossener Gesellschaft*, 50–86.
215. Millar, "Little Deal," 704. While Brezhnev initially supported material incentives in Kosygin's reforms, he began to favor party control over workers' discipline, and thus stronger "moral" incentives, as early as 1967. From this viewpoint, socialist and other competitions were a means of strengthening discipline. Nonetheless, both forms coexisted throughout the Brezhnev era. Breslauer, *Khrushchev and Brezhnev as Leaders*, 167, 188, 208.
216. Shlapentokh, *Normal Totalitarian Society*, 70. "There was a deal of reformism evident in Soviet policy in the 1960s, which gradually faded along with Brezhnev's health and the rise of the conservatives." Bacon and Sandle, "Brezhnev Reconsidered," 209.
217. Dmitriy Vanyukov notes that the Eighth Five-Year Plan was the only one that accurately reflected economic realities. Vanyukov, *Epokha Zastoya*, 19.
218. Yurchak, *Everything Was Forever*, 14.
219. Yurchak, *Everything Was Forever*, 25.

THREE

Victory Square
The Place of Memory in Tula

ANYONE WHO HAS APPROACHED TULA from the south since October 16, 1968, could not have missed its landmark in Victory Square. Called *Tri Shtyki* (Three Bayonets), the landmark is exactly that: three triangular obelisks made of stainless steel that reach between thirty and fifty meters into the sky. Below the bayonets, the eternal flame burns, next to a pedestal with a statue of a worker and a soldier. Both still seem to defend the city against the German Wehrmacht.

The monument is dedicated to the defense of Tula in the fall of 1941. The German attack on the city was part of Operation Typhoon, which had begun on September 16 and resulted in catastrophic losses for the Red Army.[1] In early October, the Supreme Wehrmacht Command (*Oberkommando der Wehrmacht*—OKW) was confident that the fall of the capital was only a matter of time. In the aftermath of the September battles, Stalin was, in a brief moment of crisis, even ready to sue for peace.[2] The Wehrmacht attacked on a wide front from Kalinin (today's Tver') to Tula.

However, the offensive did not proceed as effortlessly as the Germans had hoped; bad weather and road conditions hampered progress. Ever more frequently, the Wehrmacht became trapped in minefields and Soviet artillery fire.[3] Still, the OKW ordered Tula's conquest on October 18.[4] The city's strategic significance, as the most important industrial center in the region, was clear to both sides. The Soviet Supreme Command (*Stavka*) had largely given up hope that Tula would hold. It evacuated industrial enterprises and workers, began preparing partisan activities in the area, and even burned grain elevators so no bread would fall into the hands of the enemy.[5]

The doubts were well-founded, as only a small garrison of 4,647 soldiers remained in the city, supported by less than a thousand hastily assembled and poorly armed members of the workers' regiment (*rabochiy polk*).[6] They withstood days of attacks from General Heinz Guderian's Second Panzer Army before they received reinforcements. At about the same time that additional forces arrived, the attack ran out of steam because of exhaustion and increasingly difficult weather conditions.[7] Tula became the first city en route to Moscow that withstood the German onslaught, and one of the most important starting points of the Soviet counteroffensive that began on December 5–6.

The monument on Victory Square, "the symbol of the city" according to Soviet historian of architecture Aleksey Zaytsev, stands for Tula's wartime history but also points beyond it.[8] It embodies official war memory and highlights the military side of Tula's identity. Similar to what Karl Qualls observed for Sevastopol', the shape and attributes of the main monument were the result of contestations between central and regional authorities, between artistic designs and economic constraints, and between demands for inclusion and exclusion from various actors.[9]

The disambiguation of the urban landscape played an important role in the implementation of official war memory in Tula. On January 8, 1965, the Tula Oblast' Party Committee (Obkom) founded an ideological commission to prepare the twentieth anniversary of Victory Day. One month later, this commission instructed party organizations to highlight "the objective laws of the Soviet Union's victory and the inevitable failure of any aggressor in a war against the states of the global socialist system" in their propaganda.[10] Regional and local cells were to organize meetings with veterans. Furthermore, newspapers and the printing house Priokskoe Knizhnoe Izdatel'stvo were to begin a publication campaign about the war.

The promotion of local history and war memory was explicitly aimed at the postwar generation. Military-patriotic education and the Komsomol's All-Union Tours of Komsomol Members and Youth to the Places of Revolutionary, Military, and Labor Glory were to create transgenerational unity and motivate youngsters to emulate their predecessors. The tour's regional staff met to discuss an integrated approach to patriotic education in Tula, developing techniques to convey official memory.[11] Youth workers were tasked with setting up a museum, room, or corner exhibiting the revolutionary and military past in every school, enterprise, and kolkhoz.[12] To tie all of these commemorative spaces together, the city needed a symbolic center.

On November 6, 1964, the foundation stone for a memorial in Victory Square, right on the former front line, had been laid. During its meeting on February 5, 1965, the Obkom approved the details surrounding the construction of the monument. It was to be completed by October 25, 1966, the twenty-fifth anniversary of the German attack on Tula.[13] In a meeting three months later, presumably because of delays in planning, the completion date was moved to November 1966.[14]

In his book on monuments in Soviet Hero Cities, Alexey Zaytsev explains that the Three Bayonets formed the center of an entire ensemble of memorials. He describes Prospekt Lenina as Tula's main axis connecting the Kremlin on Lenin Square with the monument on Victory Square. "The concentration of commemorative objects in the city center fills it with memorial content (*memorial'nyy soderzhanie*)."[15] Symbolic appropriation had been typical for Soviet city planning since Stalinism, which turned downtown areas into uniform ideological staging grounds. "The goal was to have the resultant ensemble reflect the glory of the state," writes urban historian James Bater.[16] Adelheid von Saldern explains: "Corresponding to the principle of holism, city structures were first of all to be designed as ensembles regardless of their varying functions. Secondly, the city center was to be developed as the place of central communication, and thirdly, demands were heard for safeguarding the dominance of socialist representative places and structures."[17]

The city center, then, was to represent both the city's identity and socialist or Soviet values. In the Brezhnev era, this kind of patriotic urban landscape was defined more broadly than in Stalinism, not least because of the emergence of a conservationist movement.[18] In Tula, the Kremlin was thus seamlessly integrated into the ensemble—albeit counterbalanced by the Lenin statue on the square next to it and, in 1980, the construction of a "White House" for the Obkom.

Maps were used as tools to convey Tula's cultural topography. Some were included in a 1980 atlas on Hero Cities. First published in 1975, on occasion of the thirtieth anniversary of victory, the book was aimed at a broad audience; the original edition had a circulation of thirty-five thousand. The second edition, under the tutelage of the Main Division of Geodesics and Cartography, had sixty-two thousand copies. These atlases served as a kind of coffee-table book, where the main tenets of official war memory were reproduced in a popular-historical style with many illustrations in just fewer than seventy-five A4 pages. After a general introduction presenting the official interpretation of war events, the book briefly describes the war history of every Hero City.

At the beginning of each chapter, an iconic photograph from the war is contrasted with one showing the reconstructed beauty of the present city next to the Gold Star and the Order of Lenin—the medals of the Hero City. In the following pages, large maps illustrate the courses of battles. In Tula, a red line around the city marks the front. Odd round symbols represent antiaircraft batteries, and white crosses symbolize tank barriers. From the city Kremlin right below the loop of the river Upa, Prospekt Lenina leads to the bottom of the map in an almost straight line.

Victory Square is located on the southern defense line. It literally stands on the intersection of the military and labor spheres: the red star marks the place where the workers' regiment was formed. The map's caption, "Working Tula is fighting," further reinforces this connection.[19]

Victory Square, then, ties together an ensemble that connects the Great Patriotic War, the Revolution of 1917 (the Lenin statue in Lenin Square), and Tula's historical Kremlin. Moreover, in 1965 the city renamed numerous streets around Victory Square, after heroes who had fallen during the heaviest fighting.[20] Two of the most important were Grigoriy Volnyanskiy and Grigoriy Ageev. Lieutenant Volnyanskiy served in the 732nd Air Defense Brigade, one of the largest formations in Tula in 1941, with 1,687 soldiers. On October 30, 1941, when forty or fifty German tanks rushed toward the city, he commanded two antiaircraft guns on Prospekt Lenina, which the unit used because antitank guns were unavailable.[21] Before the battery was destroyed and Volnyanskiy and most of his unit died, they managed to repel three attacks and destroy between twelve and fourteen tanks. He was awarded the Order of Lenin posthumously for his "wisdom, courage, death defiance and heroism."[22]

Ageev also died on October 30. He had been a member of the Red Army since 1918 and a participant of the Civil War. Ageev was named commissar of the workers' regiment on October 28, 1941. According to the official account, he carried seven wounded soldiers from the battlefield under German fire and was killed trying to save the eighth. For this feat, he was named Hero of the Soviet Union on May 8, 1965.[23]

The workers' regiment would become a centerpiece of official war memory during the Brezhnev era. It was uniquely suited to represent the unity of workers and soldiers, of the party and the people. Its track record, however, was mixed—not surprising considering that it had received minimal training and fought with old or subpar guns.[24] When German tanks first attacked Tula from the village of Gosteevka in the south, "the regiment was scattered and fled in an unknown direction," according to Ivan Kravchenko, the commissar of the

Southern Military District.[25] Of the 380 members of the second battalion, 68 were left by the morning of October 31. Only a few had been killed or taken prisoner—the vast majority simply deserted.[26] Throughout the defense, the regiment was reformed six times and sent back into battle. Other units also retreated without permission, but party and NKVD units made sure that more than two thousand soldiers returned to the front line.[27]

Official histories of the defense of Tula from the Brezhnev era merely state that the workers' regiment resisted heroically and was removed from the front line after suffering heavy losses.[28] Exact numbers of Soviet casualties, particularly in the first two days of the siege, when one German attack followed another, are difficult to establish.[29] In the 1960s, the idealization of the fight served to create a symbolic topography of heroism: By naming streets after war heroes, authorities literally set it in stone. Furthermore, the deaths of Volnyanskiy and Ageev made the entirety of loss more palpable. They acted as highly condensed symbols of the valor, but also of the suffering and death, that made up the vague "mass heroism" defining the Hero City collective. Julie deGraffenried's observation about children in the war applies to the entirety of a traumatized nation: a handful of manageable martyrs were used to exclude discussion of people's traumatic experiences.[30]

HALF-VISIBLE WOMEN

On March 1, 1965, the Obkom asked the party's Central Committee in the RSFSR and the Council of Ministers RSFSR to approve gathering funds for the monument from among the city's workers, through "voluntary" additional workdays (*subbotniki*) and the collection of scrap metal and paper by youth organizations.[31] The Central Committee granted this request on May 7, setting an upper limit of 30,000 rubles.[32] Subsequently, the head of the Tula Oblast' Committee, Ivan Yunak, would highlight the "private" (*chastnyy*) source of the funds as proof for official war memory's profound popular appeal.[33] The project also proceeded without funds from the All-Union program for the construction of monuments that would reshape the Soviet Union's memorial landscape after 1967.[34]

By May 1965, the City Committee (*Gorkom*) of Tula had organized a competition for a memorial project, which the Moscow sculptor Boris Dyuzhev won.[35] Dyuzhev envisioned a monument with three figures on a pedestal next to a circle made up of five bayonets: a soldier, a member of the workers' regiment, and a woman with a gun in her hand. On February 1, 1966, the expert artistic council of the Ministry of Culture RSFSR approved the project, and the City Committee signed a contract with Dyuzhev.³⁶

Soon after—the archival materials do not indicate the exact moment—the planners decided to remove the woman from the pedestal.³⁷ They chose the figure that had the smallest "lobby," since the removal of the soldier would have caused resistance in the military. Leaving out the worker would have contradicted one of the tenets of official war memory in Tula—the intimate cooperation between the Red Army and the labor front—and weakened the message of emulation aimed at workers of the 1960s.

The omission is symptomatic of women's marginal position in official Soviet war memory. Their role during the defense of Tula was central: because virtually all men capable of carrying a weapon had joined the front or been evacuated along with the industrial enterprises, women, children, and old men were left. Women kept some of the production going and resupplied the troops.³⁸ They also built barricades before and during the German attack, accounting for three-quarters of the labor force.³⁹ Women not only served in "traditional" roles such as nurses but also conducted a great number of reconnaissance missions.⁴⁰ Nonetheless, no monument in the city of Tula commemorates their wartime role.

Those sculptures in Tula that depict women do so in allegorical form. The most prominent example is "To the Tulyaki: Heroes of the Soviet Union" on Prospekt Lenina: in front of a wall containing the names of 249 heroes of the Soviet Union—all but three of which are male—stands a Motherland (*Rodina-Mat'*) figure that guards the fallen. Other monuments feature mourning mothers—following the Christian *Pietà*.

Roger Markwick and Euridice Charon Cardona's claim that Soviet women remained "half-hidden" from official war memory, then, rings true.⁴¹ This ambivalence had already started during the war, when women and girls were mobilized for many "male" tasks but were not always portrayed in this manner.⁴² After victory, many heroines, such as the feared "night witches," an all-female bomber regiment, were forced back into traditional roles.⁴³

The interviews with Tulyaki whose families had survived the war in or around the city showed that it was primarily the mothers who stayed behind. The mothers of Evgeniy Stepunin, Raisa Molchanova, and Marina Neizvestnaya (a pseudonym) lived in the outskirts of Tula during the war—and thus briefly also lived under German occupation. The stigma associated with this meant that they talked little of their experiences; as women, they were especially defenseless against the invading army. Neizvestnaya, who was born in 1954 in the village of Myasnovo, said her mother only mentioned the airplanes flying overhead and explained that the entire time had been "horrible" (*strashno*).[44]

Still, Neizvestnaya's mother's depiction of the German soldiers was quite neutral, if also somewhat nondescript. "She said that there were good and bad Germans."[45] Evgeniy Stepunin, whose mother lived in the village of Pervomaysk during the war, recounts that she described most Germans as "indifferent" toward the population. According to her, some Germans were even helpful: "There were good Nazis, this is how she called them, there was one good one, who helped her and gave her food."[46] Molchanova recounted that her mother lived in an occupied village near Plavsk. She described her as "young and beautiful" and explained that "the Germans were not there for very long, but it was difficult for her."[47]

It is at least possible that the connection between her mother's beauty and her "difficulties" under German occupation points to sexual violence. This was another taboo in the Soviet Union.[48] Sexual relations in occupied areas were stigmatized as "horizontal collaboration" after the war. Even the casual, everyday interactions between the population and the occupiers described above were not openly shared with the war generation's descendants. Still, unlike in Ukraine or Belarus, the National Socialists did not occupy Tula Oblast' for long enough to establish a systematic occupation regime. No SS forces were active in the region, and partisan resistance remained comparatively limited.[49]

The limited presence of women in official war memory also meant that females in the postwar generation had a limited range of roles to identify with. Irina Sycheva, a professor of economics at Tula State University, was born in the city in 1949. She proudly recounts that she is from a family of native Tulyaki and weapons manufacturers. In order to illustrate the importance of war memory for her generation, she told a revealing story about childhood games in Tula in the 1950s: "The children played war.... There were white ones and black ones, you took turns, there were fascists and ... Soviets. Today you were the fascist, tomorrow we were. We only played this way.... The girls were medics.... This is why I originally wanted to study medicine. That is where it came from. [IM: And the women were never partisans or soldiers?] No, the women were all instructors and medics (*laughs*). [IM: And were there medics for the fascists?] No, only for the Soviets. You only killed fascists."[50]

Sycheva's account relates the symbolic violence of postwar children's games and their reinforcement of a Manichean worldview. They emulated the games children had played during the war, such as "Red Army versus the fascist dogs."

Child's play reflected national content, writes deGraffenried, and the games played after the war attest to its continued, transgenerational presence in everyday life.[51] Additionally, the games reproduced the clearly delineated gender roles, which the war had blurred.

Asked about her personal heroes, Sycheva names Dunyasha, full name Matushka Evdokiya. Dunyasha, whom the Orthodox Church in post-Soviet Russia beatified, still has a community of religious followers. Her grave is surrounded by a chapel-like metal enclosure. Women visit it regularly to pray for the dead and also for children, if they are unable to conceive. Even today in the middle of winter, fresh flowers, burning candles, and icons surround the grave.

The story Sycheva tells, she insists, she heard from her mother and from Fedor Khramaykov, former first secretary of the Gorkom, who had taken part in the battle as a member of the Tula workers' regiment.[52] According to local folklore, Evdokiya was a kind of holy fool, destitute and possibly mentally ill, whose clairvoyant powers women would consult. When the battle for Tula began, the authorities, fearing unrest, put her in jail.

Soon after, all male prisoners were released and were armed to fight the Germans. Only Dunyasha was left, and she told the director, "Free me, I have the keys to the city." She then disappeared. Soviet soldiers, including Khramaykov, subsequently said they had seen Dunyasha in the no-man's-land between attackers and defenders. "She walked all around the city, walked, stopped, bowed, walked on, while the Germans were shooting at her. She locked up the city from the Germans," recounts Sycheva. She claims that when Dunyasha died in 1970, "the whole city paid her last tribute."

One of the very rare diaries that survived the war corroborates the story: Nina Yakovleva, a Tulyak who was born in 1924 and whose notes local historian A. Lepekhin published, wrote on October 16, 1941, that a friend had told her about Dunyasha's prophecy: "The Germans will not enter Tula, I locked up Tula tightly (*ya zaperla Tulu na zamok*), and I lost the keys."[53]

Even if this story is very close to the realm of fables, it reflects a hero figure who was not present in official war memory. The existence of Dunyasha can be proven, but the qualities she was endowed with contain religious and superstitious elements, passed down by older to younger people through postmemories whose veracity is dubious.[54] Her story, however, does illustrate that many inhabitants saw the successful defense of Tula as bordering on the miraculous. This supernatural explanation shares some similarities with official hero worship: many heroes were endowed with superhuman qualities and thus came to represent the gigantic effort and suffering of the soldiers and the population.

THE MYSTERY OF THE THREE BAYONETS

Local historian Irina Paramonova claims that the omission of the female figure was not the only change to the monument's design: originally, there were supposed to be five bayonets forming a Soviet star.[55] Archival materials for the early planning phase are spotty and do not mention this change. If the story is true, it highlights the arbitrariness of cultural memory's media, which are not independent from pragmatic and financial considerations. In order to disambiguate the significance of the monument, guides and history books described it consistently: "On a low pedestal stand a Soviet soldier and a militiaman (*opolchenets*), shoulder to shoulder, with machine guns in their hands. They embody (*olitsetvoryat*) the brotherly unity of Tula's defenders and national character (*vsenarodnyy kharakter*) of the fight against the fascist hordes."[56]

The figures' symbolism was obvious—unlike the three bayonets, whose significance is less clear than that of a five-cornered Soviet star.

One can trace this confusion also in the monument's reception. Paramonova and others relate they were told in school that the three bayonets represented the socialist generational "trinity"—Pioneers, Komsomol, and the party. This interpretation is not specific to Tula's history, even if it highlights the importance of transgenerational unity. Raisa Molchanova suggests a different meaning: "We beat back three of Hitler's attacks near Moscow. Three bayonets."[57] It is not entirely clear why she mentions three attacks. There were only two: one at the end of October 1941 and another when the Wehrmacht attempted to take Tula in mid-November by circumventing it and cutting it off.[58] Possibly, she meant the three invasions that Tula had beaten back during its modern history—those of Napoleon in the Patriotic War, Denikin in the Civil War, and Hitler in the Great Patriotic War. Still, the interpretation appears contrived.

Dyuzhev himself wanted the three bayonets to signify "the military glory of Soviet arms."[59] Official publications followed this interpretation, but it does not seem to have stuck with Tulyaki, perhaps not least because it is not directly tied to the number three.[60] Still, its role as a weapons producer is a crucial element of Tula's historical identity. "From time immemorial (*isstari*), Tula has been an armory, and the bayonets that the Tulyaki forged have repelled many invaders. It is thus only logical that the motif of the three-cornered steel bayonets is used for the obelisk on Victory Square."[61]

Ever since the settlement of the first gun makers in the early seventeenth century, the city had played an important role as a weapons producer. The establishment of the first proto-industrial factory by Peter the Great in 1712 turned Tula into the center of the arms industry. Tula's defense is thus connected to

Figure 3.1. Victory Square in December 1966: the groundwork is laid. No copyright, Soviet source

its wider historical role as a city of weapon makers, with the events in 1941 portrayed in a line with wars ranging from the sixteenth to the twentieth century.[62] Each time, the city is presented as a fortress and as the capital's southern foremost post, with a weapon production that contributes to the war effort of the entire nation.

By January 1966, the planning process for the monument was well on its way. The Obkom reported to the Central Committee and the Council of Ministers RSFSR that the project would cost 120,000 to 130,000 rubles. Roughly half of the money, 67,700 rubles, went into sketches and models; 50,000 into the production of the figures and the bayonets; and another 10,000 into the groundwork. The Obkom had already collected 31,700 rubles from the population.[63]

It is likely that problems with financing the project also led to the delay in its completion. By 1966, internal communication no longer maintained the twenty-fifth anniversary as the completion date.

In August, only sketches and some models had been completed.[64] Newspaper articles about the twenty-fifth anniversary do not address the delay. The front page of *Kommunar* shown in figure 3.1 features an image of Victory Square in which the groundwork appears done. Instead of an explanation, the caption reads quite simply: "Victory Square. Here, fights against the German fascists took place in 1941."

The new plan was to begin installation in 1967. As it turned out, an opening date in that year was equally unrealistic. It would take until October 16, 1968, for the monument to be unveiled. One day before, a commission of experts sent by the Council of Ministers RSFSR had praised the monument's high artistic and ideological value and stated that it reflected "the heroic deeds of Tula's defenders" in an expressive fashion.[65]

Somewhat awkwardly, the unveiling was celebrated on the twenty-seventh anniversary of the oath that Tula's Communists had taken to defend the city. This oath by one thousand Communists on October 16, 1941, was an important aspect of official war memory, as it underlined the claim that the CPSU was always ready and willing to defend the city—even before the battle had begun: "We, the Bolsheviks of Tula, assure the Central Committee VKP(b) that all of us will fight like one man, with the weapon in our hands and to the last drop of blood for our homeland (*Rodina*), for our beloved city, and we will never give up Tula to the enemy."[66]

This oath allowed Vasiliy Zhavoronkov, the wartime head of the Gorkom and an important source for Tula's official war memory, to present himself as the driving force behind the defense. Zhavoronkov would later become Soviet trade minister and the head of the influential Historical-Literary Society of Old Bolsheviks under the Central Committee.[67] A 1988 account by E. Kassin sums up the preparations for the German attack: "Tula turned into an impregnable fortress, in which revolutionary order ruled. . . . The Party organization was the spirit behind all this."[68] This description projects the exemplary Hero City collective under the leadership of the party back to the beginning of the war.

It also covers up serious shortcomings in the preparation for the battle, for which Zhavoronkov was mainly responsible. According to Aparin, Zhavoronkov neglected the construction of trenches and tank ditches on Tula's southern outskirts, which were too shallow as a result. All-out mobilization of the population to build fortifications took place only a few days before the Germans' arrival.[69] Aparin writes somewhat dramatically that valuable time was "needlessly wasted during the city's preparation. The fighters and commanders of the 50th Army paid for this in blood."[70] For him, it was the Red Army under general Arkadiy Ermakov who had saved Tula in the decisive phase. Zhavoronkov, however, saw Ermakov as a competitor, which was symptomatic of the power struggles between the military and the party during and after the war. He managed to remove Ermakov and became a member of the city Military Council in late November.[71]

Official war memory nonetheless presented the Red Army, the party, and the population as an indivisible unit. To symbolize this, representatives from numerous work collectives gathered in front of the monument in Victory Square on October 16, 1968. Army units had formed a guard of honor. At three in the afternoon, an armored personnel carrier arrived from Moscow, carrying fire from the eternal flame on the Tomb of the Unknown Soldier.[72]

Through this transfer, Tula received "holy" fire, which had once originated from Mars Field in Leningrad. It ritualistically connected the city not only to the other eternal flames in the country but also to the October Revolution. Moreover, it signified the direct link between the capital and Tula. Quite akin to religious ceremonies, this sharing of fire consecrated the *Tri Shtyki* monument. In a scripted declaration, the participants vowed that Tula's workers would meet Lenin's upcoming one hundredth birthday in a "worthy" fashion—which meant additional work obligations. They would "do their part in further strengthening the economic and military power of the Soviet state," thus creating discursive continuity between the oaths of 1941 and 1968.[73]

The feat of Tula's defenders lived on in the new generation, wrote local historian Aleksandr El'kin. He also drew a direct line between today's "imperialists" and the Nazi invasion in 1941: "The participants of the meeting declare in all decisiveness that the revanchists will suffer the same fate as their fascist predecessors that rot (*sgnit'*) in Tula's earth."[74] After the speeches and a minute of silence for the fallen, G. Safronov, second secretary of the party Obkom, lit the eternal flame to the Soviet national anthem. The meeting ended with local inhabitants laying flowers and wreaths at the foot of the monument, reinforcing the notion of continuity.

THE ALLURE OF VICTORY DAY

Curiously, none of my respondents could remember the grand celebration, even though all of them regularly spent time in Victory Square. The square became the central gathering place for commemorative events. The most important date was May 9, when work collectives, student groups, youth organizations, veterans, and the city's political leadership would march down Prospekt Lenina.

After 1965, the week of May 3–9 was reserved for celebrations, exhibitions, meetings, and excursions, culminating in the official festive demonstration of work collectives and party organizations on May 8. By May 9, all of them were to have put the graves of fallen soldiers—many of which were damaged and in poor condition—in order.[75] On Victory Day 1970, the participants of the official procession laid down wreaths by the monument titled "To the Tulyaki: Heroes of the Soviet Union," after which they would move on toward Victory Square and gather for a solemn ceremony. The meeting ended with a threefold salute "in honor of the soldiers of the Soviet Army and the workers of the city of gun makers that gave their lives" during the war.[76]

Members of the postwar generation insist that they never perceived May 9 as a political holiday. Terms such as "holy," "all-people" (*vsenarodnyy*), and "organic" (versus "artificial") were prevalent in descriptions in both Soviet propaganda and people's individual assessments. One could talk of a phenomenal propaganda success—the significance of Victory Day remains central in contemporary Russia. The reverence that people felt was founded in their and their parent generation's profound personal connection to celebrations of the end of the war. Even Vasiliy Kotenev, an entrepreneur with a highly critical attitude toward many shortcomings of the Soviet Union, says that "veterans came, the schools went out, laid wreaths and flowers in front of monuments of military glory. Such a beautiful, great holiday, a nice holiday, it all came from the heart. May 9 was a holiday that they did not have to chase people to (*vgonyali*), everybody loved it."[77]

Kotenev distinguishes May 9 from Labor Day or November 7, for which participation was an unpopular obligation. The commemorative events on May 9 were not voluntary either; unions, party cells, and youth organizations mobilized their members to attend the festivities. Nonetheless, says Kotenev, "One had to go [at times], but this coincided with an internal desire to go."[78]

Vladimir Romanov was under more pressure to comply with expectations. He worked in the prestigious and privileged armament industry, in a collective that was obliged to send a delegation to the official march. Romanov saw this process as a negotiation: "I didn't have to go every year on 9 May. They told me for example: 'Romanov, ah, Volodya, ok, you can relax with your family this year... we let you be. You are active, it is all good (*normal'no*), we find someone else this year....' There were these kinds of compromises."[79]

Authors like Boris Dubin would criticize this attitude as an expression of the conformism that made the Brezhnev era so intellectually oppressive.[80] But the episode shows that people had room to maneuver, even under the conditions of a highly mobilized, authoritarian society; while they were expected to publicly demonstrate their loyalty to the system, this participation left space for a more personalized ritual culture.

People would spend May 9 with their families, visit their neighbors, and drink the "100 grams" frontline ration of vodka to connect them to the war. They sat and ate meals at a *russkiy stol* full of food. It was often in these informal gatherings that the veterans told wartime stories, and for big anniversaries, they would congregate from all over the USSR to remember the past together.

Members of the postwar generation like Sergey Stepuzhin and Vasiliy Kotenev "ritually" watched the Moscow parade on television and the firework salute in downtown Tula in the evening but avoided going to official meetings whenever possible. Stepuzhin seems to have gotten away with this, as he had served in the army and held regular lectures on the war. The behavior of the considerably younger Kotenev was considered "not normal" (*nenormal'nyy*), by his own account: he was a classical "hooligan."[81] As a teenager, he even smashed the window of a militia station in order to be sent to a construction brigade to do hard work in remote regions. These brigades were mostly reserved for young delinquents, in order to reeducate them through labor, but the work was relatively well paid. Kotenev's reasoning: "I had to buy a bicycle, a camera, jeans and books."[82]

As Kotenev likes to cultivate the self-image of the rebel who tricked the system, it is possible that he exaggerated the scale and purposefulness of his actions. Still, the connection between his "abnormality" and problems with the authorities is relevant: nonparticipation was accepted only if it was not part of a general pattern of abstinence from official, collective activities. Particularly in Hero Cities, youngsters' participation was proof that their behavior was "worthy" and showed reverence to past generations.

For respondents, the personal and political significance of May 9 was often blurred. Elena Bozhenko was born in 1954 and moved to Tula from Siberia with her family when she was seven years old. Bozhenko at first struggled to get used to a city that she perceived as much more infused with a working-class spirit than the scientific community in which she had lived in Irkutsk. Nevertheless, she involved herself in the activities of youth organizations and became a member of the Komsomol with privileges like access to exclusive food packets. She regularly organized celebrations on holidays. She vividly remembers Victory Day 1978: "Our planes, fighter planes, flew in the sky. And after the parade, we danced with the veterans and the pilots, a waltz, a military waltz, almost all the way to Victory Square.... Music was playing from all the speakers; Prospekt Lenina was closed for traffic. Us young girls danced with the veterans, and their youthful spirit baffled me, even though they were tired from standing on the tribune all day.... That really was the unity of generations."[83]

The dance illustrates that reverence toward the older generation was both inherently part of official propaganda and genuinely felt. Bozhenko's uncritical usage of a term that appears so clichéd to an outsider reflects this, especially since she showed herself immune to feelings of Soviet nostalgia. Raisa Molchanova used the same terminology to describe her feelings, which testifies to the longevity of war memory.[84]

As long as they participated in its reproduction, veterans enjoyed a privileged symbolic role in official war memory and Soviet society. They endowed the rituals on Victory Square with sacral meaning; they were the living counterparts to the monument.[85] Veterans talked in schools, meetings, and anniversaries. Moreover, many worked as unsalaried deputy directors in schools, in charge of patriotic education and discipline, engaging in the same "societal work" expected from everyone, which was voluntary only in theory.[86]

Veterans were also present at the opening ceremony of the *Zarnitsa* games' finals July 2–9, 1979. Of the 150,000 children who had taken part in militarized competitions, 1,980 made it to the finals.[87] Through their successes, attained through exemplary behavior in the emulation of war heroes, they had moved up in the Soviet heroarchy. As a reward, they met in the city to visit museums, be photographed with the banner of Tula's workers' regiment, practice shooting and grenade throwing, and meet veterans.

The *Zarnitsa* games, in which millions participated, were part of the *pokhody*. The opening ceremony on July 3 started outside Tula's Kremlin.[88] Youngsters followed Prospekt Lenina on a route that reproduced Soviet "traditions," stopping at the Square of Communards (dedicated to the nineteenth-century revolutionaries), the monument "To the Tulyaki: Heroes of the Soviet Union," and the two antiaircraft guns.

At Victory Square, whose surrounding buildings were decorated with Lenin portraits in honor of his 110th birthday, the procession came to a stop. Hundreds of soldiers, Pioneers, and Komsomol members were already assembled. The microphone, where the "commander" officially opened the games, was flanked by the state and party leadership—and by numerous veterans. The voice of a *diktor*, analogous to a radio broadcaster, led the ceremony.

> "Here ran the defensive line
> Where the heart of the Eternal Flame beats
> Tell us, square, tell us,
> About those distant and harsh days...
> When the worker became a soldier
> When the city became a soldier."[89]

As the ceremony proceeded, a group of actors, the "platoon of memory" (*vzvod Pamyati*), "[moved] across Victory Square as if it were alive" under the sounds of an orchestra, symbolizing the wartime spirit. Suddenly, the orchestra and the platoon of memory died down, as the *diktor* said, "Orchestra, be silent, bow the flags to the ground! In front of us are those who fell in battle." Veterans and youth lay a wreath by the monument for the defenders of Tula, followed by a minute of silence for the fallen. Once the minute was over, a young recruit moved to the microphone and said: "In the name of those who are here today, on Victory Square, in the name of those who get ready to relieve their old comrades from the post of battle (*boevoy post*), we assure the Communist Party, the Leninist Komsomol that ... we will defend our beloved homeland, will be worthy of the heroic glory of our fathers and grandfathers."[90]

This oath, subsequently taken by all of those present, marked the climax of the ceremony. The festive setting reinforced the surface of idealized war memory. At Victory Square, "the best representatives" of the postwar generation formed the "platoon of memory," thus physically performing the continuity of generations. They were supposed to emerge as something different, "worthy" to succeed the wartime heroes.[91]

Elena Bozhenko was a member of groups that dressed in wartime uniforms, sang songs, read poems, and competed with other collectives. She considered recognition and praise from veterans to be the highest form of appreciation "because they knew the price of war." She never participated in the postwar generation's competitions to write new works on the war because she considered this "vulgar" (*poshlyy*).

Bozhenko perceived wartime creative works—and by extension the veterans—to be on a fundamentally different level: the experience of war had exalted them. For her, war was a cleansing experience, in which sacrifice and suffering turned its participants into better human beings.[92] This moral power was fundamental to the presentation of veterans as exemplars for the postwar generation. But it also limited the extent to which that generation could strive to emulate their forebears. Moreover, wartime creative works exposed Bozhenko to aspects of the war not admitted in public:

> Many poems that dealt with the unpleasant (*nepriyatnye*) sides of the war, those that Soviet power (*Sovetskaya vlast'*) wanted to suppress, were nonetheless read. And they were also published, but only quietly (*po-tikhonichku*), independently, written on a typewriter. Only few people read them ... unfortunately. Because someone can only analyze [the war] fully, if he or she saw and read everything. The positive and the negative. ...
> This gung-ho patriotism (*urra-patriotizm*), that everyone had been exceptional heroes, omitted how people had acted under occupation, in the rear. ... No one wrote about that.[93]

TABOOS AND WHISPERS

Bozhenko was not the only one in the postwar generation who was aware of the discrepancy between official memory as staged on Victory Square and historical truth. For her, it led to a veritable crisis of faith: during a trip to Munich in 1979 with a group of teachers, she bought an uncensored copy of Mikhail Bulgakov's novel *Master and Margarita*. She realized for the first time how the edition published in the USSR in 1966 had been mutilated. "This did not only make me feel mortified (*obida*), but I wanted to learn more about the reasons why so much remained hidden."[94]

She applied for a permission to do research on Bulgakov in archives that were only open to reliable activists like herself in Moscow. She used the opportunity to look into the history of her grandfather, who had been repressed under Stalin, and found "many unpleasant things." Shortly after, she left the Komsomol.[95]

Evgeniy Stepunin also had a half-hidden family history of repression. His father and his relatives had been deported to Siberia from Tula Oblast' in 1941 because they were ethnic Germans. They returned in the 1950s, presumably after Stalin's death. Viktor Shcheglov, a radio journalist born in 1950 in Akmolinsk near Astana, grew up in a camp for the wives of "traitors to the motherland."[96] He remembers the fearful atmosphere and the Stalin portraits in the barracks. A careless word could lead to denunciation. One time, his mother got pale when he asked her in front of strangers whether Lenin's name was derived from the word *len* (flax), since Stalin's originated from *stal'* (steel).[97] After the death of his father, who had served in a Siberian division during the defense of Tula, his mother decided to return to her own family in the city.[98]

Sergey Stepuzhin's father underwent dekulakization when he was thirteen. As "middle" Kulaks, the family lost its possessions but was not deported.[99] It was able to keep its cow, which was very important for survival during the war. Talking about these taboos within families was difficult, but the same could be said about the war experience in general.[100] Stepuzhin's father apparently felt inferior because he did not fight in the Red Army. "He did not participate in the war, so he had nothing to tell."[101]

Stepuzhin's statement contradicts his following explanation—that his father repaired railroad tracks damaged by German attacks all over the western USSR. Apparently, this did not qualify as "real" participation. Underlying the official heroarchy were clear, hierarchic ideas about what constituted memorable actions during the war—with fighters at the top, support units like railroaders or nurses somewhere in the middle, and stigmatized groups like penal battalions or evacuated Jews at the bottom.[102]

But even war heroes stayed silent among their families. Vladimir Yurchikov's father carried the Order of the Patriotic War. Nonetheless, he almost never talked about the war: "They were all *frontoviki*. What was there to talk about?"[103] Raisa Molchanova's father was a highly decorated officer as well—in an artillery guard unit. He was seriously wounded in the battle for Königsberg (Kaliningrad) and almost bled to death, losing a hand and an eye. In photos, Molchanova said, he always hid his hand out of shame. Still, his daughter did not know what had happened to him for three decades. He first spoke about Königsberg during a serious eye operation in the late 1970s: "When he lay there with closed eyes for three whole days ... it was a complicated operation. I sat there, and he told me about it, perhaps to kill time. How he had fought, at the front, he told me a lot. The difficulties and problems, the dirt, the blood (*slozhnosti, trudnost', gryaz, krov'*). What can I say—in the trenches. He spent the entire war in the trenches. It was always dirty on the front lines, with the artillery. (*long pause*). Such was life."[104]

Only in a seriously weakened state did her father honestly address the difficult aspects of his war experience. His memories next broke through in the post-Soviet period, right before his death in May 1997, when he was no longer lucid. "Sometimes he screamed 'Battery!' 'Commanders!' 'Fire!' The memories just surfaced in his mind (*vsplyvali v pamyat'*)."[105]

This uncontrolled appearance of memories points to heavy psychological trauma that was repressed for decades and that resurfaced in moments of great vulnerability and old age. The phenomenon of the "reactivation" of trauma is well known to psychologists from Holocaust survivors and American and German World War II veterans.[106]

Vladimir Romanov said that his father could never find any benefit in talking about the war. But once he told him that he had spent time in a hospital in Erevan after being gravely wounded. Immediately, however, he added some levity by saying that young women visited the wounded soldiers, sang, and danced. "He did not like to talk about the war. He said it would have been better if this shit (*gad*) had never happened, that you know nothing about this shit. It was hellishly difficult (*adskiy trud*), blood, not pretty to look at (*nepriyatno smotret'*), he said, some people got used to it, others almost went insane when they saw this nightmare."[107]

Romanov uses crass language when relating his father's words about the war. It is miles away from that of official war memory during the Brezhnev era, marked by a "lyrical tone" and "generalizing clichés, rhetorical formulae and a normative, 'elevated' official language about war events," in Lev Gudkov's description.[108]

Except in extreme situations, the war generation struggled to find a language to convey their experiences to their children and grandchildren. Traumata and irreconcilable feelings of victory and personal loss inhibited them.[109] At the same time, the postwar generation had difficulty relating to the war period because their own living conditions were so radically different.

CHILDREN CARING FOR VETERANS

Outside the family, members of the postwar generation only occasionally heard different stories—before the collapse of the Soviet Union revealed the dark sides of history all at once. Vladimir Romanov remembers that he spoke to a seventy-year-old man in 1976 about a book on the defense that had just come out. "According to the official account, the NKVD had everything under control, but according to the non-official account, the way the older people talked about it, when I told him about this book . . . he said: 'what are you talking about? . . . They smashed windows, pillaged stores.'"[110]

Conditions in Tula had indeed been chaotic before the battle began. When the great Soviet author Vasiliy Grossman passed through on October 6, 1941, he found "Tula, seized with that deadly fever, the tormenting, terrible fever we've seen in Gomel, Chernigov, Glukhov, Orel and Bolkhov. Is this really happening to Tula? Complete confusion. . . . The streets are filled with people, they are walking on pavements and in the road and still there isn't enough room. Everyone is dragging bundles, baskets and suitcases."[111]

The passage is from Grossman's diary, which was repressed by Soviet censors for decades and published in English by Anthony Beevor in 2005. Its direct style, with its mixture of fear, confusion, and doubt, directly contradicts official war memory.

Aparin shows that panic broke out on October 14. A wave of theft and looting followed, hampering the evacuation effort. By the time the attack began, four thousand tons of metal and seventy railway carriages with industrial goods remained in Tula. During the defense, further unrest ensued when rumors concerning plans to evacuate the party and government leadership began to circulate. As the police forces either were drafted into the Red Army or had left the city, local authorities did not restore order until early November, after executing seven "ringleaders."[112]

Local knowledge about the unheroic pages of the defense was often inaccessible to the postwar generation because of its systematic public suppression. Journalist Viktor Shcheglov emphasizes that veterans did not always reproduce official war memory voluntarily.[113] "If someone let something slip, said something [he was not supposed to], nobody printed it in memoirs, and he was no longer invited to meetings, gave no more interviews in newspapers and magazines."[114]

Such public ostracism could have serious consequences for veterans, as they relied on veterans' organizations for their privileges in housing, medical services, and pensions.[115] One can interpret this situation through the lens of both the "socialist contract" and transgenerational unity: in order to receive their benefits, they had to serve the state and act as living examples of the values to be emulated by the younger cohort. The only disturbing aspect was that they had—not only in their eyes but in those of many in the postwar generation—already made plenty of sacrifices in the war.

The system disgusted Vasiliy Kotenev. "They [the veterans] did not merely have to ask when they needed something, but they also had to make friends (*polizat'*), please somebody, for example the head of a department. And if he liked you, he put you on the list."[116] Veterans' benefits thus often depended on the same *blat* practices that determined access to scarce goods in the rest of society.[117] The state did not hesitate to use these benefits as leverage.[118]

In Kotenev's retelling, it was the *blat* practices that made him rebel against the Soviet system—interestingly enough, through black-market practices that were not too far removed from it. In the 1980s, he acted as a speculator, selling black-market goods, which led him to become an entrepreneur after the collapse of the Soviet Union, The fact that veterans enjoyed such an elevated discursive position but were not provided for accordingly made him realize the discrepancy between official ideology and unofficial social practices.[119]

The situation of many veterans in Tula in the 1960s and 1970s was indeed difficult. Although their care had improved greatly since the end of the war, problems remained. A large-scale survey of living conditions in 1974 showed that 12,005 disabled veterans and 10,037 families of fallen soldiers lived in the Oblast'. The report concluded that the state provided well for them on the whole. In 1973 and 1974, 923 families had received new apartments. Nonetheless, there were 1,509 families—15 percent—still on the waiting list, with 900 of them in Tula alone; only 100 to 120 apartments became available each year.[120]

Although veterans were entitled to 10 percent of the housing stock, this provision was not always applied. A 1974 report by the Oblast' People's Control Committee (*komitet narodnogo kontrolya*) found numerous violations and judged that the city of Tula in particular was "weak" in fulfilling its housing obligations. In Tsentral'nyy Rayon, 67 families of disabled veterans and fallen soldiers had been waiting for housing since 1965—50 percent of the total.[121]

The topic was politically sensitive: a state that built its legitimacy on victory struggled to explain why it could not provide for its veterans decades after the end of the war. Ivan Yunak had to justify this state of affairs even in 1984, explaining that the party had already decided to improve the living conditions and medical situation of veterans in the 1960s and reprioritized the issue in 1975. "However, this does not mean that we have resolved the problem as a whole."[122]

Where the state failed, it mobilized youngsters to assist aging veterans. For this purpose, it reactivated the Timurov movement, which had emerged spontaneously during World War II, inspired by a fictional hero from a novel. Quickly incorporating the movement into the structures of the Pioneer organization, its members took over important tasks from absent adults:[123] they collected scrap metal and herbs for the front, cleaned streets, gathered firewood, and escorted children and old people to air-raid shelters.[124]

By the early 1970s, its tasks had only changed slightly. The main addition was veteran care. The division of social services in Tula Oblast' defined the movement's tasks as follows: "They regularly visit their wards (*podopechnye*), assist them where necessary in preparing fire, sawing firewood, in agricultural work, the renovation of houses, apartments and outbuildings, the improvement of living conditions, the transportation of groceries and domestic affairs. They help to clean apartments, bring water, [and] care for the sick."[125]

Elena Bozhenko spoke at length about her time as a *Timurovets*. For her, unlike others, this work was very meaningful. She remembers that many aging veterans lived in individual houses instead of in modern apartments, and she would go see two of them once a week. One was a man without legs, while a former military nurse would treat the Pioneers to cookies and tea.

The relationship between the postwar generation and the veterans, then, changed between the 1960s and 1970s. Respondents described the imposing presences veterans had been in the workplace and at schools in the 1960s. Later on, many became increasingly frail and needed caretaking. Statistics on the *Timurovtsy* illustrate the rising significance of this movement: whereas there were only 731 veterans in the Tula Oblast' under their care in 1970, this number increased to 5,796 by 1980.[126]

It is hard to imagine how children dealt with the task of taking care of old, sick, and often disabled veterans. What they encountered contradicted veterans' heroic public personae. The Timurov movement continued to face problems, as is evident from Komsomol files: there were numerous complaints that members exercised only "weak patronage" (*slabo shefstvuyut*) over veterans.[127] The gap between idealized official war memory and encounters with the war's physical consequences was large—and it went much beyond the public displays of generational unity that was normally requested.

WEDDING RITUALS AND POSTCARDS

As the roles of veterans and the postwar generation changed, so did that of Victory Square in everyday life. Vitaliy Savchenko describes it as follows: "Since the opening of the monument, the square has become a holy place for Tulyaki. Soldiers take their oath here, student brigades assemble here as well as those that enter professional life. Newlyweds bring flowers here, thankful to those that did not spare their lives for the happiness of the people."[128]

The postwar generation began to use Victory Square in idiosyncratic ways. It is impossible to establish a strict separation between its political, official appropriation and its private, unofficial usage. Respondents who married in Tula always laid flowers at the Three Bayonets. On the one hand, official institutions organized the ritual in this way: as in many other cities, wedding parties could book state-organized cars for standardized routes.[129] My respondents presented these rides as far less controlled than Brezhnev-era literature suggests. They paid money to a driver they knew, who would take them where they wanted to go.

Still, the route was mostly the same—less because someone supervised it than because that was how "it was done." The "traditional" procession always led from the wedding palace to Victory Square and to Yasnaya Polyana, Lev Tolstoy's country estate. "All couples absolutely had to go to Victory Square and lay down flowers by the Eternal Fire," recounts Vasiliy Kotenev. Afterward, they would drink champagne[130] and walk along the treelined paths of Yasnaya Polyana park.

Depending on a couple's financial status, the wedding dinner would take place at home or at a café. Because of the *defitsit* economy, meat had to be procured in Moscow or was absent from the menu. "Only those who had a privileged position in the distribution system could afford a big wedding," says Kotenev.[131]

Wedding parties' official route, then, connected recreational aspects with commemoration. "To lay down flowers by the monument was a ritual; we were used to it. No one told us, 'Go there! Lay down flowers!' We felt a genuine urge (*na dushe treboval*) to go to the monument, which came from a feeling of responsibility toward the participants in the war," explains Evgeniy Stepunin (pictured in fig. 3.2).[132] Here, the naturalizing effects of official war memory's hegemonic societal status become evident. People did not question why they took their wedding pictures near the war monument; it was just the "normal" thing to do. The connection of official propaganda, personal rituals, and family history remains an important factor in the transgenerational relevance of war commemoration in Soviet and Russian society.

Figure 3.2. Evgeniy Stepunin with his father and during his service in the Red Army (1972). Courtesy of Evgeniy Stepunin, private archive

Still, the route did not remain "natural" on its own. Romanov got married for a second time in the late 1980s and did not follow the accustomed path. Instead, he took the wedding party to a spring outside of town, where they all went swimming.[133] In the perestroika era, individualization grew and the boundaries of what was considered "normal" broadened.

As Antonio Gramsci points out and Romanov's statement illustrates, hegemony is not static but has to be continually reproduced through the propagation of its main tenets. In an authoritarian society like the Soviet Union, the transgression of official war memory's boundaries did not go unpunished. During his lectures, Sergey Stepuzhin walked a fine line between voluntary participation, self-censorship, and repression: "There were forbidden topics. But no one had to impose them (*navyazat'*). I understood myself that it was better to simply circumvent something that was not universally known. Or something that rarely entered the discussion (*byla maloargumentirovana*).... I always chose topics that ... (*breaks off*)."[134]

Stepuzhin's omission at the end is interesting because he goes on to talk about how, during perestroika and after the collapse of the Soviet Union, everybody spoke negatively about the war and tried to negate the existence of heroic deeds. By contrasting Brezhnev-era official war memory with the sensationalist and controversial discussions of glasnost, he justifies his own reproduction of an idealized discourse, even though he knew he was telling a one-sided story.

The repetition and reproduction of official war memory in various media in Tula was most intense in the wake of the conferment of the Hero City title in 1976.[135] Two books, aimed at a wide popular-historical and tourist audience, were published as part of a series explicitly dedicated to the country's Hero Cities. Savchenko's book focused primarily on architectural aspects and was published in 1979 by *Stroyizdat'*, which belonged to the State Committee for Construction (*Gosstroy*).[136] Anatoliy Galitsan and Dado Muriev's volume appeared in a parallel series by *Voenizdat*, the Defense Ministry's publishing house.[137]

All books had print runs of tens of thousands of copies. They were inexpensive, costing sixty and eighty kopecks. Both series told the histories of the respective cities, one with a focus on the "revolutionary, military and labor traditions" (*Voenizdat'*) and the other on buildings and monuments (*Stroyizdat'*).[138] The focus lay on the Great Patriotic War. The architectural volumes were also supposed to serve as tourist guidebooks: they were small enough to be easily portable, and their narrative followed individual streets through various sections of town. Interested out-of-towners would use them to explore the Hero City and its history. As Tula—unlike tourist centers like Moscow, Leningrad, Odessa, or Novorossiysk—hosted very few tourists, however, it is doubtful whether it was used frequently for this purpose. It seems more likely that the city simply got its own volume because every Hero City did.

Similarly, in 1978, the Moscow publisher Plakat printed a collection of fifteen postcards—in an edition of two hundred thousand copies. The same series existed for the other Hero Cities. All of them have a title image that shows the Gold Star and the Order of Lenin before the city's main war monument. In Tula, as shown in figure 3.3, the two awards are arranged in front of a red surface and the orange-black ribbon of the Order of Glory that was awarded for "bravery in the face of the enemy."[139] These insignia of the city's hero status are reminiscent of a half-drawn curtain that reveals Victory Square. The bayonets, the statue of the worker and the soldier, and the people visiting the monument are harmoniously arranged.

The inhabitants visible in the picture have gathered for a holiday, judging from their clothes. An honorary guard watches as a mother and her son place flowers at the foot of the pedestal. Others have laid down wreaths. In the background, more people have assembled to pay tribute. The image thus contains

Figure 3.3. Title page of the postcard collection *Hero City Tula*. No copyright, Soviet source

various segments of the population—children, youths, men, and women, as well as soldiers—all united in commemoration.

The fifteen postcards, edited by former first secretary Vasiliy Zhavoronkov, show various places of contemporary life. The images serve as business cards that depict the things Tula was known. In this sense, they resemble the stamps discussed in the previous chapter. One of them depicted the statue of Tolstoy, another samovars, a third weapon makers, and a fourth the Tula Kremlin. The majority, however, features various war monuments inside and outside the city, often in front of newly built apartment houses and integrated into a modern, urban landscape.

Additionally, each postcard is subdivided into three images: one showing a wartime photograph, one an architectural landmark or monument, and one a contemporary city scene. In the one pictured in figure 3.4, which is an especially striking assembly, the authors juxtapose Victory Square with children playing in Belousov Park and soldiers, most likely members of the 732nd Air Defense Brigade, on a truck that is camouflaged with twigs and earth.

Figure 3.4. Postcard showing Victory Square, with children playing and soldiers defending the city. No copyright, Soviet source

The image of the postwar generation, with its peaceful life and ostensibly happy childhood, contrasts with the grim soldiers keeping the Wehrmacht at bay. The wartime picture is in black and white, which further accentuates the difference. All the children are dressed colorfully, and the girls have bows in their hair. The boy in the middle holds red carnations. The bouquet clearly indicates that the children are in the park on a holiday: red carnations were traditionally given to veterans as a sign of reverence.

The children are playing with water, which reinforces the metaphor of life. At the same time, they are well supervised by their parents. The two pictures thus visually represent the continuity of generations and the postwar citizens' peaceful life, which can be attributed to the sacrifices of the wartime generation. The Three Bayonets monument stretches across both pictures, thus unifying not only the images but also two generations.

Victory Square is presented as an inherent part of the urban landscape. A bus passes by, and cars are visible in the foreground. The square, which stands in front of Tula's university building, is almost empty, but people are going about their business in the streets. The war is only visible in its representation in the Three Bayonets. The rest of the city is full of markers of welfare (cars), peaceful everyday life, and scientific pursuits.

The two postcards, then, present Victory Square in different contexts. On the title page, it is the embodiment and ritual center of official war memory. In the second picture, it is part of the city's everyday life. Both are united by a strong emphasis on the unity of generations. The monument provides a symbolic bracket for various population groups, all of which revere the memory of the war and owe their lives to those who died defending their country.

POST NOMER 1

Still, the popularity of the square and its use by various groups—wedding parties, tourists, visiting delegations, and strolling young people—left traces. In Moscow, officials started to demand increased control over its usage. Prompted by the complaint of Dr. A. Egorov, that young tourists had shown "disrespect" toward a monument to Yuriy Gagarin (presumably in Shchekino), the Komsomol Central Committee sent a commission to investigate the situation in Tula Oblast'.[140] On February, 22, 1971, retired colonel of the guards I. Geller wrote a report to the Central Committee about his recent inspection of Victory Square: "The monument is not kept in order. The inspection of the monument revealed numerous inscriptions that had been left with markers and chalk on all sides of the monument. They included the following: 'Kharuzin,' 'Alla,' 'the villagers of Boevo, city of Voronezh,' 'Irina,' 'Elena Mariyka, I love you.'"[141]

The colonel called on the Oblast' Komsomol organization to take immediate measures. Because of the cold, it was only able to remove the inscriptions made with chalk, not those left with marker. Obkom Komsomol secretary A. Kostyurin assured Geller that the organization would do everything necessary to efface the inscriptions as soon as possible.

The problem of neglect and hooliganism was not limited to *Tri Shtyki*. In the campaigns surrounding the twentieth anniversary of victory in 1965, putting neglected war graves back in order was one of the principal tasks. More surprisingly, even in January 1974, a report to the Obkom CPSU identified the lack of care for war monuments and graves among the chief problems confronting military-patriotic work.[142]

The acts of "hooliganism" Geller found appear rather harmless. The names had only been left with marker or chalk, not even carved into the monument. They would leave no lasting damage. Still, Geller and others perceived these inscriptions as signs of a rising tide of unruliness among youths, who participated in patriotic campaigns but did not show the necessary reverence. They feared that participation was limited to "formalism" rather than actual identification with the values conveyed.[143]

Geller felt that decisive measures were necessary to safeguard the monument and to stem this tide. He demanded that a permanent guard of honor (*Pochetnyy Karaul*) be established as soon as possible, thus advocating for a more strictly militaristic definition of Victory Square's significance. The fact that it only operated on holidays and during mass meetings enabled such scribbling, writes Geller.[144] Just over a year later, on May 19, 1972, a so-called Post Nomer 1 was opened (see fig. 3.6).[145] The original post had been Lenin's Mausoleum; after his death, an honorary guard of military personnel was established in Red Square. Starting in 1968 in Volgograd, the concept was transferred to children and youth patrols—to emphasize the unity of generations.[146] By 1985, it had become a mass "movement" in 130 cities.[147]

Post Nomer 1 was an elaborate, ritualized institution. Next to the monument, a large building was constructed to prepare the honorary guard for duty. One room served as a classroom for military-patriotic education. The leader and his assistants used another space, which also served as a "room of military glory," with artifacts from the war.[148] Young guards prepared for duty in two additional rooms.

According to official documents, and at least in the early years of the Post Nomer 1, schools competed with one another for the right to serve as guards of honor and climb the steps of the heroarchy. Students' grades, the schools' participation in *pokhody*, and the quality of their military museums and rooms all played a role in these competitions. Once a school was picked, a thirty-day preparatory program began, full of meetings with veterans and military units, lectures about the revolution and the war, essay competitions, and excursions, in which Pioneer and Komsomol units competed for the right to stand guard.[149] Those who had "good grades and high marks in discipline and societal work," thus indicating that they followed the canon of values established during Stalinism, were allowed to participate, their names published on wall newspapers.[150]

Komsomol organizers considered Post Nomer 1 to be a crucial tool. A. Kostyurin wrote that it "improved the content of military-patriotic education in the higher classes considerably. It developed in them discipline und an interest in military service."[151]

Duty itself was indeed highly regimented. Forty-two children and youth—boys and girls—served each day, in different functions. As figure 3.5 shows, they did so in military uniforms and with guns. Girls participated

Figure 3.5. Guard of honor marching in Tula. Courtesy of the Russian State Archive of Socio-Political History

within clearly circumscribed gender roles: the "soldiers" wore skirts and high heels. Youths were paired with younger children.

During the school year, each institution served four days a week; during holidays, the honorary guard continued seven days a week. The first shift lasted from 9:00 a.m. to 2:00 p.m., the second from 2:00 p.m. to 6:00 p.m. The changing of the guard was staged as a solemn ceremony, in which youngsters also received awards if they had excelled.[152] Tens of thousands of Tulyaki—more accurate numbers are not available—served in the two decades of Post Nomer 1's existence.

Vasiliy Kotenev, depicted in figure 3.7 at a youth camp, was the only respondent who had participated. He is younger than most of the others and was thus at the right age when the campaign was kicked off. He claims that every school in Tula sooner or later was called up for duty. He himself, in spite of his poor track record as a "difficult youth," was also meant to serve. He describes how he entered the building next to the monument. He changed his clothes and waited to go out, next to a kind of ritualistic drawer (*tumbochka*). "While I

Figure 3.6. Guard of honor in front of Tula's main war monument in Victory Square. Courtesy of the Russian State Archive of Socio-Political History

Figure 3.7. Sixteen-year-old Vasiliy Kotenev in a military preparation camp. Courtesy of Vasiliy Kotenev, private archive

was standing there, for about half an hour, next to the drawer, I felt the urge to snack (*perekusit'*). But the drawer was holy, you were not allowed to, you were neither allowed to walk up nor to sit down. But I sat down on the drawer and ate a sandwich. And that was a stinging (*zhguchayushchiy*) violation of order, they threw me out (*vygnali*)."[153]

Kotenev violated the basic tenets of official war memory: showing reverence for the war generation. By his behavior, he denied the commemorative ritual its legitimacy; by engaging in a trivial act like eating, he physically undermined it. At the same time, he rendered the claim that only the "worthiest" served at Post Nomer 1 absurd by his refusal to act accordingly. His teenage rebellion thus not only violated official expectations but also constituted a refusal to take at face value the added symbolic significance that ritualization endowed objects with.

His story illustrates the contradictory nature of Brezhnev-era Soviet society. Transgressions were no longer as severely punished as in Stalinist times: Kotenev was excluded from the collective and never had a conventional Soviet career. He was humiliated in public because he had refused to follow the expected means of self-fashioning, which Oleg Kharkhordin describes as "self-programming and hero-identification, eventually judged by the relevant community."[154]

Whether this was because of his own unwillingness or his misconduct is impossible to ascertain in retrospect. Still, his rebellion neither had lasting consequences nor prevented him from successfully running semi-illicit activities in the 1980s. Unlike frail veterans, who relied on the state and could not afford ostracism, the postwar generation had new options—and was less stifled by the memory of past horrors and the fear of their return.

During the Brezhnev era, those who stuck out were nevertheless met with distrust, rejection, and sometimes repression.[155] As a result of this limited freedom, the postwar generation was more willing than its predecessors to push the boundaries of the system.[156] However, it also developed a keen sense for where these lay and drew a clear line between public and private behavior.[157] Kotenev's case is so exceptional because violations of public political correctness, the socialist contract, and the expectation of "worthy" behavior, particularly in an emotionally charged field like official war memory, were so rare. Whatever people may have thought and said in the privacy of their homes, they knew the role they had to play in public.

NOTES

1. Ziemke and Bauer, *Moscow to Stalingrad*, 37.
2. Bonwetsch, "Der 'Grosse Vaterländische Krieg' und seine Geschichte," 185.
3. Guderian, *Erinnerungen eines Soldaten*, 220.
4. Hartmann, *Wehrmacht im Ostkrieg*, 312.
5. Gusev, *Tayny Tul'skikh Ulits*, 46–48.
6. Aparin, *Na Tul'skom Napravlenii*, 71–73.

7. Stahel, *Operation Typhoon*, 258.
8. Zaytsev, *Memorial'nye Ansambli*, 184.
9. Qualls, *From Ruins to Reconstruction*, 46–47. DeHaan illustrates the tensions between ideological constructs and urban reality in her study of Nizhnyy Novgorod in the 1920s and 1930s. DeHaan, *Stalinist City Planning*, 13–14.
10. Tsentr Noveyshey Istorii Tul'skoy Oblasti (TsNITO), f. P-177, op. 34, d. 31, ll. 290–92. On January 20, 1959, the Central Committee CPSU allowed the Tula Writers' Union the construction of their own publishing house. The Prioskoe Knizhnoe Izdatel'stvo became an important publisher of educational and historical materials. See *Rossiyskiy Gosudarstvennyy Arkhiv Noveyshey Istorii* (RGANI), f. 5, op. 55, d. 24, l. 65.
11. TsNITO, f. P-188, op. 1, d. 1076, l. 82.
12. TsNITO, f. P-188, op. 1, d. 1076, l. 159.
13. TsNITO, f. P-188, op. 1, d. 31, l. 293.
14. TsNITO, f. P-188, op. 1, d. 35, l. 171.
15. Zaytsev, *Memorial'nye Ansambli*, 184.
16. Bater, *Soviet City*, 30.
17. Von Saldern, "Einleitung," 14 (my translation).
18. See Kelly, "Shock of the Old."
19. Kutuzov et al., *Goroda-Geroi Velikoy Otechestvennoy Voyny*.
20. See TsNITO, f. P-1295, op. 1, d. 498, l. 53; *Gosudarstvennyy Arkhiv Tul'skoy Oblasti* (GATO), f. R-3306, op. 3a, d. 353, l. 1.
21. Soviet historians mention eighty tanks, illustrating official war memory's penchant for exaggeration. Aparin, *Na Tul'skom Napravlenii*, 87; Galitsan and Muriev, *Tula*, 57. The Wehrmacht, according to Ivan Kravchenko, lost thirty-eight tanks between October 30 and November 2, when it gave up its initial attempt to take the city. *Tsentral'nyy Arkhiv Ministerstva Oborony RF* (TsAMO), f. 208, op. 2511, d. 1034, l. 103, accessed September 8, 2020.
22. Quoted from the deed of the award in Gusev, *Tayny Tul'skikh Ulits*, 62.
23. Osovik, "Grigory Antonovich Ageev," accessed September 8, 2020; Finogenov, *Tula-Gorod Ordenonosnyy*, 13–14.
24. Gusev, *Tayny Tul'skikh Ulits* 2, 230.
25. TsAMO, f. 208, op. 2511, d. 1034, l. 99.
26. Gusev adds that even fourteen-year-olds were fighting in the trenches of the workers' regiments, until they were relieved by regular troops on November 11. Gusev, *Tayny Tul'skikh Ulits* 2, 232, 239.
27. Aparin, *Na Tul'skom Napravlenii*, 87.
28. Galitsan and Muriev, *Tula*, 63.
29. Kravchenko mentions 84 killed and 212 wounded. This number appears low and would fit into Soviet army commanders' tendency to underreport losses

because they were afraid of persecution for sustaining high casualties. TsAMO, f. 208, op. 2511, d. 1034, l. 104. Aparin only writes that the lack of preparation cost "hundreds of human lives." Aparin, *Na Tul'skom Napravlenii*, 65, 100.

30. DeGraffenried, *Sacrificing Childhood*, 13.

31. TsNITO, f. P-177, op. 34, d. 50, l. 3.

32. *Gosudarstvennyy Arkhiv Rossiyskoy Federatsii* (GARF), f. A-501, op. 1, d. 5006, l. 8. These kinds of collections were tightly regulated and limited to specific use—such as monument construction—hence the official request.

33. Yunak, *Vernost' Geroicheskim Traditsiyam*, 21.

34. The "plan for the construction of monuments with federal significance in the years 1967–1970" was an initiative by the Central Committee and the Council of Ministers SSSR from January 21, 1967.

35. GARF, f. A-501, op. 1, d. 5006, l. 24. The competition lasted from March 25 to April 20. TsNITO, f. P-3, op. 32, d. 17, l. 52. The architects N. Milovidov and G. Saevich were also involved in the projection and execution of the monument.

36. *Rossiyskiy Gosudarstvennyy Arkhiv Literatury i Iskusstva* (RGALI), f. 3151, op. 1, d. 419, l. 9.

37. Paramonova, "Nachal'nik GAI Sgorel na Rabote," 4.

38. Finogenov, *Tula-Gorod Ordenonosnyy*, 14.

39. Aparin, *Na Tul'skom Napravlenii*, 61.

40. Gusev, *Tayny Tul'skikh Ulits 2*, 255.

41. Markwick and Cardona, *Soviet Women on the Frontline*, 230. See also Alexijewitsch, *Der Krieg hat kein weibliches Gesicht*.

42. DeGraffenried, *Sacrificing Childhood*, 95. See also Krylova, *Soviet Women in Combat*, especially chap. 4.

43. See the case study by Carmen Scheide, "Bild und Gedächtnis."

44. Marina Neizvestnaya, interview with the author, Tula, April 17, 2013, 29.01 min. (name altered upon request of the interviewee). Neizvestnaya was born in 1954 and worked for the postal office until her retirement.

45. Neizvestnaya, interview, 17.59 min.

46. Evgeniy Stepunin, interview with the author, Tula, May 18, 2012, 97.30 min. Stepunin, born in 1947, worked at the data center for *Prioksstroi*, one of Tula's construction trusts. He was a party secretary but emphasized that he just did what was expected of him without strong motivation.

47. Raisa Molchanova, interview with the author, Tula, April 18, 2013, 64.03 min. Molchanova emphasized the poverty in which she had grown up and the improvements that the Brezhnev era had brought. As an activist in the Komsomol, she profited from small privileges and was entitled to an apartment.

48. Until recently, German historians ignored the topic too. Mühlhäuser, "'Mannestrieb' und 'Manneszucht.'"

49. A report from the Obkom in Tula to the Central Committee in connection

with the city's application as Hero City from April 30, 1970, maintains that the partisans destroyed 15 tanks and 102 other vehicles and "annihilated" (*istrebili*) up to 1,600 soldiers and officers in November and December 1941. TsNITO, f. P-177, op. 55, d. 110, l. 56.

50. Irina Sycheva, interview with the author, Tula, May 17, 2012, 35.35 min.

51. DeGraffenried, *Sacrificing Childhood*, 75. Catriona Kelly adds that these war games were common and politically somewhat sensitive, as roles between "fascists" and "Communists" might be reversed. She believes that the games counteracted the consistent attempts by the authorities to keep the children's world apolitical. DeGraffenried maintains that the state pushed children into a highly political role during the war. Kelly, *Children's World*, 432.

52. Sycheva, interview, 54.45 min.

53. Lepekhin, *Srazhenie za Tulu*, 567. I was not able to verify that Evdokiya's death in 1970 was indeed a major event. Tula's *Kommunar* newspaper did not report it.

54. It is thus also reminiscent of some Russian heroes from the First World War. Boris Sokolow, "Von Mythen des Kriegs zu Mythen der Literatur."

55. Paramonova, "Nachal'nik GAI Sgorel na Rabote," 4.

56. Ashurkov, *Tula*, 106.

57. Molchanova, interview, 61.34 min.

58. Guderian, *Erinnerungen eines Soldaten*, 233.

59. RGALI, f. 3151, op. 1, d. 419, l. 6.

60. Garbuzov, "Tula's Military Feat," 14; Savchenko, *Gorod-Geroy Tula*, 89.

61. Ashurkov, *Tula*, 106.

62. Lincoln, *Red Victory*, 213–14. See also the 1919 poster by Aleksandr Apsit that visualizes this notion. Apsit, "Vrag Khochet Zakhvatit' Tulu," accessed September 9, 2020.

63. TsNITO, f. P-177, op. 35, d. 60, l. 19.

64. GARF, f. A-501, op. 1, d. 5006, l. 24.

65. GARF, f. A-259, op. 45, d. 7599, ll. 55–58.

66. Quoted in Savchenko, *Gorod-Geroy Tula*, 55.

67. In 1965 he became an honorary citizen of Tula, and Leonid Brezhnev named him Hero of the Soviet Union during his visit in January 1977. Blatov, *Vydayushchiysya Podvig Zashchitnikov Tuly*, 60.

68. Kassin and Vozbranniy, *Tula*, 63.

69. Kadchenko and Lamzin, *Goroda-Geroi Velikoy Otechestvennoy Voyny*.

70. Aparin, *Na Tul'skom Napravlenii*, 60. The Fiftieth Army had been partially encircled in the weeks preceding the Battle of Tula. As the front stabilized, some units returned to strengthen the defense, along with limited reinforcements that the *Stavka* sent to the city.

71. Aparin, *Na Tul'skom Napravlenii*, 14.

72. Paramonova, "Molodomu Kommunaru Otvechaet Sovmin," 4.
73. El'kin, "Geroyam Slavnogo Podviga," 1.
74. El'kin, "Geroyam Slavnogo Podviga," 1.
75. TsNITO, P-177, op. 34, d. 31, ll. 290–92; d. 33, ll. 112–14.
76. Viktorov and El'kin, "Tula Salyutuet Prazdniku Pobedy," 1–2. On big anniversaries like the twenty-fifth in 1970, a celebration followed in the city's stadium.
77. Vasiliy Kotenev, interview with the author, Tula, May 21, 2012, 14.55 min.
78. Vasiliy Kotenev, interview with the author, Tula, May 21, 2012, 17.56 min.
79. Vladimir Romanov, interview with the author, Tula, April 17, 2013, 18.13 min.
80. Dubin, "Gesellschaft der Angepassten," 68.
81. He was born in 1962, Stepuzhin in 1951. Sergey Stepuzhin, interview with the author, Tula, May 28, 2012. For Stepuzhin, his service in the Red Army presented a particularly important period. After leaving the army, he became a history teacher.
82. Kotenev, interview, 131.07 min. One such construction project was the Baykal-Amur main line. There, as elsewhere, the hope to reeducate the hooligans through hard labor failed, producing instead a microcosm of violence and crime. Ward, *Brezhnev's Folly*, 47, 130.
83. Elena Bozhenko, interview with the author, Tula, May 17, 2012, 50.38 min.
84. This is only one example that puts in question Nina Tumarkin's findings that "the near quarter-century-long campaign of military-patriotic upbringing ... had been, almost from the beginning, a spectacular failure." Tumarkin, *Living and the Dead*, 155. Tumarkin conducted her research during the turbulent times of the late 1980s and early 1990s, which most likely colored her views and those of her respondents.
85. Hornsby points out that the tours also provided an opportunity for veterans to network with one another and with functionaries. Hornsby, "Soviet Youth on the March," 430.
86. In a meeting of patriotic educators on March 16, Lieutenant-General Solomatin, who was a member of the *Znanie* society's presidium, said that the number of talks on "military patriotic topics" had doubled between 1964 and 1965 in the Oblast'. He praised the positive effect that former officers had had on discipline in schools and on the military preparedness of youth. In his estimation, Tula's schools still used such officers much too rarely, something that was corrected in later years. TsNITO, f. P-188, op. 1, d. 1076, ll. 56–58.
87. Yunak, *Vernost' Geroicheskim Traditsiyam*, 107.
88. TsNITO, P-177, op. 82, d. 9, ll. 32–40.
89. TsNITO, P-177, op. 82, d. 9, l. 39.
90. TsNITO, P-177, op. 82, d. 9, l. 39.

91. This transition fits Victor Turner's concept of liminality. Turner, "Betwixt and Between."

92. This is reminiscent of older Christian Orthodox beliefs that suffering had a cleansing effect. Furthermore, Lev Gudkov points to a widespread notion in Russia that the people exhibited its best qualities during wartime. See Gudkov, "Pobeda v Voyne."

93. Bozhenko, interview, 92.41 min.

94. Bozhenko, interview, 39.39 min.

95. Bozhenko, interview, 95 min.

96. Barnes, *Death and Redemption*, 103.

97. Viktor Shcheglov, interview with the author, Tula, May 17, 2012, 45 min. He worked as a correspondent from various factories and participated actively in programs for "patriotic education."

98. Shcheglov, interview, 65 min.

99. Stepuzhin, interview, 9.44 min. Once Stepuzhin had grown up, he insists, these kinds of questions were less important, and he never felt at a disadvantage as a child of a former "Kulak."

100. Other publications also report this hesitance to talk about wartime events. See, for example, Osipov and Rostovtseva, *My Pomnim*.

101. Sergey Stepuzhin, interview, 14.55 min.

102. Members of this last group were often associated with the city of Tashkent and considered to be shirkers. Stronski, *Tashkent*, 123.

103. Vladimir Yurchikov, interview with the author, April 16, 2013, 8.22 min. Yurchikov, born in Tula in 1948, was not a forthcoming respondent. His family has lived and worked in Tula for over one hundred years, always in armament factories. Yurchikov spent his entire career—forty-eight years—at the weapons factory Tula. He brought his daughter to the interview, and she prompted him repeatedly to talk about the past. She knew that her grandfather almost died during the war, when he had to liberate himself from his burning tank. Yurchikov, interview, 10 min.

104. Molchanova, interview, 62.30 min, 62.30 min.

105. Molchanova, interview, 62.30 min, 12.57 min. Her description fits Judith Herman's: "Traumatic memories lack verbal narrative and context; rather, they are encoded in the form of vivid sensations and images." Herman, *Trauma and Recovery*, 38.

106. Psychologist and neuroscientist Hans-Joachim Markowitsch writes that humans are less able to repress memories in old age because many brain cells die. The result is the kind of "surfacing" that Molchanova describes. Quoted in Charisius, "Traumatische Erlebnisse." See also Markowitsch, *Dem Gedächtnis auf der Spur*.

107. Romanov, interview, 42.48 min.

108. Gudkov, "Die Fesseln des Sieges," 60.

109. DeGraffenried, *Sacrificing Childhood*, 158.
110. Romanov, interview, 90.07 min.
111. Beevor and Grossman, *Writer at War*, 55.
112. Aparin, *Na Tul'skom Napravlenii*, 62–64, 87.
113. Shcheglov, interview, 45 min.
114. Shcheglov, interview, 5.35 min.
115. Beate Fieseler and Mark Edele published two monographs that deal with the issue extensively: Fieseler, *Arme Sieger: Die Invaliden des 'Grossen Vaterländischen Krieges' der Sowjetunion 1941–1991*; Edele, *Soviet Veterans of the Second World War*.
116. Kotenev, interview, 43.21 min. Bernd Bonwetsch also found that, while veterans enjoyed great reverence, their privileges were at times resented. The dismissive term *vovy* (deriving from the Russian abbreviation of Great Patriotic War—*Velikaya Otechestvennaya Voyna*) was applied to those veterans who secured themselves advantages that were thought to be illegitimate. Bonwetsch, "Der 'Grosse Vaterländische Krieg,'" 179.
117. See the book on blat' by the political scientist Alena Ledeneva: Ledeneva, *Russia's Economy of Favours*.
118. This was partially already the case in the 1930s, as Kotkin describes: "Scarcity, far from being the Soviet political system's Achilles heel, was one of the keys to its strength. The tighter the overall balance of services of supplies, the more leverage the authorities could exercise." Kotkin, *Magnetic Mountain*, 246.
119. Gabriele Rosenthal would call this issue a central sequence of the gestalt of his life story, which shapes his autobiographical narrative. Gabriele Rosenthal, *Erlebte und erzählte Lebensgeschichte*, 18–20.
120. TsNITO, f. P-177, op. 69, d. 69, ll. 1–5.
121. TsNITO, f. P-177, op. 74, d. 93, ll. 1–2.
122. Yunak, *Vernost' Geroicheskim Traditsiyam*, 47.
123. DeGraffenried, *Sacrificing Childhood*, 60.
124. On the Timurov movement, see also Kelly, *Children's World*, 554–55.
125. TsNITO, f. P-177, op. 74, d. 93, l. 16.
126. *Rossiyskiy Gosudarstvennyy Arkhiv Sotsial'no-Politicheskoy Istorii* (RGASPI), f. M-1, op. 38, d. 463, l. 7; TsNITO, f. P-188, op. 1, d. 1378, l. 9; d. 1737, l. 1.
127. For example, in a report from E. Klobukov, head of the *pokhody*'s Oblast' staff from April 12, 1972. TsNITO, f. P-188, op. 1, d. 1236, l. 12. In a statement from October 24, 1975, Komsomol Secretary A. Artem'ev claimed that the "patronage" of youth had been improved recently, thanks to the same 1974 "raid" (*reyd*) by the People's Control Committee that brought many of the problems in veteran care to light. The timing leads one to suspect that this improvement might have been the result of a campaign for the thirtieth anniversary of Victory, rather than of a sustainable improvement. TsNITO, f. P-188, op. 1, d. 1378, l. 5.

128. Savchenko, *Gorod-Geroy Tula*, 89–90.

129. These services were organized as part of the campaign following the January 1964 resolution on nonreligious festivals and rituals. Binns, "Changing Face of Power," 173–75.

130. "Champagne, not vodka," insists Vladimir Romanov, "you did not want to be wasted at the reception." Romanov, interview, 69 min.

131. Kotenev, interview, 94.24 min.

132. Stepunin, interview, 122.56 min.

133. Romanov, interview, 69 min.

134. Stepuzhin, interview, 46.34 min.

135. Silke Satjukov and Karl Qualls emphasize repetition in their analyses of hero myths in the Soviet Union: Qualls, *From Ruins to Reconstruction*, 12; Satjukow and Gries, "Zur Konstruktion des 'sozialistischen Helden,'" 27.

136. Savchenko, *Gorod-Geroy Tula*.

137. Galitsan and Muriev, *Tula*.

138. Galitsan and Muriev, *Tula*, 2.

139. Kolesnikov and Rozhkov, *Ordena i Medali SSSR*, 86–91.

140. RGASPI, M-1, op. 38, d. 505, l. 3. They found that tourists had left their "autographs" on the monument, including statements like "Vovik and grandmother (*babulya*) Nadya were here" and "Nina, I love you!"

141. RGASPI, M-1, op. 38, d. 505, l. 110.

142. TsNITO, P-177, op. 66, d. 141, l. 16.

143. The authors complain that even though more than eighteen thousand new monuments had been built all over the Union, they were often poorly executed, constructed of low quality, and poorly supervised. "Formalism" was detected, especially in connection with the "history of the establishment of Soviet power, the Civil War and the labor tradition of the Soviet people." RGASPI, M-1, op. 38, d. 505, l. 2.

144. RGASPI, M-1, op. 38, d. 505, l. 113.

145. RGASPI, M-1, op. 38, d. 623, l. 10.

146. RGASPI, f. M-1, op. 145, d. 56, l. 19.

147. RGASPI, f. M-1, op. 145, d. 34, l. 3.

148. RGASPI, f. M-1, op. 116, d. 508, l. 1. The establishment of rooms, corners, and museums of "revolutionary, military and labor glory" was among the main goals of the *pokhody*; by 1982, three thousand of them had been installed in the Tula Oblast'. For the most part, they consisted of materials that children and youth had gathered from veterans, in local archives, and (rarely) during organized digs to former battlefields. A report from April 23, 1979, complains that, first, "the majority of dormitories" had no such corner and that, second, those that did had no visitors. TsNITO, f. P-188, op. 1, d. 1648, l. 10.

149. See, for example, the report from 1972: TsNITO, f. P-188, op. 1, d. 1236, l. 38.

150. RGASPI, f. M-1, op. 66, d. 710, l. 88.
151. RGASPI, f. M-1, op. 66, d. 710, l. 88.
152. RGASPI, f. M-1, op. 66, d. 710, l. 89–90. The various functions at the honorary guard often corresponded with military ranks: each shift had a political officer (*zampolit*), six relief commanders (*razvodyashchie*), six sentries (*chasovye*), and orderlies and controllers.
153. Kotenev, interview, 55.06 min.
154. Kharkhordin, *Collective and the Individual in Russia*, 357.
155. Dubin, "Gesellschaft der Angepassten," 67.
156. Stephen V. Bittner has analyzed this mix of repression and relaxation in his study of Arbat Street in Moscow. He shows, for instance, how the dissident trial against the writers Andrei Sinyavskiy and Yuliy Daniel was indicative of both growing repression and increasing societal freedoms, since public criticism prevented excessive harm. According to Bittner, this kind of resistance would not have been possible ten years earlier. Bittner, *Many Lives of Khrushchev's Thaw*, 178–80.
157. Elena Zdravomyslova and Viktor Voronkov conceptualized this two-sidedness of society through the notion of the "informal public"—neither entirely private nor public—in which many of the most significant social processes took place. Zdravomyslova and Voronkov, "Informal Public in Soviet Society."

FOUR

Great Expectations
A Worthy Life

IN THE LATE 1970S, A new element appeared in Victory Square: a row of black granite stones that carried the names of all the Hero Cities. Tula joined their ranks on December 7, 1976, as the last city to receive the highest Soviet award during the Brezhnev era. The general secretary visited in January 1977 in honor of this momentous occasion—for the first and only time. He emphasized the significance of Tula's elevation: "The Hero Cities, whose names are forever tied to the most memorable wartime events, greet you. Moscow, Leningrad and Volgograd, Sevastopol' and Odessa, Kiev and Minsk, Novorossiysk, Kerch', and Brest Fortress have sent you their representatives—to welcome Tula to their glorious and heroic family. . . . Today, all Soviet people share your pride and joy."[1]

Brezhnev brought not only kind words and symbolic privilege but also tangible material promises from a party leadership that claimed to value the welfare of the Soviet population above all else:

> When I got ready to come here, I was especially interested in how the Tulyaki live, how the city is developing. I was told that every year, comfortable new houses are built in Tula, that the number of places in schools and kindergartens grows, that new hospitals and clinics are opened. I know you say, "This is not enough." You say, "We need more apartments, larger facilities for children, more goods and stores." Well, you are right. Demand exceeds our possibilities. But it is not like we remain standing in place—we move ahead. Let us balance some numbers. If 474 million rubles were invested into Tula's development during the eighth Five-Year Plan, it was 718 in the ninth, and for the tenth 903 million rubles are planned. But why don't you applaud? (*Applause. Animation in the hall.*)"[2]

Following a surprisingly self-critical assessment of Tula's problems, Brezhnev tried to gain applause for the proposed remedies. But the audience of honorary guests, mostly regional party and state functionaries, only praised him after explicit encouragement. This constituted an unparalleled éclat.

The remarkable incident shows that there existed considerable discontent with Tula's socioeconomic situation in the mid-1970s. This was due to the slow progress in the decades since the end of the war, which will be discussed below. The inhabitants of the industrial city felt that the "socialist contract" had not been in their favor, while Moscow's focus lay on the shortcomings of the regional economy. Expectations in connection with the award were correspondingly high—from both the party and the population. The award was to serve as a mobilizing tool, which coexisted uneasily with popular anticipation of tangible rewards.

War and economic reconstruction had become intimately tied as soon as Tula Oblast' was liberated in January 1942. Soviet propaganda extensively talked about material damage but remained largely silent on human losses; these were only disclosed in front of a select audience much later.[3] On December 8, 1971, in a speech to party activists in honor of the thirtieth anniversary of Tula's defense, Ivan Yunak, First Secretary of the party's Oblast' Committee, mentioned that 38,500 Soviet soldiers had fallen. This number would only be revealed to a nonparty public a decade later.[4]

The Stalinist regime would not allow for mourning in the postwar years—economic reconstruction was the main goal. Tula, which produced not only weapons but also metal and coal, had strategic significance. The Soviet Council of Ministers thus prioritized the reconstruction of its heavy industry. By 1950, it had reassumed a dominant position in the regional economy;[5] workers were moving to Tula in large numbers. Because Tula had not been destroyed during the war, however, it was not included in the list of fifteen Russian cities that received special funds for development, and living conditions remained precarious until the late 1950s.[6]

The hardest year, according to Sergey Stepuzhin, was 1947: the postwar economic crisis reached its climax, and people were suffering from severe food shortages.[7] His father was unable to pay his taxes on time, and the state even took away the family's cow.[8] Like Stepuzhin, Raisa Molchanova relies on family memories when retelling the postwar situation. Her parents moved to Tula in 1946 and at first rented a half-destroyed apartment. One year later, they were able to relocate to a *kommunalka* that had running water and gas—a significant improvement.

As a decorated war hero and member of the Communist Party, her father was entrusted to run the bread combine (*kombinat*) in Suvorovskiy Rayon near Tula. He left his family in the city because the countryside was too dangerous. Molchanova's mother told her that bands of criminals and demobilized soldiers roamed the area near the combine, which was heavily guarded because of its strategic significance. "There was hunger after the war, great danger because there was a lot of theft, and one had to feed people. It was a dangerous time."[9] This lawlessness marked many areas of the USSR.

The return of Red Army soldiers often exacerbated social tension. In his work as a journalist, Viktor Shcheglov frequently talked to veterans. One of them told him privately about their disappointment when they saw Tula again: "These soldiers had marched halfway across Europe, through Germany, Poland, Czechoslovakia . . . and suddenly they, who had ploughed across all these beautiful streets with their tanks, saw these pathetic shacks (*ubogye lachugi*) . . . and they began to compare without wanting to. . . . [They] saw that the defeated Germans had such roads, and how they were here. . . . That was of course difficult, but no one spoke about it, you were not allowed to."[10]

In Shcheglov's assessment, the Soviet authorities not only censored veterans but also initially ignored their economic and social needs, forcing them into poverty and petty crime. "The veterans came back after the war, some without feet, some without hands, others as invalids. . . . Some did not have families anymore; some died, others went away. Veterans did not have houses; they had burnt down, or neighbors had simply moved in during the war. As a result, they either joined gangs—no real gangs but petty crooks (*melki-vorishi*), pickpockets, you know. . . . And they sold what they had."[11]

Even once the situation became more stable, the war remained visible. Conditions varied depending on the level of destruction. From his childhood in the village of Pervomaysk outside of Tula, Evgeniy Stepunin remembers the traces of armed conflict, such as fortifications. The houses, however, were mostly intact, as there had only been limited fighting. Still, some villagers were living in dugouts when he was a child, Stepunin recalls.[12]

Marina Neizvestnaya vividly remembers the tank ditches and craters in her native village of Myasnovo: "As children, we ran around in them. . . . And in winter, we went sledding in them. . . . Near our house, there was this crater (*kotlovan*), perhaps from an explosion; perhaps there had been a structure there during the war. The children (*rebetizhki*) dug and dug there. They found boxes with grenades at the bottom."

According to Neizvestnaya, parents immediately called the authorities, and the military commissariat had the ammunition removed.[13] Children's lives among the remnants of the world war were dangerous at times. In a collected volume containing memories of the postwar era in Tula, one witness mentions that a significant number of them lost limbs because they were playing with blind shells.[14] Even in 1975, a history textbook for fourth graders warns students of unexploded ammunition and recommends that they "tell adults, or even better, the local military commissariat" if they come across them.[15]

By the 1960s, new apartment buildings had been built over the former battle scars, and newly planted forest covered old trenches in Myasnovo. Vasiliy Kotenev saw this tendency to build over remnants in Tula's Proletarskiy Rayon critically. He recounts that a dilapidated German war cemetery fascinated him and his friends: "I remember how we ran around there. Skulls, bones, and crosses were lying on the ground. . . . Afterward, they built a cooperative on top of the cemetery. . . . I did not understand this. . . . They could at least have reburied them elsewhere."[16] This unease about the authorities' unceremonious approach to reconstruction, even on former battlefields and cemeteries, was shared by other respondents, in both Tula and Novorossiysk. The authorities' actions contradicted the emphasis on reverence in official war memory and showed the selectivity of this reverence.

Yet the need to build new housing was great, as the population grew rapidly during the economic upswing. After forced industrialization under Stalin had increased the number of Tulyaki to 285,000 on the eve of the war, this number dropped drastically during the conflict but increased again to 351,000 in 1959. Before 1989 it would grow to over half a million (see fig. 4.1).[17]

The 1950s also saw marked growth in the Oblast's agricultural industry. It would become one of the most important suppliers of the Moscow region. For its achievements in agriculture, the region received the Order of Lenin on December 27, 1957. On February 17, 1959, Nikita Khrushchev visited in honor of this award and was welcomed by more than fifty thousand Tulyaki.[18]

Khrushchev's reforms, combined with rural depopulation, nonetheless created recurrent supply problems.[19] During the Seven-Year Plan, Tula's agricultural output fell short, and in 1964–65 the entire USSR experienced harvest failures, some of which were the result of the unsustainable measures employed to develop the virgin lands. People in Tula had to line up for basic commodities like bread. Vasiliy Malinichev, a cadre in the Oblispolkom, writes in his memoirs that the newly appointed Ivan Yunak feared bread riots like those in Novocherkassk in 1962 and even met with the commander of the local garrison to discuss countermeasures.[20]

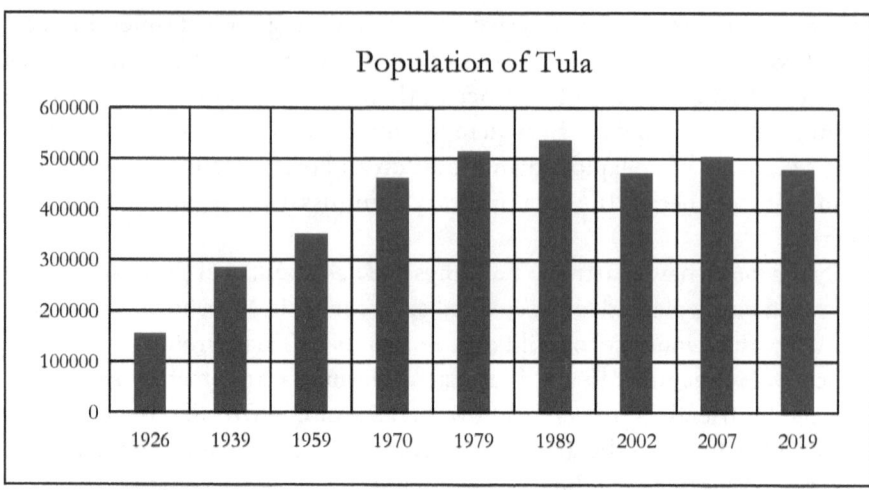

Figure 4.1. Population in Tula, 1926–2019. Graph drawn by the author

Irina Sycheva well remembers the "long breadlines" and the rationing in Tula during this time.[21] Sergey Stepuzhin said that in 1963 there was not enough bread—particularly "almost no white bread." He explained: "They of course gave black bread, but white bread—they rationed it (*davali po spisku*). I was still little, twelve years, so I stood in line at one store, bought some, went to another one, bought some because they did not give it out freely."[22] The rationing of bread, then, appeared to the Soviet population as a particularly striking violation of Khrushchev's promise of a bright communist future—and of the socialist contract.

Trying to extricate itself from this socially explosive situation, the Obkom began to advocate economic reforms in line with those of Evsey Liberman and Premier Aleksey Kosygin, which suggested the introduction of limited market mechanisms. The Shchekino method, a model that created incentives to lay off unproductive workers, was developed right outside Tula.[23] In spite of initial success and Brezhnev's support, the reforms were never implemented consistently. Instead, they were vulnerable to accusations of introducing capitalist methods into the socialist economy. Moreover, they had to compete ideologically with those that advocated "moral" instead of "material" incentives—the strengthening of Soviet values, increased party control, and awards to motivate workers.[24]

Neither approach promised to defuse tensions in Tula Oblast' in the short run. Yunak understood that he needed more funds from Moscow to improve the population's lives—and that the twenty-fifth anniversary of the Battle of Moscow and Tula provided a welcome opportunity.

REWARDS FOR TULA'S ANNIVERSARY

On January 8, 1966, the Obkom not only planned the upcoming festivities but also asked the Central Committee CPSU and the Council of Ministers to "award the city of Tula with a government order for the self-sacrifice and the courage that the city's inhabitants displayed during the fight against the German-fascist occupiers."[25] Yunak and the head of the Oblispolkom, Gerontiy Kamaev, justified this demand with the will of the people: "Currently many requests are arriving at the Obkom CPSU and the central organs from workers [and] former soldiers who defended Tula—for a decoration of the city and the immortalization of the memory of its heroic defenders."[26]

The Obkom also forwarded to Gosplan SSSR and the Council of Ministers RSFSR its suggestion on how to improve Tula's infrastructure, housing, and services.[27] A day earlier, Yunak and Kamaev had described Tula's drastic situation in a letter to the Council of Ministers RSFSR: 4,345 families in the city still lived in damaged houses and sheds. Electricity, water, and medical facilities were insufficient to supply the quickly growing population, and numerous schools still operated in three shifts because of the lack of space.[28]

On March 1, 1966, Kamaev and Olimp Chukanov, Second Secretary of the Obkom, linked their demands even more explicitly to the anniversary. "In connection with the upcoming celebration of the twenty-fifth anniversary of the city of Tula's defense against the German-fascist invaders, a large volume of work is being carried out in Tula and the Oblast'—renovating, rebuilding and enlarging public amenities buildings, local hospitals, schools, etc." [29] Because the Oblast' lacked the necessary building materials, they asked for a broad range of commodities, such as fifteen thousand square meters of window glass and five hundred thousand table slates.

On April 24, 1965—immediately before the twentieth anniversary of victory—the Council of Ministers decided to build a sewage system in Tula for 19 million rubles. Moreover, the city was to receive new trams and buses for 5.4 million rubles, and houses were to be equipped with gas pipes at a cost of 12.6 million rubles. Nonetheless, in June the Obkom complained that Gosplan had provided only 25.3 million rubles for public amenities from 1966 to 1970—almost 5 million less than during the preceding five-year period. Tula's leaders asked for 40 million.[30]

As a result of these large-scale infrastructure projects, Tula doubled the number of water pipes and improved its public transportation network between 1960 and 1970.[31] The Brezhnev era saw a fivefold increase in state investments in communal services.[32] Tula's airport opened in 1970 and offered new options for travel.[33]

The coincidence between anniversaries and large infrastructure projects in the 1960s is striking. It shows that the political authorities—and the population—saw the two as connected. An anniversary was seen as a legitimate foundation for material demands—a practice that dated back to Stalinism, following the Soviet authorities' custom of handing out financial or material benefits to the population in general and to veterans in particular near big holidays.[34] In a society that prided itself on its egalitarianism, heroism was a significant factor that justified material privileges.

The Obkom is rather vague in its demand for a "government award," but it may have hoped for an elevation into the ranks of Hero Cities in 1966. The initial request seems to have set an application process in motion. On October 29, Ivan Yunak sent additional background information (*spravka*) to the Central Committee, explaining why Tula deserved a government award: the city had stopped General Heinz Guderian's tanks, and sixty thousand workers joined destruction battalions (*istrebitel'nye batal'ony*) and the workers' regiment. Finally, the city's remaining inhabitants had repaired a lot of military technology in the vacated shop floors of evacuated enterprises during the war.[35]

On December 7, 1966, Tula was awarded the Order of Lenin, one of only thirty-five cities to receive that distinction.[36] The event was widely propagated in the national media but also overshadowed by the anniversary celebrations in the capital. On the day Tula received the award, Moscow's official meeting in honor of the counteroffensive's twenty-fifth anniversary filled *Pravda*'s front page. The feats of Muscovites, who "stood until death" to stop the Wehrmacht, were discussed at length.[37]

Tula and other cities that played an important role in the battle sent representatives. Smolensk, which had received the Order of the Patriotic War First Degree, was mentioned first, followed by Tula: "The Wehrmacht encountered particularly steadfast resistance near Tula. The renowned (*proslavlennye*) Tula weapon makers demonstrated in those days that they are not only capable of forging weapons but also of crushing (*razit'*) enemies with them. Their heroic feat will never be forgotten. The Muscovites today heartily greet their fighting comrades and brothers in arms, the workers of glorious Tula. They warmly (*goryacho*) congratulate them on their high award—the Order of Lenin."[38]

Tula's special role was thus recognized—albeit only along with that of a number of other cities and primarily in reference to its contribution to Moscow's defense. The *Short History* of the Great Patriotic War, published in 1965, only mentions Tula in passing. The same goes for Maksim Kim's history textbook for tenth graders.[39] Only the more extensive publications on the war—the six-volume *Istoriya Velikoy Otechestvennoy Voyny Sovetskogo Soyuza 1941–1945*, initiated under Khrushchev, and the Brezhnev-era twelve-volume *Istoriya Vtoroy Mirovoy Voyny 1939—1945*—discuss Tula extensively. Both emphasize that it stabilized the left wing of Moscow's defense, an assessment that is widely shared in Western historiography.[40]

The elevation of the significance of the Battle of Moscow and the Hero City award to the capital in 1965 nonetheless created controversies. Under Stalin, the battle was rarely mentioned because it pointed to the leadership's mistakes at the beginning of the war. During the Thaw era, the disorganized nature of the initial Soviet defense, the huge casualties, and the leadership's poor decision-making led to debates.[41]

In a speech in 1966, the writer Mikhail Granin openly addresses this point. Granin deplores that the significance of the Battle of Moscow had not been recognized properly. With Leningrad blockaded and the Wehrmacht advancing in the South, the fall of the capital would have ended the war: "the fundamental turning point occurred here, and not in Stalingrad."[42] Granin's statement, then, denies even Stalingrad a sense of exceptionalism. Moscow moved to the top of the official wartime pantheon, firmly embedding other Hero Cities below it in the heroarchy. Tula's position was also strengthened: as a crucial staging ground for the offensive, it was presented as one of the places where the tide turned toward victory, thereby advancing to the second row of the heroarchy.

On December 9, Tula's Order of Lenin received a front-page story in *Pravda*. The paper had sent two correspondents to cover the festivities. Eight thousand people gathered in Tula's *Luzhniki* Stadium. They took a solemn oath to contribute to the fulfillment of the Twenty-Third Party Congress's decisions, thereby highlighting transgenerational unity.[43] On the following day, a more exclusive gathering of party, union, and Komsomol members took place in the Cultural Palace of the Railroad Workers (*Dvorets Kul'tury Zheleznodorozhnikov imeni V. I. Lenina*). Also present were Hero City representatives. Dmitriy Ustinov—Politburo candidate, secretary of the Central Committee, and subsequently minister of defense—was the guest of honor, who handed over the Order of Lenin and attached it to the city banner.[44]

In his speech Ustinov emphasized the collaboration between the Red Army and the city's workers. He presented the Order of Lenin as a "symbol of the feat of arms and the glorious revolutionary traditions of Tula's proletariat."[45] He moved on to praise the defense of Tula, in which "the entire city, from young to old, participated." Somewhat surprisingly, he also dwelled on the role of women, who shouldered most of the workload and also supplied the front lines. Finally, he mentioned youth, who volunteered for the Red Army in large numbers: "The self-sacrifice of youth in those days remains an example for the generation that is growing up now."[46]

Wartime youth, as an example for the postwar generation and the party as the "leader and organizer of all our victories," provided the discursive bridge to the socialist contract in the present.[47] "The highest goal of the Communist Party is the elevation of the material welfare of the workers, the full satisfaction (*udovletvorenie*) of their cultural and everyday demands. How this task is being fulfilled is evident in the example of your city and region."[48]

In reality, however, Ustinov's priorities lay less in the light consumer industry than in the armament sector.[49] Between 1965 and 1968, he was in charge of recentralizing the military-industrial complex, an extremely important project for the USSR's growing ambitions. This economic realm had been fraught with competition among different ministries and design bureaus.[50] Regional actors, including Tula's leadership, were reluctant to give up power.

By 1978, Tula had thirty-two enterprises producing military goods, and thirteen military research institutes. Every month, they produced two hundred thousand Kalashnikov rifles, as well as commodities such as mopeds or televisions.[51] In spite of its relative privilege in material supplies and cadres, the military-industrial complex suffered from the same problems that had been endemic throughout the Soviet economy since the 1930s. In his study of the Soviet military industry, Peter Almquist names unreliable supply lines, "storming" (the concentration of output at the end of the month), and problems with product quality.[52]

Ustinov openly criticized the technical level of manufacturing, the lack of accuracy and electronic technology in the production process, even though he said that "it is normally not pleasant to talk about these kinds of facts on a holiday."[53] He found "serious deficiencies" (*nedostatki*) in the work of the Obkom, which was especially weak in promoting "socialist discipline" in the enterprises.[54] Nonetheless, he expressed confidence that "you will understand these critical remarks in the right way."[55] Moreover, he suggested using the "moral incentives" inherent in official war memory to motivate workers and keep them aware of the ongoing danger of war with the West.[56] The award recognizing Tula's contribution to the Battle of Moscow was used as a mobilizing device.

However, no large-scale mobilization of the population took place after December 1966: the archives contain no programs or campaigns for harder work in honor of the award. The moral pressure to show oneself worthy of the Order of Lenin was not as strong as Dmitriy Ustinov's statements indicate. The Oblast' authorities did not have to show activity or justify the lack thereof.

On the other hand, the award's prestige was comparatively small. It could not compare to that of the Hero City or even the Order of the Patriotic War; the capital and Smolensk, which, unlike Tula, had fallen, were mentioned before it in the anniversary festivities. Ustinov's open criticism reinforced this sense. "I always thought that [the Order of Lenin] was enough for Tula, and I found it strange (*chudno*) that the city also got the Hero City award later on," Vasiliy Kotenev explains, confirming the distinctions within the Soviet heroarchy.[57]

In the memory of my respondents, the Hero City award overshadowed the Order of Lenin completely. Those recollections of the Order of Lenin that exist are decisively prosaic. Raisa Molchanova worked as a Komsomol activist in the factory Tula, which also produced military equipment. She used to read the news to other workers during meetings, and she also told them about the Order of Lenin: "There was a lot in the papers, of course, and I read that. And there were political talks (*politbesedy*). [IM: Ustinov was here, right?] I can't remember that, I don't know about that.... We passed on information as well, one told [the workers] about the news for three to five minutes before work started."[58] Judging from her contextualization, the award ceremony was only one item of news among many others, which activists simply read out to the workers.

This perception stands in contrast to the tangible results of the city's elevation. Tula's leadership took Ustinov at his word when he promised that the party's main priority lay in safeguarding the welfare of Soviet workers. This was not an easy feat for a regional capital outside of the privileged centers of Moscow and Saint Petersburg, which traditionally received the lion's share of funds and attention. It placed the regional leadership in a position to articulate demands and catch the ministers' attention—not least because of extensive press coverage.

Yunak's relative closeness to Brezhnev was an additional benefit. Born in Poltava Oblast' in 1918, he made his career in Ukraine, sharing parts of Brezhnev's path. He had been the head of the Dnepropetrovsk Oblispolkom from 1954 to 1961 before he was transferred to Tula. As one of Khrushchev's and Brezhnev's protégés (part of the "Dnepr-Mafia," in John Dornberg's words), he was tasked with securing the First Secretary's hold on the strategically important Tula

Oblast'.[59] In a tense social situation, the Order of Lenin helped him to secure real everyday improvements.

A WORTHY HOME

The Obkom subsequently based its official lobbying explicitly on the Order of Lenin. In a letter to the Council of Ministers SSSR, Ivan Yunak and Gerontiy Kamaev expressed their "profound gratitude" for the "high estimation of the courage and steadfastness displayed by the defenders of Tula during the heroic defense."[60] The Obkom then joined the call of other Soviet institutions to award Leonid Brezhnev with a Gold Star Medal on the occasion of his sixtieth birthday for his contribution to victory, which he received.[61]

After this formalistic gesture of respect and deference to the leader, Yunak and Kamaev continued with a description of Tula's difficult living conditions: ninety-four thousand people in the city were waiting for new apartments, they wrote; total demand was estimated at 2.7 million square meters. Planned construction in the ninth Five-Year Plan (1971–75) was only 404,000 square meters, half as much as the Obkom had asked, which meant that it would take twenty-five to thirty years to meet the population's needs.

Yunak and Kamaev asked for an additional 60 million rubles for housing. They succeeded: almost 1.2 million square meters were built during that time.[62] The direct link between wartime heroism and entitlement to better living conditions is a striking illustration of the socialist contract.

Although Tula had not sustained massive wartime destruction, the shelling of the city and the significant population shifts nonetheless created a housing crisis that lasted well into the Brezhnev era. Until the late 1950s, housing was low on the list of priorities. Large parts of the city still consisted of pre-revolutionary, one-story wooden houses in the mid-1960s. According to Ivan Yunak, these buildings made up half of Tula's housing stock and were in poor condition. Another 15 percent consisted of barracks, basements, and damaged apartments.[63] In a letter to the Council of Ministers on January 16, 1965, the First Secretary of the Obkom maintained that there had been "practically no housing construction" before 1957.[64]

That marked the year when Nikita Khrushchev's campaign for the construction of apartment buildings (1956–63) took off. Mark Smith calls it "one of the greatest social reforms of modern European history," in spite of its many problems and shortcomings.[65] Thirty-five million apartments were assembled in the Soviet Union between 1955 and 1970.[66] Following the ideological unrest of de-Stalinization, the Soviet leadership wanted to firmly entrench its legitimacy

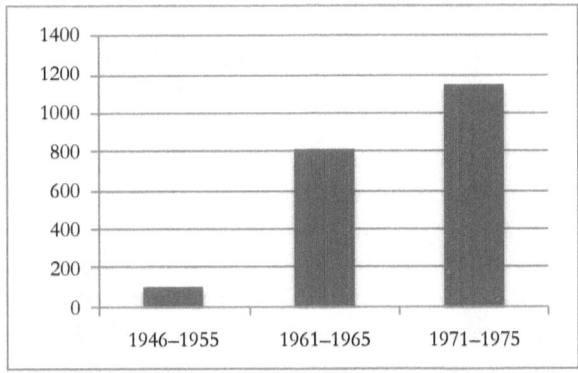

Figure 4.2. Housing construction in Tula. Graph drawn by the author

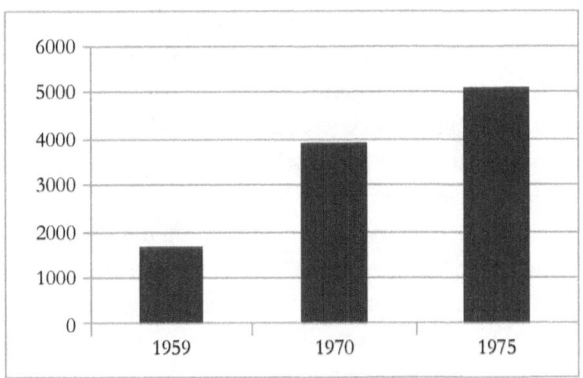

Figure 4.3. Total housing space in Tula (in thousands of m²). Graph drawn by the author

through a socialist contract that foresaw the provision of worthy housing conditions to all segments of the population.[67]

In 1957 alone, more housing was built in Tula than in the years between 1946 and 1955. Until the mid-1970s, construction accelerated, with the largest increase during the ninth Five-Year Plan, between 1971 and 1975.[68] Leonid Brezhnev's claim that "a second Tula" had been built between 1966 and 1976 was no exaggeration (see fig. 4.2).[69]

In 1970, the 3.9 million square meters of overall housing stock (see fig. 4.3) provided each of the 520,000 inhabitants with 7.5 square meters, considerably less than the legal minimum of 8.5 square meters of living space (*zhiloy ploshchad'*).[70] Additionally, communal services often worked poorly. Malinichev writes that the Oblispolkom received almost three thousand complaints every year in the late 1960s and early 1970s: "People write about the poor work of transport, broken roads, bad water supply, the lack of necessary commodities in the stores, the long lines."[71]

In a meeting on June 19, 1970, the Obkom discussed serious problems with water supply: for months, various *mikrorayony* had received water only six to seven hours a day. An important cause was that thirteen thousand to fifteen thousand cubic meters of drinking water seeped away daily because the pressure in the pipes was not high enough. Industrial enterprises used a fifth of Tula's drinking water and received priority treatment. The Obkom concluded that the authorities in charge had so far dealt poorly with the issue, and it promised improvements.[72]

Moreover, Tula's construction enterprises lost millions of rubles between 1967 and 1972 because of the poor quality of their bricks[73]—another problem that was familiar to various cities from Stalinist times.[74] Tula almost consistently failed to meet plan targets throughout the Brezhnev era.[75]

As a result, the number of uncompleted buildings grew, and authorities, lacking labor and material resources, could not use funds assigned to new construction. By 1971, investments for 1,135 buildings lay idle (*nedosvoena*). Moreover, 242 buildings were only partially built.[76]

Still, the improvements in living conditions during the Brezhnev era dominated the accounts of my respondents. The move to a family's own apartment often signaled the beginning of a new, better life phase, something that Donald Raleigh also found in interviews with members of the same generation in Saratov.[77] Raisa Molchanova spent her childhood in a cramped communal apartment in Tula's Proletarskiy Rayon, then a socially disadvantaged area. Vasiliy Kotenev lived in a one-story house in the same neighborhood, twenty-eight square meters lacking running water, with five other people and frequent visits from relatives. Irina Sycheva's five family members inhabited one room in a workers' dormitory, sharing a total of twenty square meters.

A childhood picture of Kotenev (fig. 4.4) shows a small boy in a Tibetan cap (*tibetechka*), which was, according to Kotenev, fashionable at the time. The rest of his clothes look handmade. He stands on an unpaved road in a seemingly rural area on the outskirts of Tula's Proletarskiy Rayon. Fences in the background separate the houses. There was no running water, so people carried drinking water from a central fountain and went to the bathroom in an outhouse. To clean themselves, Kotenev and his family visited the *banya* twice a week.[78]

He never moved to a city apartment, preferring his house and garden to urban conveniences. Whereas this kind of suburban living is considered

Figure 4.4. Vasiliy Kotenev on the street in front of his house, 1964.
Courtesy of Vasiliy Kotenev, private archive

prestigious in today's Russia, it was tied to numerous inconveniences in the 1960s, often lacking public transport and communal services. The most peripheral areas of cities were the last to be connected to the gas and water supply. The move to an urban apartment was seen as an inherent part of a worthy standard of living, which illustrates how closely this notion was connected to the socialist contract. For Marina Neizvestnaya, it was a much-coveted change for the better, even though she loved the nature surrounding the house she grew up in: "I had lived in a private house until I was eighteen, and how I had wanted a bathtub! In the apartment there was water right there; in the private house we had to go to the standpipe; there were no provisions.... I was glad that I ended up in an apartment (*v kvartiru popala*)."[79]

She considers the lack of agency implied in the last phrase to be a positive thing. Unlike today, when one can buy an apartment, she said, one waited "not long, only four to five years" at the time and then received a "surprise on a platter" (*syurpriz v tarelku*); this system was much "simpler."[80] Neizvestnaya preferred the paternalistic Soviet system of housing assignment to the "complicated" and expensive capitalist one. This reflects an expectation that the state will take care of its citizens, who are entitled to these services by virtue of being Soviet.

As a disabled war veteran and officer, Raisa Molchanova's father received an apartment from the military commissariat in 1960, when she was in eighth grade. When both she and her brother got married, it became "tight" in the apartment, and her father was assigned a new place. "In those days there were lines at the enterprises for apartments. But because I had already worked there for a long time and was involved in societal work... I went ahead in the line and received living space (*zhilploshchad'*). I moved into the two-room apartment where my parents had lived."[81]

In Molchanova's view, then, the members of her family received apartments because of their service both during the war (father) and in the enterprise (Molchanova). Patriotism and loyalty complemented state paternalism; service to the country was part of the socialist contract that entitled Soviet citizens to an apartment.

Not all enterprises were equal, however. Housing stock depended on a person's economic significance—with strategically important enterprises under the control of the Council of Ministers at the top. Sergey Stepuzhin began his studies at the Pedagogical Institute in 1973 and first lived in a dormitory. Later on, as a teacher, he did not benefit from construction of the large industrial conglomerates but could only apply for city housing, which was in short supply. He had to find an apartment by informal means.[82]

The experiences of my respondents illustrate both the centrality of the housing question under Brezhnev and the great differences in quality depending on social status, personal connections, and employment.[83] In a shortage economy, city authorities had to provide housing, communal services, and infrastructure because they were part of a political system that justified its legitimacy by raising the population's living standards. Particularly the period from the mid-1960s to the early 1970s improved Tulyaki's everyday lives.

DEFITSIT, PRIYANIKI, AND THE SAUSAGE TRAIN

The advancement was also linked to the booming economy: industrial production during the eighth Five-Year Plan increased by 163 percent, light industry by 243 percent.[84] This growth, however, did not necessarily benefit the population, as most of the industrial and agricultural production did not remain in Tula. Average income rose by one-third between 1965 and 1970, but the significance was limited.[85] The USSR suffered from "hidden inflation," since many commodities were not available in stores.[86]

Tula consistently struggled with this problem, although basic goods could be bought. Starting in the late 1960s, a broad range of commodities was for sale in Tula's markets. Milk, meat, fruits, and vegetables were offered by merchants from Moscow or by Kolkhozes and Sovkhozes who were selling off their surplus production. According to Malinichev, the KGB closed down this system of "speculation" soon after and thus reduced the goods on offer. The trade subsequently moved through informal channels.[87] This system was highly unreliable, and recurring bad harvests in 1972, 1974, 1975, and 1978 led to shortages even in vegetables.[88]

The *defitsit* in meat and milk was an oft-mentioned topic in my conversations with Tulyaki. Acquisition of these products took significant time and effort. Marina Neizvestnaya remembers that she would regularly get up very early to stand in line for hours before work to buy milk for her young daughter. She was lucky as far as meat was concerned; in 1973, she received an apartment right above one of the city's main stores: "We saw the store from the window. . . . When the car came that brought the sausages, I went down . . . that was very convenient, people ran, there was a line all around the store. All I had to do was look."[89]

Komsomol nomenclature member Elena Bozhenko (see fig. 4.5) was privileged in a different way. She received a weekly package with two to three sausages, preserves, and sweets: "We were not paid much, and I had no privileges.

Figure 4.5. Elena Bozhenko in the Komsomol (*middle row, fifth from right*). Courtesy of Elena Bozhenko, private archive

[IM: Except sausage.] Except for sausage! But don't make fun of this. Sausage at the time was . . . that was the time of the *defitsit*."[90]

That she paused to highlight the significance of sausage is telling. Both Bozhenko and Vasiliy Kotenev resented that salesmen with access to meat products enjoyed more prestige in Tula than engineers or doctors. The lack of meat products emphasized the disparity between Moscow and Tula: multiple meat plants in and around Tula processed the Oblast's agricultural production—only to send it straight to the capital.

Those who did not possess Bozhenko's privileges were forced to travel to Moscow to buy meat. Vladimir Romanov even began the interview by comparing Tula's supply situation to those of other regional cities: Tula was similar to Vladimir, Kaluga, and Ryazan', while Orel was better provided for. Romanov was employed in the military-industrial complex and earned high wages of over 300 rubles a month.[91] Still, he had to take the "sausage train," as he jokingly called it: "What is long and green and smells of sausage? The suburban train (*elektrichka*) from Moscow to Tula." Similar quips were told in other provincial cities.[92]

Politically, the sausage train was no joke. The Obkom demanded additional and cheaper trains. On July 8, 1965, Yunak and Kamaev asked the Moscow Railroads to include Tula in the suburban railway zone, which would have lowered prices. More than three thousand commuters a day took the train to Moscow, many of them to procure items of everyday usage, and they should receive the "best opportunities" on the trip. B. Beshchev, minister of tracks and communications, denied the request on July 31, citing 420,000 rubles in income loss and the necessity of granting the same privileges to Vladimir and Ryazan' because they were approximately equidistant from Moscow.[93]

In another letter, from April 6, 1970, Yunak and Kamaev asked I. Karpov, head of the Moscow Railroads, to increase the daily number of trains traveling between the two cities from five to ten. Yunak complained that the cars were packed, particularly in the morning, and that they often lacked basic services such as toilets and newspaper trolleys.[94] They succeeded, as Malinichev concludes that additional trains were Yunak's pragmatic solution to the *defitsit* problem. "This way the people received the opportunity to travel to Moscow and back in one day and bring back sausage, meat and fish."[95]

Even if Tulyaki adjusted to this arrangement, they were not happy about it. The fact that they told jokes about it reflects the mixture of resignation and gallows humor with which they accepted the poor supply situation. They helped themselves with *blat* practices.

One product in particular was available locally and valued highly, even in Moscow and Leningrad, where it was sold only in specialized stores for the nomenclature or foreigners: the *Tul'skie priyaniki*, a kind of gingerbread. It was a symbol of the city and a popular gift in ceremonies, not least for veterans on May 9.[96] More importantly for Tulyaki, the priyanik could be used for barter. Romanov would therefore stand in line at the factory store for three hours before it opened at nine o'clock in the morning, along with "two hundred or three hundred others . . . everyone waited in the cold or in the heat, but they waited."[97]

A friend of Romanov's was a seaman from Feodosiya who regularly traveled abroad, where he bought popular commodities like jeans or shoes. As the Feodosiya-Moscow train passed through Tula, he would meet Romanov at the station and exchange clothing for priyaniki. "Jeans cost two hundred rubles," Romanov remarked, providing an idea of the high value of Tula's gingerbread. Romanov also used them as bribes on business trips: "We get to a hotel, there is no room. 'Young lady (*devochka*), you don't know whom you're dealing with. We congratulate you, we come from Tula—with priyaniki!' . . . Before there were no rooms, now there are rooms. . . . Priyaniki from Tula were, how shall I put this, a present.... That was the showcase for our city: that we are Tulyaki who come with Tula priyaniki.[98]

For inhabitants of Tula, then, access to priyaniki provided a comparative advantage that enabled them to obtain rare goods. Financial value in the Soviet Union was relative; depending on a commodity's availability, it could be worth much more than its "objective" money value. While these practices certainly made some lives easier, they were a long way off from officially propagated "exemplary" values that Soviet citizens were supposed to exhibit.

THE HERO CITY APPLICATION

Improvements in everyday life had defused social tensions, but Yunak was not satisfied with Tula's symbolic status. In the early 1970s, the Obkom began the process to become a Hero City. It petitioned the Presidium of the Supreme Soviet three times—always on war anniversaries: 1970, 1975, and 1976.[99] Each application contained a formal request and a document with background information justifying the claim. The latter was relatively short for the two unsuccessful applications in 1970 and 1975 and considerably longer in 1976. The fact that Tula had already received the Order of Lenin was a key argument.

Each application referred to the "numerous wishes and demands by the city of Tula's working people (*trudyashchiesya*), veterans of the war, workers, Kolkhoz workers, members of the intelligentsia and servicemen" to underline its broad popular support.[100] Pride of past achievements was connected to dedication to the country and the most recent Party Congress decisions. In award applications, official war memory was thus connected to present political requirements in exemplary fashion.

If one tries to identify formal clues as to what constituted a successful versus an unsuccessful application, one notices two distinctive aspects: the progressive idealization in descriptions of Tula's wartime achievements and the growing inclusion of postwar labor accomplishments into the applications—in order to demonstrate the city's "worthiness." Whereas the first two *spravki* mention sixty thousand Germans fighting near Tula, the 1976 version speaks of eighty thousand. The number of tanks also grows from three hundred to six hundred. German superiority in field guns increases from threefold to sixfold.[101]

The accounts highlight Tula's role as an "impregnable fortress," the "Southern fore post of the capital," the unity of workers and the Red Army, the Communists' role as the "soul of the defense," the "mass heroism" and the "iron discipline" of the entire population, and the "exemplary order" in the city.[102]

The 1975 and 1976 accounts, unlike their predecessor, explicitly mention the role of youth and pensioners;[103] these two groups grew in importance because the war generation was aging and youth were the target of patriotic education programs. Their contribution may have thus been made more explicit than before. The 1976 application newly emphasizes that "Tulyaki made a worthy contribution (*dostoynyy vklad*) to our country's economic and defense potential in the postwar period."[104] It goes on to enumerate that the population had fulfilled the ninth Five-Year Plan ahead of schedule. Moreover, the city was highly successful in socialist competitions in 1974 and 1975, thereby multiplying "the glorious labor, revolutionary and military traditions of the old generations."[105]

In part, this statement reads like a confirmation of Dmitriy Ustinov's demands in 1966. However, there is an additional element: by emphasizing the direct link between Tula's "worthiness" of a high award and its achievements as well as future intentions in contributing to the Soviet economy, the application created a bond of obligation discursively. Through the acceptance of the award, Tula would commit itself morally to fulfilling the party's goals.[106]

The applications demonstrate the learning process the regional authorities went through. By progressively exaggerating the scale of the battle for Tula, they followed the logic of the Soviet heroarchy. Because of the growing competition for recognition in the escalating war cult of the 1970s, heroism had to be expressed in impressive numbers—even if their veracity was doubtful. Wartime feats were then connected to those of the present to illustrate transgenerational unity of purpose and patriotic service.

This was the discursive currency with which to claim recognition. It is striking how similar the approach of the Hero City applicants was to those of housing petitioners described by Christine Varga-Harris: "Within the socialist contract, citizens conjoined their individual sacrifices with the radiant future of the collective, while simultaneously presenting their contribution as valuable currency in the realm of state recognition and reward."[107] Both "spoke Bolshevik," to cite Kotkin, and both learned in their negotiations with the center which strategies were most promising.

Tula's third application succeeded. A letter from Ivan Yunak to the Central Committee on October 6, 1976, must have met with an encouraging response, as he wrote a second one on November 18, this time addressed to "Leonid Il'ich" personally. Attached was a joint resolution of the Obkom and the Oblispolkom to "ask the CC CPSU and the Presidium of the Supreme Soviet to award to Tula the honorary title 'Hero City.'" In his personal letter to Brezhnev,

Yunak added that this request was connected to the thirty-fifth anniversary of the city's heroic defense.[108]

Stalin's wartime speech from November 7, 1942, in which he mentioned Tula alongside other Hero Cities, is featured in all applications. Dmitriy Ustinov and Andrey Grechko are both also quoted. Last but not least, Vladimir Lenin's praise for Tula as "Russia's arsenal and shield" during the Civil War represented the central endorsement.[109] His words are employed as "proof" of Tula's worthiness in 1976: "Tula, Moscow's peer (*rovesnitsa*) . . . which had earned V. I. Lenin's high appraisal, is worthy of sharing the glory that the Hero Cities received."[110]

Almost equally important was Marshall Georgiy Zhukov's 1966 estimation that "Tula's role for the general course of the battle for Moscow is difficult to overestimate." The quoted passages included this: "The glory of Moscow as a Hero City is rightfully also the glory of Tula and the Tulyaki."[111] Zhukov also appears to have played an important role in advancing Tula's claim behind the scenes.

Journalist Yuriy Kirilenko claims that the city had to thank Viktor Pastukhov, First Secretary of the Tula Gorkom, and Ivan Yunak for the award. In his account, their connection to Brezhnev and Georgiy Zhukov was decisive. Kirilenko says that Pastukhov had met Zhukov in 1966, where the retired marshal lauded Tula's contribution to the defense of Moscow. He promised to ask Brezhnev, along with four other marshals, to award the Gold Star to Tula.[112]

Kirilenko claims that Brezhnev denied the request, while Timofey Dubinin, a high-ranking veteran of the defense of Tula, sees the general staff behind the rejection; they considered the operation "not significant enough."[113] The stories appear plausible because Tula received the Order of Lenin in 1966 (possibly as a "consolation prize") and because the applications repeatedly cite Zhukov's 1966 article.

Personal connections continued to play an important role in the ten years that followed. In a 2008 interview, Pavel Potekhin, a former member of the Obkom Buro and head of the Oblast' KGB, claims that Yunak's proximity to the Moscow elite, first and foremost to Yuriy Andropov, were the decisive factor in overcoming the resistance.[114] Opponents were not wary only because of the scope of the battle but also because the Hero City Tula would further heighten the symbolic significance of Moscow.

Finally, the controversial elevation of Novorossiysk, discussed in the next two chapters, fueled fears that the "family" of Hero Cities was getting too big. Dubinin, conversely, claims that the former First Secretary of the Tula Obkom, Vasiliy Zhavoronkov, who enjoyed considerable prestige as a historian,

Figure 4.6. Newspaper article entitled "Hero City: The Continuation of the Feat." No copyright, Soviet source

used Novorossiysk; he argued that if the Southern port city deserved a Gold Star, so did Tula.[115] Possibly in a coordinated campaign with Zhavoronkov, Yunak placed a personal call to Andropov—"and then the signatures were collected."[116]

Yunak's status as a member of Brezhnev's Dnepropetrovsk circle and the resulting political and personal connections to the elite played a crucial role in getting Tula Hero City status. The war record certainly mattered, but in a country where hundreds of cities had suffered and fought "worthily" against the Wehrmacht, it was not enough. This applied particularly to high state awards, which carried considerable political prestige and economic weight.

The formal decision by the Presidium of the Supreme Soviet to name Tula a Hero City was made on December 7, 1976. One day later, a festive assembly (*torzhestvennoe sobranie*) thanked party leadership and Leonid Brezhnev personally. The assembly assured (*zaveryat'*) the Central Committee that the people of Tula would "make a worthy contribution" to the socialist economy.[117] This oath by party activists, just like its counterpart ten years earlier, referred back to October 1941 and underlined the unity of generations and values.

The coverage in Tula's newspaper *Kommunar* thus focused on the workers' readiness for the "continuation of the feat" in the factory. Commentators underlined that Tula would show itself worthy: "In response to the high honor, the workers of Tula are ready to use all of their strength toward fulfilling and over-fulfilling the tasks of this year and of the Five-Year-Plan as a whole, toward the steadfast elevation of efficiency, quality, the organization of production and labor discipline."[118]

In the newspaper's arrangement of four pictures (fig. 4.6), the workers have different ages and work at different factories, but all of them are heroes of labor. The man to the right, the metal turner N. Kuznetsov, works at one of Tula's

Figure 4.7. Title page of *Kommunar*: "Glory to Tula—the Hero City!" The image depicts the meeting at Tula's stadium. Workers carry posters with portraits of Brezhnev, Kosygin, and other members of the Politburo. No copyright, Soviet source

armament factories. N. Pavlova, to his left, works at the factory Priboy, which produced acoustic equipment for radios and the military. The man and the woman on the left work at a metallurgy and toy production factory.

The images create the impression that an even balance existed between consumer and heavy industries in Tula's economy. In fact, the latter predominated, but Tula's production is presented as geared toward the satisfaction of the population's and the country's industrial and defense needs. Vigilance against enemies and the welfare of the population are equal priorities in the Hero City. Moreover, the generations work together to reach both goals: "brigadier" N. Pavlova is instructing a younger colleague, sharing knowledge and presumably values with her.

In political speeches, appreciation toward the leadership was the dominant theme. Yunak said that the award "filled our hearts to the brink with a feeling of great gratitude toward the Party."[119]

Kommunar's title page depicts this gratitude (fig. 4.7). A large group of workers has assembled at Tula's stadium to celebrate its new status and the country's leaders: the workers carry politicians' portraits, next to banners reading "Glory to the CPSU" and "Tula—Hero City." They celebrate the new connection that the award has created between the city and the leadership. To the right of the picture, moreover, reprints of the congratulatory telegrams that Tula received from other Hero Cities celebrate its ascension to their "family."

BREZHNEV IS HERE

While the event dominated the headlines of *Kommunar* for weeks, *Pravda* reported relatively sparsely on the festivities, although it featured the award on its front page once. This changed in January, when Leonid Brezhnev visited Tula with his entourage. His sojourn between January 17 and January 19, 1977, was a national media event.

The general secretary arrived by train at 1:00 p.m. A delegation headed by Yunak and Pastukhov met him at the station. Also present were representatives of other Hero Cities. Brezhnev's visit included meetings with party activists and trips to factories and to Yasnaya Polyana, Lev Tolstoy's estate. Tens of thousands of Tulyaki were mobilized to line the streets, carrying posters and slogans, as Brezhnev's motorcade sped into the city.

The population was carefully supervised. More than a thousand KGB officers were present, in addition to numerous soldiers and militiamen.[120] They also made sure that the workers and students did not leave prematurely because of the cold; the temperature on January 17 was minus twenty degrees Celsius.[121] Brezhnev, however, did not meet the population outside of formal events.[122]

Accordingly, Tulyaki mostly remember the cold and the traffic chaos. The main routes were more or less consistently closed for almost three days.[123] Sergey Shcheglov, deputy editor in chief of *Kommunar* at the time, remembers trying to return home: "I had to go to Prospekt Lenina to take the bus. The cars were stuck in the side streets, roadblocks closed off everything.... I had to walk to Lenin Square, where I finally found an exit and could go home. It took me an hour and a half."[124]

To some, like Evgeniy Stepunin, the visit felt like a distant event for politicians, which he only read about and saw on television.[125] Multiple respondents complained that they had not even gotten the day off from work.

The climax of Brezhnev's visit was the award ceremony in Tula's Gor'kiy Dramatic Theatre on January 18. The chairman of the Gorispolkom opened the ceremony, followed by the national anthem. Then, war veterans carried the banners of the Oblast', the city, the workers' regiment, the 732nd air defense, and the 156th NKVD brigade to the podium, thereby contributing local symbols of the defense.[126]

In his speech, Brezhnev congratulated the city's inhabitants on receiving the "highest award of the Homeland." He welcomed Tula into the "glorious, heroic family" of Hero Cities.[127] He said: "Your city is one of the oldest in the country. Over the course of the centuries Tula was the shield and arsenal of the Russian state. On this ancient earth matured the character of the Russian man—tireless worker and skillful craftsman, steadfast defender of the Homeland, adamant fighter for a happy future."[128]

He connected Tula's defense in 1941 to the city's century-old traditions of fighting and resistance on its "ancient earth," reflecting the increased significance prerevolutionary symbols had attained by the late Brezhnev era.[129] As evident in the speech and in Tula's applications, this historical link also extended the notion of transgenerational unity further into the past.

After this excursus, Brezhnev explained the significance of Tula's heroic past for current society. He began with a minute of silence in honor of the fallen, then declared that these fighters and the people as a whole had "transformed their Homeland into a powerful, thriving great power."[130]

Two consequences ensued from victory. The current generation had to be vigilant against revanchist and pro-fascist regimes. Simultaneously, Brezhnev lauded détente, underlining the peacefulness of Soviet foreign policy, with its proposals for stopping the arms race and limiting the expansion of the Warsaw Treaty and of NATO. Because of US resistance, however, the Soviet Union could reach its goals "only by fighting, exactly by fighting, comrades."

For the first time, Brezhnev publicly revoked the USSR's nuclear first-strike policy passed under Khrushchev[131]—not least because of the strain that the arms race put on its economy. Brezhnev's "Tula speech" is thus well known in foreign policy circles, only rarely being connected to its occasion.[132]

The speech, however, failed to bring about a "reset" of détente: Brezhnev, who had pursued relaxation policies with great energy in the first half of the 1970s, was no longer able to control more militaristic and isolationist forces. Moreover, the new US president, Jimmy Carter, had little interest in improving relations, instead emphasizing Soviet human rights violations while continuing the arms race.[133]

Brezhnev's program in Tula contradicted his peaceful message, pointing once more to official war memory's ambiguity as a peace symbol. His visit to the weapons factory, in particular, created controversy: because of its significance to the military-industrial complex, it was an important stop. According to Brezhnev's adviser Anatoliy Chernyaev, some in Brezhnev's entourage tried to dissuade him because of how the visit would be perceived in the West, but the general secretary would not listen:

> Oh, come on! (*kak zhe tak!*) I came to Tula. They have given me hunting rifles for so many years, according to my specifications. And I don't go to them. That is not good!" ... He loved guns, pistols and similar things. (In the famous weapons factory Tula, by the way, there remained at this time only one small production facility that built hunting weapons, and the others produced—you know what). In the end we agreed that he would visit there, but that we would say in public appearances and press releases that he had visited a "mechanical factory.[134]

Kremlinologists were not fooled, but the episode illustrates how acutely aware Soviet advisers were of their image in the West. It also shows the pitfalls of Brezhnev's carefully arranged public appearances, where every gesture, even if it was the stubborn decision of an old man, was read into.

Straightforward by Brezhnev's standards was his description of domestic problems. He not only admitted crop failures but also conceded problems in supplying the population with meat and milk products.[135] Moreover, he admitted shortcomings in housing and public services. As the lack of applause, discussed at the beginning of this chapter, showed, his proposed remedies did not convince the audience.

The crowd applauded throughout Brezhnev's speech, but not at its climax. In Soviet leaders' minutely staged appearances, applause during the strategic moments in the speech—*udarnye mesta*, the punch lines—defined and reinforced the hierarchical relationship between leader and audience.[136]

There were various qualities of acclamation: "applause" was the lowest form, topped by "long-lasting applause" (*prodol'zhitel'nye aplodismenty*) and "exuberant applause" (*burnye aplodismenty*). At the pinnacle of the applause hierarchy was either a combination of the former two, "uproarious ovation" (*goryachaya ovatsiya*) or cries of "hooray" (*ura*). The end of Brezhnev's speech in Tula was met with "exuberant applause, which did not quiet down for a long time."[137]

Chernyaev describes the speech's preparations in detail. The second reading was fully dedicated to the punch lines. Nervous about his delivery, Brezhnev anxiously asked his advisers, "Will it work out? Yes, I think it will work out. They will clap."[138] Brezhnev's increased financial commitments to Tula were supposed to form the central punch line, but it fell flat. The silence of the audience, then, constituted a serious breach of political correctness and amounted to an open show of disrespect toward the general secretary.

One reason for the silence was that, aside from assigning more money, Brezhnev mostly asked Tulyaki to work harder and produce goods of higher

Figure 4.8. Postcard showing Brezhnev's visit, during which he attached the Gold Star to Tula's city banner. No copyright, Soviet source

quality—thus showing themselves worthy of their predecessors and securing better living conditions for themselves. "I am convinced that each one will draw the right conclusion: in order to live better and earn more, one needs to work better."[139] Because of the structure of Tula's industry, this link, however, was not evident to Tulyaki; they had little use for the weapons and industrial goods they produced, and the food was exported to Moscow.

The mood improved when Brezhnev redirected his attention to the honorary task at hand: "Comrades! The Order of Lenin has adorned Tula's banner for more than ten years. Now I am entrusted with an honorable and pleasant mission—to attach to your banner the Gold Star, the symbol of heroism, steadfastness and courage, the symbol of the entire people's recognition of the extraordinary feat of Tula's defenders. . . . (*an uproarious ovation flares up as Leonid Il'ich attaches the medal 'Gold Star' to the banner of the city. . . . a loud 'Ura!' resounds.*)"[140]

After he had completed the gesture (see fig. 4.8), Brezhnev stepped off the podium, and Ivan Yunak, holding the banner, spoke the concluding words "in the name of the Hero City's inhabitants": "Thank you, dear Leonid Il'ich, thank you, dear representatives and heads of the Hero City delegations, the delegations of our older brothers and sisters, for accepting us into your family of Hero Cities."[141]

NEGOTIATING THE SOCIALIST CONTRACT

To assess the effects of Tula's elevation, it is crucial to take a look at both the officially prescribed reaction and the award's popular reception. The question of what constituted a "worthy" Hero City lay at the center of both. Official discourse raised high hopes in the population. Promises included new fast public transport and better roads. One publication even quoted the extremely unlikely number of an additional four million square meters of housing as a result of the award.[142] The signifier "worthy" is particularly ambiguous, since it left open the question of whether the onus of delivery lay on the authorities or the population. As parties to the socialist contract, both had to deliver.

In the archives, no documents show a connection between the new status and improved communal services or additional housing construction—in striking contrast to 1966. Omnipresent instead are programs to increase labor productivity and output. Ivan Yunak's statement in a meeting of the Obkom's Buro on January 20, 1977, is telling: Brezhnev's speech was to be interpreted "as a program of concrete acts aimed at the mobilization of workers to fulfill and over-fulfill the tasks of the tenth Five-Year-Plan." Among the goals were higher productivity and quality, as well as better educational work in the collectives.[143]

There was no shortage of problems: in 1976, 29 of 303 enterprises in the Oblast' had failed to reach their production targets. A year later, this number more than doubled—to a record of 61.[144] Even more worrisome, losses due to inferior quality grew steadily beginning in the early 1970s, offsetting the improvements of the late 1960s. Absenteeism, which amounted to a total of 5.2 million days in 1972, was also on the rise.

The slogan of the tenth "Five-Year Plan of efficiency and quality," Brezhnev's speech, and the upcoming sixtieth anniversary of the October Revolution were combined to serve as "moral incentives." The party spared no resources for this purpose, instructing its departments to direct "immediately all organizational and mass-political work" toward distributing and explaining the labor tasks emanating from the speech.[145]

On July 1, 1977, the Obkom's Department of Agitation and Propaganda reported that the organization Znanie had already held 1,903 lectures.[146] The Cultural Department wrote that its institutions were organizing exhibitions featuring Tula's new status and the revolution, Brezhnev's peace policy, and lectures at universities and in clubs. The plan was to attract 290,000 visitors to a total of one thousand lectures and four thousand excursions in 1977.[147] In the same year, approximately two-thirds of all people between ten and thirty years of age participated in a lecture titled "Labor Feat for the Military Feat" (*podvigu ratnomu—podvig trudovoy*), dedicated to Tula's Hero City award.[148]

In the workplace, this discursive connection between the past wartime feat and the present labor feat was implemented primarily through the campaign "For Yourself and for That Lad" (*za sebya i za togo parnya*), which the Komsomol had launched in Tula on July 4, 1974.[149] Work brigades would compete for the honorary right to name their brigade after a fallen military hero who had worked in the enterprise before the war. Then they would fulfill that hero's annual norm in addition to their own. By 1975, it had become a widely instituted campaign. In Tula Oblast', over a thousand collectives participated.[150] By 1977, every third collective in the Oblast' had added one of Tula's wartime or revolutionary heroes to its roster.[151]

Most respondents could not remember these programs or uttered platitudes about the plan always being fulfilled in their enterprises. Vladimir Romanov, former worker at the Arsenal arms factory, however, illuminates some limits of the campaigns' acceptance. The Hero of the Soviet Union who would accompany Romanov as a moral point of reference was Oleg Matveev, a lieutenant in a tank brigade who fell in Poland in 1945. School number 29, which Matveev had attended, was named in his honor. Ivan Yunak highlighted the institution as a positive example for the utilization of Tula's "glorious traditions" for youth's patriotic education.[152]

As a member of the school Komsomol committee, Romanov visited Matveev's parents multiple times, inviting them to holiday celebrations that honored their dead son. They would all gather around the desk where Matveev had sat as a child, which had become a kind of shrine. Romanov participated "with pleasure." After he finished school in 1969, Romanov went to work at the Arsenal weapons factory, which, as he emphasized, lay literally "across the bridge."[153]

Many of his fellow students also worked at the factory. This created a sense of local community. The name of Matveevich was added to Romanov's brigade, and he and his colleagues accepted it. Only the steady expansion of the program created resistance:

> Oleg Matveevich was our hero, and we are proud of him.... So each brigade [added a hero]. But when they added (*zapisyvayut*) two to our roster, we told

the management, "Aren't two a bit too many?" Because we did work, but you have to understand, thirty people worked in our brigade, we had a big brigade, and if it was thirty-one, OK. If the brigade was complete. But if one half . . . one part is on a business trip, one part on vacation, and one part on a Kolkhoz, and only half left, and two additional people are added, then our wage dropped by two people. . . . And we thought this was not right. . . . But they only told us, "What do you want? These people died for their homeland, they defended us, they gave their lives. What do you want?" That was it (*vse, vse, vse*). . . . There was nothing to add.[154]

Romanov's statement reveals not only the tension between moral and financial incentives but also the contradictions inherent in official war memory. Resistance was not motivated by opposition to the system or a lack of reverence for the war dead. Workers simply struggled to see the direct connection between their labor and war memory but nonetheless had to give in to their superiors' moral pressure.

There were clear limits to their opposition, but the mere fact that they complained shows the ambiguity of programs that extended official war memory into the work realm of the postwar generation. To Romanov, this economization meant that the value of a hero could be expressed in rubles: "We received the plan, we produced five items (*izdelii*). . . . We earned about 400 rubles on average. . . . This meant: fifteen people—if you added a sixteenth, this was no longer 400 rubles but 380 or 370."[155]

Even though Romanov subsequently insisted that the program's significance went beyond this pecuniary aspect, he nonetheless had an exact idea of its financial impact. This monetary focus could not but cheapen war memory.

It is thus not surprising that the programs appear to have done little to increase the intrinsic motivation of the postwar generation at work. Neither Romanov nor the other respondents said that these programs or the new status as inhabitants of a Hero City made them perform better, even though that was their explicit purpose.

DISAPPOINTMENT

Respondents accepted that the new status was closely linked to notions of dignity and worthiness in everyday life. The nature and causality of this connection was much less clear. "Hero City is an honorary title," explained Elena Bozhenko, "and you have to live up to it. The streets have to be cleaner. . . . You have to clean the streets and build new houses."[156] Her response points to the responsibility of all individuals in the city to prove themselves worthy of their new status. The postwar generation, then, had to participate in urban beautification, through their societal activism. She thus partially reflects official demands, which are reminiscent of the large-scale campaigns for "culturedness" during the 1930s.[157]

There is, however, a second aspect. Not just the inhabitants but also the authorities were responsible for providing a worthy urban environment. Most respondents connected the new status to the hope for higher quality of life. Vladimir Romanov said he had hoped not to have to take the "sausage train" to Moscow anymore.[158] In his opinion, stores without meat were not worthy of a Hero City. He was especially annoyed by the fact that cities with a far less heroic wartime performance were better supplied—especially the regional rival Orel. Orel had been given up without a defense—"offering bread and salt" to the Wehrmacht, as a local historian comments.[159] It was thus less "deserving" of a "worthy" standard of living.

Marina Neizvestnaya went a step further: "We were so happy and thought we would receive some kinds of privileges (*l'goty*)."[160] She argued that veterans who had served their country through military or labor also received such benefits—for instance, paying less for electricity. She now expected a similar arrangement for all the inhabitants of Tula as a result of the official discourse's insistence on the Hero Cities' collective heroism.

Vladimir Yurchikov showed no understanding of this position: "I work—what kinds of privileges are there supposed to be? All right, Hero City, great, and now? Are you supposed to pay less for electricity? . . . That is not right. Hero City is just a name; it was moral, just moral."[161] He reasoned that the postwar generation had done nothing to deserve the distinction and was thus not entitled to benefits analogous to those of war veterans.

Both statements reveal an idiosyncratic interpretation of the "continuity of generations." They reflect the ambivalence toward transferring heroism from the individual to the collective and from one generation to the next. The anthropomorphization of the Hero City only works to an extent; the vagueness it contains raises dilemmas about who is entitled to benefit and on what basis. Expectations and the tools available to fulfill them were mismatched in Tula—not least because of the gap between official rhetoric and economic opportunities.

The importance of the moral aspect, or, more to the point, the symbolic elevation of Tula, should not be discounted. Aside from Vasiliy Kotenev, who is skeptical of local patriotism, all respondents expressed pride—primarily because the defenders had stopped the German tanks. Yet this pride has a defiant undertone. Sergey Stepunin defended himself against the position that Tula did not deserve the title: "The award was completely justified.... I am proud and have always been."[162] His justification reveals a fear that Tula might not be worthy of the title. Elena Bozhenko encountered this opinion soon after the reception of the award:

> The only thing people asked when one met them was, "Where are you from?"—"From the Hero City Tula!" Because "Hero City Tula" was something one said often, particularly at the beginning. Then the question, "And what did you become a Hero City for?" ... I said, "what do you mean, what for? ... We stopped Guderian! ... We are Tula! The southern gate, we did not let anything get to Moscow from Tula!" (*laughs*) Yes, especially at first we said that. But it is true: I live in Tula; this is why I defend the city.[163]

The statement reveals a latent inferiority complex—especially since Bozhenko adds that people from Leningrad (Saint Petersburg) often exhibited a dismissive attitude. Tula may have been important, but it paled in comparison to the bloodiest battles of the war. Even Yunak had admitted this implicitly, when he referred to the "older brothers" in the family of Hero Cities. Tulyaki would visit places like the Hero Fortress of Brest (like Vasiliy Kotenev, standing all the way to the right in fig. 4.9) as representatives of their city, but not as equals. Tula had waited long for the recognition of its achievements, but when it came, doubts remained on whether the award placed them on the same level as other Hero Cities.[164] Aside from the official heroarchy, there remained an unofficial one, which placed Leningrad and Stalingrad at the top.

Irina Sycheva also attests to the existence of doubt when she tells the story of her celebration of the news at her dormitory. A German exchange student who entered the room quickly lowered the jubilant mood: "He just stood there and said cynically, 'You guys have nothing but Hero Cities, looks like they are giving out awards to everyone.' And I said, 'Yes, but if it wasn't for those heroes, I would serve your food now.' ... We never spoke again."[165]

Sycheva's outrage over this episode contains an element of Soviet-German tension. At the same time, it points to a perception of award inflation, not surprising in view of the general secretary's weakness for excessive decoration. Because the award's symbolic value was unclear, Tulyaki seemed to have looked for other indicators to confirm it.

The question of additional privileges—and more specifically improved communal services and supply—was one of these indicators. In Marina Neizvestnaya's opinion, the award should have put Tula on par with Moscow:

Figure 4.9. A delegation from Tula (with Vasiliy Kotenev, *far right*) visits the Hero Fortress of Brest in 1978. Courtesy of Vasiliy Kotenev, private archive

> With an honorary title like Hero City you can basically compare yourself to the capital.... We are of course smaller than the capital, but nevertheless, they gave us the Hero City title, and this means that we deserved it. If we had not deserved it, they would not have given it out. There are so many factories in Tula that produce weapons. The city can be proud of this, of the Samovars and the weapons. Our city was worthy of the title, deserved it.... We live worthily here, because it is a Hero City. We are proud of it.[166]

Again, the notion of worthiness appears—this time in connection with the city's economic specificities. Traditional weapons production and other locally made commodities become part of local pride, just like the Hero City status.[167]

In spite of these great expectations, the hoped-for benefits only materialized around Brezhnev's visit. On New Year's Day 1977, prices for clothes, refrigerators, and televisions were lowered by 10 to 15 percent.[168] For his visit, the streets were repaired, and stores even sold sausages and oranges.[169] "When Leonid Il'ich himself came, immediately after the award, they did everything well here;

for a while we had everything. As soon as Leonid Il'ich had left, however... it was basically the same, if not worse, in terms of groceries," confirms Vladimir Romanov.[170]

Bozhenko also commented on the deterioration of the supply situation: "We laughed about it. There was a joke (*anekdot*) at the time that said: 'Well, which one is it now? Either the Hero City award or groceries!'"[171] Both Raisa Molchanova and Vasiliy Kotenev said that the only sustainable change in everyday life comprised new monuments—the marble blocks depicting all the Hero Cities in Victory Square or neon lights reading "Hero City" on roofs. Other than that, there were, in Kotenev's words, no "substantial (*sushchestvennye*) changes" in people's lives: "I understand that the Hero City award changes the status.... But on the level of the everyday... they did not open any new bus routes, the trams did not go further. [IM: Did the people hope for such changes?] There were hopes. The title of Hero City was supposed to signify that things would get better, that they would do something for the city, build a bridge, something was supposed to get better, widen the prospect [Prospekt Lenina], the riverside, something."[172]

The more than 900 million rubles that Brezhnev had promised for new communal services were, according to Yunak, used to reduce the backlog of unfinished construction sites.[173] In 1977, only fifty-eight thousand square meters of new housing was built, which was less than half the average of the 1960s. The other years in the late 1970s were not much better.[174] The fact that Brezhnev only met with Tula's leaders and that the award reaped few tangible benefits turned it into a matter concerning primarily the political elite rather than the city population as a whole. This elitism rested uneasily with official war memory's continued insistence that Tula's defense was an achievement of the entire city, of workers, soldiers, and the party.

As successors to the war generation—and even more as inhabitants of Tula—many considered themselves worthy of a better life. Local historian Irina Paramonova, commenting on Tulyaki's reaction to Brezhnev's suggested increase in funds, shares this interpretation: "Tulyaki are proud people with a strongly developed sense of their own dignity. This is why their reaction to the increase in budget allocations was justified. They saw them as owed to Tula."[175]

Unfortunately for Tula, its elevation to Hero City status occurred at a time when social and economic problems in the Soviet Union were starting to accumulate. In the second half of the 1970s, and particularly in the early 1980s, the costs of drastic loss in economic dynamism, low birth rates, alcoholism, imperial overreach, and the arms race could no longer be concealed.[176] In contrast to earlier periods (in Tula but also in Novorossiysk, which had received the Gold Star four years earlier), the accruing problems limited the availability of funds for extraordinary investments—funds that the Tulyaki had expected.

As a result, the state was less able to uphold its side of the socialist contract—the improvement of living conditions. The lack of balance between demands and rewards ultimately undermined the power of official war memory as a "moral incentive," which had never been seen as entirely separate from its material counterpart. Under these circumstances, it failed to raise the intrinsic motivation of workers.

NOTES

1. Quoted in Blatov, *Vydayushchiysya Podvig Zashchitnikov Tuly*, 13.
2. Blatov, *Vydayushchiysya Podvig Zashchitnikov Tuly*, 21–22. The newsreel of Brezhnev's appearance tellingly does not feature this particular moment: Mikhail Tentser, "1977 god. Prisvoenie Tule Pochoetnogo Zvaniya 'Gorod-Geroy,'" YouTube, accessed September 26, 2018, https://www.youtube.com/watch?v=zpaPoD2lpYo&t=4s.
3. Galitsan and Muriev quoted statistics indicating that Tula Oblast' had suffered 5 billion rubles in damage; 625 villages, 316 industrial enterprises, and 37,000 Kolkhozes were destroyed; and 15,700 horses, 16,400 pigs, and hundreds of thousands of fowl were killed and confiscated. Galitsan and Muriev, *Tula*, 140, 148.
4. *Tsentr Noveyshey Istorii Tul'skoy Oblasti* (TsNITO), f. P-177, op. 87, d. 1, l. 19. A 1976 report to the Central Committee mentions that 38,409 people fell "on Tula's soil," and a third of Tulyaki who joined the Red Army died. TsNITO, f. P-177, op. 72, d. 96., l. 13. This document was intended only for communication within the party. The number, however, appears in Viktor Golikov's widely distributed volume *Podvig Naroda* in 1980. Golikov, *Podvig Naroda*, 166.
5. Golikov, *Podvig Naroda*, 148.
6. TsNITO, f. P-177, op. 34, d. 13, l. 24.
7. Southern Russia was even plagued by famine.
8. Sergey Stepuzhin, interview with the author, Tula, May 28, 2012, 17.54 min.
9. Raisa Molchanova, interview with the author, Tula, April 18, 2013, 17.35 min.
10. Sergey Shcheglov, interview with the author, Tula, May 16, 2012, 42.59 min.
11. Shcheglov, interview, 45.09 min. Jeffrey Jones showed that the wealth of weapons available in the postwar Soviet Union also gave rise to more serious crimes. Jeffrey W. Jones, *Everyday Life and the 'Reconstruction' of Soviet Russia*, 54.
12. Evgeniy Stepunin, interview with the author, Tula, May 18, 2012, 94.30 min.

13. Marina Neizvestnaya, interview with the author, Tula, April 17, 2013, 29.01 min.
14. Osipov and Rostovtseva, *My Pomnim*, 192.
15. Pen'kov and Stekunov, *Kray Nash Tul'skiy*, 69.
16. Vasiliy Kotenev, interview with the author, Tula, May 21, 2012, 48.41 min.
17. The wartime dip is invisible, as there was no census. The sense of continuous growth is thus misleading.
18. Paramonova, *Tula: Khronika XX Stoletiya*, 131–32.
19. Breslauer, *Khrushchev and Brezhnev as Leaders*, 126.
20. Malinichev, *Na Puti k Krakhu*, 289.
21. Irina Sycheva, interview with the author, Tula, May 17, 2012, 1.21 min.
22. Stepuzhin, interview, 25.03 min.
23. See Vanyukov, *Epokha Zastoya*, 29.
24. Roesler, "Reaktionen der politischen Eliten der realsozialistischen Länder auf den 'Prager Frühling,'" 203.
25. TsNITO, P-177, op. 35, d. 41, l. 20.
26. Kamaev was the head of the Oblispolkom between 1962 and 1970. After the war he worked in Zaporozh'e and Dnepropetrovsk in Ukraine—the same places where Brezhnev began his postwar career. He was part of the Soviet leader's network of clients. TsNITO, P-177, op. 35, d. 60, l. 16.
27. TsNITO, P-177, op. 35, d. 41, l. 20.
28. TsNITO, P-177, op. 35, d. 60, l. 2.
29. TsNITO, P-177, op. 35, d. 59, l. 23.
30. TsNITO, P-177, op. 35, d. 61, ll. 61, 64, 72.
31. The total length of water pipes in the city increased from 59.6 to 115.2 kilometers. The number of trams grew from 169 to 231 and that of buses from 90 to 321 by 1970. The expansion of the sewage system was finished in 1968. *Gosudarstvennyy Arkhiv Rossiyskoy Federatsii* (GARF), f. A-374, op. 39, d. 967, ll. 7, 11, 17–18. Moreover, a citywide heating scheme (1971), telephone lines (1972), power lines (1974), and a system for the supply of gas (1974) were installed.
32. GARF, f. A-411, op. 3, d. 7506, ll. 39–41; op. 5, d. 3758, ll. 12–14. Growth slowed considerably in the early 1970s.
33. Baybakova, "Yubiley Pobedy i Gastrol'nyy Bum," 7.
34. Additional goods were made available to consumers at lower prices during holidays, beginning in the mid-1960s. Chernyshova, *Soviet Consumer Culture in the Brezhnev Era*, 38.
35. TsNITO, P-177, op. 35, d. 61, ll. 161–62.
36. Kolesnikov and Rozhkov, *Ordena i Medali SSSR*, 40.
37. TASS, "Podvig Moskvy," 1–2.
38. TASS, "Podvig Moskvy," 1.

39. Pospelov et al., *Velikaya Otechestvennaya Voyna Sovetskogo Soyuza 1941–1945*, 53.

40. Pospelov et al., *Istoriya Velikoy Otechestvennoy Voyny Sovetskogo Soyuza 1941–1945*, 251; Andronikov et al., *Istoriya Vtoroy Mirovoy Voyny 1939—1945 v Dvenadtsati Tomakh*, 101; Stahel, *Operation Typhoon*, 258; Hartmann, *Wehrmacht im Ostkrieg*, 312. During the Cold War, Eastern and Western historians were locked in a bitter dispute about the reasons for the German failure before Moscow. German historians in particular argued that the mud in which Wehrmacht tanks became stuck in the fall of 1941 contributed more to their defeat than did the Red Army. Maksim Kim dismissed references to the weather as a political ploy by "bourgeois falsifiers of history." In keeping with official war memory, Kim highlights ideological steadfastness as the decisive element. Kim, *Istoriya SSSR*, 54.

41. Sokolow writes that the Red Army had a ratio of ten dead for every wounded, which indicates that most injured soldiers were left on the battlefield to die in the chaos of the retreat. Sokolow, "Von Mythen des Kriegs zu Mythen der Literatur," 726.

42. *Rossiyskiy Gosudarstvennyy Arkhiv Sotsial'no-Politicheskoy Istorii* (RGASPI), f. M-1, op. 38, d. 39, ll. 68, 70.

43. Finogenov, *Tula-Gorod Ordenonosnyy*, 1.

44. Finogenov, *Tula-Gorod Ordenonosnyy*, 4–5.

45. Quoted in Finogenov, *Tula-Gorod Ordenonosnyy*, 10–11.

46. Quoted in Finogenov, *Tula-Gorod Ordenonosnyy*, 14.

47. Quoted in Finogenov, *Tula-Gorod Ordenonosnyy*, 15.

48. Quoted in Finogenov, *Tula-Gorod Ordenonosnyy*, 18.

49. Cooper, *Soviet Defence Industry*, 30.

50. Zubok, *Failed Empire*, 205. In 1962, 599 military-industrial enterprises and 367 military research institutions existed in the Soviet Union. They employed 3.7 million workers. Nikolay Simonov: *Voenno-Promyshlennyy Kompleks SSSR v 1920–1950-e Gody*, 276.

51. Malinichev, *Na Zakate*, 64. This number is not entirely comparable to that quoted above, but it gives the reader an impression of the proportions.

52. The industry's employees earned 20–30% above average but had to sign a vow of secrecy. Almquist, *Red Forge*, 51, 64. Vladimir Yurchikov held true to this promise: even though he worked at a weapon's factory, he only said that it produced bicycles and Vespas and would not divulge the exact nature of his work during the interview.

53. Quoted in Finogenov, *Tula-Gorod Ordenonosnyy*, 21–22.

54. Quoted in Finogenov, *Tula-Gorod Ordenonosnyy*, 22.

55. Quoted in Finogenov, *Tula-Gorod Ordenonosnyy*, 22. *Pravda*, unlike the regional Tula publication, did not print the details of Ustinov's criticism. *Pravda* and TASS, "Za Podvig Ratnyy i Trudovoy," 2.

56. Quoted in Finogenov, *Tula-Gorod Ordenonosnyy*, 22.
57. Kotenev, interview, 70.04 min.
58. Molchanova, interview, 46.32 min.
59. Dornberg, *Breschnew*, 19, 281.
60. TsNITO, P-177, op. 35, d. 61, l. 173.
61. TsNITO, P-177, op. 35, d. 61, l. 173.
62. TsNITO, P-177, op. 35, d. 61, l. 176.
63. 440,000 m², to be exact. TsNITO, f. P-177, op. 34, d. 19, l. 24.
64. TsNITO, f. P-177, op. 34, d. 19, l. 24.
65. Mark Smith, *Property of Communists*, 4. Between 1956 and 1989, the urban population in the Soviet Union increased from 87 to 188 million, which provides an idea of the scale of the challenge. Khrushchev's approach, which Brezhnev continued, comprised the hasty construction of standardized, prefabricated houses in so-called *mikrorayony*. Even though these houses often fell short of lofty promises, they still form the backbone of housing in the post-Soviet space today. French, *Plans, Pragmatism and People*, 70, 81–82.
66. Lovell, *Shadow of War*, 151.
67. Varga-Harris, *Stories of House and Home*, 13–15.
68. Inexplicably absent are the statistics for 1966–70, but judging from the total housing space, construction must have been higher than in the first half of the decade. Brezhnev maintains that central investment in Tula's communal services stayed at 474 million during this period, considerably lower than the 718 million between 1971 and 1975. V. Ashurkov maintains that the ninth Five-Year Plan's main focus in Tula was housing construction. Ashurkov, *Tula*, 194.
69. Quoted in Blatov, *Vydayushchiysya Podvig Zashchitnikov Tuly*, 22.
70. Savchenko, *Gorod-Geroy Tula*, 168.
71. Malinichev, *Na Puti k Krakhu*, 313.
72. TsNITO, f. P-177, op. 55, d. 77, ll. 103–4.
73. Deputy Minister of Finance RSFSR A. Kamenskov's complaint from 1970 is quite characteristic. "In the [Oblast's] four brick factories . . . quality of the production is low, 34,000 bricks were unusable." The enterprises in the construction sector complained about high fluctuation in personnel and low work discipline. GARF, f. A-411, op. 5, d. 359, l. 8. In another case from Novomoskovsk in Tula Oblast', the industrial construction trust only fulfilled 85% of its plan for 1969 and needed one million additional rubles to reach it—half of its total annual budget. TsNITO, f. P-177, op. 55, d. 74, ll. 148–49.
74. For instance, in Nizhnyy Novgorod in the 1930s, as described by DeHaan. DeHaan, *Stalinist City Planning*, 130.
75. In the Oblast's reports to the Finance Ministry RSFSR, the shortcomings in the realm of housing construction were a constant cause for concern. Every

year, Tula lost millions in unused construction funds. GARF, f. A-411, op. 5, d. 359, l. 10; GARF, f. A-411, op. 5, d. 3334, l. 2.

76. The city was awarded 200 million rubles from the Council of Ministers but also received additional construction assignments. By 1977 the backlog in housing construction amounted to 900 million rubles—equivalent to the sum that Brezhnev promised for the Tenth Five-Year-Plan. Malinichev, *V Romanticheskom Tumane*, 182–83.

77. Raleigh, *Russia's Sputnik Generation*, 16.

78. Kotenev, interview, 15 min.

79. Neizvestnaya, interview, 40.05 min.

80. Neizvestnaya, interview, 43.27 min.

81. Molchanova, interview, 42.35 min. Aleksandr Senyavskiy estimates that the city administrations on average only controlled about 3–5% of the total budget that was at the disposal of enterprises in their territory. The latter thus played a central role in housing construction. Senyavskiy, *Rossiyskiy Gorod v 1960-e—80-e Gody*, 68. After 1957, the city Soviets started to play a bigger role in the distribution of living space.

82. Stepuzhin, interview, 83.20 min. Because of the housing shortage, Thomas Bohn maintains, illegal and corrupt practices were common in the process of registering people in cities, which was the decisive criterion for receiving housing. Bohn, *Minsk*, 185.

83. Even the privileged armament industry was not immune to shortages. In a letter from September 16, 1966, Yunak and Kamaev described the difficult situation of workers: 920 families lived in apartments without plumbing, 943 in damaged houses or sheds. At the Mashinostroitel'nyy Zavod, 2,625 families were waiting for housing. The Defense Ministry, the Party leaders complained, had only assigned a third of the necessary funds for the period of 1966 to 1970. TsNITO, f. P-177, op. 35, d. 61, l. 122.

84. Galitsan and Muriev, *Tula*, 151.

85. Baybakova, "Yubiley Pobedy i Gastrol'nyy Bum," 7. In the rest of the USSR, the eighth Five-Year Plan also brought advancements. Vanyukov, *Epokha Zastoya*, 24.

86. Zaslavsky, *In geschlossener Gesellschaft*, 54.

87. Malinichev, *Na Puti k Krakhu*, 380–81.

88. See Malinichev, *Na Zakate*, 4.

89. Neizvestnaya, interview, 44.31 min.

90. Elena Bozhenko, interview with the author, Tula, May 17, 2012, 9.28 min.

91. An excellent income considering that the average wage in 1975 was 146 rubles. Meier and Meier-Rust, *Sowjetrealität in der Ära Breschnew*, 80. In Tula, it was even lower, at 126.3 rubles in 1971. Malinichev, *V Romanticheskom Tumane*, 85.

92. Vladimir Romanov, interview with the author, Tula, April 17, 2013, 5.52 min. The "sausage train" or "salami train" was a phenomenon that was quite widespread in the vicinity of large cities. Chernyshova, *Soviet Consumer Culture in the Brezhnev Era*, 80.

93. TsNITO, f. P-177, op. 34, d. 50, ll. 43, 52.

94. TsNITO, f. P-177, op. 55, d. 110, l. 12. That Yunak put toilets and newspapers on the same level of basic amenities illustrates the importance that cultural services had in the Soviet Union.

95. Malinichev, *Na Puti k Krakhu*, 387.

96. Molchanova, interview, 49.47 min.

97. Romanov, interview, 17.21 min.

98. Romanov, interview, 17.47 min. Priyaniki's high symbolic, if not financial, value persists today. Inhabitants insist that any guest of the city must buy priyaniki before leaving and that they must be fresh. Naturally, each local knows a different "best place" to get them.

99. As the Party Archive in Moscow (*Rossiyskiy Gosudarstvennyy Arkhiv Noveyshey Istorii*—RGANI) has not declassified the vast majority of Politburo and Central Committee documents, the process cannot be documented in its entirety.

100. *Gosudarstvennyy Arkhiv Tul'skoy Oblasti* (GATO), f. R-2640, op. 12, d. 587, l. 160.

101. TsNITO, P-177, op. 55, d. 110, l. 55; op. 72, d. 96, l. 9.

102. These terms are consistently employed throughout all three applications, which can be found in TsNITO, P-177, op. 55, d. 110, ll. 52–58 (1970); TsNITO, P-177, op. 69, d. 84, ll.1–6 (1975); and TsNITO, P-177, op. 72, d. 96, ll. 1–15 (1976).

103. TsNITO, op. 72, d. 96, l. 12.

104. TsNITO, op. 72, d. 96, l. 15.

105. TsNITO, op. 72, d. 96, l. 15.

106. Bruno Frey and Jana Gallus argue that acceptance of an award not only creates a "special bond of loyalty" but also reinforces existing hierarchies. Frey and Gallus, "Awards Are a Special Kind of Signal," accessed on September 13, 2020, 4–5.

107. Varga-Harris, *Stories of House and Home*, 207.

108. TsNITO, f. P-177, op. 72, d. 96, ll. 6–8.

109. TsNITO, f. P-177, op. 69, d. 84, l. 5; op. 55, d. 110, l. 54.

110. TsNITO, f. P-177, op. 72, d. 96, l. 14.

111. Zhukov, "V Bitve za Stolitsu," 58.

112. Kirilenko, "Yanvar' 1977 Goda."

113. Evgeniy Zhirnov, "'Komanduyushchego Armiey Predat' Sudu," accessed on September 13, 2020.

114. Afanas'eva, "Tula Stala Gorodom-Geroem Blagodarya Yunaku." Vasiliy Yunak, the son of the Obkom's First Secretary, corroborates Yunak's phone call. See Ryabikova, "Gensek i Tula," 16.

115. Zhirnov, "'Komanduyushchego Armiey Predat' Sudu."

116. Quoted in Afanas'eva, "Tula Stala Gorodom-Geroem Blagodarya Yunaku."

117. TsNITO, f. P-177, op. 72, d. 96, ll. 1–3.

118. *Kommunar*, December 10, 1976, 1.

119. Quoted in "Nepristupna, kak Krepost'!," *Kommunar*, December 1976, 1.

120. Kharlashkin, "Byla li Bomba?," 10.

121. Ryabikova, "Gensek i Tula," 16; Maslov, "Ozhivlenie v Zale," 10.

122. Three hundred guests, most of them representatives of the party and the trade unions, attended the banquet in his honor. Maslov, "Ozhivlenie v Zale," 10.

123. Pavlenko, "Brezhnev Privez v Tulu Apel'siny i Kol'basu," 10.

124. Shcheglov, interview, 51.49 min. He had to cover four kilometers.

125. Stepunin, interview, 107.55 min.

126. Blatov, *Vydayushchiysya Podvig Zashchitnikov Tuly*, 12.

127. Quoted in Blatov, *Vydayushchiysya Podvig Zashchitnikov Tuly*, 13.

128. Quoted in Blatov, *Vydayushchiysya Podvig Zashchitnikov Tuly*, 14.

129. Tula Oblast' would continue to play an important ceremonial role in anniversaries highlighting the Soviet state's Russian roots. Yitzhak Brudny points to the celebrations commemorating the six hundredth anniversary in 1980 of the Battle of Kulikovo near Tula, which marked the high point of nationalist circles' influence in Soviet politics. Brudny, *Reinventing Russia*, 181–83.

130. Quoted in Blatov, *Vydayushchiysya Podvig Zashchitnikov Tuly*, 16.

131. Quoted in Blatov, *Vydayushchiysya Podvig Zashchitnikov Tuly*, 22–25.

132. Philip Roeder even talks of a "Tula line" that emerged from the speech. Roeder, "Dialectics of Doctrine," 93–95.

133. Zubok, *Failed Empire*, 255.

134. Chernyaev, *Sovmestnyy Iskhod*, 259. Indeed, the brochure on Brezhnev's Tula trip noted that he visited the "largest machine construction factory in Tula" (*krupneyshiy Tul'skiy Mashinostroitel'nyy zavod*). Blatov, *Vydayushchiysya Podvig Zashchitnikov Tuly*, 8.

135. Quoted in Blatov, *Vydayushchiysya Podvig Zashchitnikov Tuly*, 20. According to Schattenberg, the shortages in milk and meat were Brezhnev's figurative "problem children," which preoccupied him over years. Schattenberg, *Leonid Breschnew*, 368–69.

136. On applause in the Stalinist leader cult, see Sarah Davies, "Stalin and the Making of the Leader Cult," 30–31.

137. Quoted in Blatov, *Vydayushchiysya Podvig Zashchitnikov Tuly*, 31.

138. Chernyaev, *Sovmestnyy Iskhod*, 259.

139. Quoted in Blatov, *Vydayushchiysya Podvig Zashchitnikov Tuly*, 21. This is a reversal of his argument in 1970, which indicates growing frustration.

140. Quoted in Blatov, *Vydayushchiysya Podvig Zashchitnikov Tuly*, 30–31.

141. Quoted in Blatov, *Vydayushchiysya Podvig Zashchitnikov Tuly*, 48.

142. This was to "improve the housing conditions of approximately four hundred thousand people." As this was an English-language publication, it may have exaggerated the number for propagandistic effect abroad. Garbuzov, "Tula's Military Feat," 14.

143. TsNITO, f. P-177, op. 74, d. 127, l. 4.

144. TsNITO, f. P-177, op. 77, d. 82, l. 12; Malinichev, *V Romanticheskom Tumane*, 182.

145. TsNITO, f. P-177, op. 77, d. 82, l. 3.

146. TsNITO, f. P-177, op. 77, d. 82, l. 107.

147. GATO, f. R-3306, op. 5, d. 477, ll. 1–6.

148. TsNITO, f. P-188, op. 1, d. 1491, l. 4.

149. In the trade sector, which was notorious for its poor service and supplies, 400 out of 3,828 Komsomol members participated in a similar campaign called "Exemplary Service to the Hero City," improving work discipline and service quality. RGASPI, f. M-1, op. 38, d. 764, l. 204.

150. RGASPI, f. M-1, op. 38, d. 833, l. 92.

151. TsNITO, f. P-188, op. 1, d. 1491, l. 3.

152. Yunak, *Vernost' Geroicheskim Traditsiyam*, 29.

153. Romanov, interview, 46.45 min.

154. Romanov, interview, 48.51 min.

155. Romanov, interview, 53.25 min.

156. Bozhenko, interview, 170.20 min.

157. DeHaan's description is very close to Bozhenko's: "Train curtains, clean store shelves, polite service, and sophisticated systems of retail trade were all deemed 'cultured', as were tidy city streets." DeHaan, *Stalinist City Planning*, 151.

158. Romanov, interview, 12.22 min.

159. Irina Paramonova, email message to author, October 12, 2012.

160. Neizvestnaya, interview, 40.58 min.

161. Vladimir Yurchikov, interview with the author, April 16, 2013, 32.18 min.

162. Stepuzhin, interview, 55.33 min.

163. Bozhenko, interview, 183.15.

164. Viktor Shcheglov and Vladimir Yurchikov both expressed this opinion.

165. Sycheva, interview, 58.52 min.

166. Neizvestnaya, interview, 50.47 min.

167. Compare also Raisa Molchanova's statement: "I live in Tula, in the city of weapon-builders, of priyaniki, in which there are many industrial

enterprises.... Whether it is a Hero City or a hero—it is just my native city." Molchanova, interview, 67.51 min.

168. Malinichev, *V Romanticheskom Tumane*, 160.

169. Maslov, "Ozhivlenie v Zale," 10; Pavlenko, "Brezhnev Privez v Tulu Apel'siny i Kol'basu," 10.

170. Romanov, interview, 7.09 min.

171. Bozhenko, interview, 170.20 min.

172. Kotenev, interview, 72.03 min.

173. In a Buro meeting of the Obkom on January 20, 1977. TsNITO, f. P-177, op. 74, d. 127, l. 3.

174. See, for instance, GARF, f. A-411, op. 5, d. 3758, l. 8. In 1976, 75,400 m^2 were built, only 80% of the plan, according to the Buro of the Obkom, because Glavprioksstroy, the Oblast's general contractor, had not fulfilled its obligations. GARF, f. P-177, op. 77, d. 82, l. 20.

175. Paramonova, email.

176. One drastic example is the rising mortality due to alcoholism, which lowered labor productivity by 15–17% on average in the Soviet Union—with a concomitant rise of social expenses by the state. Between 1979 and 1982, production stagnated. Vanyukov, *Epokha Zastoya*, 56, 64, 197.

FIVE

Novorossiysk as a Monumental Ensemble
Little Land and the Ideal of War

IN HIS BOOK *HERO-CITIES OF THE BLACK SEA*, the editor in chief of the newspaper *Sovetskiy Krym*, Konstantin Kinelev, quotes a saying about Novorossiysk: "When you pass *Ploshchad' Geroev* [Hero Square], continue on to Malaya Zemlya, and from there, stop at the wagon monument. At each monument—bow down to the soldiers, comrade!"[1] Kinelev outlines a commemorative topography that reproduces the three battles of Novorossiysk: the wagon monument stands next to the line of defense in 1942, where the German attack was stopped. Malaya Zemlya, "Little Land" in English, is the area in which the landing operation of February 1943 succeeded unexpectedly. Hero Square, finally, lies in the city center and symbolizes its liberation on September 16, 1943. Vicky Davis fittingly calls it the city's "center of remembrance."[2]

Historians of architecture conceptualized these main monuments as the "face" (*fasad*) of the city and as the elements that unify its space. "The ensembles consolidate (*ob"edinyayut*) the arc of Tsemess Bay, including in its sphere all objects that are located along the coastal line."[3] Architects lauded Novorossiysk for its combination of everyday and commemorative structures.[4] Official accounts presented its urban landscape as a successful fusion of the past and the present, the reverence for war memory and the well-being of the population.[5]

In Novorossiysk, the task of homogenizing the memorial landscape was more closely tied to the Great Patriotic War than in Tula because it had left a much larger imprint. Politicians and planners made enormous efforts to construct this homogenous surface and thus fixate the city's identity—before but especially after it became a Hero City in September 1973. They tried to smoothen the inherently pluralistic significance of urban space to reinforce dominant discourses. Not least, this meant idealizing a battle that had involved numerous strategic blunders by the Soviet leadership in a phase of the war that was particularly difficult and bloody.

The loss of the Battle of Moscow and the Soviet counteroffensive in the winter of 1941–42 had beaten the Wehrmacht back but had not defeated it. It had sustained unprecedented losses, but those on the Soviet side were even larger.[6] In order to regain the initiative, the German high command (OKH) launched a new offensive in the South on June 28, 1942. The Wehrmacht conquered the Donbas, Voronezh, and Khar'kov. After the fall of Sevastopol' on July 4 and the subsequent hasty retreat from Crimea, Novorossiysk became the Soviet Navy's most important Black Sea port. The Luftwaffe conducted regular bombing raids.[7] Farther east, the attack on Stalingrad began on July 17. By mid-August, the Wehrmacht had taken more than half a million Soviet soldiers prisoner, and the Red Army had lost more than four thousand tanks.[8]

Torn between Stalingrad's huge psychological value and access to the Black Sea coast and to the oil fields in the Caucasus, Hitler split the Wehrmacht forces between Stalingrad and the Caucasus.[9] German historians see this decision as a crucial mistake that doomed the Wehrmacht, as neither battle group had enough resources to reach its goals.[10] The conquest of Novorossiysk was crucial, as the city held the "key to the Transcaucasus": its port was significant, and it opened the door to the main road on the Black Sea coast.[11]

During my interviews, the bombings came up repeatedly. Vladimir Gusev (pseudonym) was born in 1942—"under bombs," as he emphasizes.[12] Gusev is my only respondent with firsthand experience of the war. His mother, a native Novorossian, told Gusev that "the sky was black with airplanes" in the summer of 1942, an image that has stayed with him until today.[13] Even though Gusev has few conscious memories from the war years, they continue to haunt him. He still hates the sound of airplanes. "Until I was ten years old, I would start shaking when I heard an airplane, the 'ooOOOOOOOOVROOOOMmm!' Such fear! I would hide."[14] Julie deGraffenried observed similar symptoms in an entire cohort: "Today, the war children are in their seventies and eighties, suffering, often silently, from the post-traumatic stress disorder, depression, social phobias, and the lingering physical effects of wartime scarcity."[15]

Another "native Novorossian," Natal'ya Grigor'eva, was born on November 13, 1954, in the Mefodievka neighborhood. Her grandmother had survived the war in Novorossiysk. She was working as a janitor at the port in 1942 when the bombing started. "She saw how they bombed our ships, how the sailors jumped into the water, how they were ... burning alive. She saw the war, and she told us all about this, how terrifying it was. I can't talk about this calmly."[16]

Even if the details are difficult to verify, the interviews convey a sense of the helplessness the civilian population felt in the face of German bombings; the Luftwaffe enjoyed almost complete air superiority in the South in 1942.[17] Equally important, the immediacy of Grigor'eva's emotions illustrates how present these traumatic memories remained in families, passed across generations, even if the grandchildren did not experience the incidents personally. The psychologist Angela Moré even maintains that there are no indications these traumata get weaker in following generations.[18]

Conversely, official Soviet historians like Ivan Shiyan, a participant in the fights for Novorossiysk and the author of multiple books on the Hero City, described the defense of the city as a great success. His volumes had print runs of hundreds of thousands of copies in the 1970s and 1980s and thus to a significant extent shaped the image that a broad Soviet readership had of the battle—even if less propagandistically minded historians did not take this type of idealized description seriously.[19] Differentiated discussions, however, often remained limited to military academic circles—and to the period between Stalin's death and the propagation of official war memory under Brezhnev, starting in the 1960s.

Shiyan writes that Soviet order 227, *Ni Shagu Nazad!* (Not One Step Back!), strengthened resistance.[20] According to him, the construction of defensive lines in Novorossiysk exemplified the smoothest possible collaboration of civilians and the military.[21] The two acted in perfect harmony under the guidance of the Communist Party, which was "the soul of all deeds and initiatives."[22]

Shiyan only admits that "at the beginning of the opponent's attack on Novorossiysk the construction of the defensive line was not finished and continued during the course of the fight for the city."[23] Local historian Tamara Yurina is more blunt; according to her, the organization of Novorossiysk's defense was poor. In the course of the southern front's reorganization, as a result of order 227, purges removed numerous senior commanders, creating chaos and undermining soldiers' confidence in their commanders.[24]

Moreover, writes Yurina, the *Stavka* did not recognize Novorossiysk's strategic significance and thus failed to assign sufficient forces for the defense. On August 19, the city and its surroundings held about fifteen thousand troops, who faced four times as many Romanian and German soldiers. Only 20 percent of the planned defensive structures were in place, and thousands of refugees and wounded soldiers flooded the city. Only on August 23 did the authorities begin to evacuate people and materials.[25]

Two days later, the Wehrmacht began its ground attack. In spite of continued resistance, German troops broke through. Street battles ensued on September 6, 1942. Only six thousand defenders remained, and they fought a desperate battle.[26] Some were evacuated by sea, but most were killed or taken prisoner. On September 10, the Germans reported the fall of the city; one day later, the Soviet Information Buro confirmed it.[27]

However, a small group of fighters managed to entrench itself in the Proletariy cement factory on Novorossiysk's easternmost edge, denying the Germans access to the coastal road.[28] The "half-victory" in Novorossiysk caused a profound shock in the German High Command:[29] the stagnation of the front and the mounting losses led Hitler to sack a number of leading generals. The Wehrmacht's plight only worsened after the defeat in Stalingrad in February 1943. German forces in the Caucasus became increasingly vulnerable.

Some generals advocated for a retreat from the Caucasus. Hitler, however, wanted to hold on to the bridgehead in Novorossiysk to use it as a stepping-stone for a new attack.[30] The Wehrmacht held this "Blue Line," or "Gotenkopf," until October 1943. Starting in January, it mined Novorossiysk with thirty-two thousand explosives and amassed up to three divisions.[31] It built a multilayered defense structure, forcing the local population to assist and shooting those who refused.[32] The Germans were turning Novorossiysk into their own "impregnable fortress."

In late January 1943, the Red Army had finalized its preparations for a vast landing operation in Yuzhnaya Ozereyka, a small village fifteen kilometers west of Novorossiysk. Early in the morning on February 4, 1,427 soldiers landed, with tanks and heavy weaponry. The operation turned into a disaster.[33] A few kilometers to the east, however, a small detachment under the command of Major Tsezar' Kunikov successfully landed near the village of Stanichka. Intended as a distraction, the landing troops at Malaya Zemlya (Little Land) succeeded against all odds and established a bridgehead.[34] Realizing the opportunity to salvage the botched invasion of Yuzhnaya Ozereyka, Rear Admiral Nikolay Basistyy sent reinforcements.[35]

Their position was unfavorable: surrounded by hills held by the Germans, the "Malozemel'tsy," as the landing troops were called, were shelled daily. Over the next seven months—or 225 days, according to official Soviet historiography—German artillery and planes dropped 1.25 tons of metal for each soldier—without managing to liquidate the beachhead.[36] As German troops and their allies had withdrawn into the "Blue Line" fortifications,

Malaya Zemlya constituted a thorn in their side, or right flank. The Wehrmacht thus launched Operation Neptune on April 17, attacking the beachhead with twenty-seven thousand men, as well as hundreds of guns and airplanes.[37] The attack failed again—because of the Soviet soldiers' resistance and fresh airplanes from the *Stavka* reserve, but also because of poor weather conditions. It would be the last large-scale attack by German forces in the Caucasus.

OCCUPATION AND DEPORTATION

Unlike military events, civilians' fates in occupied Novorossiysk remain largely unarticulated in official war memory. Life under occupation—not to speak of topics such as collaboration—was taboo. The wartime history was portrayed as a succession of heroic defense, dedicated underground resistance under occupation, and, in September 1943, glorious liberation: "The underground organization expanded its work, and the partisan units began their military activities. . . . During the year [of occupation] the Novorossian partisans conducted 125 fights, completed 150 ambushes in the rear of the enemy and annihilated (*unichtozhili*) about 2,000 Hitlerite soldiers and officers as well as a large quantity of the enemy's weapons and military technology. During occupation the fascists annihilated over 7,000 civilians and sent more than 40,000 people into forced labor in Germany. The Hitlerites destroyed factories, port buildings and apartment houses."[38]

The account obscures as much as it reveals. In 1940, Novorossiysk had a population of around one hundred thousand, which shrank to forty thousand by September 1942.[39] According to a Soviet special commission installed in 1945 to investigate German crimes, inhabitants were subsequently deported in three waves: the first two in November 1942 and May 1943. Deportees went through "filtration camps" in Ukraine and Crimea, and many were sent to Germany as forced laborers. The five thousand men who remained in the city after May were forced to build fortifications and were deported in August.[40]

Four out of my ten interview partners' parents experienced occupation or deportation. They spoke at much more length about deportation than about life under occupation. Vladimir Gusev's mother and her two sons were removed from the city in 1943. Two barges took them to Crimea. According to his mother, the Soviet Air Force bombed the transports because they saw the National Socialist flag but did not know that Soviet civilians were on board. "But what can you do? This was war. Beat the German!"[41] Gusev's statement reveals fatalism and even cynicism, as he ironically repeats Soviet wartime slogans.

Natal'ya Grigor'eva's grandmother and mother, who was still a child at the time, were also brought to Ukraine. Grigor'eva said that she once asked her grandmother about how the Germans had behaved—a sensitive topic even in today's Russia:

> I'm not sure.... Are we allowed to talk about this? (*laughs nervously*) [IM: Of course—you can talk about anything.] Yes, I don't know.... Well, she said that there were those that, when they sent them to Ukraine, I don't even know where to, some there, some here, she said there were those Germans who ... also felt sorry for the Russian children, gave them bread.... And there were evil ones.... But others were good, they gave the children harmonicas, or bread. So it seems that among the soldiers there were also good ones, who understood that war was unnecessary.[42]

The admission that not every enemy soldier was evil would appear to be commonplace. Still, Grigor'eva's hesitation underscores the longevity of Soviet-era taboos. Similar stories surfaced in other interviews. Georgiy Shcherbakov is a Novorossiysk native, born and raised in the Tsemdolina neighborhood on its northern edge. His father was deported to Germany at the age of fourteen. Shcherbakov explained: "He talked a lot about Germany, about his time as a prisoner. But I would like to say that according to his stories, they were not really in captivity but kept to work. As he told it, the relationship was not swinish (*khamskaya*), it was all right (*normal'no*). He worked at a factory and almost got married to the director's daughter." [43]

Shcherbakov could not name any details about this almost-marriage. However, he did remember that American soldiers had liberated the factory and confronted his father with the choice of returning to the USSR or staying in the West. His father chose the Soviet Union. The veracity of this story is difficult to judge. Perhaps Shcherbakov's father did not want to tell his son about his traumatic experiences and so stuck to a fairy tale, in which he almost married a rich German girl. Maybe he was treated as well as he claimed. It is clear, however, that good treatment of Soviet laborers was the exception, as the level of violence against them was great, not least because of the National Socialist regime's racist notions of superiority toward Slavs.[44]

Perhaps tellingly, Shcherbakov does not know whether his father, like many other forced laborers, encountered problems with Soviet authorities upon his return. Valeriy Sviderskiy's father, Valentin, who had lived under German occupation and had been deported in 1943 as a minor, did face repercussions: he could not join the navy when he returned to Novorossiysk. "Having lived under the occupation meant that you were a second-class person, under constant suspicion," explained Sviderskiy.⁴⁵ As a result, his father moved to the Donbas, where Valeriy was born in 1951. The family only returned to Novorossiysk in 1954.

Soviet counterespionage units (*Smersh*) checked prisoners of war and civilians coming back to Novorossiysk for over a month after the end of the war.⁴⁶ Eight hundred soldiers who had returned from German captivity did forced labor in the reconstruction for two years. They received permission to settle permanently only after their construction brigades were dissolved in 1947. According to Elena Burik, the participation of prisoners of war was a taboo in official historiography, as it points to Stalin's paranoia about returning prisoners, suspected of being spies.⁴⁷

Still, verifications mostly applied to groups considered suspicious. They left out others, such as young mothers. Vladimir Gusev explains that his mother "was nobody. She was a mother with two children. How could she have talked to the Germans? As a spy, or what? I asked for grub (*zhrat'*) the whole time! I screamed of hunger—aaaahhh!"⁴⁸ Gusev's disturbingly direct articulation of his hunger underscores how preoccupied he remains with his war experience. It illustrates the high price the population paid, through occupation, deportation, postwar deprivation, and stigmatization.

The parents of my respondents told them many fewer details about everyday life under German occupation. This was due not only to the suspicion that inhabitants of occupied territories were subject to after the war but also to extremely blurry moral categories:⁴⁹ Soviet citizens who were deported had only a minimum of agency; they were victims of overwhelming forces. This was no different in an occupied city like Novorossiysk, yet everyday life appears to have made many more compromises necessary. Novorossians lived with the Germans, housed them, and interacted with them. They certainly did not do this voluntarily. But the few available sources indicate that relations were not generally hostile.

Local historian Sergey Novikov conducted an in-depth interview with Klotilda Shtirts, a woman who had experienced occupation in Novorossiysk when she was young. She talks about hunger and death, but she also mentions various Germans her families housed, with whom they had amicable relations. According to her, the occupiers were "little interested" in the civilian population, unless they "created problems for the occupiers."⁵⁰

The Germans appear to have pursued a policy that combined neglect with episodic campaigns of terror against certain groups of the population. They refused to investigate violence against Soviet civilians, as a matter of principle, creating an atmosphere of impunity.[51] Seven thousand people were killed, but it is unclear how many died of neglect. Valentin Sviderskiy, father of Valeriy, writes in his memoirs that wounded Red Army soldiers in hospitals in the occupation zone received no medical aid.

He almost certainly came across this information after the war, as he was a minor during it. This illustrates the extent to which different temporal levels converge in any oral history source[52]—the time of experience and the moment of writing it down. The information nevertheless appears plausible. Once conditions worsened for the Wehrmacht after February 1943, civilians began to starve, as a result of the poor supply situation—and the low priority the Germans attributed to Soviet civilians.[53]

However, the Germans did target two groups: Jews and partisans. According to Il'ya Al'tman, one of the foremost Russian specialists on the Holocaust, more than one thousand Jews were killed in Novorossiysk in the fall of 1942.[54] Historians like Yuriy Zhurkin mention the massacre but not the Jewish identity of its victims;[55] Soviet historiography never granted any group a claim to exceptional victimization—least of all the Jews. In Novorossiysk and elsewhere, they were only part of the "Soviet people."[56] Vicky Davis found that the memory of Jewish suffering in Novorossiysk remains "on the periphery of the war myth" even today.[57]

Partisans featured more prominently in official historiography because they were the symbols of continued resistance in occupied territories. According to Ivan Shiyan, they summoned the population when it became clear that the city could not be defended on September 10, 1942: "Do not fulfill orders by the German command.... Hurt the Hitlerites at every step, do not appear at work, fight and destroy equipment, settle your scores (*raspravlyaytes'*) mercilessly with German occupiers and traitors, help the Red Army with all your strength." The workers, Shiyan maintains, followed this call.[58]

For civilians, however, partisan activity created the kinds of problems with the Germans mentioned above—problems they tried to avoid. Lyudmila Dorosh's family members told her stories to this effect. Her stepmother (*machekha*) had lived in the village of Vasil'evka right outside Novorossiysk during the occupation. She told Dorosh that even though the Germans would requisition food, partisans were the main problem: "My machekha said that nothing really bad ever happened during the occupation. When did the problems come? They came with the partisans. Something exploded, and this affected the population right away."[59]

Houses were burned, and civilians suspected of harboring or feeding partisans were arrested or executed.[60] An order from the German city authorities from May 4, 1943, stated that ten male civilians were to be shot if a soldier was attacked.[61] The Nazis, then, tried to rob the civilian population of all incentive to support the partisans. Rather than being part of a unified resistance, as Soviet historiography maintained, the civilians were stuck between the hammer of the occupiers and the anvil of the partisans.

The lines between resistance and collaboration were even blurred for partisans. Yuriy Zhurkin, the First Secretary of the Gorkom between 1978 and 1985 and the supposed coauthor of a seminal book on the city's history, highlights the feats of a group headed by Stepan Ostroverkhov.[62] The group consisted of twenty to twenty-five people. According to Shiyan and Zhurkin, Ostroverkhov managed to place various members among the occupation authorities.[63]

Those members saved numerous people from deportation by issuing false passports and waivers. In early 1943, thirty wounded soldiers were freed from a hospital and handed over to partisan groups. As a result of the deportation of the population, the organization's chances of hiding among civilians became smaller. Its members were betrayed, explains Shiyan, although he fails to elaborate by whom. On June 10, 1943, the Gestapo arrested, tortured, and shot most of them. Ostroverkhov was posthumously awarded the Order of the Patriotic War on May 10, 1965.

The story provides one of Soviet historiography's most detailed descriptions of the inner workings of the German occupation authorities.[64] It unwittingly admits that Novorossians collaborated—even if they did so to help the Red Army. The reader may nevertheless derive that significant numbers of local inhabitants, aside from the underground agents, worked for occupation authorities.

Although some details of interviewees' statements are difficult to verify, their combination with other sources illuminates various aspects of life under occupation in considerable detail. Davis found that "collaboration with the enemy is suspected amongst some interviewees, if largely unspoken."[65] My respondents also hesitated to address topics that sit uneasily with official heroism.

But beneath the surface, the stories shared within the intimacy of family circles and passed down to the next generations remain relevant—even if they do not undermine the feeling of pride. They existed for decades, unarticulated in public and only partially revealed since the collapse of the Soviet Union. Oral history as a source is all the more important in this context, as it supplements the available historical research and enables the historian to purposefully read between the lines of official Soviet sources.

UNITY OF GENERATIONS IN HERO SQUARE

The Wehrmacht's defeat in the Battle of Kursk in July 1943 meant that the "Blue Line" lay hundreds of miles east of the central and northern front line. The

Seventeenth Army was cut off. Hitler nevertheless hesitated to authorize the retreat until September 4.[66] By then, the Red Army was ready for an attack on the fortified German positions: the main strike was to be directed against the harbor of Novorossiysk, as the first step toward liberating the Taman Peninsula and cutting off the retreating enemy.[67]

At 2:44 a.m. on September 10, 1943, Soviet artillery opened fire on the port with eight hundred guns.[68] For almost six days, Soviet, German, and Romanian forces fought for control of the city. The supporting attacks from the front line near the cement factories and from Malaya Zemlya provided cover for the troops in the harbor. By 10:00 a.m. on September 16, the last German units had left Novorossiysk. After 393 days of fighting and occupation, the city was liberated. Nevertheless, the Red Army missed its goal of encircling significant enemy forces. Instead, even Soviet sources admit that the Wehrmacht left the city of its own accord on September 15.[69]

According to the bulk of Soviet and post-Soviet Russian historiography, the liberation of Novorossiysk was a great victory. Marshal Andrey Grechko, one of the top commanders in the Caucasus, wrote the canonical, if highly propagandistic, account of the battles: "The victory that the Soviet soldiers won at Novorossiysk had great significance for the general course of fighting on the Soviet-German front. An important military Navy base was completely liberated. Our Black Sea Fleet received the opportunity to attack the opponent's maritime communication more effectively."[70]

Shiyan sees the liberation of the city as the first step toward freeing the Taman Peninsula and later on Crimea from occupation.[71] Tamara Yurina argues that it "enabled the completion of the fundamental turning point (*korennyy perelom*) in the course of the Great Patriotic War," especially since it happened at virtually the same time as other crucial events like the forcing of the Dnepr near Kiev.[72] German historians with Wehrmacht sympathies, writing primarily in the 1970s and 1980s, highlighted the success of the German retreat, which "ran with the precision of clockwork." Roland Kaltenegger goes so far as to call the landing in Novorossiysk useless. In his interpretation, the fighting in Novorossiysk covered the German retreat because it forestalled Soviet attempts to attack elsewhere.[73]

More recent works on the battle put greater focus on its long-term effects. Rauh points out that the defensive battles on the Taman Peninsula drained the forces of the Wehrmacht, depriving it of the opportunity to reinforce its rear positions.[74] Moreover, the successful retreat did not go far enough, according to Schönherr: after the loss of Novorossiysk, the commanders of the Seventeenth Army wanted to evacuate Crimea, but Hitler would not agree. As a result, the Red Army managed to trap it on the peninsula. It was evacuated from Sevastopol' only in May 1944 and was not able to play a role in the battles in central Ukraine.[75]

Two months after Novorossiysk's liberation, in November 1943, the Gorispolkom decided to erect a modest monument in Hero Square. In 1958, Davis points out, Hero Square became only the third place in the Soviet Union to receive a permanent eternal flame, which at that time only existed in Leningrad and Sevastopol'.[76] On September 16, thousands of people gathered to await its arrival, and "a delegation from the Hero City of Sevastopol' brought a bit (*chastitsa*) of Eternal Fire on a cruiser of the Black Sea Fleet from Malakhov Kurgan, which is holy to the entire Soviet people."[77]

The transport of fire through the water symbolically reproduced the wartime kinship of the two cities. The provenience of the flame from a Hero City, which had, in its turn, received it from Mars Field in Leningrad, served to underscore the continuity and connection between Hero Square and the revolutionary and military traditions.

One of the commanders of the storm on Novorossiysk, vice admiral and Hero of the Soviet Union, Georgiy Kholostyakov, lit the eternal flame.[78] He thus literally passed the torch from the past to the present in a gesture of transgenerational unity, endowing the ritual with authenticity because of his crucial role in the battles. Less than two years later, another element was added to the square: at the request of the Gorkom, the famous composer Dmitriy Shostakovich wrote the piece *Novorossiyskie Kuranty* (Novorossiysk Chimes), which would henceforth play at the top of each hour.[79]

These different elements impressed members of the postwar generation. The historian Tamara Yurina remembers arriving in the city from Siberia in 1966, when she was nine years old. The family had moved because of her mother's poor health. Novorossiysk appeared as a kind of wonderland to her. Yurina remembers well how she marveled at the variety of fruits and vegetables, which were easily available in Novorossiysk, in stark contrast to Siberia. On one of the first days, a neighbor took them to Hero Square. "And when I saw the eternal flame, I was so amazed (*porazhena*), I did not know such a thing existed. 'How, eternal? Is it really eternal? Lifelong? How?' And when I heard Novorossiysk Chimes, that was so unusual! That was the first encounter with this unusual place, dedicated to such a heroic event."[80]

The solemn combination of music and fire helped reinforce the notion that this was a special place. Schoolbooks, newspapers, and historical publications consistently told the postwar generation that it was exactly in *this* place that

Novorossiysk's liberation had been completed. Like Victory Square, its counterpart in Tula, Hero Square derived its authenticity from the wartime events that had taken place there. The ritualistic retelling underscored Novorossiysk's heroism—even to a stranger who was not acquainted with its history. War memory helped to integrate newcomers and make them identify with their new hometown.[81]

On May 9, 1975, three years later than in Tula, a Post Nomer 1 was established in Hero Square. A guard of honor, composed of students from various schools, stood there every day from 9:00 a.m. to 6:00 p.m. They swore to keep the graves of those who had died during the war safe: "I swear to be worthy of the memory of the heroes that gave their lives in the fights for Novorossiysk as long as I live. I swear by the holiness (*svyatost'*) of these graves that I will be steadfast, as befits a Komsomol member and a Pioneer, and guard the peace of the soldiers who died in the fights for Novorossiysk. I will not leave this post, not even if my life is threatened by deadly danger. If I break this oath, not only my comrades but all Novorossians shall punish me."[82]

Death was immediately present in the square in the shape of "holy" graves, but through Post Nomer 1 and the oath, service was ritualistically transformed into an obligation for the postwar generation. The youths guarded the memory of the war heroes and reproduced their feats with their own service to the fatherland. The honorary guards swore that their "worthiness" as successors also included the will to sacrifice themselves for the defense of the fatherland.

The images in figure 5.1 were published in 1978 and were most likely taken on September 16 of that or the previous year. Young men and women in sailor's uniforms—probably cadets, judging from their age—stand behind the eternal flame. They pay tribute to the fallen heroes of the Great Patriotic War.

One cannot help but notice the lush vegetation, which stands in stark contrast to the tombstone and the eternal flame. Arranged next to one another, they convey the message that life depends on the sacrifices of the past. An official description of the solemn mood reproduces the same message in a different medium of memory; it projects an ideal ritual practice for the square: "A considerate silence always reigns on Hero Square. Sprawling woods subdue the street noise, people do not talk loudly, children make no noise. In the festive silence the hammered steps of the honorary guard of the Komsomol-Pioneer Post Nomer 1 resound. Young Novorossians in a sailor's uniform and with automatic guns in their hands stand guard over the holy memory of [the events that unfolded on] Hero Square."[83]

Figure 5.1. Soviet honorary guard in front of the eternal flame in Hero Square. No copyright, Soviet source

For all its trees and solemn architecture, Hero Square is not as sheltered as this description leads one to believe, as it lies right between two busy streets. Still, the ritualistic ensemble of monuments and honorary guards creates an atmosphere that is different from everyday life.

The square's goal was to ritualistically establish a direct connection with heroes, transcending time and space. Students in the honorary guard wore real uniforms and were armed with real rifles.[84] The handling of a gun, then, performatively enacted the unity of generations.

N. Borshch' insists that only the best students stood guard in Hero Square. In the first five years, 13,500 youths had served in Post Nomer 1, 360 of whom later became officers.[85] As in Tula, however, the sheer number of students manning the permanent guard makes one doubt how selective the process could have been in reality.

Some members of the postwar generation interpreted the elitism of this hero cult in a different way than it was intended. Natal'ya Grigor'eva talks about her jealousy of the students who were in the honorary guard, of which she was never part. As she was already twenty-one years old by the time Post Nomer 1 was established, she was too old to be considered. Still, in her recollection, her lack of participation was linked to something different: "It was mostly the central, city schools that took part. Children who were good at school. And we went to admire them, with so much jealousy. My school was in the hills, far away, but they were so beautifully dressed... like those that stood next to the Kremlin, I went to the mausoleum in Moscow as a child and saw the honorary guard. Our girls and boys looked just like that."[86]

The "chosen-ness" of the honorary guard, in her recollection, is defined not only by their worthiness as good students but by a vague notion of privilege linked to the difference between center and periphery. Because they stood guard over Novorossiysk's eternal flame, Grigor'eva also saw them as closer to the ritual center of the Soviet Union—Red Square. By extension, they are also higher up in the heroarchy, which Soviet citizens associated with material privilege—in Novorossiysk as well as in Tula.

This interpretation is less based on historical facts than on a projection of symbolic differences between the city center and the peripheral Mefodievka neighborhood where she grew up; archival documents as well as local historian and former Komsomol activist Sergey Novikov state that all the city's schools were called to serve Post Nomer 1.[87]

DANGEROUS GAMES IN OLD TRENCHES

The symbolic extension of Hero Square is Malaya Zemlya. The grave of Tsezar' Kunikov, the most important Novorossian war hero and leader of the landing at Malaya Zemlya, lies on Ploshchad' Geroev. Soviet-era accounts highlight that Kunikov both received military training and worked as a fitter and machinist before the war. He had already received awards for his labor heroism, before he volunteered for the Red Army, becoming a *politruk* (political instructor)—like Leonid Brezhnev, incidentally. According to official Soviet historiography, Kunikov selected an elite troop of 262 volunteers, all of whom he had fought with previously.[88]

The writer Georgiy Sokolov had commanded a reconnaissance unit on the beachhead and was wounded twice. He began writing about the battle in the late 1940s and founded an organization of Malaya Zemlya veterans in 1950.[89] His heavily embellished books did much to shape and disseminate a mythologized account of the battle. He was not the first, however. In November 1943, the Red Army newspaper *Za Kommunizm* had published a description of the heroes of Malaya Zemlya and called the battle "one of the remarkable pages of the self-sacrificing fight of the Soviet people against the German-fascist Barbarians."[90]

In Sokolov's narrative, Kunikov comes to occupy a central position. He "recounts" Kunikov's last speech before the landing: "Each one of you knows what awaits us—cold, icy water, enemy fire. It will be very hard."[91] Kunikov then said that anyone who wished could leave without shame. No one budged. One soldier suggested they take less food and more grenades and ammunition instead. Then the entire unit swore: "Going into battle, we give an oath to the Motherland that we will act quickly and daringly, not sparing our blood, which we shed drop by drop for the happiness of our people, for you, dearly beloved Motherland. Our law is and will always be only to move forward!"[92]

This account is highly problematic. The oath reproduces order 227—"Not One Step Back!" It thus has to be seen more as a ritualized declaration of loyalty to Stalin and less as an expression of the soldiers' intensions. In its Brezhnev-era retelling, the figure of Stalin is replaced by that of people and country. Considering that Sokolov's book *Malaya Zemlya* was first published in 1949, the presence of Stalinist tropes is unsurprising.

Even more dubious are Kunikov's elite "volunteers." Why would the Red Army send elite forces to a landing that was intended as a diversion? Conversely, the historian Roman Taldykin has shown that penal battalions fought at Malaya Zemlya. They, however, belonged to units that landed after Kunikov's initial three waves.[93] Still, Kseniya Shapoval points out that the commander of the landing, Kholostyakov, knew he was likely sending Kunikov's men to their deaths. This disregard of soldiers' lives was nothing out of the ordinary among wartime commanders. At least Kholostyakov had chosen an officer who did his utmost to avert a failure. According to Shapoval, Kunikov had a reputation as a "surprisingly calm and prudent" officer.[94]

Kunikov stepped on a mine on the night of February 11–12 while coordinating the evacuation of the wounded and the intake of reserves. Because of the heavy fighting, it was impossible to evacuate him to a hospital for two days. He died on February 14 and was named a Hero of the Soviet Union posthumously.[95]

The extreme odds against the success of the operation augmented Kunikov's feat. His biography was told in such a way as to illustrate the interchangeability of labor and military heroism, with the same qualities—discipline, intelligence, and initiative—serving him well in both realms. The fact that he died while evacuating wounded soldiers underlined his compassion as a commander. He thus served as an exemplary Soviet citizen for the postwar generation to emulate through labor in peacetime. His feat and its ritualized reproduction gave Kunikov an almost saintlike status.[96]

The place of his feat remained a wasteland for almost three decades. Located outside the city center, the landscape was full of duds, half-destroyed bunkers, rusting military equipment, and bones. Malaya Zemlya was a dangerous place. Vladimir Gusev tragically lost his brother there in 1944. According to him, there were warning signs, but his brother, who was ten years old, could not read. "He stepped on a mine (*podorvalsya na mine*). It so happened that a scrap cut a vein. He was alive; he lived through all of it. No organs were injured. But he bled to death. There was no one there. So no one came to get him."[97] Natal'ya Grigor'eva's grandmother would tell stories about how the earth would turn red from all the blood in it when it rained.[98]

As the city was repopulated, Malaya Zemlya appears to have almost magically attracted children and youth with its mix of adventure and terror. Teenagers who were mobilized for reconstruction would meet on the edge of town because there were no adults. As the areas were not yet cleared of mines, many accidents occurred.[99] Galina Bozhok used to go out to Malaya Zemlya with her father, who was a fisherman and sought a quiet spot. She said: "The trenches always astounded (*porazhali*) me. My brother was older than us, and he and his friends always went out to dig for ammunition.... And I look at it now, and there are houses and all, and I compare that to my childhood impressions. There were the trenches. And so many spent shells, there was all of that. We saw all of this with our own eyes."[100]

Little Land still resembled a battlefield in the 1950s and 1960s. Bozhok also mentions that her brother would go out to "dig for ammunition." This appears to have been a veritable sport and a rite of passage in many cities, and also in Tula and Novorossiysk. Along the former front lines, the earth was filled with old weapons and ammunition.

The main motivation for the dangerous activity was adventure and boredom: "What were we supposed to do? We had nothing else to do," explains Georgiy Shcherbakov. "We just needed ammunition."[101] The fun thing to do with the ammunition, apparently, was to put it on a bonfire and watch it explode. Shcherbakov, like many others, had friends who lost fingers and eyes during these adventures, although deaths appear to have been rare. Shcherbakov nevertheless insists that they were not scared—except when they found soldiers' bones.[102]

Lyudmila Dorosh tells an even more adventurous and dangerous story about Vasil'evka, a village north of Malaya Zemlya. She and her friends would go on "tours" (*pokhody*), as she calls them—albeit not those that the authorities sanctioned. One day they found the remnants of a German bunker—"with a uniform and a biscuit. It was still whole, and you could even eat it."[103] They dug around some more but then got tired and decided to go back another time.

When they did, some weeks or months later, the ground had shifted, so they lost their bearing. Suddenly, they stumbled upon a large aerial bomb.

"We carried it, laid it on the bonfire (*koster*), burnt it, and just barely managed to run away. There was such an explosion! For about five minutes, shreds were flying through the air, there was this howling sound, black smoke. We were in this trench—some trench from the war that had remained—into which we had jumped. I remember thinking, 'Dear Mama, how do people manage to remain alive during a war?'"[104]

After they had recovered from the initial shock, they approached the fire and saw that, not far away, a woman was standing with two children. There was a house nearby, and Dorosh realized how foolishly they had acted. She does not elaborate on whether the authorities noticed the explosion, which would seem likely.

On the one hand, these games were and are typical for teenagers testing boundaries and enjoying the allure of the forbidden. On the other hand, they illustrate how omnipresent the war and its traces were in the lives of the postwar generation. As Pioneers and Komsomol members, they were constantly reminded of it through rituals, speeches, and meetings with veterans. In their semi-illicit games, they experienced the proximity of the war in a less mediated manner.

For Dorosh, the terrifying experience of the bomb blast provided an emotional approximation of the wartime situations that her parents had gone through. These games were, then, a rebellious, youthful, possibly alcohol-infused interpretation of official war memory. The scarred and dangerous postwar landscape of Malaya Zemlya is perhaps a much more suitable metaphor for the war's presence than the smooth landscape of official commemoration that would be created in Novorossiysk during the Brezhnev era.

The lack of supervision, with parents working and then participating in state-sponsored societal organizations in their free time, enabled this youthful foolishness. Sergey Tsymbal's mother, however, was at home to make sure he stayed out of trouble. He remembers the shell craters at Malaya Zemlya in the 1950s: "The boys rode their bicycles around the holes and played catch. There were so many shells, and so many children and also adults set off mines, because this was outside of the city.... After I had gone there with my bicycle, my mama beat me so hard that I never went there again in my life! Because all parents were scared that their child would go there and get blown up."[105]

The mother's violent reaction illustrates how perilous Malaya Zemlya was. Natal'ya Grigor'eva was also kept under close observation by her grandmother, who would not let her play in dangerous areas.

Still, the lines between official and illicit exploration were sometimes blurry. Just as everywhere in the Soviet Union, the Tours to the Sites of Revolutionary,

Military, and Labor Glory took place in Krasnodar Kray. According to the Komsomol archives, more than forty-three thousand of them had been organized there by 1977, with millions of participants.[106] Novorossiysk was one of the primary destinations. Thus, students also spent time digging in Malaya Zemlya under official instruction, as Galina Bozhok confirms: "We were not allowed to dig that deep. We were also constantly under surveillance by the teachers so we would not dig up any live shells. They told us that we were only allowed to take ammunition (*patrony*), some metal, 'but please, nothing big, if you find that, go to the side and tell the teacher!' That is how they warned us; safety techniques were always observed."[107]

It seems that the search for bigger ammunition would not have felt like a significant transgression. Moreover, Komsomol brigades were also regularly sent out to gather metal with which to finance their activities. Particularly on the edge of town, the easiest places to get large amounts of scrap metal were the former battlefields.[108]

COMMEMORATING MALAYA ZEMLYA

Malaya Zemlya was also a wasteland in terms of war monuments: no plaque or sculpture reminded people of its history. By the late 1950s and early 1960s, however, veterans of the battle had begun to advocate for more conscious and prominent commemoration. The driving forces were Georgiy Kholostyakov and the writer Georgiy Sokolov.

They used the twentieth anniversary of the beachhead's establishment to lobby the Soviet leadership for a monument. In 1962, Kholostyakov, Sokolov, and Admiral Filipp Oktyabr'skiy, commander of the landing operations in February 1943, had already pointed out Malaya Zemlya's crucial importance for the subsequent breakthrough at the "Blue Line" in a letter.[109]

Even though thousands of veterans and excursionists traveled there every year, the men remarked, "there are no travel guides on Malaya Zemlya, no one tells people about the battles that took place there, no particular place exists, like Sapun-Gore in Sevastopol', Mamaev Kurgan in Stalingrad, and Brest Fortress." The letter's authors thus compared Malaya Zemlya to the key battles of the war, at around the same time as the writer and television presenter Sergey Smirnov mentioned earlier—a significance that would be further inflated in Brezhnev-era historiography.[110]

The letter was possibly addressed to the authorities of Krasnodar Kray, although this is not clear from the available material. Either way, it does not appear to have produced any results, given that Sokolov wrote another one on January 29, 1963, this time directly to Leonid Brezhnev, then chairman of the Presidium of the Supreme Soviet USSR. Sokolov begins by claiming to have received a letter from Malaya Zemlya veterans, in which they showed themselves "outraged" (*vozmuzhen*) by the absence of a monument. He had turned to the Kray authorities with his request but had been met by a "wall of indifference." He writes: "Dear Leonid Il'ich! You were a front soldier (*frontovik*), a 'Malozemelets.' And Nikita Sergeevich [Khrushchev] was a front soldier. Why do you pay so little attention to monuments for the Great Patriotic War?"[111]

Sokolov clearly wanted to shame Brezhnev. Even though he does not use the word, he indicates that the lack of a monument is *unworthy* of the great significance of Malaya Zemlya. Once more, we see how negotiations for symbolic recognition were clothed in politically correct language for lobbying purposes. The strategy apparently worked. On February 7, Brezhnev forwarded the letter to the First Secretary of the Krasnodar Kraykom, Georgiy Vorob'ev. Vorob'ev assured Brezhnev that the "necessary measures," including possibly a monument at Malaya Zemlya, would be taken by the anniversary of the city's liberation in September.[112] As in Tula, anniversaries played an important role for such measures.

On September 16, 1963, a stela was indeed opened, nine meters tall and made of reinforced concrete. Its text read: "On 4 February 1943 the sailors of the Black Sea Fleet and the soldiers of the North-Caucasian Front landed on these frontlines. The heroic Soviet sailors and soldiers held the bridgehead, which they called Little Land, for 225 days. From here began the decisive storm on the positions of the Hitlerite occupiers, which ended in their expulsion from the city on 16 September 1943. Glory to the defenders of Novorossiysk."

The text on the stela maintains the central importance of Malaya Zemlya. Figure 5.2 depicts its carefully arranged surroundings. It stands about one hundred meters from the shoreline, on a concrete pedestal. Steps lead up to it from all four sides. The carefully crafted, smooth surface of the monument starkly contrasts with the trenches and dugouts, which still today form an uneven, wild landscape. The lush vegetation planted around the stela provides an additional counterpoint to the scars of war.

The image visually arranges the continuity of generations. The weather is clearly warm and sunny; people wear light clothes. In the foreground, a young family appears with a child. Presumably, some are vacationers; others have come to pay tribute. Below the stela, somebody has laid down flowers. The picture shows that tourism was an important aspect of Malaya Zemlya's usage. However, the wreath seems to show that it was a "rational" kind of tourism, in

ГОРОД-ГЕРОЙ НОВОРОССИЙСК

Figure 5.2. The stela for the defenders of Malaya Zemlya in Brezhnev-era Novorossiysk. No copyright, Soviet source

keeping with *turizm*, which showed reverence for the fallen heroes of the Great Patriotic War.[113]

Because of its location on the Black Sea, Novorossiysk was in the midst of a tourist area that experienced a veritable boom in the 1960s and 1970s. Sochi, but also smaller *kurorty* (spa towns) in Novorossiysk's immediate vicinity, like Gelendzhik and Anapa, developed rapidly; although there were 140,000 tourists in 1959, this number had quadrupled to 600,000 in 1966. In 1972, 4.5 million people had visited Krasnodar Kray.[114] Because Novorossiysk's heavy industry and busy port did not predestine it for tourism, large hotels were only built in the second half of the 1970s, presumably to handle the sheer mass of visitors. Until then, most excursions to Novorossiysk, which was on all major tourism routes, had departed from other cities.

Itineraries were standardized and developed by the Central Soviet for Tourism, in collaboration with Kray- and Oblast'-level suborganizations. "Around the Caucasus" (*Vokrug Kavkaza*), one of the most frequented routes, was opened in 1963. It departed and ended in Sochi. In eighteen days, tourists traveled to Gelendzhik and Novorossiysk along the Black Sea coast. They then ventured inland to Krasnodar and the Georgian capital, Tbilisi, to return to Sochi along the shoreline through Sukhumi. In Novorossiysk, tourists went on a city tour by bus.[115] Organizers praised the Caucasus's attractions, as in a May 1969 report by the Krasnodar Kray Soviet for Tourism and Excursions: "The rich nature of the Northern Caucasus, the Caucasus State Nature Reserve, the many unique parks, the historical and cultural monuments, legendary Malaya Zemlya, the gigantic achievements of the Soviet people in transforming the *kurorty* of the Black Sea coast—all of this exerts a great compelling force and contributes to the patriotic education of the Soviet people."[116]

By then Malaya Zemlya was one of the central attractions of the entire Caucasus region, which attests to its prominence as a symbol of the Soviet victory and a tourist destination. Buses always stopped at Malaya Zemlya. Visitors were also shown the Line of Defense and Hero Square. Tourists on the All-Union Route 81 from Krasnodar to Ashe stayed in the resort town of Kabardinka, a few miles southeast of Novorossiysk, for six days. In this time, they visited "heroic Malaya Zemlya, Hero Square, the museum of local history and diorama," according to a description by the Krasnodar Tourism Soviet. Many other routes featured the same program.[117]

In 1973, when Novorossiysk became a Hero City, more than 265,000 tourists visited. During high season, the city hosted 5,500 guests daily.[118] The

Novorossiysk Bureau for Travel and Excursions not only handled all the tourists but also sent guides out to schools to give lectures on the city's patriotic past. After 1973, the number of tourists increased by 50 percent—within only five years.[119] New excursions were added, such as "Novorossiysk: Hero City," "Through the Memorials of Novorossiysk," "Heroes and Feats," and "Malaya Zemlya: Legendary Bridgehead of Courage."[120]

The connection to the award is clear—and the city stands in marked contrast to Tula, where archival evidence provides no indication of a tourism boom, in spite of the fact that Tula is close to popular routes, such as the Golden Ring around Moscow. A city's position in the heroarchy was thus only one of multiple factors that determined whether it was considered suited for tourist development.

Novorossiysk was also a destination for excursions to places of military glory. Figures 5.3 and 5.4 are from a 1978 "operation" for cadets from Kiev. The cadets traveled from their hometown to Odessa, Sevastopol', Feodosiya, and Novorossiysk. As part of their training, they also practiced landing operations.[121]

The captions to these pictures read: "Landing on 'Malaya Zemlya': The second wave of young guardsmen attacks" and "Young Navy infantrymen brigade after the landing on Malaya Zemlya." The young "troops" emulated their predecessors, attacking in successive waves like the original heroes of Malaya Zemlya. The preserved trenches added to the authenticity. Once the "fight" was over, the cadets marched by the stela erected in honor of their forefathers, orderly and solemnly, in a "worthy" fashion. After the reenactment, it appears that this ritual march reestablished temporal difference, as a kind of transition back to the present. At the same time, it reinforced the notion that the youngsters were marching on graves, symbolized by the stela.

Novorossians' new status gave them opportunities for travel. In 1974, for instance, a new patriotic train trip to the "constellation of cities" (*sozvezdie gorodov*)—to the Hero Cities of Ukraine and to Volgograd—was added. More than forty-five hundred students, workers, and veterans took this and similar excursions in the same year. The participating classes had spent months studying the history of the Hero Cities and exchanging letters with schools in Kerch', Sevastopol', Odessa, and Kiev.[122]

Participants were reminded that they were "tourists from the Hero City of Novorossiysk, and we fulfill the citizen's 'mandate' (*nakaz*) of the city of Novorossiysk through our behavior in all cities."[123] This mandate was used in tourism and in the workplace.[124] The mandate conveys the obligation to study and work well, to be true to the cause of communism[125]—and to show oneself worthy of citizenship in the Hero City when traveling. Rather than simply

Figure 5.3. Youngsters on an "invasion" of Malaya Zemlya in 1978. Courtesy of the Russian State Archive of Socio-Political History

enjoying themselves, young Novorossians had to represent the best sides of their city during their travels.

Judging the popularity of these patriotic excursions is difficult. Clearly there existed a tension between the desire of Soviet citizens to simply relax at the seaside and the tourist authorities' intention of providing *turizm*. The problem of "wild tourism"—independently organized trips in cars and with tents—preoccupied state experts for decades.[126]

Tourists often complained about the quality of trips to Novorossiysk, but there was only one suggestion to delete the excursion.[127] Most problems were linked to transport and the low level of customer service. One traveler noted that the buses were dirty. "The drivers do not behave respectably. They curse, do not fulfill the demands of the guides and do not prepare their vehicles beforehand."[128] Clearly, this comportment was miles away from the propagated ideal of cultured travel.

More specific to Novorossiysk were complaints about the quality of the excursions. As the city lies in a narrow valley between mountains and the sea,

Figure 5.4. "Young Navy infantrymen on Malaya Zemlya."
Courtesy of the Russian State Archive of Socio-Political History

there is little room for transport. All the tours followed the same main route, which led to congestion and delays, while groups waited their turns. A guide complained that the excursions were repetitive.[129] More damning was his complaint that the main attraction, Malaya Zemlya, was boring. He bemoaned the "absence of good exhibition objects" because the stela remained the only monument.[130]

THE RITUAL OF THE SAILOR'S HAT

Tourists' complaints about the emptiness of Malaya Zemlya did not necessarily coincide with the perceptions of the local population. The absence of an official program of commemoration at Malaya Zemlya gave other social practices room to emerge, not in opposition to official war memory, but at least partially autonomous from it.

The most prominent was *Beskozyrka*. It evolved from a literary club called *Shkhuna Rovesnikov* (Schooner of Peers) founded by local journalist Konstantin Podyma. On November 1, 1965, "the captain of the Shkhuna Rovesnikov, K. Podyma," appealed to "boys and girls, romantics, dreamers, fidgets!" to join up. There was only one rule: "We do not take those aboard that are indifferent." Various youths began to meet at *Novorossiyskiy Rabochiy* every Monday to produce one page of the newspaper. They wrote poems, drew pictures, and collected photographs. The goal, according to local historian Raisa Sokolova, was to "get to know the truth about the war, the one 'you do not learn in school.'"[131]

Browsing the pages of Shkhuna Rovesnikov, one does not get the impression that it differed from official war memory; the same hero stories are told, while other, unknown wartime episodes are discovered—incidents that nevertheless fit the heroic template of heroism, self-sacrifice, and loyalty to the fatherland. It appears that Podyma's originality lay less in his views than in his initiatives.

Tamara Yurina was well acquainted with him. She says that Podyma's activism drove the Komsomol *nomenklatura* mad and recounts an amusing episode that she heard from the former Third Secretary of the Komsomol Gorkom, Tatyana Mitina. One day Podyma ran into her office, telling her that he had ordered a steamship for an excursion and that it was on its way to Novorossiysk's port. Because of his good relations with officials, he never got into trouble, but his organization was highly unusual, Yurina maintains: "The Gorkom Komsomol had nothing to do with this campaign. It was all done by Shkhuna Rovesnikov, an organization that existed in parallel to it. . . . Of course they knew what Shkhuna did, they tolerated and tried to support it, but according to the traditions of that time, all initiatives were supposed to come from official organizations and be approved by the party. But here, everything worked from the bottom up. This was a completely unique phenomenon."[132]

Podyma's masterpiece was to follow on the twenty-fifth anniversary of the landing at Malaya Zemlya. He organized twenty-two young men to gather secretly at 1:30 a.m. on February 4, 1968, at Hero Square. Podyma had invited a veteran, the former nurse Elena Ostapenko, to light the boys' homemade torches from the eternal flame. The men began to march quietly toward Malaya Zemlya. There, they released a single sailor's hat into the water, accompanied by flowers.[133]

The ritual caused a big stir among officials.[134] There were good reasons to be skeptical of such an undertaking, which involved considerable risks. According to one of the earliest members of Shkhuna Rovesnikov, Tatyana Prokopenko, the girls in the group were scared and did not join the boys in the first year: "Go to Stanichka [on Malaya Zemlya] at night? . . . This is where the *marshrutka* line ended. And further on—nothing but trenches from the war."[135] The area still had an unsafe reputation.

Still, the ritual "took roots," as Sviderskiy puts it. After a brief ban in 1969, it was quickly reinstated.[136] In 1970 there were already a few thousand participants. In the following years, the Komsomol increasingly appropriated the grassroots initiative—a mechanism familiar from the Timurov movement during the war.[137] It became an "All-Union event" (*vsesoyuznaya aktsiya*) in the 1970s, with honorary guests from all over the USSR. New elements were added: troop carriers brought the eternal flame, and groups reenacted the landing. In 1978, veterans from Tsezar' Kunikov's units took an oath with members of the postwar generation to serve their country. In the late 1970s, winners of socialist competitions began to participate.[138]

Most of my interview partners have participated in Beskozyrka for decades, today often with their children or grandchildren. Galina Bozhok says that she was too young to partake in the first years. In the early 1970s, the schools did not yet send their students to Beskozyrka, and she left for Kiev in 1972. Since her return, she has participated "without fail! (*obyazatel'no!*)" She is particularly touched by the newly added practice of the inhabitants who live along the route, who put candles in their windows in honor of the fallen.[139]

Georgiy Shcherbakov also considers the ritual an important part of the city's life. He likes the reenactments: "This landing in general—if you watch Beskozyrka, they sometimes stage it. Just imagine: into the cold water, then the fight, there is shooting, bombs are flying—what a nightmare."[140] For him, the reproduction of wartime events created an emotional connection, not least because the ritual takes place during the same season as the landing. In her oral history interviews with Novorossians, Davis also found that the emotional attachment to Beskozyrka is widely shared among the population.[141]

Beskozyrka, then, became part of the *pokhody* in Novorossiysk, but Podyma had arranged official war memory in a creative new way. He used the axis between Hero Square and Malaya Zemlya, which is central to the city's cultural topography, as the route for his march. The fact that Beskozyrka, unlike many other Soviet traditions, is alive and well today speaks to its adaptability. At the same time, the ritual attests to the hegemonic status of official war memory, which absorbed new moments without redefining its basic tenets.

The official memorial landscape, centered on Malaya Zemlya and Hero Square and reproduced in patriotic rituals, tourism, and monuments, does not suffice to cover the polysemy of everyday urban life. The postwar population used these spaces in their own way, through dangerous childhood games and grassroots rituals like Beskozyrka. Family history and official war memory—and also the inevitable realization that one was living on ground that was both sacred and contaminated because of the war—convened to make the memorial landscape a steady presence in Novorossiysk.

The public elevation of war memory in the Soviet Union under Leonid Brezhnev formalized this presence—and literally set it in stone: dozens of memorials were built in Novorossiysk, particularly on big anniversaries of liberation. Still, city leaders wanted a marker that was worthy of the significance they were convinced Novorossiysk had in the canon of official war memory. The scale of the monument they envisioned was such that it would be impossible to finance it without support from Moscow.

Fortunately for their ambitions, the political climate was favorable, and the construction of monuments enjoyed a high priority. On June 24, 1966, the Central Committee of the CPSU and the Council of Ministers of the USSR passed the "Plan for the construction of monuments with federal significance between 1967 and 1970." The program set off a veritable avalanche of projects, also from Novorossiysk. The Second Secretary of the Krasnodar Kraykom, Aleksandr Kachanov, and the head of the Krayispolkom, Ivan Ryazanov, proposed a new monument in a letter to the Council of Ministers on February 24, 1967.[142] The suggestion was the result of a letter from Malaya Zemlya veterans that the Novorossiysk Gorkom had forwarded to the Kray authorities.[143]

The regional rulers made their demand not only with the knowledge that federal funds were available but also with the confidence that they were representing a city in the second row of the heroarchy: on May 7, 1966, Novorossiysk had received the Order of the Patriotic War First Degree.[144] In their letter, they highlighted the impending twenty-fifth anniversary of liberation. They also pointed out Malaya Zemlya's great "educational significance for the Soviet people" who visited the city, thus emphasizing the tourism aspect. They asked for 2 million rubles for the construction of a monument and a museum.[145]

Nikolay Kuznetsov, culture minister of the RSFSR, backed the plan. On August 11, 1966, he had voiced his support for a new monument at Malaya Zemlya because of its national significance. On February 15, 1967, his deputy expressed a favorable attitude toward the project as well, referring to Novorossiysk's recent Order of the Patriotic War.[146] The Council of Ministers RSFSR, however, had the last word. Its deputy chairman, V. Kochemasov, expressed doubts about the necessity of the construction. For him, monumental ensembles in Ulyanovsk (Lenin's birth city) and Volgograd enjoyed higher priority. The project was shelved.[147] Novorossiysk did not yet have the backing and symbolic significance to elevate it into the first league.

MONUMENTAL IDEAS AND SHORTAGES

It also appears that the Union authorities were not prepared for the boom in monuments their campaign had created. By 1968, officials were complaining constantly about the flood of requests: of 260 projects in the first semester of 1969, 60 were turned down. The rest suffered from chronic cost overruns.[148] The Council of Ministers RSFSR maintained that funds were spent on unrelated projects, hinting at corruption and ordering investigations.[149]

Moreover, many projects were delayed because of a nationwide shortage of granite.[150] Additional problems included soaring prices for high-quality materials and the lack of cadres at the factories making the monuments. This led to production times of two to three years for individual orders.[151] This state of affairs persisted until at least the early 1980s.

The Novorossian authorities were not discouraged by the setback. They managed to put their monumental ensemble back on a list of projects recommended by the Council of Ministers RSFSR on October 6, 1971.[152] On February 24, 1972, the council approved construction in Malaya Zemlya and other important historical places. The Council of Ministers mandated a competition by artistic collectives. They presented ideas for four topics: "Line of Defense," "Malaya Zemlya," "Hero Square," and "Monument to the Sinking of the Black Sea Fleet."[153]

Sixteen artistic collectives submitted suggestions for the monument design. Three of them were exhibited in September 1973 at the F. E. Dzerzhinskiy

Pioneer Club.[154] The citizens of Novorossiysk got to vote for their favorite project. According to Soviet sources and my respondents, an overwhelming majority chose a design by Vladimir Tsigal'.[155] The sculptor and painter had himself served at Malaya Zemlya. Lyudmila Shalagina, a journalist who moved to Novorossiysk as a child in the 1950s, believes that the "city voted for Tsigal'."[156]

In the archives, the decision process is presented differently: as the result of evaluations by expert committees like the Artistic Expert Council for Monumental Sculpture of the Culture Ministry RSFSR and the decisions of Kray and city authorities. The public exhibition is mentioned only in passing. In May 1974, a jury approved Tsigal's project, which he implemented with the architects Yakov Belopol'skiy, Roman Kananin, and Vladimir Khavin. The Council of Ministers RSFSR gave its approval on May 15, 1975. Construction was to be completed in 1978.[157]

Vladimir Tsigal' intended three monumental ensembles: one commemorating the sunken fleet, one on the former line of defense, and one at Malaya Zemlya.[158] The initial budget from August 18, 1975, foresaw total expenses of 3.8 million rubles, including 2.299 million for Malaya Zemlya. Compared to 1967, costs had already doubled. They were to be covered by the reserve fund of the Council of Ministers.[159]

The complications and cost overruns resulted from problems with supply, oversight, and organization. According to Lyudmila Kostornova, then a city official in the cultural department, Tsigal' was charming and communicative but very inflexible when it came to his work. "It was useless to argue with him. He set a task—and asked for its fulfillment at any cost."[160] Tsigal's prioritization of artistic decisions over pragmatic and financial concerns led to problems. Still, the fact that the monument was built mostly according to Tsigal's plans attests both to Malaya Zemlya's high political priority and to his prestige as an artist and a veteran.

Tsigal's ideas for the monument at Malaya Zemlya were particularly extravagant, which meant that the problems this sculpture caused—and also the attention it received—overshadowed those of the other two ensembles. He envisioned a twenty-two-meter-tall wedge rising out of the waves to symbolize the penetration of the enemy front line. Journalists looking at the completed monument would write that it was shaped like the "nose of a huge landing vessel. . . . It seems like the landing troops are plunging into the attack right here, smashing the hated enemies on their way."[161]

The sculpture's "landing" shows six soldiers materializing from the "vessel's" left side (see fig. 5.5). On its right (pictured in fig. 5.6), reliefs depict troops coming

Figure 5.5. Monument at Malaya Zemlya with the sculpture's "landing," September 2013. © Ivo Mijnssen

out of the water. Ivan Shiyan was reminded of "knights from a fairytale (*skazochnye bogatyri*)."[162] Zen'kov and Yartsev write that, looking at the "landing," "you can feel the mass heroism of the Soviet soldiers of different ages and nationalities, united by one goal—to rout and smash the fascist beast (*gadina*)."[163]

The inside is hollow, with a semicircular corridor that features stone reliefs of Malaya Zemlya's most important heroes. A red heart that contains capsules with the names of the fallen fighters is located at the center. Because of the project's steadily rising costs, planned tourist amenities at Malaya Zemlya, such as a special train station and piers for small passenger boats, as well as additional paths and squares around the monument, were not realized.[164]

The main reason for the steadily rising costs was the location at Malaya Zemlya. As the wedge was to emerge from the waves, it had to be built right on the water. Because of Novorossiysk's climate, especially its notorious "Nordost" winds in winter, which caused storms and high waves, special measures were necessary. Moreover, the monument was built inside a protection zone—the trenches are a historical landmark—which necessitated further precautions.

Figure 5.6. Relief of landing troops emerging from the water (detail of the monument). © Ivo Mijnssen

The Council of Ministers and Ministry of Culture RSFSR, Gosplan, Kray authorities, the architects, and the sculptor weighed various options. They discarded the construction of a jetty against the waves because of its high price.[165] Culture Minister Yuriy Melent'ev thus ordered them to move the monument thirty to fifty meters away from the shore and to use reinforced concrete for the body. The additional high-quality materials and new plans led to further delays and costs.[166]

LITTLE LAND ACCORDING TO BREZHNEV

By the end of 1977, the original plan of opening the monument at Malaya Zemlya in 1978 was beyond reach—a fact that was officially admitted in June.[167] The stakes were rising. In 1978, Leonid Brezhnev's ghostwritten memoir *Malaya Zemlya* was published; the bridgehead was becoming the central symbol of official war memory in the political elite—bypassing even Stalingrad and Leningrad in terms of propagandistic attention.

The circle around Brezhnev developed the idea for the book en route to awarding Tula the honorary title of Hero City in January 1977—a surprising connection between the two Hero Cities in this book. While there is disagreement about the details of authorship, Leonid Zamyatin, the director general of the official news agency TASS, penned the final version. Brezhnev was involved with comments and corrections.[168] His "autobiography" has become the epitome of the Soviet war cult's excesses. In his biography of Brezhnev, Roy Medvedev criticizes the "coarse and un-ceremonial exaggeration" of the role of the general secretary, who was presented as an important leader at Malaya Zemlya.[169]

The book's publication in February 1978 in the magazine *Novyy Mir* set off a gigantic campaign that included the second and third part (of ultimately eight) of Brezhnev's memoirs, *Vozrozhdenie* (Rebirth) and *Tselina* (Virgin Lands), in May and November of the same year. Each copy cost only 15 kopecks and was thus about four times cheaper than other heavily promoted books. Every volume had a print run of fifteen million. The actor Vyacheslav Tikhonov made an audio recording on vinyl, and *Malaya Zemlya* became part of the literature curriculum in all schools.[170] A postcard collection with a distribution of 575,000 copies was published in 1980, featuring monuments in Novorossiysk and quotes from the autobiography.[171]

All over the USSR, agitators gave tens of thousands of lectures and exhibitions. The publisher Plakat printed twenty-five thousand copies of a ready-made poster collection as templates.[172] In Novorossiysk, a big conference with political and military representatives discussed the lessons of the book, insisting that it had been sold out moments after it got to the stores and that it provided an example of how to emulate the heroic general secretary in order to serve the homeland and communist ideals.[173]

The overwrought hero worship for the aging Soviet leader invited ridicule and disbelief. That Brezhnev received the Order of Victory in 1978 appears to have cheapened the latter's value in the eyes of many, as did the fact that he won the Lenin Prize for a book everybody knew he had not written. Just three days after his death in 1982, the books were quickly removed from libraries and curricula and used as scrap paper.[174]

While Brezhnev was alive, however, the completion of the monument enjoyed the highest priority. In this case, political clout and Novorossiysk's firm position in the heroarchy created considerable pressure. By March 7, 1979, it had become clear that the plan to open the monument in time for the thirty-fifth anniversary of victory in 1980 was also failing. Construction was even partially interrupted: the sculpture's "landing" could not be completed, because of the lack of copper and bronze. With a hint of resignation, the deputy head of the Culture Ministry's Department of Culture, Art, and Publishing, A. Belyakov, concluded that the work was "unique in its complexity and scope in the practice of monument construction."[175]

On June 21, work had stopped again because the 480 tons of metal needed to build the reinforced concrete foundation had not arrived. Neither did 350 cubic meters of granite for the reliefs.[176] Essentially, monument construction had not yet really started in earnest. On March 13, 1981, the Council of Ministers had to move the opening to 1982.[177] As in preceding years, the Krayispolkom, which was responsible for the project, reported problems to the Culture Ministry, which passed the additional demands on to the Council of Ministers RSFSR. This body grudgingly approved the additional costs and delays—including reprimands from Gosplan to the lower authorities to stick to budgets and plans.

Nerves, however, were increasingly raw. The fact that the round anniversary of victory in 1980 had been missed was serious: these jubilees carried not only memorial but also political significance, especially for a highly prestigious monument like the one at Malaya Zemlya. In April 1981, a special regional council, which included the artists and the deputy minister of culture, E. Zaytsev, said at one and the same time that the artists' sketches were too extravagant and that they did not reflect the "greatness and immortality of the feat" at Malaya Zemlya. The council thus decided to eliminate granite plaques and mosaics on walls and ceilings. Instead, it added twenty-six reliefs of the Heroes of the Soviet Union who had fought at Malaya Zemlya, including Brezhnev (see fig. 5.7).[178] Quotes from his autobiography were added in various places.

This concession to the general secretary's personality cult further complicated the finalization of the project and led to a blame game between Tsigal' and the Krayispolkom.

In June, the authors' collective wrote a letter to deputy chairman V. Kochemasov, in which it expressed its great concern over the slow progress, the many missed deadlines, and the lack of materials. Tsigal' and his colleagues bemoaned that the final decision on the interior design was being dragged out, even though they had submitted their revised plans. They finished their letter with a denunciation: "This monument, which is dedicated to heroic 'Malaya Zemlya' and connected to the work (*deyatel'nost'*) of comrade Leonid Il'ich Brezhnev, General Secretary of the CC CPSU and Chairman of the Presidium

Figure 5.7. Inside of the monument, with the relief of Leonid Brezhnev (*right*).
© Ivo Mijnssen

of the Supreme Soviet, also has huge political significance. For the operative decision about all questions arising in the final stage of construction, it would be expedient to establish a staff under the Council of Ministers RSFSR because the direction that exists in Novorossiysk is not capable of handling the scale of the tasks at hand—in spite of its decision authority."[179]

The reference to Brezhnev and the political significance of the monument served as a warning to the Krayispolkom. The denunciation appears to have succeeded: the head of the Krayispolkom, Georgiy Razumovskiy, lost his post in the same month the letter was sent. The timing is striking. Razumovskiy's successor, Nikolay Golub', was a close associate of the Kraykom's powerful First Secretary, Sergey Medunov, and Razumovskiy was an opponent.

Medunov, who had built a veritable fiefdom in the region, was fighting for his political survival at the time. Yuriy Andropov, the chairman of the KGB, had targeted the mafia-like structures surrounding Medunov to set an example in his anti-corruption campaign and to position himself in the struggle for Brezhnev's succession.[180] As long as Brezhnev was still alive, however, he protected Medunov, and the first attempts to attack him through corruption charges in the resort town Sochi in the late 1970s backfired.

In 1981, it appears, the Kraykom First Secretary went on the attack against his intra-party opponents, using the problems in Novorossiysk's monument construction against them. Tsigal's letter, a copy of which was addressed to Medunov, most likely served as ammunition against Razumovskiy; former Politburo member Egor Ligachev writes in his memoirs that Razumovskiy asked to be transferred so he would not have to work with his rival anymore.[181] The Krayispolkom was made responsible for the bulk of the problems and was forced to transfer an additional 150,000 rubles of its own reserves—from health care funds—to make up for the deficit.[182]

Subsequently, the completion of the monument went comparatively smoothly, presumably thanks to the time-tried Soviet practice of "rushing" to attain plan goals. The monument was finished in 1982. Its final costs, judging from the last available budget in 1981, were over 8 million rubles—more than four times the originally planned amount—and sixty times the costs of Tula's Victory Square monument.[183]

COMPLETING THE MEMORIAL LANDSCAPE

Medunov's victory was nevertheless short-lived. The weaker Brezhnev got, the less he was able to protect Medunov. Andropov, assisted by Mikhail Gorbachev, then First Secretary of the neighboring Stavropol'skiy Kray, removed Medunov from office on July 23, 1982, only months before the general secretary's death.[184] In 1983, Razumovskiy would take Medunov's place. When the monument was opened in a grand ceremony on September 16, 1982, Medunov was not present. The frail general secretary was also unable to attend but sent his best wishes by telegram to the 120 guests of honor.

The organizers used the various monuments' significance to geographically reinforce the unity of revolutionary, military, and labor traditions. Already at eight o'clock in the morning, silent meetings were held to honor the fallen throughout the city. They followed Novorossiysk's memorial axis.

The political leadership then assembled at the Lenin monument in front of city hall and boarded buses to the *Line of Defense*. This monument, opened on the thirty-fifth anniversary of liberation on September 16, 1978, symbolized not only the Germans' farthest advance but also the link between war and labor. The fists clasping rifles signified the front line, while the factory in the background, canonized already in 1925 in Fedor Gladkov's novel *Tsement*, reinforced the imagery of the "concrete defenders," the human equivalent of the "impregnable fortress."[185] This objectification of humans could be considered the counterpart to the anthropomorphization of the Hero City. The connection between "military and labor traditions" expressed in the ensemble was crucial to any commemorative event.

By 4:00 p.m., the cortege had moved to Malaya Zemlya. A troop carrier, escorted by an honorary guard, a veteran, and a carrier of the Order of Lenin, brought the city's banner, which was adorned with the Golden Star.[186] Malaya Zemlya's territory had been outfitted with flags. The leaders stepped onto a podium in front of the portraits of Lenin, Brezhnev, and members of the Politburo.

The First Secretaries of the Gorkom and the Kraykom, Yuriy Zhurkin and Medunov's successor, Vitaliy Vorotnikov, both thanked Brezhnev.[187] Vorotnikov even claimed that the monument had been built on Brezhnev's initiative. He then read Brezhnev's telegram, which was greeted with "tempestuous applause," according to *Pravda*:[188] "It embodies the indestructible bond of generations—the fighters for the great cause of Communism—and glorifies those that defended the right of our people to freedom, independence and a happy life during the fiery days of the Revolution and the terrible days of the Great Patriotic War."[189]

Vorotnikov opened the monument. The honorary guard marched past him, and the hymn of the Soviet Union and a salute followed. Then the monument was made accessible to the population, which laid down wreaths and flowers. Novorossians acknowledge no memories of the opening; this was an official affair of the Communist Party and its honoraries, just as Tula's Hero City award celebration had been. However, this lack of memory does not keep them from visiting the monument and expressing their pride in it.

The opening signified the completion of Novorossiysk's idealized memorial landscape, the creation of which had lasted almost the entire Brezhnev era. For its construction, no efforts or expenses were spared—even in the late 1970s, when the economy had become stagnant. The fact that it was completed nevertheless illustrates Novorossiysk's and Malaya Zemlya's towering position in official war memory—on par with ensembles in Volgograd, Brest Fortress, and Leningrad.

NOTES

1. Kinelev and Medvedev, *Goroda-geroi Chernomor'ya*.
2. Davis, *Myth Making in the Soviet Union and Modern Russia*, 178.
3. Zaytsev, *Memorial'nye Ansambli v Gorodakh-Geroyakh*, 196.

4. For example, during a meeting of the Kuban region's architects, artists, and sculptors in 1974. *Gosudarstvennyy Arkhiv Krasnodarskogo Kraya* (GAKK), f. R-1792, op. 1, d. 35, l. 4.

5. Steven Maddox describes a similar strategy of uniting commemoration and restoring the necessities of everyday life in urban space for postwar Leningrad. Maddox, *Saving Stalin's Imperial City*, 69.

6. German archival sources document losses of 1.3 million. Overmans, "Menschenverluste der Wehrmacht an der 'Ostfront,'" accessed September 15, 2020. Post-Soviet research, based on declassified field reports, estimated irretrievable Soviet losses at 4.65 million men between June 1941 and 1942. Krivosheev, *Soviet Casualties and Combat Losses*, 89.

7. Yurina, *Novorossiyskoe Protivostoyanie*, 90–91.

8. Rauh, *Geschichte des Zweiten Weltkriegs*, 111.

9. Boog et al., *Das Deutsche Reich und der Zweite Weltkrieg*, 1095–96.

10. Boog and his coauthors call the fragmentation of forces "disastrous." Boog et al., 1099.

11. Tieke, *Caucasus and the Oil*, 95.

12. Vladimir Gusev, interview with the author, Novorossiysk, September 25, 2013, 1.51 min. Gusev worked as an engineer in a refrigerator factory.

13. Gusev, interview, 2.22 min.

14. Gusev, interview, 4.01 min.

15. DeGraffenried, *Sacrificing Childhood*, 170.

16. Natal'ya Grigor'eva, interview with the author, Novorossiysk, September 23, 2013, 5.22 min. She repeatedly burst into tears during our conversation. Because of her family's experiences, the war remains emotionally charged for her. Since the Brezhnev era, she has worked as a saleslady: "I always just wanted to be a saleslady." Grigor'eva, interview, 67.09 min.

17. Shiyan, *Novorossiysk*, 48. On July 2, 1942, alone, sixty-four German planes dropped 170 bombs on Novorossiysk, killing more than a hundred sailors. The head of the port's radiolocation was shot on Stalin's order. Yurina, *Novorossiyskoe Protivostoyanie*, 91.

18. Moré, "Die unbewusste Weitergabe von Traumata und Schuldverstrickungen an nachfolgende Generationen," 26.

19. Including Zav'yalov and Kalyadin, *Bitva za Kavkaz*; Kirin, *Chernomorskiy Flot v Bitve za Kavkaz*. For a detailed overview of Soviet historiography, see the introduction in Yurina, *Novorossiyskoe Protivostoyanie*, 9–54.

20. Shiyan, *Novorossiysk*, 34. The order forbade commanders from retreating without orders. It also created penal battalions (*shtrafbat*) and barrier troops (*shtrafnoy battalion*) to stop retreating soldiers. Merridale cites estimates that 158,000 Red Army members were sentenced to death. Merridale, *Ivan's War*, 157.

21. Shiyan, *Novorossiysk*, 36–37.

22. Shiyan, *Novorossiysk*, 22.
23. Shiyan, *Novorossiysk*, 38.
24. Yurina, *Novorossiyskoe Protivostoyanie*, 68. Lavrentiy Beriya traveled to Sukhumi on August 23 to oversee the reorganization and the purges. Shirokorad, *Bitva za Chernoe More*, 450.
25. Yurina, *Novorossiyskoe Protivostoyanie*, 77–78, 96. Among them were 1,967 tons of industrial materials, 5,501 civilians, and 6,520 soldiers, of which 1,400 were wounded. Shirokorad, *Bitva za Chernoe More*, 447–49.
26. Yurina, *Novorossiyskoe Protivostoyanie*, 84.
27. Sovetskoe Informatsyonnoe Buro, "Operativnaya Svodka za 11 Sentyabrya," accessed September 15, 2020.
28. The battalion that held the Proletariy factory was cut off from the Soviet command and formed spontaneously from the remnants of other units. They only received reinforcements after days of fighting in isolation. Beredin, *Malaya Zemlya*.
29. Boog et al., *Das Deutsche Reich und der Zweite Weltkrieg*, 936.
30. Schönherr, "IV. Der Rückzug der Heeresgruppe A über die Krim bis Rumänien," 451, 456.
31. Yurina, *Novorossiyskoe Protivostoyanie*, 201–2.
32. Saneev, "Golubaya Liniya," 68. By early 1943, about four hundred thousand troops were concentrated in the Kuban bridgehead and Crimea. Schönherr, "IV. Der Rückzug der Heeresgruppe A über die Krim bis Rumänien," 452.
33. For a detailed account of the ill-fated landing, see Yurina, *Novorossiyskoe Protivostoyanie*, 202–28; Shiyan, *Novorossiysk*, 77–80; Tieke, *Caucasus and the Oil*, 329–35. Fewer than 200 Soviet soldiers managed to fight their way through to the Soviet lines; 594 were taken prisoner, and at least 620 died. Recent research by Novorossiysk historian Evgeniy Lapin only lists 58 soldiers who broke through. Lapin, "Byl li Predan Otchayannyy Desant?"
34. See the account of the battle by one of its participants, Egor Larikov, who was wounded eight times while at Malaya Zemlya. Quoted in Kolesov, *V Pamyati i v Serdtse*, 44.
35. By February 9, seventeen thousand men had landed. Yurina, *Novorossiyskoe Protivostoyanie*, 244–45.
36. Like many such symbolic numbers in official Soviet historiography, their veracity is questionable. It is beyond doubt, however, that Malaya Zemlya was one of the battlefields that experienced the most concentrated military action in a very small space. Grigor'evich, *Gorod-Geroy Novorossiysk*.
37. Yurina, *Novorossiyskoe Protivostoyanie*, 260.
38. Kutuzov et al., *Goroda-Geroi Velikoy Otechestvennoy Voyny*, 59.
39. Turchin, "O Zverstvakh Nemetsko-Fashistskikh Zakhvatchikov i ikh Soobshchnikov v Okkupirovannom Novorossiyske," 144.

40. *Gosudarstvennyy Arkhiv Rossiyskoy Federatsii* (GARF), f. R-7021, op. 148, d. 61, l. 2; d. 62, ll. 3–4. Yurina, *Novorossiyskoe Protivostoyanie*, 315.
41. Gusev, interview, 20.31 min.
42. Natal'ya Grigor'eva, interview, 6.09 min.
43. Georgiy Shcherbakov, interview with the author, Novorossiysk, September 20, 2013, 16.54 min. Shcherbakov was born in Novorossiysk on May 26, 1957. His parents met while his father was working in the Urals. The family waited for decent housing in Novorossiysk for almost thirty years because the state railroads were not among the privileged enterprises. Georgiy Shcherbakov moved to the far-northern city of Chukotka in 1980. There, he worked as an engineer in a gold-mining company. He was an active Komsomol member but never joined the Communist Party. "It was one thing to be a patriot but another to be a Communist. If you wanted to join the Party, you had to be a real Communist. I was not such a person." Shcherbakov, interview, 63.30 min.
44. Sergey Novikov, email message to author, March 4, 2019.
45. Valeriy Sviderskiy, interview with the author, Novorossiysk, September 23, 2013, 12.46 min. Sviderskiy, a lawyer, is proud that his family has lived in Novorossiysk since 1888—with some interruptions. The low prestige and pay of the legal profession during the Brezhnev era made it difficult for him to feed his family. Judging from his office, he has done well in the port city in the post-Soviet period—not least because maritime law is his specialty.
46. Burik, "Byvshie Sovetskie Plennye na Vosstanovlenii Novorossiyska," 218.
47. Burik, "Byvshie Sovetskie Plennye na Vosstanovlenii Novorossiyska," 219–20.
48. Gusev, interview, 79.42 min. Single mothers were especially vulnerable to poverty in the immediate postwar era. Jeffrey W. Jones, *Everyday Life and the 'Reconstruction' of Soviet Russia*, 55.
49. In many areas, the CPSU conducted purges after the war to determine who had remained "loyal." Weiner, *Making Sense of War*, 85.
50. Sergey Novikov, email message to author, March 4, 2019.
51. Sviderskiy, "Divizii Vermakhta v Novorossiyske," 140.
52. Haumann, "Die Verarbeitung von Gewalt im Stalinismus am Beispiel ausgewählter Selbstzeugnisse," 386–88.
53. Sviderskiy, "Divizii Vermakhta v Novorossiyske," 142.
54. The *Einsatzgruppe D* murdered twenty-seven thousand Jews in Krasnodar Kray. Al'tman, *Kholokost na Territorii SSSR*, 661.
55. Zhurkin, *Gorod-Geroy Novorossiysk*, 203.
56. The most famous case is of course Babiy Yar, where more than thirty thousand Jews were executed in September 1941. Their identity was not mentioned after the war. The commemoration became a public issue when the city tried to build a sports stadium on the site. Protests by writers and artists led

to the cancellation of the project. On the Jewish question and the aborted efforts to create a "Black Book" of atrocities against the Jews in the USSR, see Grüner, "Die Tragödie von Babij Jar im sowjetischen Gedächtnis"; Bergman, "Soviet Dissidents on the Holocaust, Hitler and Nazism."

57. Davis, *Myth Making in the Soviet Union and Modern Russia*, 199.

58. Shiyan, *Novorossiysk*, 60.

59. Lyudmila Dorosh, interview with the author, Novorossiysk, September 21, 2013, 98.03 min. Dorosh was born on January 15, 1955, and still lives in Vasil'evka. Her family moved there in 1959. Her mother died of cancer soon after, and her father married a woman who had lived in the village during occupation. "An apartment would be the death of me," she says. Dorosh, interview, 64.10 min. Having had her first child in 1978, she lived as a single mother near Novorossiysk, working as a saleswoman in various stores.

60. Zhurkin, *Gorod-Geroy Novorossiysk*, 202–3.

61. GARF, f. R-7021, op. 148, d. 62, l. 12.

62. The real authors were the writer Aleksandr Eremenko and the editor of the local newspaper, V. Tyshenko. Zhurkin did not contribute; his name was only necessary for the book to be published by the Moscow publisher Mysl'. I am grateful to Sergey Novikov for pointing this out.

63. The descriptions can be found in Zhurkin, *Gorod-Geroy Novorossiysk*, 205–6; Shiyan, *Novorossiysk*, 60–61, 115.

64. For a post-Soviet account, see Novikov, "Podpol'e na Peredovoy."

65. Davis, *Myth Making in the Soviet Union and Modern Russia*, 204.

66. Tieke, *Caucasus and the Oil*, 365.

67. See Sivkov, "Novorossiysko-Tamanskaya Nastupatel'naya Operatsiya Krasnoy Armii."

68. On details of the battle, see Yurina, *Novorossiyskoe Protivostoyanie*, 293–98, 303.

69. Shiyan, *Novorossiysk*, 147.

70. Grechko, *Bitva za Kavkaz*, 380.

71. Shiyan, *Novorossiysk*, 155.

72. She nevertheless emphasizes "the high price" for the breakthrough, which resulted in 14,564 dead and 50,946 wounded Red Army soldiers between September 10 and October 9, 1943. Yurina, *Novorossiyskoe Protivostoyanie*, 318, 285.

73. Kaltenegger, *Gebirgsjäger im Kaukasus*, 253, 247–48. During the Cold War, it was mostly former Wehrmacht participants who wrote books about the war in the Caucasus. These are heavily slanted, however well researched. Only in the last quarter century have German historians written more objective and encompassing regional studies.

74. Rauh, *Geschichte des Zweiten Weltkriegs*, 212–13.

75. Schönherr, "IV. Der Rückzug der Heeresgruppe A über die Krim bis Rumänien," 466, 476.

76. Davis, *Myth Making in the Soviet Union and Modern Russia*, 178. One might add the village of Pervomaysk outside Tula, where Evgeniy Stepunin grew up. The fire in Pervomaysk, however, was not, strictly speaking, "eternal," as it was only lit periodically.

77. Zhurkin, *Gorod-Geroy Novorossiysk*, 300.

78. Sokolova, *Beskozyrka*, 6.

79. Zhurkin, *Gorod-Geroy Novorossiysk*, 300. Hear the song here: https://www.youtube.com/watch?v=vxQnc2kBUQY (accessed September 27, 2018). Shostakovich had composed it as an entry for a competition to write a new Soviet national anthem in 1943.

80. Tamara Yurina, interview with the author, Novorossiysk, September 18, 2013, and Krasnodar, October 9, 2013, 157.22 min. With the help of friends, the family bought a tiny house, which they later sold for a cheaper one in Malaya Zemlya. The family was settled with debt. "That built character." Yurina, interview, 145 min. Yurina became a history teacher in School 2 (named after Tsezar' Kunikov)—where she had studied herself.

81. Maddox observed this in postwar Leningrad as well. "By offering the Leningrad identity to newcomers . . . Leningrad's authorities sought to create a sense of attachment to the city that would make people sacrifice more to restore it." Maddox, *Saving Stalin's Imperial City*, 146.

82. *Rossiyskiy Gosudarstvennyy Arkhiv Sotsial'no-Politicheskoy Istorii* (RGASPI), f. M-1, op. 66, d. 707, l. 55.

83. Zhurkin, *Gorod-Geroy Novorossiysk*, 300.

84. Zhurkin, *Gorod-Geroy Novorossiysk*.

85. RGASPI, f. M-1, op. 66, d. 707, l. 53.

86. Grigor'eva, interview, 23.17 min.

87. Sergey Novikov, email message to author, October 5, 2018.

88. Shiyan, *Novorossiysk*, 81.

89. Lapin, "Malaya Zemlya Georgiya Sokolova," accessed September 27, 2018. See also Davis, *Myth Making in the Soviet Union and Modern Russia*, 53–58.

90. Al'tshul', "Malaya Zemlya."

91. Sokolov, *U Yungi tozhe Serdtse Moryaka*, 12.

92. Sokolov, *U Yungi tozhe Serdtse Moryaka*, 14.

93. Taldykin, "Iskupit' Vinu Krov'"yu."

94. Shapoval, "Bol'shaya Lozh' o 'Maloy Zemle.'"

95. Lapin, "Byl li Predan Otchayannyy Desant?," 3.

96. Nina Tumarkin traces this quasi-religious status of heroes as secular martyrs in Russia's Orthodox tradition: Tumarkin, *Living and the Dead*, 76.

97. Gusev, interview, 7.26 min.

98. Grigor'eva, interview, 6.07 min.

99. Novikov, "Strategii Vyzhivaniya Naseleniya Osvobozhdennogo g. Novorossiyska," 124.

100. Galina Bozhok, interview with the author, Novorossiysk, September 26, 2013, 16.29 min. Bozhok went to Kiev in 1972 to study and then work as an engineer. She returned to Novorossiysk after the collapse of the USSR to take care of her aging parents.

101. Shcherbakov, interview, 27.40 min, 31.30 min.

102. Shcherbakov, interview, 28.54 min.

103. Dorosh, interview, 88.13 min.

104. Dorosh, interview, 89.56 min.

105. Sergey Tsymbal, interview with the author, Novorossiysk, September 23, 2013, 6.31 min. Tsymbal was born in Novorossiysk on November 24, 1950, and grew up in one of the first houses built after the war; his grandfather worked at a cement plant. Living conditions were nonetheless cramped—with five people sharing two rooms. Tsymbal studied in Moscow to become a meat and milk specialist after his military service.

106. RGASPI, f. M-1, op. 66, d. 64, l. 155.

107. Bozhok, interview, 28.42 min.

108. Dorosh, interview, 57 min.

109. *Tsentr Dokumentatsii Noveyshey Istorii Krasnodarskogo Kraya* (TsDNIKK), f. 2, op. 1, d. 252, l. 7, quoted in Upravlenie po Delam Arkhivov Krasnodarskogo Kraya, *Stranitsy Istorii v Dokumentakh Arkhivnogo Fonda Kubani*.

110. "The significance of the bridgehead can hardly be overstated." Shiyan, *Novorossiysk*, 94.

111. TsDNIKK, f. 2, op. 1, d. 252, l. 4.

112. TsDNIKK, f. 2, op. 1, d. 252, l. 4.

113. Gorsuch and Koenker, Introduction to *Turizm*.

114. GAKK, f. R-1624, op. 1, d. 126, l. 1; d. 400, l. 2; d. 812, l. 2.

115. GAKK, f. R-1624, op. 1, d. 299, l. 65.

116. GAKK, f. R-1624, op. 1, d. 533, l. 161.

117. GAKK, f. R-1624, op. 1, d. 397, l. 50. The diorama of the battle, built in 1970, is located inside the local history museum.

118. GAKK, f. R-1624, op. 1, d. 820, ll. 38–39.

119. To 430,000. GAKK, f. R-1624, op. 2, d. 309, l. 102.

120. GAKK, f. R-1624, op. 1, d. 905, l. 3.

121. RGASPI, f. M-1, op. 66, d. 639, l. 25.

122. RGASPI, f. M-1, op. 66, d. 639, l. 28.

123. RGASPI, f. M-1, op. 66, d. 639, l. 28. Anne Gorsuch points out that the notion of behaving in a "cultured fashion" was also emphasized when Soviet tourists traveled abroad in organized groups. Gorsuch, "Time Travelers," 221.

124. Novorossiyskiy Gorodskoy Sovet Deputatov Trudyashchikhsya, *Kompleksnyy Plan Sotsial'no-Ekonomicheskogo Razvitiya g. Novorossiyska na 1976–1980 Gody*, 136.
125. Eremenko and Podyma, *Imenem Rossii Narechennyy*, 348–49.
126. Noack, "Coping with the Tourist."
127. In a book in which tourists could list their complaints and suggestions for improvement. GAKK, f. R-1624, op. 1, d. 252, l. 1. Many thanks to Christian Noack for pointing out this passage.
128. Complaint from June 19, 1976. GAKK, f. R-1624, op. 2, d. 175, l. 8.
129. GAKK, f. R-1624, op. 1, d. 905, ll. 45–46.
130. GAKK, f. R-1624, op. 1, d. 905, l. 45.
131. Sokolova, *Beskozyrka*, 7–10. Vicky Davis points out that the club was inspired by the example of a similar circle founded at the *Komsomol'skaya Pravda* in 1962. Davis, "Time and Tide," 106.
132. Yurina, interview, 128.50 min. Vicky Davis interviewed Podyma before his death in 2013. He admitted Komsomol encouragement and organizational support but insisted that the initiative had come from below. Davis, "Time and Tide," 108.
133. Eremenko and Podyma, *Imenem Rossii Narechennyy*, 349. The sailor's hat was "the symbol of the sailors' boldness, their devotion to their homeland. So many of them died valiantly here, on the shores of Novorossiysk, in their sailor's uniform and sailor's hat." Sokolov, *U Yungi tozhe Serdtse Moryaka*, 6.
134. Sviderskiy, interview, 18.33 min.
135. Quoted in Sokolova, *Beskozyrka*, 12.
136. Davis, "Time and Tide," 108.
137. DeGraffenried, *Sacrificing Childhood*, 61.
138. Shiyan, *Novorossiysk*, 167. The organizers also changed the location of the event. For a number of years, it took place at a different monument, and in the post-Soviet era, a ritual at Yuzhnaya Ozereyka was added.
139. Bozhok, interview, 30 min.
140. Shcherbakov, interview, 49.37 min.
141. Davis, *Myth Making in the Soviet Union and Modern Russia*, 149–73.
142. GARF, f. A-259, op. 45, d. 6652, l. 13.
143. TsDNIKK, f. 821, op. 14, d. 4, ll. 228, 240.
144. Andryushenko, *Novorossiysk*.
145. GARF, f. A-259, op. 45, d. 6652, ll. 14, 17.
146. GARF, f. A-501, op. 1, d. 5005, l. 78; GARF, f. A-259, op. 45, d. 6652, l. 19.
147. GARF, f. A-259, op. 45, d. 6652, l. 15.
148. GARF, f. A-259, op. 45, d. 8471, l. 36.
149. GARF, f. A-259, op. 45, d. 8471, l. 4.
150. GARF, f. A-501, op. 1, d. 5910, l. 172.

151. GARF, f. A-259, op. 46, d. 848, ll. 28–29.

152. GARF, f. A-259, op. 46, d. 848, l. 25.

153. GARF, f. A-259, op. 46, d. 5661, l. 114. The monument refers to the sinking of the Black Sea Fleet in Novorossiysk on Lenin's orders to keep it from falling into the Germans' hands as part of the peace treaty of Brest-Litovsk. In Yuriy Grigor'evich's interpretation, the fact that the sailors fulfilled Lenin's command constituted an act of loyalty to the party. Grigor'evich, *Gorod-Geroy Novorossiysk*.

154. Kislyakov, "Novorossiysku Posvyashchaetsya."

155. Zen'kov and Yartsev, "Potomkam na Pamyat'." Kislyakov, the chairman of the competition, mentions two other artistic collectives running against Tsigal's and submitting sketches. One suggested a monument for Malaya Zemlya with an obelisk at its center, and the other consisted of three gigantic figures attacking from the ocean.

156. Lyudmila Shalagina, interview with the author, Novorossiysk, September 27, 2013, 69.50 min. Shalagina was born on November 12, 1953. Her father was a career officer. When they moved to the Black Sea, she immediately "fell in love with Novorossiysk . . . and even though [she] tried to get away from [there] often, [she] always came back." Shalagina, interview, 9.32 min.

157. GARF, f. A-259, op. 46, d. 5661, ll. 107–15.

158. Tsigal's also made plans for Hero Square, but they were never implemented. The reasons are unclear.

159. GARF, f. A-259, op. 46, d. 5661, ll. 90–93.

160. Quoted in Shalagina, "Granitnyy Dozor Novorossiyska," accessed September 20, 2018.

161. Zen'kov and Yartsev, "Potomkam na Pamyat'," 3.

162. Shiyan, *Novorossiysk*, 168.

163. Zen'kov and Yartsev, "Potomkam na Pamyat'," 3.

164. GARF, f. A-259, op. 46, d. 9056, l. 35.

165. It would have cost 700,000 rubles. GARF, f. A-259, op. 46, d. 5661, l. 58.

166. By December 29, 1977, when this decision was made, the costs had already amounted to 5.431 million rubles. GARF, f. A-259, op. 46, d. 7893, l. 10; GARF, f. A-259, op. 46, d. 9065, ll. 6–7.

167. GARF, f. A-259, op. 46, d. 5661, l. 40.

168. According to Zamyatin, Chief Ideologist Mikhail Suslov was the driving force behind the project. A recent article also claims that Arkadiy Sakhnin, correspondent of the newspaper *Komsomolskaya Pravda*, was the initial author but that Brezhnev did not like the draft and had Zamyatin rework it. Filippov, "Zhivopistsy 'Maloy Zemli.'" Tamara Yurina identifies the author as Anatoliy Agranovskiy, who penned the second part of the autobiographical trilogy *Vozrozhdenie*. She also writes that Lieutenant Colonel Pakhomov's diary

served as the basis for the factual accounts in the book. Yurina, *Novorossiyskoe Protivostoyanie*, 21.

169. Medvedev, *Lichnost' Epokha*, 43.

170. Scherrer, "Siegermythos versus Vergangenheitsaufarbeitung," 644–45. Schattenberg points out that Brezhnev, whose salary as a general secretary was modest, made a lot of money from royalties—180,000 rubles. Schattenberg, *Leonid Breschnew*, 601.

171. Karavaeva, *Komplekt Otkrytok po knige L. I. Brezhneva 'Malaya Zemlya.'*

172. Chernyakhovskiy, *Al'bom-Vystavka po Knige Leonida Il'icha Brezhneva Malaya Zemlya*. The collection cost seven rubles—a low price considering its high-quality finish.

173. Pridius and Filimonov, *Bol'shaya Sud'ba Maloy Zemli*, 62.

174. Studio Galakon, *Malaya Zemlya Leonida Brezhneva*.

175. GARF, f. A-259, op. 46, d. 5661, ll. 28–29.

176. GARF, f. A-259, op. 46, d. 5661, l. 8.

177. GARF, f. A-259, op. 48, d. 3366, l. 50.

178. GARF, f. A-259, op. 48, d. 3366, ll. 45–47.

179. GARF, f. A-259, op. 48, d. 3366, ll. 41–42.

180. William Clark, *Crime and Punishment in Soviet Officialdom*, 169.

181. GARF, f. A-259, op. 46, d. 5661, ll. 42; Ligachev, *Kto Predal SSSR*.

182. GARF, f. A-259, op. 48, d. 3366, ll. 14–17.

183. GARF, f. A-259, op. 48, d. 3366, l. 39.

184. William Clark, *Crime and Punishment in Soviet Officialdom*, 170.

185. Kolesov, *V Pamyati i v Serdtse*, 23.

186. Zakiev and Yartsev, "Vchera v Novorossiyske."

187. Vorotnikov had played an important role in the campaign against Medunov, as first deputy prime minister of the RSFSR. William Clark, *Crime and Punishment in Soviet Officialdom*, 170. As the deputy head of the Council of Ministers, he was also involved in the planning of the monument at Malaya Zemlya. GARF, f. A-259, op. 48, d. 5661, l. 47.

188. Kalishevskiy and Shcheglov, "Simvol Muzhestva i Otvagi," 3.

189. "Priumnozhat' Slavnye Revolyutsionnye, Boevye i Trudovye Traditsii," 2.

SIX

Brezhnev's Beloved Novorossiysk
Wartime Glory and Window to the World

NOVOROSSIYSK WAS NAMED A HERO City on September 14, 1973. One year later, Leonid Brezhnev visited the city to award it the Gold Star and to celebrate. The event remains alive in people's memories as a turning point: "The city totally transformed itself after Leonid Il'ich's visit," says Georgiy Shcherbakov, a sober and analytical man. "Ask any native Novorossian, and they will tell you that the city would not be what it is without Brezhnev.... He had a very good influence on Novorossiysk's development."[1] Virtually all respondents shared this enthusiastic assessment, something Vicky Davis also found in her much larger-scale sample of interviewees.[2]

Novorossiysk was a boomtown in the 1960s and 1970s. Its population rose from 110,000 to almost 190,000 between 1964 and 1979. It became the new location for the civilian Black Sea Fleet and a major terminal for the oil and gas industry. What made it truly extraordinary in comparison to other developing cities was that it received thousands of new apartments as part of two special programs. These also improved the water supply and the educational and medical infrastructures.

Brezhnev's visit is a good lens through which to explore the interaction between economic development and official war memory in Novorossiysk. As in other towns, this nexus contained the question of what a Hero City was entitled to in terms of status, political prestige, and quality of life, as well as what its new obligations entailed.

In a paternalistic political system like the Brezhnev-era Soviet Union, these entitlements fundamentally depended on clientelist relations. Personal ties between Novorossiysk and Brezhnev, mediated by his adviser, the native

Novorossian Viktor Golikov, played an important role in the awarding of special development programs and the Hero City title.

Malaya Zemlya was the key to Brezhnev's relationship with the city. The territory became not only the city's main memorial place but also the primary vector for its expansion: the thousands of new apartments built on the former battlefield symbolized a return to life from the ruins of war. Malaya Zemlya thus signified Novorossiysk's wealth and the Soviet leadership's concern for the population. Commemoration, the "socialist contract," and the notion of "worthiness," however, did not coexist without tension; just as in Tula, Novorossians, regional authorities, and Moscow struggled to reconcile opposing interpretations of privilege, obligation, and entitlement.

Novorossiysk received the Hero City award in 1973, together with Kerch' on the thirtieth anniversary of the two cities' liberation. They were part of the second wave, following the first in 1965. Because of Brezhnev's personal connection to Novorossiysk and particularly to Malaya Zemlya, the general secretary viewed the naming of his "own" Hero City as a personal honor and a means of distinguishing himself from the rest of the Soviet elite.[3]

Leningrad and Stalingrad were the only other Hero Cities that were so closely associated with individual Soviet leaders. While Novorossiysk undoubtedly played an important role in the war, the connection to Brezhnev made the decisive difference in the competition with other, equally deserving cities. For Novorossiysk, war memory, which had been an important source of local identification, became inextricably tied to the general secretary's past. He had fought as a soldier on Malaya Zemlya, but his role had not featured prominently in official depictions prior to May 1966, when Novorossiysk received the Order of the Patriotic War. Subsequently, however, the general secretary's propagandistically inflated presence overshadowed other heroes in official war memory.[4]

In 1973, Brezhnev was at the peak of his power.[5] Tolerating competing "clans" in the Politburo in the 1960s, he had largely neutralized his rivals by the early 1970s, sending Petro Shelest into forced retirement and sidelining powerful figures like Aleksandr Shelepin. Since Brezhnev had overcome a challenge to his leadership in 1970 with the help of the military its influence in the Politburo grew as well, most notably with the elevation to full membership of Defense Minister Andrey Grechko.

Grechko was not only an important representative of the military establishment but also the country's "top historian." The twelve volumes of the *History of the Great Patriotic War* were written under his tutelage, closely supervised by his deputy minister, Alexey Yepishev.[6] Moreover, Grechko's own memoirs,

The Battle of the Caucasus, published in 1967, had become the canonical work on the war in the South and the battle for Novorossiysk.

Novorossiysk was an important station in both Brezhnev's and Grechko's biographies. On September 7, 1942, Grechko had replaced General Major Grigoriy Kotov as commander of the Novorossiysk Defensive Area because of the latter's inability to beat back the German assault.[7] As commander of the Fifty-Sixth Army, Grechko was subsequently heavily involved in the winter offensives and the liberation of Novorossiysk in September 1943.

Archival material shows that both men intervened directly to make Novorossiysk and Kerch' Hero Cities. On September 13, 1973, they wrote a letter to the Central Committee CPSU asking for the honorary title. Brezhnev and Grechko's request was much shorter than the complicated application process Tula had to go through. It is, unfortunately, impossible to trace the communication between the two and the city section of the Communist Party, as the files for the period are not accessible.[8] For this reason, we do not know if the request to the Central Committee was the only document or if others preceded it.[9] It is nevertheless highly likely that patronage from the most powerful person in the USSR smoothed the path to the heroarchy considerably.

My interviews provide access to some of the stories told in Novorossiysk about the decision-making. Valeriy Sviderskiy, whose father, Valentin, was a close friend of Vice Admiral Georgiy Kholostyakov's, claims that the latter, along with Brezhnev's adviser Viktor Golikov, was the main initiator of Novorossiysk's Hero City bid. This appears plausible considering Kholostyakov's central role in promoting monuments at Malaya Zemlya. Sviderskiy says that the officer often talked about struggles within the leadership, where many opposed awarding Novorossiysk the title.[10]

Sviderskiy believes that part of the opposition was personally linked to Kholostyakov, who had been arrested during the purges and who carried a bad reputation among some members of the leadership. Perhaps more significantly, there was real concern that opening the "family" of Hero Cities to further members would set off a veritable avalanche and compromise its exclusive status. Many cities could feel entitled, as there were only the vaguest parameters for determining an honoree's "worthiness." Aside from prestige, widening the heroarchy also raised economic questions, as the notion of the socialist contract continued to play an important role in the public legitimation of the Soviet regime.

In their application letter, Brezhnev and Grechko focused exclusively on Novorossiysk's and Kerch's wartime significance. They reiterated the region's strategic importance and highlighted the "supreme (*velichayshiy*) heroism, steadfastness and self-sacrifice" exhibited by the defenders of Novorossiysk in general and those of Malaya Zemlya in particular.[11] The two politicians concluded with a specific demand: "The heroic fight of the Soviet soldiers and the workers of the cities of Novorossiysk and Kerch' during the Great Patriotic War and the postwar period deserves high appreciation (*vysokaya otsenka*). In recognition of the extraordinary merits, mass heroism, courage and steadfastness in the fight against the German-fascist invaders and of the 30-year anniversary of these heroic events, we ask for the consideration of the question of whether to award to the cities of Novorossiysk and Kerch' the honorary title 'Hero City.'"[12]

With these advocates backing the claim, the Central Committee and the Presidium of the Supreme Soviet did not deliberate long. Just one day later, both cities received the award. Brezhnev and Grechko's request was a pure formality. The decision had already been made in an informal setting.

JOY TO THE HERO CITY

News of the award came as a complete surprise to all those outside a small circle of insiders. The September 15, 1973, issue of the newspaper *Novorossiyskiy Rabochiy* contains the text of the decree at the top of the front page but does not mention it anywhere else. This indicates a last-minute arrival of the news. For Tamara Yurina, the decision amounted to a "sensation" (*chudo*). "Because there had been a lot of talk about why Novorossiysk was not a Hero City. There was some discussion, but the issue appeared to be closed. There already were Hero Cities, and there would be no others.... And suddenly this decree!"[13]

Later in the day, city authorities organized a festive assembly. As was the custom with high awards, those gathered first and foremost thanked the leader personally. Brezhnev sent a letter and a telegram from Crimea lauding the significance of the city and recognizing the great losses that were the price of victory. Brezhnev wrote, "I am proud to have been its [the battle for Novorossiysk's] direct participant," and he apologized for the fact that "official circumstances" (*sluzhebnye obstoyatel'stva*) prevented him from participating in the celebrations. He continued: "The beauty of Novorossiysk, returned to life by the self-sacrificing labor of the Novorossians for the sake of our Homeland, is the best monument to those who fell gallantly at its walls.... I wish you good health, personal happiness and great successes in labor, comrades Novorossians, friends-in-arms (*boevye druz'ya*)!"[14]

That Brezhnev apologizes for his absence appears to be a break with the formalism of the rest of the letter. It can be interpreted as an expression of the personal connection he felt; there are numerous anecdotes about Brezhnev's emotionality. When they first met in Moldova in 1950, he told Golikov about how much his wartime experience in Novorossiysk had shaped him: "Victor . . . I almost died multiple times in Novorossiysk. Believe me, I went through the entire war, but my true inferno was your hometown."[15] This personal relation, as well as the notion of Novorossiysk's rise from the ashes to its contemporary beauty, would often be emphasized in official war memory.

Festivities involving the population took place on September 16. Many of my respondents do not really remember them; Brezhnev's visit one year later appears to have eclipsed them from memory. Yurina, however, had already moved away in 1974 and thus recalls the evening well: "There was the salute. . . . Beautiful stars over Tsemess Bay, people screamed 'Ura!' I don't even remember how many people there were on the shore. It was very hard to get back, all the buses were full, and people were so happy. It was very tight in the crowd . . . but everyone was smiling, people were smiling at each other. . . . There was this unity, like everybody was together, everybody was . . . it was a completely wondrous (*udivitel'nyy*) feeling."[16]

Yurina remembers the salute as the emotional climax of the holiday. She recounts a truly collective experience—crowded, not necessarily comfortable, but strangely comforting. Particularly the end of her quote is astonishing: she is clearly struggling to find words to describe her feelings. She first uses the word *unity*; then, fearing that the expression is clichéd and overused, she just leaves the description blank. It appears that this omission contains the personal and local pride Novorossians felt at the recognition. The fact that everyone was smiling in spite of the discomfort well illustrates the "completely wondrous" feeling.[17]

Yurina does not mention the official meeting or the celebration at the stadium, but *Novorossiyskiy Rabochiy* featured it all the more prominently.

Figure 6.2 shows the participants of the official public rally (*miting*) on September 16. In contrast to the night before, no one smiles. The workers are dressed in their Sunday best; many of the men have taken off their coats, and some wear sun hats. They seem to be listening to a speech. In the background, children are sitting on the steps of a war monument. A girl and what appears to be a young man hold up a sign saying "Hero City." To their left, some participants hold red flags and banners.

Figure 6.3 depicts the meeting of the Komsomol Kraykom. The young activists are dressed somewhat more casually as they listen to a speech by Georgiy Kholostyakov. The picture features mostly young women with stylish haircuts;

Figures 6.1/6.2/6.3/6.4. The workers, Komsomol members, and Pioneers celebrate Novorossiysk's new honorary status with a salute. No copyright, Soviet source

the lone young man appears to have pomaded his somewhat long but properly cut hair, looking confidently ahead.

Figure 6.4 shows the city's Pioneers assembled in the stadium for a "sports celebration." Lined up in perfect military order, they applaud the Hero City. In the background, the Gold Star, the Order of Lenin, and the Order of the Patriotic War appear. The message on the banner underneath them presumably contains a patriotic slogan. The signs look more professional than those at the workers' rally. In various groups, the Pioneers show their athletic prowess and skills as a well-trained and patriotic young generation.

Taken together, the pictures depict the unity of generations in the moment of celebration, symbolized by the fireworks in figure 6.1. It includes the workers, the Komsomol members, and the young Pioneers. All collectives are orderly, politically conscious, and confident, declaring their reverence for their fallen forefathers and their faithfulness to the party. A letter from the participants reasserts this loyalty to Brezhnev personally.

> Dear Leonid Il'ich!
>
> We, the participants of the public rally, dedicated to the thirtieth anniversary of the destruction (*razgrom*) of the fascist armies and the awarding of the honorary title of "Hero City" to Novorossiysk, heartily thank you for the warm words to the workers of the city and the participants of the fights in Novorossiysk in your welcome letter and telegram.
>
> Especially dear to us was the reception of greetings on this day from You, an active participant and organizer of the battles for Novorossiysk.
>
> Your high estimation of the soldiers of the Soviet Army's, Military Maritime Fleet's and Aviation's steadfastness and valiance, as well as the labor achievements of the Novorossians, evokes in us a feeling of pride and a passionate striving for new achievements in labor in the name of further strengthening the power of our beloved Homeland.
>
> The Novorossians pledge to you that they will not spare their strength in implementing the decisions of the twenty-fourth Congress of the CPSU, in honor of fulfilling the high responsibilities the workers of the Hero City Novorossiysk have taken upon themselves on the third and decisive year of the Five-Year Plan.
>
> From all of our hearts, we wish you, dear Leonid Il'ich, good health, great successes in your lofty (*blagorodnoy*) and titanic activity as the leader of Communist construction and the strengthening of the cause of peace in the whole world.[18]

This official "oath" is admittedly long and thoroughly formalistic. It is still worthwhile to quote it in full because it provides an impression not only of Alexei Yurchak's authoritative discourse in action but also of official war memory in its Novorossian peculiarity. Addressing Brezhnev as an "active participant" is a direct quote from his earlier letters. Calling him an "organizer" of the battles fits into the increasingly exaggerated representation of his wartime role. The heartiness highlighted in mutual communication emphasizes his personal connection to the city.

Moreover, the oath creates continuity over time. The Hero City's labor feats of the 1970s are the continuation of wartime heroism, and its inhabitants shoulder the responsibility of showing themselves worthy. Under the slogan "Carry high the banner of the Hero City, be in the first lines of the fighters for the cause of our Party," Novorossiysk swore to overfulfill the goals of the Five-Year Plan.[19] Aside from the note that the city had entered into a socialist competition with Armavir, a regional city, no concrete additional obligations are mentioned.

BREZHNEV MEETS HIS CITY

The emphasis on Brezhnev's affection for Novorossiysk had given rise to the expectation that he would visit soon. Still, it remained unclear for months whether he would actually come. The reasons are not entirely known. Vicky Davis quotes three interview partners who claimed that Brezhnev had vowed only to return to the city once it "looked worthy of its new status." The general secretary supposedly criticized its appearance and vowed to solve its problems at the national level.[20]

If this is true, it would indicate how closely official war memory and "worthiness" were linked in Brezhnev's mind. The connection also helps to explain why the special development programs for Novorossiysk discussed below became reality: to an extent, it was a question of Brezhnev's own prestige. What is clear is that Viktor Golikov had to intensively lobby to get Brezhnev to make the trip. He reminds the general secretary on May 8, 1974, that "the Novorossians have been in a state of active tension and expectation of your arrival." As a result of a trip taken by Golikov and other advisers to Novorossiysk in late March, during which they had discussed the possibility of a visit, the expectation had "risen especially."[21]

Viktor Golikov is a central mediator in the relationship between Novorossiysk and Brezhnev. One of the Soviet leader's closest advisers, Golikov worked with him for more than three decades. Born in Novorossiysk in 1914, he became a teacher there before embarking on a Komsomol and party career in 1940, during which he was responsible for questions of ideology and agriculture in Brezhnev's entourage.[22] He wrote many of Brezhnev's speeches.

Golikov's seemingly dispassionate report about the "rising expectations" in Novorossiysk was not entirely selfless, as he remained intimately connected with his hometown and maintained good relations with the local leadership.[23] Moreover, a visit organized by Golikov would also elevate his prestige as an adviser. The polite but persistent pressure was necessary: the general secretary did not visit the city of Kerch' alongside Novorossiysk, sending Andrey Grechko to award the honorary title instead. Furthermore, while Brezhnev would visit subsequent Hero Cities in the mid- to late 1970s, this practice had yet to be established for the first cities of the second wave.

Golikov suggested that Brezhnev combine the trip to Novorossiysk with one to Krasnodar, where Sergey Medunov, the powerful First Secretary of the Kraykom, had been named a Hero of Socialist Labor. Medunov carefully guarded his fiefdom in Southern Russia, which he ran like a mafia state, largely undisturbed by Moscow. He skillfully and publicly cultivated his close relationship with Brezhnev—flattering his vanity with numerous congratulatory addresses and even an ode to the general secretary.[24] Brezhnev thus avoided any impression that his special relationship with Novorossiysk stood in competition with the hierarchies in Krasnodar Kray, which Medunov guarded jealously.[25]

Golikov added that everything was ready for a trip in mid-May, that the speeches were written, and that a maximum of one million rubles had been earmarked. He closed the letter with a comment about the good weather forecast for May and a plea to "excuse my intrusiveness (*nazoylivost'*). But this is what our work is like."[26] The formulation indicates that this was not the first time Golikov had to nudge Brezhnev, possibly also because the latter's addiction to pills was starting to affect his work habits by 1974.[27]

Golikov would have to wait another four months for Brezhnev to finally make the trip. His helicopter landed at Malaya Zemlya on September 6. The regional party elite—including Medunov and Mikhail Gorbachev, then First Secretary of neighboring Stavropol'skiy Kray—met him in the pouring rain. A young couple in traditional Kuban dress brought him the host present of bread and salt. The journalist Nikolay Kolesov, who would publish a sycophantic report of the visit under the tutelage of Viktor Golikov, captured the "holiday atmosphere": "The rain stopped as suddenly as it had started. Again, the sun peeked out (*vyglyanulo*), illuminating the bay in bright light, the lush greenery, the white buildings and the smooth asphalt of the roads. And at first glance nothing reminds one of the terrible battle that lasted for 225 days here, on 'Malaya Zemlya.'"[28]

Exactly because of its embellishments, the report indicates the messages that Golikov wanted to get across. It was the story of Brezhnev's triumphant return to the place of his wartime heroism, a city rebuilt and reborn as an exemplar of untiring labor and high quality of life.

Still, the visit has a fond place in the hearts of many respondents. It has become so central to the city's identity that it has taken on a mythical quality. Even those who were not there at the time would look at pictures with family members when they came home—in a classic example of postmemory. One of Davis's respondents was convinced that an old woman meeting Brezhnev in a well-known photograph was her own grandmother, in spite of overwhelming evidence to the contrary.²⁹

One can gather from various sources that most enterprises had declared a holiday during the visit. Lyudmila Dorosh, nineteen years old at the time, says that everybody relaxed and took walks (*gulyali*) at the expense of the state.³⁰ People realized what was expected of them, as they lined the streets to meet Brezhnev. Even though multiple respondents said there was no official obligation to do so, they wanted to see the general secretary. Dorosh says that people were proud of the visit, which is why the mood was relaxed and joyful. Vladimir Gusev also observed a general atmosphere of excitement in what he describes as a rather provincial city at the time. Personally, he experienced the event as stressful and discomforting: "There was a crowd. It was a nightmare. Everyone was running, everyone watching."³¹

Official propaganda presented the proximity between Brezhnev and the people as greater than it really was. Images published in Nikolay Kolesov's book show the general secretary riding through the city in an open car, with Sergey Medunov on his left and Eduard Polyakov, First Secretary of the Gorkom, on his right. The crowds appear very near. Unpublished pictures (see fig. 6.5) reveal that the population stood behind a police barrier. Brezhnev waves at them, while Polyakov and Medunov make stern faces. To Brezhnev's left, a car with a beacon on its roof serves as an escort. Another follows close behind. Judging from the angle at which the picture is taken, the photographer was in the car in front of Brezhnev's. Other images show that an additional dozen cars followed.³²

The Novorossians I interviewed provided contradictory accounts of Brezhnev's ability to move freely around the city. Lyudmila Dorosh's is particularly remarkable. She remembered that there were many KGB officers—"plain-clothed people" (*lyudi v shtatskom*), as she called them. She claims, however, that Brezhnev's security was relatively easy to bypass:

> He mostly met with Pioneers. They did not let anyone else close to him. But he stayed at the hotel Brigantina and took walks around the city. . . . We were also just taking a walk. Suddenly, my friend said, "Look, there goes Brezhnev!" Well, we were still young girls. We see Brezhnev, and there are lots of "plain-clothed people," but we do not see that. We go and watch. From afar. They did not let us get up close. He is talking to some policemen, to members of the Gorkom and probably Medunov. He asks, "What is this? And that?" Of course the stores were full at that time. . . . Wherever he went at any moment, everything was great. We keep going, and then he says, "Girls, are you not done watching?" He noticed us and said, "Come on, girls, come

Figure 6.5. Security detail behind Brezhnev's car during his visit to Novorossiysk. © http://nvrsk-kostomarovo.ru/

here!" And he gave us some candy; he gave a box of candy to anyone who saw him.... His assistants did. He asked us how things were.... We told him that everything was good with us, that we liked everyone, *Komsomoltsy, Komsomoltsy,* well done (*molodtsy*), candy to us, and forward with a song (*vpered s pesen*)![33]

The story reflects Brezhnev's charm and spontaneity, which lay at the heart of his popularity but also contrasted so strangely with his public persona, particularly in later years. The folksiness and simplicity with which he supposedly greeted the girls is markedly different from the grueling dullness with which he delivered his speeches at party congresses.

Whether this meeting took place as described by Dorosh is a difficult question. That he "took walks" is an often-shared local legend, which was even immortalized in a statue in 2004 (fig. 6.6). Davis describes the legend as "a narrative trope whereby an important personage dons common dress to mingle with the people.... Here is a potent example of the robustness of a legend, even when faced with virtually no evidence of individual corroborative memory, perhaps

Figure 6.6. Statue of Brezhnev on his mythic walk in Novorossiysk's city center.
© Ivo Mijnssen

just a wish that has developed into collective consciousness and so-called historical fact."[34]

According to Davis, then, the stroll never took place. Her main arguments against it are the tight security arrangements surrounding Brezhnev's visit. It is possible that Dorosh misremembered or was an unreliable narrator—a danger always inherent in oral history. She may have embellished or even constructed this meeting in her mind later on.

Still, the fact that she is an actual eyewitness who describes the encounter in great detail lends her memory credibility. She could have approached Brezhnev in a lucky moment in front of his hotel, even if he was not on a walk. She also mentions the numerous KGB agents surrounding Brezhnev, an accurate representation of the high level of security.

Furthermore, her retelling does not fit the clichéd accounts that Davis describes. He does not "[don] common dress," and the encounter is not as saccharine as the one Davis mentions, in which an old woman who knew him from the war but no longer recognized him moved Brezhnev to tears. Instead, Dorosh presents the meeting as both spontaneous and extremely scripted. The supposed exchange between the girls and Brezhnev is deeply embedded in Yurchak's authoritative discourse: he asks a stereotypical question, and they give a well-rehearsed answer.

It also reveals the deeply paternalistic nature of Soviet society and the relations between power and the population. Brezhnev, the patriarch, treats the young women—Dorosh was nineteen at the time—like children by giving them candy. Other roles were not on offer—something that was already evident in Tula, where young women lacked powerful role models. The continuity of generations was highly hierarchical.

Dorosh ironically reflects this from today's point of view, when she retells the story in shorthand, in the style of the slogans of the Soviet youth organizations—"*Komsomoltsy, Komsomoltsy*" and "forward with a song." The memory also shows, then, the overlay of various temporal levels.

Dorosh's account points to Brezhnev's role-play, which marked his entire visit to Novorossiysk. He played his part on a stage that regional leaders had set for him. It included freshly laid asphalt, shops full of the greatest variety of goods, happy people waving, and young people showing their ideological dedication. Medunov had even made sure that a bunker that Brezhnev had used during the war was rebuilt.[35]

Brezhnev was a victim of his own propaganda and style of leadership. His policy of "stability of cadres" meant that regional leaders had a wide berth in the management of their affairs. His laissez-faire leadership and unwillingness to tackle problems contributed to the increasing corruption among the nomenclature and the stagnation of the system.[36] Brezhnev's visits were limited to increasingly ritualized meetings with the population.[37]

PROJECTING THE SOCIALIST CONTRACT INTO THE PAST

Brezhnev spent most of his time meeting carefully selected strata of Novorossiysk's population. On the first day, he met with veterans. The second day was dedicated to the official reception at the stadium, where he also awarded the Gold Star. On the third day, he ventured out to meet the managers and workers of Novorossiysk's most important enterprises, first and foremost the cement factories and the port.

Viktor Golikov had arranged for more than two hundred veterans of the battles to travel to Novorossiysk. Most of them lived far away in other cities.[38] Again, all accounts in the press stressed the heartiness of this meeting, thirty years after the end of the war.

Nikolay Kolesov describes the contrast between the men who had once defended their homeland and the group of older veterans now gathering around Brezhnev in a prosperous city.[39] Kolesov also emphasizes that "Brezhnev remembers everything." The picture of general Grechkin informing Brezhnev about the battle in 1943 (the caption of fig. 6.7 is most likely misleading, considering Brezhnev's lower rank) is thus the historical basis for the general secretary explaining the military situation to a group of veterans in front of the map. In both images, Brezhnev stands at the center of attention, gathering and sharing information. On the left, two radio operatives are ready to pass on knowledge; on the right, the Soviet media accompanying him fulfill this task.

Whereas Brezhnev had been in a subaltern position to General Grechkin during the war, he was the final arbiter in judging the significance of the battles for Novorossiysk by 1974. Kolesov writes that the visit was the first time "the truly crucial significance of the city of Novorossiysk in the fight for the Caucasus was unveiled so clearly and solidly, so profoundly argued."[40]

The exaggeration of the Soviet leader's role would be taken to the extreme in his "autobiography," *Malaya Zemlya*: its most notorious passage concerns an apocryphal conversation between Brezhnev and Georgiy Zhukov in April 1943. In Zhukov's memoirs, which he was only allowed to publish in 1969 after much bending to political demands, the former supreme commander wrote that the *Stavka* was unsure whether the defenders would hold out during the German

Figure 6.7. Brezhnev reporting on the situation in Malaya Zemlya—in 1943 and 1974. No copyright, Soviet source

Operation Neptune: "We wanted to consult with the head of the politotdel of the 18th Army, L. I. Brezhnev, about this, who had been there multiple times and knew the conditions well, but he was on Malaya Zemlya where extremely heavy fights were raging."[41]

Brezhnev "confirms" this request: "To be frank, I also wanted to talk with him: we were all very worried about enemy air superiority."[42] In the end, however, he declined the request: "I remained with the fighting men on Little Land."[43] Hence, Brezhnev presented himself not only as the leader who had foreseen the need for additional airplanes, which the *Stavka* sent a few days later, but also as a man of the people who remained with the soldiers rather than answering the flattering request from the supreme commander. It is clear that a colonel would never have taken the deadly risk of refusing a direct order from Zhukov.

Brezhnev's role as a military planner is also exaggerated, although less in his autobiography than in other publications. Nikolay Kolesov writes that the plan to storm Novorossiysk was thought up by the commanders of the Eighteenth Army, which included Brezhnev. In reality, the heads of the political department were not involved in military decisions. Still, Brezhnev is named as "one of the initiators and passive advocates" of the plan.[44]

Brezhnev gives credit to General Konstantin Leselidze. Nevertheless, he insists he was present when it was first conceived—during a lull in the fighting, when commanders were relaxing on a "Caucasian blanket."[45] The book describes in great detail the many times he was on the beachhead. During one of these crossings, Brezhnev's boat hit a mine, and he was hurled into the water. The jaw injury he sustained would trouble him until the end of his life and make it difficult for him to speak in later years.⁴⁶ Brezhnev relates how he came to consciousness in the water, hearing an angry shout from Petty Officer Second Class Zimoda: "'Are you deaf or something? Give us your hand!'... He couldn't see my shoulder-tabs in the water, and it really made no difference at such a moment.... And in this tragic setting lit by explosions and tracer bullets a song suddenly welled up.... It was a song born on Little Land and was about the iron will and strength of just such fighting men as were on board the boat at that moment."⁴⁷

Once again, Brezhnev is presented as an egalitarian man who does not insist on hierarchies. Zimoda and the men on the boat personify the "Russian lads" who bore their harsh fate patiently and—in keeping with the kitschy romanticism that often marked official war memory—with a song on their lips. The earlier setting of the commanders on a "Caucasian blanket" was supposed to illustrate their closeness to "the people" as well.

Veteran testimonies during his visit were to emphasize the respect Brezhnev enjoyed. They agreed that not only was he a capable strategist and ideologist but he also cared deeply about the men's well-being. Kolesov's book is full of accounts in which Brezhnev organized the supply of food and the building of facilities like baths on the beachhead: "He acted with deep respect toward each soldier and officer, their food, rest, cultural services (*kul'turno-bytovoe obsluzhivanie*), military and hygienic well-being."⁴⁸

These statements can easily be dismissed as propaganda; there were no sanitary installations or even sufficient food supplies on Malaya Zemlya.⁴⁹ More interesting, however, is the role they played in the politics of history by presenting Brezhnev as a compassionate leader who understood the people, not least because of his wartime service. This image fit neatly into the Brezhnev regime's strategy to legitimize its rule through a socialist contract for popular welfare and projected this concern back onto the war years.

POSTWAR WOUNDS

In Novorossiysk, as elsewhere, the socialist contract was intimately tied to the housing problem. The war had annihilated the city. Official estimates placed the destruction at 96.5 percent⁵⁰—much higher than the average of around 40 percent across all occupied cities in the Soviet Union, not to speak of Tula, which had remained largely unscathed.⁵¹ "In Novorossiysk, the image of destruction exceeds anything seen before. This is a dead city," wrote Sergey Borzenko, correspondent for the Red Army newspaper *Krasnaya Zvezda*, on September 18, 1943.⁵² The wreckage included 11,315 buildings, and the total damage was estimated at between 1.2 and 2 billion rubles.[53] According to a report from October 18, 65 percent of all housing lay in rubble, a further 20 percent required fundamental renovation, and only 15 percent could be used in some way. All schools and cultural institutions had been completely eradicated. According to Nikolay Kolesov, only four out of one hundred thousand inhabitants were left.[54]

Official Soviet historiography maintains that reconstruction began right away; the battleground shifted from the military to the labor realm. Aleksandr Eremenko and Konstantin Podyma write that "the entire postwar story of the Hero City is a feat as well, the labor feat of Novorossians in the name of life and the flourishing of their hometown."[55] Nikolay Kolesov speaks of a "second battle" for Novorossiysk that began when the war was over: the struggle to return to life, which soldiers and civilians fought together.[56]

Stories of returning veterans served to underline this narrative. The authors of the book *Hero City Novorossiysk* recount the arrival of a train of soldiers on July 22, 1945. One of the men, a certain V. Kiselev, thanked those workers who had already begun reconstruction: "Today, we, the front soldiers (*frontoviki*), tell you that we will now cure the wounds together. We will work here, like we did on the front lines. Heroes of labor, you deserve our front line thank you (*frontovoe spasibo*)."[57] Kolesov echoed these words: "The first to touch the painful (*tyazhkie*) wounds of Novorossiysk were the caring hands of soldiers and partisans, yearning for peaceful work."[58]

The most "painful wounds" in Novorossiysk were the tens of thousands of mines the Wehrmacht had left. Unexploded bombs and shells created an additional problem. In the first weeks, sapper and engineer units of the Red Army stayed behind to defuse explosives.[59] The most elaborate booby trap was attached to the Lenin monument. Upon investigating it, the sappers found a system of underground explosives that was connected to the electricity grid and was supposed to detonate once the engineers turned the power back on. There were enough explosives to take out the entire neighborhood.[60]

By November 10, 1943, the civilians were on their own. On that day, the Society for the Promotion of Defense, Aviation, and Chemical Industry took control of the mine-clearing effort, employing teenagers, many of them girls. Poorly trained and equipped, they did the lion's share of the work for years. This certainly represented a continuity of generations, albeit different from the one highlighted in propaganda. Lyudmila Dorosh's stepmother was seventeen when Novorossiysk was liberated. She was drafted for mine-clearing work right away. Dorosh explained: "All the fields were mined. They had a three-day course, where they trained them. And the girls, all the young girls were sappers and miners (*minery*). During the entire first year, they cleared all the mines. They did no work in the fields. ... They also cleared all the mines in the city itself, and they said, how many explosions there were, how many died."[61]

Her account complements the available sources. In his book on the Hero City Novorossiysk, Yuriy Zhurkin only briefly mentions the "girl-miners" (*devushki-minery*). He confirms Dorosh's stepmother's account about the courses they took. According to him, the first of them "graduated" on May 26, 1944. Before this date, instruction was likely even less systematized. The number of young people who died remains unknown. They were buried near the train station.[62]

By December 15, 1943, 809 people, including 343 women, were working to clear mines.[63] By mid-1944, regular units were active. All over the region, they cleared a total of three or four hundred thousand mines and duds, one thousand explosives each on average.[64] Their truly heroic feats were mentioned only in passing; the inhuman conditions under which they worked precluded them from inclusion in the Soviet pantheon. Admitting to them would have forced the propagandists of the war to admit to the cynicism of a leadership that sent unequipped youngsters to do the dirtiest and most dangerous work of reconstruction, often sacrificing them needlessly. Their cruel fate stood in stark contrast to the Communist Party's claim that the welfare of Soviet citizens always enjoyed priority. Finally, the case of the "girl-miners" illustrates how helpless the overwhelmed leadership often was in dealing with the war's horrific traces.

Aside from the port and the reestablishment of rail transport into the cutoff city, the party prioritized the reconstruction of the cement factories. According to Serafim Shurin, First Secretary of the Novorossiysk Gorkom, four of them were producing concrete again within a year of liberation.[65] By the end of 1944, forty enterprises were back in business. The Soviet leadership, recognizing the strategic and economic significance of Novorossiysk, had already invested 1.4 million rubles a day after liberation.

The lack of workers remained a problem for years. By March 1944, 25,000 people had returned to the city, living in barracks and huts (see fig. 6.8), but even at the end of 1945, only 3,800 were workers. Among them were 1,300 German prisoners of war and 800 former Soviet prisoners of war. The first people to return were women, children, and senior citizens—some of whom received modest state support as relatives of Red Army members.[66] The men only started coming back once the war was over. Many were either physically or mentally impaired. Still, on January 1, 1947, Novorossiysk's city architect complained to the Council of Ministers RSFSR that most of the projects that

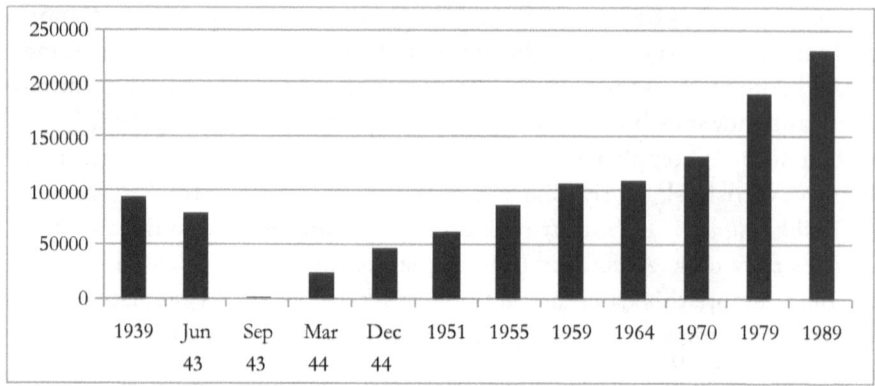

Figure 6.8. Population of Novorossiysk (1939–89). Graph drawn by the author

had been approved and financed could not be implemented because of the lack of architects and workers.[67]

The stories that members of the postwar generation heard from their parents about the first years of reconstruction provide a tangible impression of these difficulties. Vladimir Gusev remembers that for years, only the city center was remotely habitable—the last house lay a few blocks south of Hero Square. "In the city center, the frogs croaked so loudly that you could not talk because you could not hear what was said."[68] Presumably because of the destruction of drainage systems, parts of Novorossiysk were boggy. Only once the swamps were drained were the conditions for reconstruction created. Transport was another problem. Natal'ya Grigor'eva's grandmother and mother had to walk everywhere for years—a tiring task considering that the center is very hilly. Because the Wehrmacht had removed all buses to Germany, no public transport existed. The first tramline was opened only on August 10, 1948.[69]

The weight of the war also affected human interactions. Vladimir Gusev's father had suffered a severe head trauma because one ton of explosives detonated only twenty-five meters away from him: "He came back from the war deaf and nervous (*nervnyy*)." Gusev says that his father terrorized the family with breakouts: he would jump up and smash all the plates, then sit back down as if nothing had happened. Still, Gusev considers himself lucky his father came back alive.[70] His own childhood memories appear to have traumatized him as well: "I know what war is, what soldiers are. When half a city of healthy men, half a city, imagine, half a city, [is] without hands, without eyes, without feet, can you imagine? There were so many invalids. It was terrible. Terrible. Heroes of the Soviet Union everywhere. Now they carry them on their hands, but then he begged, 'Give me a kopeck.' Nobody gave anything. Nothing. Because there was nothing. The country was poverty-stricken (*nishchaya*)."[71]

Novorossiysk's poverty left a lasting impression on Gusev. He sees nothing romantic about this period. Galina Bozhok, on the other hand, born on February 24, 1953, and living in Novorossiysk since 1959, sees positive aspects. Both of Bozhok's parents fought in the war, and they met when her father was recovering from injuries in a hospital in Vilnius. They got married in 1944. Her father served in Germany afterward. After being dismissed from the Red Army, he struggled to find work, having no real education. The family had to rent a tiny apartment.

Nevertheless, Bozhok maintains, relations with the neighbors were friendly. They knew each other; "there were no locked doors."[72] Other respondents (Luydmila Dorosh, Natal'ya Grigor'eva) repeated the notion that "everybody lived poorly but friendly."[73] It nevertheless appears highly likely that this interpretation stems from respondents' experiences since the collapse of the Soviet Union rather than their feelings in the 1950s; Russians of this generation tend to juxtapose the relative lack of social differences in the USSR with post-Soviet inequality.

The case of Sergey Tsymbal, today the chairman of the city's Civic Chamber, demonstrates this in exemplary fashion. Tsymbal freely admits that he did not believe in communist ideology as an adult and that he joined the Communist Party for reasons of career advancement. In his school days, on the other hand, "things were easier. There were no rich and poor people, no stratification of society."[74] Equality in poverty, then, comes to symbolize a kind of simplicity and solidarity that many respondents seem to believe has vanished in the course of Novorossiysk's rapid development in the Brezhnev era and beyond. Still, most have no memories before the mid-1950s, when life was more miserable and less suited for ex post facto romanticizing.

"THE DREAM OF THE MALOZEMELTSY"

On November 1, 1945, Novorossiysk was added to the fifteen cities that received priority funds for reconstruction—an additional 55 million rubles.[75] In 1946, Moscow architect Boris Iofan worked out a general plan that foresaw the construction of numerous parks, broad alleys, and neoclassicist buildings in the center. Because of financial constraints and uncoordinated, spontaneous housing construction as a result of the population's dire situation, only a much-reduced version was implemented, without most of the parks and representative buildings.[76] Karl Qualls describes similar ambitions and developments in Sevastopol', where, however, local resistance against Moscow's plans appears to have been greater.[77]

The first apartment houses of the postwar era were built around 1950 for workers of the cement factories, such as Sergey Tsymbal's grandfather. The pace of reconstruction only picked up in the second half of the 1950s. According to Shurin's account, the city had rebuilt its prewar housing stock only by 1957—531,000 of 540,000 square meters.[78] This was around the same time that it reached its prewar population levels again. Because of Novorossiysk's strategic significance, economic reconstruction took priority over the needs of the population. This only changed in the early 1970s, partially as the result of changes in national policy and of the Hero City award.

The embodiment of the new, heroic, and livable Novorossiysk was, unsurprisingly, Malaya Zemlya. Here, planners found the kind of tabula rasa they needed to rebuild the city from scratch according to their ideals.[79] Brezhnev articulated this notion in his speech, when he talked about the "dream" of the fighters on Malaya Zemlya: "We imagined bright, beautiful cities, noisy schools, beautiful new factories, fertile fields and blooming gardens. But I think that not even our wildest dreams at that time compare to the reality of our days. Life surpassed them by so much. (*stormy, prolonged applause*) ... Your city, dear comrades, serves as a good example of how the face of our country has changed in the past years."[80]

Both Georgiy Sokolov and Nikolay Kolesov subsequently elaborated on "Brezhnev's dream," sometimes adding other characters to express the same message. Kolesov writes: "'Malaya Zemlya' ... Today it has become part of Novorossiysk. All of it is full of modern apartment houses, asphalted roads, burgeoning green on the flanks of the mountains ... renewed, peaceful, flourishing. But in the memory of the Malaya Zemlya veterans, it remains wounded, blackened, rampant—exactly as they wrested (*otvoevali*) it from the enemy and defended it, not sparing their blood and lives."[81]

Malaya Zemlya changed so much that it became almost unrecognizable, especially to those who had fought there. Sokolov remarks that "only the experienced eye of the *Malozemeltsy* (fighters on Malaya Zemlya) recognizes some shrapnel on the rocky ground or a half-destroyed bunker somewhere."[82] The change is, in both accounts, a sign that the dream has been fulfilled.[83]

By the end of Brezhnev's reign, twenty-six thousand Novorossians would live in houses built on the former battlefield[84]—in *mikrorayony*, which were ideologically highly charged embodiments of socialist housing.[85] K. Mikhaylov even went so far as to write that, thanks to the new construction projects, the city was becoming a single "unified organism."⁸⁶ The neighborhood was simply called *Kunikovka*, named after Tsezar' Kunikov, the hero of Malaya Zemlya. The history of the place, then, was inscribed not only in the ground but also in the name of the neighborhood.

Numerous streets were named after heroes of the battle. N. Nadykta, writing for the newspaper *Komsomolets Kubani*, thus concluded in 1973: "Kunikovka. Here, everything is intertwined (*pereplelos'*). The past—with the present. The present—with the future."⁸⁷ The schools, squares, roads, and corners that the postwar generation grew up in were literally marked by the war. "They spent their childhood on legendary earth, but it did not coincide with war," sums up Nadykta.⁸⁸ From this statement, the state's ideologists derived the demand that the postwar generation be thankful for their peaceful lives and show itself worthy of the loyalty and self-sacrifice that inspired their predecessors.

Respondents had ambiguous feelings about Malaya Zemlya as a symbol of postwar life and wealth. Georgiy Shcherbakov commented positively on the growth of the city, especially in the 1970s. Still, some had trouble reconciling contradictory identities: Malaya Zemlya was a space to be revered and protected, but it was also a space for everyday life. To Galina Bozhok, the construction of houses on a battlefield is plainly wrong: "There were these bloody fights here, and then there was not enough room, so they built an entire city, well, on bones, really, on bones. Because what the people lived through, hardly any city ever had to live through that."⁸⁹

From her point of view, housing construction there was "barbaric" (*dikiy*): "This is a very holy place and should not be built on."⁹⁰ There is a tension here about the significance of the continuity of generations. Does reverence for the dead mean preserving their graves? Or does it oblige the state to honor the socialist contract by literally building a better society on their sacrifices?

The latter interpretation certainly predominated since the Khrushchev era, as Varga-Harris has shown, assuming the status of a "tacit concordat between government and populace."⁹¹ Bozhok was not convinced. She does not grant the state ownership of the fallen at Malaya Zemlya and, by extension, of war memory. As her repeated emotional outbursts during the interview show, war memory is a deeply personal issue for her, owned only by the families of the fallen.

Tamara Yurina disagrees, on the basis of virtually identical arguments. Like Bozhok, she refers to the will of the fallen. "People died here, but I don't think that means that they did not want there to be life," she says.⁹² In her opinion, a consistent application of the logic that Novorossiysk's earth is holy would empty it. "Basically, the whole city is a memorial zone, but that does not mean that things have to be worse here. On the contrary: the better people live, the more thankful they are to those who withstood."[93] Reverence for their sacrifices means providing the postwar generation with a better life.

At its core, this discussion deals with what it means to continue living in a place that went through a deadly and deeply traumatic war. Considering the fact that Novorossiysk was only one of many Soviet cities that were destroyed, the entire country had to address this question. The answer that had come to be widely accepted by the Brezhnev era—that mass death created the preconditions for new life—appears to be the only one that could guarantee the continued existence of society.

A TOAST TO NOVOROSSIYSK'S FUTURE

Planners chose Malaya Zemlya as the site for this new life for mostly pragmatic reasons. They used it as the main vector of development because there was no room in the city's hilly eastern parts.[94] The "Third Mikrorayon" was the first of multiple neighborhoods built between 1965 and 1971 to accommodate the population.

The city's turbulent growth was directly linked to its economic development. Novorossiysk already enjoyed a reputation as a producer of cement, but transport remained a problem. In 1964, therefore, a separate tanker branch of the Black Sea Shipping Company was founded and stationed in the port. According to Yuriy Semenov, head of the Gorispolkom, the idea came from Brezhnev, who looked for a way to expand revenue from international trade. As Soviet cement was one of the most important export commodities, stationing tankers near the factory appeared logical.[95] A further argument for Novorossiysk was the large agricultural export of Krasnodar Kray. In the 1970s, the booming oil and gas industry increasingly appropriated the port.

The growth, however, created problems for the city. Quite symptomatically for Soviet policy, the authorities had not sufficiently considered housing and communal services—something also encountered in Tula.[96] Doubtlessly aware of this, Semenov used his connections to Viktor Golikov to lobby for an extra program that included housing and communal services during a visit to the city in 1967 or 1968.

Apparently going against the party line and ignoring the chain of command, Semenov gave a toast thanking Golikov for the city's economic development but also bemoaned that the only "profit" remaining in Novorossiysk comprised "cement stains" (*tsementnaya pyatna*). He asked the government to alleviate the city's housing problems and water shortage. Even though both Gorkom and Kraykom demanded his resignation as a result of this foolhardy move, Golikov unexpectedly used his political weight, secured Brezhnev's approval, and lobbied the ministries to assign the additional funds.[97]

The archives contain no files about the decision-making process, and no memoirs other than that of Semenov, who may have inflated his own role, are available. There is no doubt, however, that he played an important role through his link to Golikov and, indirectly, to Brezhnev.[98] The city's special connection to the leader allowed it to secure the "Measures for the Further Development of Novorossiysk's Municipal Services between 1968 and 1975." Such a program for a small provincial city was unique. It was all the more surprising because the Krasnodar authorities had seriously criticized the leadership for its economic incompetence in the late 1960s.[99]

The Council of Ministers SSSR nevertheless approved 35 million rubles for the program on September 9, 1968.[100] It stated that "in September 1968, 25 years have passed since the day of the German-fascist army's destruction in Novorossiysk."[101] As in Tula, then, the anniversary of liberation provided the politically correct justification for the benefits. The Soviet tradition of handing people gifts—or even apartments[102]—on high holidays was transferred to the Hero City. Only afterward does the report state that Novorossiysk had been almost fully destroyed but nevertheless had become a "harbor city of international significance and a large industrial center."[103] Economic arguments were secondary in the public representation of the decision.

The lion's share of the funds went toward the construction of an aqueduct for Novorossiysk. The water shortage had come to a head in the fall of 1968, when a drought made it necessary to transport water to Novorossiysk from Tuapse and Sochi in tankers. In this situation, the Council of Ministers' funds were welcome, but the planned completion by 1975 was too late. The historian Sergey Novikov demonstrates that the city leadership's connections to Moscow made it possible to complete construction by November 4, 1971, not least thanks to the help of the population's voluntary labor.[104]

Adequate water supply was the precondition for further development. From the end of 1971, each of Novorossiysk's inhabitants was able to consume three hundred liters of water per day, sufficient to cover demand.[105] Moreover, a system for sewage, which had thus far just spilled into the ocean, was built, as well as a further twenty kilometers of road, streetlights, and bus lines.[106] Finally, Novorossiysk received a new hospital, schools for 2,400 additional students, and preschool facilities for 980 children.[107]

The Council of Ministers' plan also provided for additional housing. Up to this point, as in the rest of the Soviet Union, housing availability depended strongly upon the enterprise at which one was employed. Those under direct control of the ministries in Moscow, which included the strategically significant port and cement factories, had large housing funds. The wait for their workers was relatively short. Others needed to be much more patient.

The new housing program foresaw the construction of 2,100 apartments between 1970 and 1975 for families that were still living in damaged houses in 1968. A further 6,500 were on waiting lists. In order to achieve this goal and create a sustainable basis for development, a special housing construction combine—Trest 12—was founded, capable of building 35,000 square meters a year.[108] The implementation did not proceed without problems. The sewage system was completed two years later than planned, and the hospital was delayed. The sudden upswing in construction created shortages in materials and bottlenecks in the port and railway facilities. Moreover, the city struggled to attract enough qualified workers.

The perspective of receiving housing was nevertheless very attractive. Mariya Inozemetseva, who was forced to move to Novorossiysk in the early 1970s when her family sent her away—she was pregnant out of wedlock—joined Trest 12 because of the incentives. She profited from childcare facilities that allowed her to work while the state took care of her child.[109] Inozemetseva spent five years at a workers' dormitory but then received her own apartment, which she had literally built herself. The members of the construction combine were entitled to 10 percent of all apartments they built.[110] For someone like her who had no connections and little education, the combine was a tool for social mobility.

The work opportunities, however, also created additional demand for communal services. In the 1970s alone, Novorossiysk's population grew from almost 133,000 to 189,000. As a result, the Hero City received a second special investment package from the Council of Ministers SSSR on February 8, 1977. It earmarked 118 million rubles for housing and communal services between 1977 and 1985, a sum more than four times larger than the preceding one. At a time of economic stagnation, these additional finances were very significant, and they underline the high priority Novorossiysk enjoyed. The city foresaw new schools for 4,704 students and kindergartens for 1,680 children, a children's hospital, and a general hospital for 1,600 patients, as well as extensions of the sewage system and the water supply.[111]

The housing problem had become even more pressing. Yuriy Semenov presented the situation with some urgency, demonstrating that 14,360 families were already waiting for an apartment in Novorossiysk—in spite of ongoing construction. At the current pace, he argued, it would take fifteen years to house those on the list alone—even without further population growth.[112]

Semenov also criticized the development policies of the party directly: "The marked disproportion between economic and social development has led to a situation in which the city cannot satisfy modern needs in many areas." He added that it could not fulfill the most pressing necessities of the city's inhabitants and guests.[113] Semenov identified a shortfall in housing of almost four hundred thousand square meters. The fact that the military automatically received a "significant portion" of housing space exacerbated the problem for the rest of the population.[114]

Again, the Council of Ministers responded to his demands. As early as February 20, 1975, it had assigned the city 183,000 square meters of housing space as part of the regular tenth Five-Year Plan, between 1976 and 1980. The special measures foresaw a further 280,000 square meters. Altogether, between 1970 and 1980 Novorossiysk received 633,000 square meters of housing, which more than doubled total square footage.[115]

Semenov's reference to "modern needs" is remarkable, as it transfers the discussion to a new level—reflecting Novorossiysk's elevated status and its position as a tourist center: "The designation of Novorossiysk as a Hero City has brought the city a lot of attention from the Soviet people. Everyone who is on the Black Sea coast wants to see Novorossiysk and its history, its feat of arms (*ratnyy podvig*) and its many monuments. Up to 60,000 guests now visit the city in summer."[116]

Semenov goes on to explain that tourism temporarily increased the number of inhabitants in the city so dramatically that the regular food supplies no longer fulfilled the annual norm: eggs, milk, and meat did not suffice.[117] Again, his request was heard—the special measures included new supermarkets (*univermagi*) and additional food deliveries.

One is tempted to speak of a rather bold set of requests, especially as Semenov also included demands for better television reception and a substation for up to ten thousand additional phone numbers. The fate of these initiatives is unclear, but they reflected the Zeitgeist: the Council of Ministers adopted the notion that urban planning needed to provide for the population's social and economic needs as official policy in 1979.[118] Two years prior, the right to housing had been anchored in the Soviet Constitution, formalizing an already widely shared expectation.[119]

This sense of entitlement was also communicated to the population. Mikhaylov explicitly interpreted the 1977 special program as "evidence of the new concern of the Party and the government for Novorossiysk and the workers of the Hero City."[120] He explained that it enabled not only the construction of new buildings but also a general "elevation of the city's social development."[121] The Hero City deserved these qualitative improvements because of its history of "self-sacrificing labor."[122]

Members of the postwar generation appropriated this discourse. Vladimir Gusev articulates it in the most tangible fashion: "There is the expression *bare minimum*. Three kinds of sausage, three kinds of cheese, three kinds of bread. [IM: That was available here, right?] Yes. In Germany you would have seventeen kinds; we had three. [IM: That is not bad, though.] No. It is enough to show off with (*shikovat'; laughs*)."[123]

Most other *defitsit*-plagued urban dwellers in the Soviet Union could only dream of a supply situation such as this, and they would certainly not have considered it the "bare minimum." There were, naturally, other factors that facilitated the supply of Novorossiysk, such as the proximity of the Kuban's "breadbasket." Moreover, the ocean provided ample quantities of fish and, perhaps more importantly, a steady flow of ships and commodities.

The combination of the Hero City award, official prioritization of social needs, political connections, strategic position, and window to the world were all relevant in securing Novorossians a high standard of living. The decisive factor is difficult to determine in retrospect, although the political priority the city enjoyed would be a promising contender. It is clear, however, that other cities that were missing one or more of these elements—including other Hero Cities like Tula—fared worse. For Novorossiysk, the factors formed a virtuous cycle.

SOVIET PEPSI

In 1977, Novorossiysk's ships traded with 240 ports worldwide.[124] Official publications presented the harbor as a source of great pride, the place where Novorossiysk's labor traditions were repeated from generation to generation. In his ghostwritten book, Yuriy Zhurkin lauded Novorossiysk's hospitality: in order to better accommodate the many foreigners, the city not only entered into a friendly exchange with Plymouth and Livorno but also built a "Sailors' Club" (*Klub Moryakov*). The club organized meetings, movie nights, and more than four hundred excursions. He claimed that the "direct conversation with Soviet people gives the foreigners an image of our way of life."[125]

One may cast some reasonable doubt on whether the foreign guests were as overjoyed about this opportunity to see the "Soviet way of life." Activists and the KGB closely monitored these exchanges—something which Sergey Zhuk also described for Dnepropetrovsk.[126] The exchange between Novorossians and foreigners was a constant headache for the authorities: the port may have been a source of pride and wealth, but it was also an entryway for illicit literature and Western music, clothes, and ideas.

Archival materials show that the Party and Komsomol Gorkoms were enveloped in a Sisyphean struggle against the harmful effects of perceived "enemy propaganda." In 1974, for instance, the Komsomol's Department of Propaganda and Agitation reports that its brigades arrested 186 people for "undesired (*nezhelatel'nye*) contacts with foreign sailors." The department bemoaned the lenient treatment of these perpetrators; only 3 were excluded from the youth organization.[127]

Violations were frequent and often tolerated[128]—because of a profound systemic dilemma. On the one hand, consumerism was considered ideologically harmful. On the other, the regime based its legitimacy on a socialist contract that increasingly included the availability of consumer goods—albeit within the context of "rational" consumption, which satisfied "real" needs instead of hedonistic pleasures.[129] Neither Khrushchev nor Brezhnev were able to resolve the tension between ideological imperatives and marketlike financial consumerist forces.[130]

A showcase port city like Novorossiysk, the Soviet Union's window to the world and a Hero City on top of that, had to be able to withstand comparison with Western counterparts. People had to be well supplied and well dressed; the official imagery of the 1973 Komsomol meeting that was discussed in the beginning of the chapter illustrates the importance of this modernity. As a consequence of this conundrum, the lines between illicit but allowed activities and the official attitude toward Western goods became increasingly blurred.

A fascinating example is the Soviet Union's first Pepsi factory in Novorossiysk. The three images below (fig. 6.9) are from the photo book *The Hero-Cities of the Black Sea*, published in 1978 by Konstantin Kinelev and Vitaliy Medvedev. It celebrates the heroism of Novorossiysk, Kerch', Sevastopol', and Odessa, demonstrating various aspects of each city's identity. Distributed in tens of thousands of copies, it contributed to shaping their image in the rest of the country.

The accompanying text highlights Novorossiysk's role as an import-export center and lauds the level of social welfare attained in the Hero City. Then, the reader sees two pictures showing Pepsi products.

The top left image depicts three Pepsi bottles and various Pepsi glasses on two Pepsi trays. Bottles, glasses, and trays have been polished and set on a shiny modern table at a stylish restaurant. They appear alluring and refreshing. If it were not for the Cyrillic labels, this image could appear in any commercial

Figure 6.9. The Hero City's very own Pepsi. No copyright, Soviet source

in the capitalist West. No ideological explanation would limit its advertising effect.

On the right, a Pepsi delivery truck turns a corner in front of the beverage's production facility. Aside from the label, it also has a bottle painted on it, which creates a moving billboard. Two female workers, clothed in spotless white dresses, are awaiting its arrival. These figures, as well as the park in which the factory is located, create an impression of cleanliness and refreshment.

This factory, at least, carries a socialist code: the mural showing a child's face and the abstract relief of a flower is clearly located within the iconography of a Soviet youth or children's organization. It would strengthen the link between Pepsi, youth, and modernity that the first picture already suggests. The message is as clear as it is puzzling: there is no contradiction between Soviet icons and those of Western consumerism; Komsomol imagery and the Pepsi logo stand side by side.

One could interpret the coexistence of imagery as an expression of parity between two superpowers. It can also be read as a kind of capitulation of Soviet ideologists before a global youth culture that did not stop at the USSR's doorsteps. Either way, Pepsi appears as an inherent part of Soviet consumption and the identity of the Hero City.

The history of Novorossiysk's Pepsi shows just how ambiguous this cooperation was. Donald Kendall, the former CEO of PepsiCo, tried for almost two decades to enter the Soviet market. During the American National Exhibition in Moscow in 1959, Nikita Khrushchev drank a bottle of Pepsi at his insistence.[131] The publicity stunt made headlines worldwide, but the Soviet leader did not agree to establish production facilities in the USSR. The efforts only gained ground once the geopolitical climate had relaxed.

In 1970, Kendall bartered with Aleksey Kosygin: Pepsi concentrate for vodka.[132] PepsiCo was allowed to build a factory in Novorossiysk and produce Pepsi locally, while the Soviet "Stolichnaya" vodka would get exclusive access to US markets. Over the next twelve years, the Soviet Union earned a total of 139 million rubles from Pepsi sales—one bottle of which cost 45 kopecks. This added up to a total of 309 million bottles sold.

Yuriy Semenov and the full PepsiCo Board of Directors opened the Novorossiysk factory on May 31, 1974. Press coverage was modest—in Sergey Novikov's opinion because the city administration did not want to create unnecessary "noise" about this ideologically sensitive affair.[133] Still, the plant appears to have been a priority for Brezhnev, as he visited it during his stay in Novorossiysk. Vicky Davis interprets the opening of the factory in Novorossiysk as a sign of Brezhnev's favoritism, even if he was not the main instigator and the city enjoyed no stable water source.[134]

The newspaper *Novorossiyskiy Rabochiy* did not write about the visit in any detail, but it did mention the name Pepsi-Cola and add that the general secretary "familiarized himself with the [factory's] modern equipment, technological processes of production and talked to workers and specialists."[135] The image that was released shows him chatting with a female worker in the same white uniform visible in the pictures above. Only the bottles' Pepsi labels were invisible.

The Pepsi-vodka cooperation was a product of détente. Russia and the United States had signed the SALT I treaty only two years earlier, on May 26, 1972. Negotiations for the SALT II treaty and the Helsinki Accords were far advanced. Furthermore, the summit meeting between Brezhnev and Gerald Ford in Vladivostok was only two months away. Brezhnev's much-publicized visit to the Pepsi factory was also a political signal—albeit one whose symbolism fit the message he wanted to send much better than his ill-fated and contradictory visit to Tula's armament factory in January 1977.

The general secretary's public support of détente was evident in the speech he held in Novorossiysk. It was noticeably devoid of belligerent rhetoric: he did not criticize Western imperialism or aggression even once. Instead, Brezhnev's "peace policy" keeps reappearing: "We are not yet able to confirm that a solid foundation for peace has been created in Europe and the whole world. That would be premature. But what has been and is being achieved in this regard opens up encouraging perspectives. . . . We see our duty in dedicating a maximum of efforts henceforth to making sure that neither us nor our children, grandchildren and great-grandchildren will ever know what war is."[136]

The victory at Novorossiysk, its reconstruction, and the transition to a comparatively high level of social welfare symbolically underscored Brezhnev's policies of détente and peace. This interpretation of continuity was neither uncontested nor without political risks since Soviet military circles used war memory as a means of justifying defense expenditures. According to Nikolay Mitrokhin, Viktor Golikov also supported this militaristic interpretation of victory.[137] Still, he demurred when he wrote Brezhnev's speech for the occasion.

During Brezhnev's visit, however, another speaker, D. Litovtsev, commander of the North-Caucasian Military District, all but disagreed with the general secretary. He pointed out that while the military supported Brezhnev's and the Central Committee's foreign policy, "we would like to remind you of your words about the fact that even under the conditions of détente (*razryadka*), international tensions continue and the process of materially preparing for a world war is even accelerated."[138]

Subsequent events would prove Litovtsev partially right: the summit at Vladivostok was largely a failure, during which Brezhnev suffered a heart attack from which he never recovered fully.[139] Because of Brezhnev's health problems, Richard Nixon's and Willy Brandt's resignations, and new international tensions, détente never regained the momentum it lost in 1974.[140] It ended with the Soviet invasion of Afghanistan—at the very latest.

NOVOROSSIANS BETWEEN *BLAT'* AND WORTHINESS

Among the postwar generation, in any case, "Novorossian Pepsi" was very popular, and they considered it a source of pride. Novikov writes that even today many insist that "their" Pepsi was better than what is sold in stores all over Russia.[141] Tamara Yurina also emphasizes its importance: in her opinion, Pepsi was the "best present." She said, "We had something that no other place had."[142] The fact that it was freely available in Novorossiysk's stores made it a popular "bribe," as Yurina admits with a smile, among her teachers at the university of Voronezh.[143] Like the *Priyaniki* in Tula, its scarcity in the rest of the Soviet Union made it a valuable currency in the widespread barter transactions of Brezhnev-era society.

These deals were not completely legal. Still, the generations that had grown up without personally experiencing Stalinist terror did not always accept the lines as drawn by the state. The semilegal economy was an inherent part of the everyday lives of the Soviet people, most of whom did not see their participation in it as criminal or even amoral. It provided a way of satisfying the "modern needs" that the leadership kept promising but rarely provided for.

In Novorossiysk, opportunities were more plentiful than elsewhere. My respondents openly admitted to buying and even selling products in illegal flea markets called *barakholki* or *tolchki*. As it was mostly sailors who sold the goods, these kinds of transactions were the main source of the "undesired contacts" mentioned above. The largest barakholka, which still exists today, took place every Sunday at Mefodievskiy Market in the eastern part of town. Lyudmila Dorosh describes a square where the sailors, many of them foreigners, laid out their commodities on newspaper. Apparently, one had to go early to get the best deals, as demand was great and quality uneven.

She also mentions that the KGB would sometimes conduct raids and arrest people. Dorosh claims that its officers merely confiscated the wares and that some even sold them subsequently.[144] Whether this is true or not, there were no systematized efforts to shut the market down.

Dorosh herself was heavily involved in black market trading. She had established an elaborate network of "business contacts." As a saleswoman, she cultivated her friendship with the head of the main storage site in Krasnodar, where imports from eastern European countries were first collected. Because she lived in a village by the seaside, she was also able to offer her partners a vacation home directly on the shore. Considering the overcrowded tourist facilities in and around Novorossiysk, this was an attractive proposal. Moreover, as a member of the Kolkhoz, she had access to foodstuffs, which she could also use to barter. She explained: "I turned this into my business. I also speculated. For example, we would get Hungarian coats for the spring season, sold them for thirty rubles. They tore them out of my hands even for a hundred. When I went through the city, there would be a crowd behind me, asking, 'Give us some too. We will pay any price!'"[145]

The scarcity of high-quality imports created strong demand for them, which someone with good connections could exploit for profit. Moreover, many in the Brezhnev era had money but no opportunity to buy anything with it because of the *defitsit*.

By her own admission, Dorosh "slily" (*khitro*) used this situation. In the interview, she chose the same word to describe the person she became during the Brezhnev era because of her constant wheeling and dealing. Still, she insists that money was not the prime motivator. Her "business contacts" were about "you for me and I for you," she says. "We helped each other out."[146]

Even though the distinction may appear academic from the outside, it would be a mistake to confuse the Soviet *blat* system, based on personal contacts and barter, with proto-capitalism. Instead, the exchange took place within clearly defined networks not based on generalized rules or currencies.[147] While this system compensated for the shortages of the Soviet economy, it can also be seen as a foundation for the corrupt networks in today's Russia.

Even those respondents who claim that they never participated in these semilegal marketplaces insist on the distinction. Vladimir Gusev got quite angry when I asked him about "gray markets" in Novorossiysk: "What do you mean, gray market! That did not exist. You are my friend; I have access to a store with good clothing. They have pants or a suit.... And another a sausage store. So it was like, 'Bring me a suit, I bring you sausage.' That is called *blat, po blatu*."[148]

To him, the difference between "homegrown" *blat* practices and the foreigners who were active on Novorossiysk's flea markets is crucial. The latter, he insisted, were involved in a more commercialized and, by extension, morally dubious activity. Other interview partners, however, did not accept this distinction. Mariya Inozemetseva argues that the sellers contributed to the status of Novorossiysk, as they helped people dress "very stylishly (*shikarnyy*)," which set them apart from residents of other places.[149]

Lyudmila Shalagina recounts that people from all of Krasnodar Kray would travel to the *tolchki* of Novorossiysk because they could buy quality foreign goods there. "The fact that foreigners were here gave the city a certain charm."[150] Novorossiysk's openness and sophistication set it apart from the surrounding Kray.

This belief in a Novorossian exceptionalism, based on the city's history and often connected to its brief existence as its own republic during the revolution of 1905, was widespread.[151] It also fit into the Hero City discourse. The semilegal activities on Novorossiysk's markets underlined this exceptionalism, reinforcing its privileged position in the heroarchy: the provision of sufficient consumer goods made for a worthy living standard.

Still, living in a city that was publicly declared to be exceptionally heroic and that had an exceptionally high level of wealth and supplies created problems. The tension between the egalitarian ideology and the constant propagation of exemplars of excellence, far above the average Soviet man, also applied to Novorossiysk. One way this tension manifested itself was jealousy, of which Sergey Tsymbal was acutely aware: "They do not love us, the Hero City of Novorossiysk, in Krasnodar or in Slavyansk because they think ... well, a sea city always has its specificities ... when we chewed gum, they thought we had bought it from foreigners. And we had jeans here. We had speculators, *fartsovshchiki*, sailors brought in things from abroad. And jeans were something unbearable (*nevynosimo*) [to them]."[152]

Tsymbal's attitude reflects the self-confidence of a cosmopolitan city dweller. He dismisses the jealousy of his provincial neighbors as ignorant resentment. His attitude also reflects the power that commodities like jeans and chewing gum still had over the Soviet imagination as symbols of Western capitalism. This emphasis on consumerism rested somewhat uneasily with official heroism. Hans Günther writes that the Soviet hero was defined exactly in contrast to petty bourgeois norms, as the embodiment of an ideal, far removed from such trite concerns.[153]

It is no surprise, then, that respondents insisted on not basing the distinction from neighboring cities purely on differences in wealth. Instead, Georgiy Shcherbakov sees the Hero City as a unique category: "Look: there is the 'spa town' of Anapa and the 'spa town' of Gelendzhik (*gorod kurorta*)—but Novorossiysk is the 'Hero City' (*gorod-geroy*). Spas are no heroes—spas are spas (*laughs*)."[154]

Again, the quote reveals a sense of exceptionalism. In this instance, however, the distinction emphasizes the presence of something that is lacking in the vacation resorts on the Black Sea coast. Shcherbakov says, essentially, that Novorossiysk has more substance than its neighbors; the heroic history served as a kind of proof that Novorossiysk was patriotic in spite of its worldly culture, that it was not hedonistic like spa towns. This was significant, as Stalinism stigmatized cosmopolitanism and associated it with "enemies of the people" and traitors—an association that appears to have lingered on until the 1970s.

The violent and heroic history of Novorossiysk, then, makes it worthy of its honorary title. Most respondents declared that they were proud of Novorossiysk's feat, and they insisted that the award was a commendation for its sacrifices.[155] Lyudmila Dorosh interpreted the government funds and the tourists flowing into Novorossiysk as expressions of the same appreciation.[156]

If one probes deeper, the issue of government recognition is not as simple as it presents itself on the outset. Novorossiysk's economically and politically privileged position inevitably also raised the question of how politicized war memory was in the city and whether this cheapened the "real value" of its heroism. Because of Malaya Zemlya's close connection to Brezhnev, this value was called into question even before perestroika.[157] Particularly painful for proud Novorossians were the jokes that began to circulate in the late 1970s. They clearly indicated that wide segments of society considered an aspect of official discourse to be ridiculous.[158]

To be fair, most jokes made fun less of the feat in Novorossiysk than of the Brezhnevite war cult. One of them mocks the fact that Brezhnev did not write his memoir personally. "Brezhnev asks Suslov: 'Did you read *Malaya Zemlya*?'—'Yes, twice. I liked it very much.'—'In this case I have to read it too.'"[159] In the most famous anecdote, Stalin asks Zhukov how the conquest of Berlin is progressing. "I don't know," he answers. "I first have to consult with Colonel Brezhnev."[160] The joke referred to the notorious quote that Zhukov was forced to include in his autobiography.

Because Malaya Zemlya and Brezhnev had, in the eyes of the vast majority of Soviet citizens, become almost synonymous, they could not be separated neatly. As a result, the reputation of the landing as a whole suffered as well. In one joke, two veterans meet up. One of them accuses the other of having relaxed in the trenches of Stalingrad while he had fought at Malaya Zemlya—a jab at official war memory's exaggeration of the beachhead's significance.

For years, politicians had told Novorossians and the entire nation that their feat equaled that of Stalingrad. During Brezhnev's visit in 1974, Sergey Medunov stated: "One can say without exaggeration that Novorossiysk and its defenders repeated the immortal feat of Stalingrad. They resisted and destroyed the enemy."[161] Respondents are ambivalent about this comparison. Yurina clearly states that, in spite of all of Novorossiysk's heroism, a comparison to Stalingrad is inappropriate. Sergey Tsymbal agrees, arguing that "Stalingrad is on a higher level."[162]

Galina Bozhok, on the other hand, defiantly insists that the comparison was justified—because of the concentrated intensity of fights on a tiny piece of land on Malaya Zemlya. She explains, however, that she had only recently arrived at this conclusion because of a fight her son had with his teacher about Brezhnev's role, and the research they subsequently did on the internet.[163] Her judgment thus reflects primarily the uncritical appropriation of "patriotic" historiography in contemporary Russia—but also a defiant reaction to the continued currency of the opinion that Novorossiysk's heroism was "not real."[164]

Georgiy Shcherbakov compares Novorossiysk to Stalingrad by virtue of their status as Hero Cities: "Of course [they are on the] same level! Because what is the difference? I do not see a big difference in what happened or in how to judge what happened in Tula, for example, and Novorossiysk. There was a feat there, and there was a feat here. The feat of Stalingrad, the feat of Sevastopol'. The feat of Novorossiysk."[165]

By reducing the category of comparison to "feats," Shcherbakov creates an equivalence between all Hero Cities. When asked why not all cities that fulfilled "feats" during the war became Hero Cities, he said that "only those who gave the awards, who made the decision, can answer this."[166] He thus implicitly admits to political factors for Novorossiysk's status.

THE REAL VALUE OF HEROISM

The search for the "real" value of heroism, independent of politicization and exaggeration, still preoccupies Novorossians today, as Davis notes as well.[167] Many exhibit a defensive attitude even when they are asked neutrally about their assessment. Vladimir Gusev occupied the most extreme position. When I questioned him about his participation in commemorative events, he would consistently look for a subtext. At the end of the interview, a question about Malaya Zemlya and Brezhnev led him to accuse me angrily of intentionally politicizing a sacred history.

Interestingly enough, he had earlier criticized Brezhnev's visit much more harshly than anyone else. To him, its "official" character contradicted the "true" meaning of Novorossiysk's heroic past. He was especially critical of the Hero City award: "These awards.... They gave them somewhere in some hall. You thought maybe this was among the people; no, it was behind closed doors (*kuluarnyy*), where Brezhnev appeared in a hall, then they broadcast it in the mass media, and that was it. They did not invite us; we did not go."[168]

Gusev thus expresses an opinion encountered repeatedly in Tula but only rarely in Novorossiysk, where the circumstances of Brezhnev's visit made people feel more involved. Still, the politicization also influenced Novorossians' interactions with people from other places. Tamara Yurina encountered jealousy regularly, as Voronezh, a city where hard fights had taken place as well, always felt slighted: "I was very insulted when people in Voronezh or other cities said that Novorossiysk did not deserve the honorary title of Hero City because Brezhnev fought there. This hurt me the most inside (*sovpala v dushu*). I endured this with trouble. I always wanted to show that him fighting here was actually not the main thing. The main thing was the events. They were not trivial ... but very, very important events ... for the entire Second World War."[169]

Yurina seems torn between her stance as a professional, detached historian and her personal attachment to the history of Novorossiysk. Still, she maintains the "objectively" crucial importance of the battle, which should not be touched by its politicization in the Brezhnev era.

Such defensiveness led to interviewees making sure to tell me that Novorossiysk deserved its position in the canon of war memory. Lyudmila Dorosh was insistent: "It was really deserved, there were such heavy battles here, and we did not only know this from newspapers and magazines but from local inhabitants."[170] This insistence on deriving knowledge not from official, state-sponsored media but from local, "authentic," personal memories appeared in various interviews. It seems to be an important yardstick by which to measure the past's real "value"; the politicization of war memory, considered sacred by many, appears to cheapen it.

Tamara Yurina, Galina Bozhok, Sergey Tsymbal, and Valeriy Sviderskiy also centered their argument for Novorossiysk's "worthiness" as a Hero City on the fact that the Germans did not manage to conquer it. They passionately rejected the objection of Gusev, who saw the hero status as unearned, because "in the city itself were the Germans, so why give the hero [the title of Hero City], right?"[171] For Bozhok, the fact that it was never completely conquered elevated Novorossiysk over Hero Cities like Kiev. Sviderskiy mentioned that even Odessa and Kerch' were given up: "This is why we thought we had a serious case [for being named a Hero City]."[172]

Local pride, then, unbroken almost eighty years after liberation, coexists uneasily with the awareness of the fact that Novorossiysk would not enjoy its symbolic or economic position without its close connection to Leonid Brezhnev. Even other Hero Cities—not to speak of the rest of the USSR—could only dream of Novorossiysk's privileges.

NOTES

1. Georgiy Shcherbakov, interview with the author, Novorossiysk, September 20, 2013, 27.40 min, 5.24 min.
2. Davis, *Myth Making in the Soviet Union and Modern Russia*, 107.
3. Dönninghaus and Savin, "Leonid Brezhnev," 187.
4. Sergey Novikov: "K Voprosy ob Ostavlenii Novorossiyska v Sentyabre 1942 goda."
5. Bacon, "Reconsidering Brezhnev," 15.
6. Bonwetsch, "Der 'Grosse Vaterländische Krieg,'" 176.
7. Yurina, *Novorossiyskoe Protivostoyanie*, 124.
8. More precisely, the documents for 1973, located at the Documentation Center for the Recent History of the Krasnodar Kray, have been declassified, but they were not accessible as of 2013, since the archivists had not vetted them for sensitive personal information. The materials for the Kraykom were available.
9. Brezhnev and Grechko, "Prosim Rassmotret' Vopros."
10. Valeriy Sviderskiy, interview with the author, Novorossiysk, September 23, 2013, 2.34 min.
11. Brezhnev and Grechko, "Prosim Rassmotret' Vopros," 150.

12. Brezhnev and Grechko, "Prosim Rassmotret' Vopros," 154.
13. Tamara Yurina, interview with the author, Novorossiysk, September 18, 2013, and Krasnodar, October 9, 2013, 171.02.
14. Brezhnev, "Uchastnikam Torzhestvennogo Zasedaniya i Vsem Trudyashchimsya Goroda Novorossiyska." Andrey Grechko also transmitted his best wishes for the city.
15. Podyma, "Viktor Golikov."
16. Yurina, interview, 172.45 min.
17. Anyone who has visited Russia can relate to her astonishment. Russians are not known for smiling a lot.
18. Quoted in *Novorossiyskiy Rabochiy*, September 17, 1973, 1.
19. "Vysoko Nesti Zvanie Goroda-Geroya, Byt' v Pervykh Ryadakh Bortsov za Delo Nashey Partii."
20. Davis, *Myth Making in the Soviet Union and Modern Russia*, 107.
21. Golikov, "Na Segodnya v Novorossiyske vse Gotovo."
22. Podyma, "Viktor Golikov."
23. Who, according to Davis, had asked him for years to organize a visit from Brezhnev. Davis, *Myth Making in the Soviet Union and Modern Russia*, 94.
24. Shishkova-Shipunova, *10 Praviteley Kubani*.
25. Semenov, "Nam Svetila Zvezda Udachi." In his speech in Novorossiysk on September 7, 1974, Brezhnev said that everyone was only talking about Novorossiysk's achievements. "But at the same time we should not forget that this city is part of Krasnodar Kray." Quoted in Tsygikalo, *Podvig Geroev Bessmerten*, 25.
26. Golikov, "Na Segodnya v Novorossiyske vse Gotovo," 168.
27. A visit in Paris in December 1974 turned into a disaster because the general secretary was no longer able to handle the physical strains of the official program. Schattenberg, *Leonid Breschnew*, 522.
28. Kolesov, *V Pamyati i v Serdtse*, 40.
29. Davis, *Myth Making in the Soviet Union and Modern Russia*, 105.
30. Lyudmila Dorosh, interview with the author, Novorossiysk, September 21, 2013, 9.51 min.
31. Vladimir Gusev, interview with the author, Novorossiysk, September 25, 2013, 8.40 min.
32. Many thanks to Vasiliy Khonin for providing me with his collection of historical images.
33. Dorosh, interview, 104.09 min.
34. Davis, *Myth Making in the Soviet Union and Modern Russia*, 125.
35. Sheudzhen: "Vzlety i Krakh Sergeya Medunova."
36. "In the relatively 'hands off' leadership style of Leonid Ilyich can once again be seen the beginnings of stagnation. In particular, in relation to the Soviet

regions, the attitude of 'autonomy with loyalty' increasingly took hold, with a subsequent slide toward corruption and mismanagement in many areas." Bacon, "Reconsidering Brezhnev," 15.

37. Dönninghaus and Savin write that in Brezhnev's later years, ritualized staging replaced his participation in the political process. Dönninghaus and Savin, "Leonid Brezhnev," 188.

38. Golikov, "Na Segodnya v Novorossiyske vse Gotovo," 168.

39. Kolesov, *V Pamyati i v Serdtse*, 24.

40. Kolesov, *V Pamyati i v Serdtse*, 19.

41. Zhukov, *Vospominaniya i Razmyshleniya*, 150.

42. Brezhnev, *Trilogy*, 44.

43. Brezhnev, *Trilogy*, 45.

44. Kolesov, *V Pamyati i v Serdtse*, 75.

45. Brezhnev, *Trilogy*, 64.

46. Schattenberg, *Leonid Breschnew*, 103.

47. Brezhnev, *Trilogy*, 16–17. Historians disagree over the number of times Brezhnev was in Malaya Zemlya. Medvedev claims he was only there twice. Medvedev, *Lichnost' Epokha*, 41. Tamara Yurina quotes Georgiy Kholostyakov's memoirs, in which he writes that he personally signed eleven crossing orders. Yurina, *Novorossiyskoe Protivostoyanie*, 270. As Kholostyakov's memoirs were published in 1976, however, it would have been unthinkable for the vice admiral to critically question Brezhnev's presence.

48. Kolesov, *V Pamyati i v Serdtse*, 15.

49. Medvedev, *Lichnost' Epokha*, 42.

50. Mikhaylov, *Gorod-Geroy Novorossiysk*, 48.

51. Varga-Harris, *Stories of House and Home*, 4.

52. Quoted in Yurina, *Novorossiyskoe Protivostoyanie*, 315.

53. This is the range provided in Soviet-era accounts. See Shiyan, *Novorossiysk*, 158; Zhurkin, *Gorod-Geroy Novorossiysk*, 245.

54. Kolesov, *V Pamyati i v Serdtse*, 99.

55. Eremenko and Podyma, *Imenem Rossii Narechennyy*, 270.

56. Kolesov, *V Pamyati i v Serdtse*, 99.

57. Quoted in Zhurkin, *Gorod-Geroy Novorossiysk*, 268.

58. Kolesov, *V Pamyati i v Serdtse*, 101.

59. Kolesov claims that during the first ten days alone, engineers and sappers removed thirty-three thousand mines and more than ten thousand unexploded aerial bombs and shells. Kolesov, *V Pamyati i v Serdtse*.

60. Romanov, "Krovotochashchie Rany Voyny," 159.

61. Dorosh, interview, 83.01 min.

62. Zhurkin, *Gorod-Geroy Novorossiysk*, 254–55.

63. Erokhin, *Novorossiysk*, 70.

64. See Zhurkin, *Gorod-Geroy Novorossiysk*, 254–55; Romanov, "Krovotochashchie Rany Voyny," 159.
65. Shurin, *Novorossiysk Stroitsya*, 3.
66. Novikov, "Strategii Vyzhivaniya Naseleniya Osvobozhdennogo g. Novorossiyska," 122.
67. *Gosudarstvennyy Arkhiv Rossiyskoy Federatsii* (GARF), f. A-150, op. 2, d. 79, l. 31. Many other cities, such as Sevastopol', encountered a similar gap between grand designs and postwar shortage of construction materials. Qualls, *From Ruins to Reconstruction*, 112.
68. Gusev, interview, 26.42 min.
69. Zhurkin, *Gorod-Geroy Novorossiysk*, 268.
70. Gusev, interview, 33.59 min.
71. Gusev, interview, 55.26 min.
72. Galina Bozhok, interview with the author, Novorossiysk, September 26, 2013, 45 min.
73. Dorosh, interview, 43.14 min; Natal'ya Grigor'eva, interview with the author, Novorossiysk, September 23, 2013, 13 min.
74. Sergey Tsymbal, interview with the author, Novorossiysk, September 23, 2013, 32.32 min.
75. Komissarov, *O Meropriyatiyakh po Vosstanovleniyu Rasrushennykh Nemetskimi Zakhvatchikami Gorodov RSFSR*.
76. Lapin, "Na Chertezhakh Iofana Novorossiysk Predstaval Grandioznym."
77. Qualls, *From Ruins to Reconstruction*, 47–61.
78. Shurin, *Novorossiysk Stroitsya*, 5.
79. In the decades after the war, planners dreamed of this kind of clean slate to build the socialist city. Bohn, *Minsk*, 12.
80. Quoted in Tsygikalo, *Podvig Geroev Bessmerten*, 24–25.
81. Kolesov, *V Pamyati i v Serdtse*, 39.
82. Sokolov, *U Yungi tozhe Serdtse Moryaka*, 5.
83. Kolesov, *V Pamyati i v Serdtse*, 69.
84. Zen'kov and Yartsev, "Potomkam na Pamyat'."
85. "Everywhere the broad aims of planners have been the same—to create an optimum living environment where enhanced productivity, social justice, and maximum satisfaction of the inhabitants would be attained." French and Hamilton, "Is There a Socialist City?," 5.
86. Mikhaylov, *Gorod-Geroy Novorossiysk*, 171.
87. Nadykta, "Kunikovka."
88. Nadykta, "Kunikovka."
89. Bozhok, interview, 16.53 min.
90. Bozhok, interview, 71.55 min.
91. Varga-Harris, *Stories of House and Home*, 207.

92. Yurina, interview, 104.26 min.
93. Yurina, interview, 105.54 min.
94. Mikhaylov, *Gorod-Geroy Novorossiysk*, 82.
95. Semenov, "Nam Svetila Zvezda Udachi," 5.
96. As well as in most other Soviet cities. See, for example, DeHaan, *Stalinist City Planning*.
97. Semenov, "Nam Svetila Zvezda Udachi," 5.
98. Davis, *Myth Making in the Soviet Union and Modern Russia*, 108.
99. Gorlizki, "Too Much Trust," 693.
100. GARF, f. R-5446, op. 102, d. 293, l. 3. I am not sure whether this was the total investment. If one adds up the items in the plan, 35 million appears rather low. Additional funds may have been contributed from other sources.
101. GARF, f. R-5446, op. 102, d. 293, l. 1.
102. Varga-Harris, *Stories of House and Home*, 56.
103. GARF, f. R-5446, op. 102, d. 293, l. 1.
104. The population dedicated a total of fifty thousand man-hours of (by Soviet standards) voluntary labor to completing the sixty-seven kilometers of pipes. Novikov, "Bol'shaya Voda," accessed March 9, 2015 (site discontinued).
105. Zhurkin, *Gorod-Geroy Novorossiysk*, 277.
106. GARF, f. R-5446, op. 102, d. 293, l. 3.
107. New schools were especially necessary, as many children were still taught in three shifts. GARF, f. A-259, op. 45, d. 7429, ll. 3–4. These measures were not sufficient. By 1977, a third of the city's students were still instructed in two or three shifts. GARF, f. R-5446, op. 102, d. 286, l. 11.
108. GARF, f. A-259, op. 45, d. 7429, l. 65.
109. In spite of continuing deficiencies, childcare facilities in the Soviet Union improved dramatically in the 1960s and 1970s and were mostly linked to the enterprises with which one worked. Kelly, *Children's World*, 393. Furthermore, in a context of labor shortage, a strategic enterprise like the Trest 12 had to offer its workers good fringe benefits.
110. Mariya Inozemetseva, interview with the author, Novorossiysk, September 26, 2013, 13.36 min. Inozemetseva was born in Ukraine in 1952 and grew up in poverty. As a single mother, she found refuge in Novorossiysk: "I came to a foreign city, with a five-year-old girl on one hand and a suitcase in another. It was risky. Many people . . . whom I met later do not know this about me." Inozemetseva, interview, 74.29 min.
111. GARF, f. R-5446, op. 102, d. 286, l. 17.
112. GARF, f. R-5446, op. 102, d. 286, l. 10.
113. GARF, f. R-5446, op. 102, d. 286, l. 8.
114. The military was entitled to 9,710 m^2 between 1973 and 1976 alone, according to Semenov. GARF, f. R-5446, op. 102, d. 286, l. 10.

115. GARF, f. R-5446, op. 102, d. 286, l. 9; Zhurkin, *Gorod-Geroy Novorossiysk*, 291; Eremenko and Podyma, *Imenem Rossii Narechennyy*, 271.

116. GARF, f. R-5446, op. 102, d. 286, l. 8.

117. According to the norm, each inhabitant of Novorossiysk was entitled to 81.8 kilograms of meat, 433.6 kilograms of milk, and 292 eggs. GARF, f. R-5446, op. 102, d. 286, l. 10. This was, however, illusory: in its internal communication, the Politburo admitted that 7 kilograms of meat per person and year was as good as it got in reality. Schattenberg, *Leonid Breschnew*, 618.

118. Ruble, *Leningrad*, 96–97.

119. Mark Smith, *Property of Communists*, 151.

120. Mikhaylov, *Gorod-Geroy Novorossiysk*, 170.

121. Mikhaylov, *Gorod-Geroy Novorossiysk*, 170.

122. Zhurkin, *Gorod-Geroy Novorossiysk*, 294.

123. Gusev, interview, 60.18 min.

124. Novorossiyskiy Gorodskoy Sovet Deputatov Trudyashchikhsya, *Kompleksnyy Plan Sotsial'no-Ekonomicheskogo Razvitiya g. Novorossiyska na 1976–1980 Gody*, 3.

125. Zhurkin, *Gorod-Geroy Novorossiysk*, 283–84.

126. Zhuk, "Religion, 'Westernization,' and Youth."

127. *Tsentr Dokumentatsii Noveyshey Istorii Krasnodarskogo Kraya* (TsDNIKK), f. 3495, op. 9, d. 17, l. 13.

128. Zhuk sees a failure to prevent "ideological pollution" in Dnepropetrovsk. Zhuk, "Religion, 'Westernization,' and Youth," 679.

129. Chernyshova, *Soviet Consumer Culture in the Brezhnev Era*, 160.

130. Tsipursky, *Socialist Fun*, 9.

131. On Soviet consumers' reactions to this exhibition, see Reid, "'Our Kitchen Is Just as Good.'"

132. Novikov, "Kak 'Stolichnuyu' na 'Pepsi' Menyali," accessed March 11, 2015 (site discontinued).

133. Novikov, "Kak 'Stolichnuyu' na 'Pepsi' Menyali."

134. Davis, *Myth Making in the Soviet Union and Modern Russia*, 109.

135. As the local newspaper printed a TASS article, it was also published in Union newspapers like *Pravda*. TASS, "Na Zemle Boevoy i Trudovoy Slavy."

136. Quoted in Tsygikalo, *Podvig Geroev Bessmerten*, 28.

137. Nikolay Mitrokhin claims that Golikov was ideologically close to the Russian nationalists. Golikov especially believed in the necessity of using war memory as a means of militaristic mobilization and supported controversial neo-Stalinist writers' projects for this end. Mitrokhin, *Die "Russische Partei,"* 107.

138. Quoted in Tsygikalo, *Podvig Geroev Bessmerten*, 48.

139. Zubok, *Failed Empire*, 246.

140. Schattenberg, *Leonid Breschnew*, 516.

141. Novikov, "Kak 'Stolichnuyu' na 'Pepsi' Menyali." Unfortunately for the taste buds of Novorossians, the Pepsi experiment was short-lived: the renewal of the production facilities in 1986 no longer enjoyed priority and was neglected. With the collapse of the USSR five years later, a Soviet brand of Pepsi had become irrelevant as the American company flooded the market.

142. Yurina, interview, 94.57 min.
143. Yurina, interview, 95.51 min.
144. Dorosh, interview, 36.34 min.
145. Dorosh, interview, 39.05 min.
146. Dorosh, interview, 40.03 min.
147. See Millar, "Little Deal."
148. Gusev, interview, 62.06 min. On *blat*, see also Dubin, "Litso Epokhi," 28.
149. Inozemetseva, interview, 48.51 min.
150. Lyudmila Shalagina, interview with the author, Novorossiysk, September 27, 2013, 55.41 min.
151. See, for instance, Shiyan, *Novorossiysk*, 7–9.
152. Tsymbal, interview, 30.17 min.
153. Günther, *Der sozialistische Übermensch*, 175.
154. Shcherbakov, interview, 57.55 min.
155. Natal'ya Grigor'eva stated this almost verbatim. Grigor'eva, interview, 8.52 min.
156. Dorosh, interview, 111.52 min.
157. Historians like Medvedev and Michael Ignatieff dismissed the battle as a "minor skirmish" in the 1980s. Ignatieff, "Soviet War Memorials," 158.
158. "An important reason for the genre's storied fecundity was its capacity to outflank, mimic, debunk, deconstruct, and otherwise critically engage other genres and texts of all stripes." Graham, *Resonant Dissonance*, 64.
159. Quoted in Vanyukov, *Epokha Zastoya*, 211.
160. "Anekdoty pro Brezhneva," accessed September 22, 2020.
161. Quoted in Tsygikalo, *Podvig Geroev Bessmerten*, 53.
162. Tsymbal, interview, 49.49 min.
163. Bozhok, interview, 83.24 min.
164. The main controversies in post-Soviet historiography revolve around the enormous price of holding Malaya Zemlya—without making progress toward the liberation of Novorossiysk for many months. Post-Soviet authors estimate that the Red Army lost about twenty-one thousand soldiers there. German losses were lower; their exact number remains a subject of contestation. See Yurina, *Novorossiyskoe Protivostoyanie*, 270; Shapoval, "Bol'shaya Lozh' o 'Maloy Zemle'"; Lapin, "Byl li Predan Otchayannyy Desant?," 3.
165. Shcherbakov, interview, 56.17.
166. Shcherbakov, interview, 57.14 min.

167. Davis, *Myth Making in the Soviet Union and Modern Russia*, 134–40.
168. Gusev, interview, 74.59 min.
169. Yurina, interview, 189.25 min.
170. Dorosh, interview, 110.18 min.
171. Gusev, interview, 9.28 min.
172. Sviderskiy, interview, 5.43 min.

SEVEN

Impossible Continuity

THE HEROIZATION AND IDEALIZATION OF war memory formed the basis for the conversion of a traumatic experience into a discourse of societal inclusion. Mass death had created the precondition for life after the war, and the heroes of official war memory symbolized and made tangible the unimaginable sacrifices. What is more, they turned them into models for shared "Soviet" values even in the Brezhnev era.

In Brezhnev-era Novorossiysk and Tula, official memory distilled the Great Patriotic War into a simple story for the younger generation: the heroic resistance of a unified collective of soldiers, workers, women, and children had stopped the German onslaught at crucial junctions of the war. Their contributions to what Soviet historiography called the "great turning points" of the war justified their elevation to Hero City status.

Novorossiysk paid a much higher price in terms of both human and material losses: it was completely destroyed, while Tula only sustained limited damage. These different experiences significantly affected postwar life: while both cities would take more than a decade to become habitable again, Novorossiysk, unlike Tula, was a truly deadly place because of unexploded bombs and shells as well as the many mines and traps the occupiers left behind.

Tens of thousands of inhabitants in the two cities did not survive. Both were emptied during the war; the Tulyaki fled or were evacuated with their enterprises, while a significant part of Novorossiysk's civilian population died or underwent deportation. Wartime violence and postwar industrial growth led to an almost complete population exchange in Tula and Novorossiysk. Most Brezhnev-era inhabitants of the Hero Cities thus did not have firsthand knowledge of the period between 1941 and 1945. They relied primarily on official memory media to access wartime events.

Tula's and Novorossiysk's "mass heroism" formed the basis of their official identity. "Unheroic" moments like looting and chaos in Tula or disorganization, mass murder, and collaboration in Novorossiysk were concealed. As a result of the cities' exemplary statuses, their inhabitants were meant to derive an obligation to show themselves "worthy" even during the Brezhnev era. The Hero City collective offered an attractive, transgenerational offer for identification.

Conversely, the metaphoric representation of wartime feats meant that the sacrifices remained vague: the postwar generation could only guess at the horrors of the past. This contributed to war memory's sacral aura and elevated its moral power but also gave it a haunting and supernatural quality. Alexander Etkind called these fragments of the past returning to the present "the uncanny," a combination of unprocessed memory and fear of future violence.[1]

Instead of confronting the past, the party leadership streamlined its interpretation—increasingly relying on official war memory to compensate for the flagging mobilizational power of socialist ideology. In both cities, the economization and politicization of the past led to popular ambivalence, particularly in the late 1970s.

The economization of war memory had surprising effects. When Tula became a Hero City in 1976, the expectation of perks was tangible, as a result of the city authorities' lobbying for additional benefits in the 1960s. They had successfully emphasized Tula's heroism on the anniversaries of victory and the Battle of Moscow. But when the honorary title was bestowed, large-scale additional benefits did not materialize; Brezhnev's limited promises were widely perceived to be inadequate and unworthy of a Hero City.

Conversely, as "Brezhnev's Hero City," Novorossiysk profited greatly from additional investments. It found itself in a sweet spot, inhabiting the highest position in the official heroarchy, playing a crucial economic role because of its port as well as its industry, and enjoying excellent connections to the leadership. As the first investment program of 1968 shows, the city needed all three for a decisive improvement in living standards. Tula at most had two: its connections to the elite were good but not excellent. Its heavy industry, moreover, was less suited for the *blat'* practices that complemented the shortcomings of the planned economy in Novorossiysk.

All of these aspects are intimately tied to the question of Tula's and Novorossiysk's "worthiness" as Hero Cities. "Worthiness" was measured in terms of obligation and reward, which formed a tenuous balance. Everyday urban life in the Hero Cities was to be "worthy" of their glorious past—in terms of continued service to the fatherland and of living conditions.

This "socialist contract," which was founded in the war and reiterated throughout the Khrushchev and Brezhnev eras, reinforced the connection between expectation and service. Official discourse encouraged the populations of Tula and Novorossiysk to feel entitled rather than obligated: Brezhnev himself had called a decent standard of living the precondition for achievements in labor.

The Brezhnev era's emphasis on consumption as an inherent part of Soviet identity contributed to this sense—life in a Hero City included "worthy" living standards. Tula and Novorossiysk profited from this alternative system of stratification based on wartime merit. While the economy expanded, funds were available for housing and communal services. The slump that was beginning in the second half of the 1970s led to stagnation in living standards or, in Tula's case, to deterioration. The "socialist contract" increasingly came under pressure. Novorossiysk was luckier, as the main decisions that assured its upswing were put in place a decade earlier.

With the economic downturn, they were increasingly reabsorbed into the fundamental laws according to which the USSR functioned: only the most well connected and politically most prevalent were able to secure improvements. This disparity testifies to the limitations of the Soviet system when it came to promoting popular welfare—and to those of the official heroarchy, which pretended to put all Hero Cities on the same level.

During the same period, the overuse of official war memory led to a sense of inflation and a loss of significance of the official heroarchy. Tulyaki and Novorossians were truly proud of their cities and their inclusion into the top tier of the USSR's finely stratified "heroarchy." Nevertheless, doubts remained whether their membership in the "family of Hero Cities" put them on the same level as their older counterparts. Neither had been part of the first wave of Hero Cities, whose feats had already been recognized during the Great Patriotic War. Because of the postwar generation's awareness of war memory's increasing politicization, a later recognition was "worth" less; there was a clear division within the Hero Cities between more important and lesser members—bigger and smaller brethren.

THE DISSOLUTION OF OFFICIAL WAR MEMORY

The embodiment of the official heroarchy's deflation was Leonid Brezhnev himself. Between 1976 and his death, he received three Gold Star medals, as well as the Lenin Peace Price for his memoirs. He was named Marshal of the Soviet Union and awarded the prestigious Order of Victory, which only nineteen military leaders had received before him—all during wartime.

Brezhnev's death on November 10, 1982, brought about corrections of official war memory's excesses. He was posthumously stripped of his Order of Victory. His death was felt acutely in Novorossiysk: the city became the object of ridicule. Malaya Zemlya's towering position in official war memory was scaled back, and Brezhnev's autobiography was removed from schools' reading lists. New publications about the beachhead omitted Brezhnev's name and focused on the defenders' collective heroism instead.

Aside from the omission of Brezhnev's personality cult, little changed in official war memory, despite the growing instability of Soviet politics. Yuriy Andropov, who recognized the stagnation of the system, died in February 1984, soon after embarking upon a reform program. His successor, Konstantin Chernenko, had been in power for thirteen months when he succumbed to heart and liver failure in 1985.[2] Only after Brezhnev's peers had literally died out did the Politburo make way for generational change, electing Mikhail Gorbachev, born in 1931, as the new general secretary.

Gorbachev initially reproduced the tenets of official war memory. The fortieth anniversary of victory in 1985 featured the ritualistic elements of its predecessors in the 1970s. For Tula, the year represented a last high point, as it hosted the Convention of Winners of the All-Union Tours to the Sites of Revolutionary, Military, and Labor Glory in an expensive and elaborate festival of patriotism. Twelve hundred champions of regional competitions met in the Hero City from May 8 to May 12.

The official logo of the convention (fig. 7.1) showed three generations of Soviet heroes, symbolized by their headwear: the *Budenovka*, worn in the Civil War, sits atop the soldiers' helmet of the Great Patriotic War and the construction helmet of the Baikal-Amur Mainline (BAM)—the signature project of the Brezhnev era. The Central Staff of the All-Union Tours in Moscow noted that Soviet traditions would be used to create greater understanding of Leninism in the service of Gorbachev's policy of *uskorenie*—acceleration.[3] Once more, the notion of transgenerational unity was put forward to legitimize a political turn.

The main event of the All-Union Tours took place on Victory Day, when a troop carrier brought holy fire from the Tomb of the Unknown Soldier in Moscow to Tula, mixing it with that of the city's weapons factory. The flame thus fused labor and military glory. In Tula's stadium, a theatrical performance retold the history of the Soviet Union in a straight line from the big industrial construction sites of Stalinism through the war to the construction of BAM.

Figure 7.1. The logo of the 1985 Convention of Winners of the All-Union Tours to the Sites of Revolutionary, Military, and Labor Glory, showing three generations of heroes. Courtesy of the Russian State Archive of Socio-Political History

During the performance, officers lauded youths' contribution to the defense of their fatherland against Western imperialists.[4] International tensions over the war in Afghanistan, rearmament in Europe, and NATO's Able Archer exercise strengthened militarist rhetoric in the USSR. Gorbachev's peace policy would only gain track in the second half of the decade.

The general secretary, in his speech in Moscow, criticized imperialism but also lauded the Hero Cities, who had received two new members just three days before: Murmansk and Smolensk. Gorbachev claimed that the entire world remembered their "unswerving courage."[5] Their ascension to the highest tier of the heroarchy had been prepared during the Brezhnev era, as Murmansk received the Order of the Patriotic War in 1982 and Smolensk in 1966.[6] Both cities were awarded the Order of Lenin in 1983. Gorbachev carried out a decision that was long in the making on the anniversary of the war, thus following a well-established tradition.

Less than a year later, official war memory was coming under increased public scrutiny. Gorbachev's glasnost policy, accelerated as a result of the dismal handling of the Chernobyl disaster, complicated the further homogenization of commemoration.[7] This was evident in the construction of the central war monument in Moscow. Planning for it had begun in 1957. It was meant to serve as a centerpiece for official war memory and to underline Moscow's position as the leading Hero City.

A closed competition in 1979 had yielded a winning project, and a staggering 190 million rubles had been collected in *subbotniki*. Construction was to begin in 1984. The more liberal public climate emboldened criticism, forcing Moscow's city authorities to hold an open competition in September 1986, for which no winner was chosen.[8] Before the monument at Poklonnaya Gora was finally built in 1993, it had gone through many detours: the Moscow Committee of War Veterans claimed in 1990 that 62 out of the 190 million rubles had been "thrown down the drain." Less than a year later, the Cabinet of Ministers had to authorize additional funds to finish the construction.[9]

The fate of the monument exemplifies the disorientation that increasingly accompanied the official assessment of the Great Patriotic War and the Soviet past. Just as during the Thaw under Khrushchev, long-suppressed controversies over Stalinist terror erupted—often along the same lines.[10] Historians debated the price of war, resulting in Gorbachev's estimation that twenty-seven million people had died. Eastern European countries demanded the truth about the shooting of Polish officers in Katyn in 1940 and the brutal Soviet annexation of Estonia, Lithuania, and Latvia. The independence movements in the Baltics claimed the right to write their own history instead of reproducing clichés about the "brotherhood of nations."[11]

The party state lost control over the interpretation of the past, while Gorbachev maneuvered hesitantly between demanding "openness" and trying to contain the mounting wave of criticism. Civil society organizations like Memorial began to uncover the "blank spots" of official war memory. A multitude of recollections that had been suppressed reached the public. Historians who were freed from the shackles of dogma began to question some of the greatest feats' veracity, including the last stand of Panfilov's men near Moscow in 1941 or Alexander Matrosov's self-sacrifice in 1943.[12]

This rapid collapse of official war memory's central tenets strongly affected patriotic education. The Komsomol discontinued the tours to the sites of glory in 1987. In June 1988, history tests for all students were canceled. A year later, the Congress of People's Deputies of the Soviet Union admitted the existence of the Hitler-Stalin Pact's secret addendum about the partition of large parts of Central and Eastern Europe between the Soviets and the National Socialists. Another taboo had been broken.

The controversies overshadowed the celebrations of Victory Day in 1990. While Minister of Defense Dmitriy Yazov, who would be one of the Putschists against Gorbachev in 1991, repeated the heroic tropes of official war memory, the president discussed the repressions in the Red Army and its unpreparedness in 1941.[13] The newspaper *Komsomol'skaya Pravda* printed statements from a veteran who accused the state of having stolen victory by abusing it for political purposes. Vladimir Kryuchkov, head of the KGB and another subsequent coup leader in August, compared such critical publications to the German attack in 1941.[14]

The deviating interpretations of the war reflected the profound tensions between orthodox communists and democratic reformers—with Gorbachev stuck in between. They would come to a head in the failed coup, which doomed the USSR: stripped of all legitimacy and political will to hold it together, the union rapidly dissolved in the second half of 1991. The unified official discourse on the war was dislocated as those institutions that had promoted it were disbanded and alternative narratives reemerged.

POST-SOVIET CHAOS

Under president Boris Yeltsin, the post-Soviet Russian state emerged in the midst of ideological confusion, political chaos, and rapidly deteriorating economic conditions. Many of the thousands of citizens who had defended him against the tanks of the old regime in August 1991 quickly became disillusioned or preoccupied with survival. In national politics, the power struggle between the reformers around Yeltsin and the nationalist-communist opposition climaxed in the president's order to shell the White House in October 1993, leaving hundreds dead and undermining public confidence in the new democratic order.

The chronologist Irina Paramonova has provided a detailed description of this period in Tula; her rich mosaic provides an impression of how dramatic and traumatic the changes were, not just in the capital but also in the provinces. The nuclear accident at Chernobyl, which had exposed eighteen subregions of Tula Oblast' to radiation, was a first caesura in 1986. Twenty-six hundred Tulyaki, most of them miners, were called to the disaster site as first responders. Three hundred of them would die subsequently because of insufficient protection against radiation during the work.[15] Three years later, the military city witnessed a humiliating retreat from Afghanistan, which affected its heroic self-image. Four thousand Tulyaki had fought in the campaign; their return to a country in turmoil left many without economic perspectives, often resulting in a life of crime.[16]

Living conditions rapidly deteriorated—only a few years after Gorbachev's 1986 promise that every family would have their own apartment by 2000. After Tula had fulfilled the plan for housing construction for the first time in many years in 1988, thanks to a new credit scheme, it came to a virtual standstill because of supply problems. At the same time, vouchers were introduced for basic goods like sugar, flour, and laundry detergent. In 1990, the supply crisis came to a head, and in October 1991, breadlines formed. The Hero City received humanitarian aid from Germany and the United States.[17] In the 1990s it would lose a fifth of its population to emigration and high mortality.

Post-Soviet Russia suffered a deep economic crisis, as the government applied shock treatment to reform the economy. Tula's experience reflected many of the national processes: the liberalization of prices led to a tenfold increase within two years. Housing costs soared for those who did not own their Soviet-era apartments. The government struggled to pay pensions, and Soviet citizens had to face the new phenomenon of mass unemployment. Under these circumstances, many were forced to sell the vouchers they had received to make them co-owners of privatized enterprises. Those with disposable cash bought the shares at low prices, often cheating the desperate sellers. To add insult to injury, naive Russians lost their savings in fraudulent investment schemes such as the Ponzi scheme MMM (named after the last names of the company's founders) and the ruble devaluation in 1998.[18]

The rapid transformation from a socialist to a highly deficient capitalist economy in the midst of a profound crisis undermined all the notions that had marked Soviet official discourse. The socialist contract was disbanded, as the state was no longer in a position to reward service, and its representatives became preoccupied with taking advantage of the new opportunities linked to privatization. As a result, living conditions for average Russians were anything but worthy.

The defense sector, crucial for the city, was hit particularly hard: the state reduced its expenses for the armed forces by two-thirds in 1992, and military industrial output fell by 80 percent between the mid-1980s and 1997.[19] Tula's weapons factory, producing arms since 1712, stood on the verge of bankruptcy in 1997. Workers' strikes only ended once Tula's governor had promised to pay wage arrears from the Oblast' budget.[20] "At the start of serious reform, both managers and workers were faced with the frightening possibility of the collapse of the regional economy," conclude Baglione and Clark.[21]

Novorossiysk was confronted with many of the same problems and similarly chaotic conditions. Its industrial base suffered, as did the port—not least because the agricultural production that went through it contracted due to reduced subsidies from Moscow.[22] Tourism shrank as the trade unions that had maintained the facilities ran out of money, patriotic excursions ceased, and the wealthier part of the population could fly abroad for the same cost as a trip to the Black Sea.[23] The political scientist Svetlana Shishkova-Shipunova describes the state of society and politics as one of "total crisis."[24]

As a result of the turmoil, both Krasnodar Kray and Tula became part of the Red Belt—a region in Central Russia where overlapping industrial and agricultural crises hampered recovery for years.[25] The disappointing results of democratic and economic reforms as well as the incompetence of many Yeltsin-appointed cadres brought Communist leaders back to power in the second half of the 1990s. In Tula, Vasiliy Starodubtsev, participant in the 1991 coup, became governor. His new counterpart, Nikolay Kondratenko in Krasnodar, had sympathized with the Putsch. They now serviced their constituents' nostalgia for the Soviet Union, running on protectionist, populist, and—in Kondratenko's case—a xenophobic and antisemitic platform.[26]

Fears of a Communist "revanche," however, remained unfounded. "The new governors quickly embourgeoised and lost all passion for radicalism. Once in the governors' seat, the Communists noticed with astonishment that they had to build capitalism," writes the journalist Maksim Artem'ev.[27] Communist slogans largely remained folklore, with the exception of stabilizing some elements of the social safety net, for instance by subsidizing bread prices. This subsidization was a far cry from worthy living conditions, but it constituted the bare minimum of a new kind of social contract. However, if these new leaders wanted any kind of financial maneuvering space, they needed to attract foreign investment. To advance their economic interests, political leaders showed remarkable ideological flexibility.[28]

Still, Starodubtsev and Kondratenko maintained state control over those sectors that they considered strategically significant—the defense industry in Tula and the port in Novorossiysk—thus reflecting the politics of the ascendant "statists."[29] Both governors created a regional "party of power" around them, which united Communist-era "red directors," new entrepreneurs, and influential officials. In Tula, the defense industry kept close political and economic connections to the capital—continuing Soviet patterns in select sectors. Enterprises maintained a paternalistic relationship to their employees, taking care of housing and other social services.[30] By the late 1990s, they also profited from increased government spending on armament as the statists' influence grew.[31]

When Vladimir Putin took power in 2000, he refined this mix of paternalism and liberalism—albeit subjected to a strong state—which marks Russia's economy still today. Putin recentralized power, considerably limiting regional elites' autonomy.[32] He broke the Communists' hold over the "Red Belt"; compared to Yeltsin, Putin improved his election results in this region by 15 to 30 percent: "Putin snatched the great-power-patriotic rhetoric from the Communists, and all those who had painfully experienced the 'capitulation' of Moscow before the West, joined the side of the new president with relief."[33]

He nevertheless left many governors in office—with some exceptions.[34] Kondratenko had to step down in 2001 under pressure from Moscow. Starodubtsev held on to power in Tula until 2005, when he was replaced by Vyacheslav Dudka, a candidate promoted directly by Putin. This heavy-handed approach did not work well: Dudka, a former deputy director of the arms company KBP Instrument Design Bureau, was removed in 2011 amid a power struggle with the mayor of Tula and subsequently was sentenced to nine and a half years in prison because of corruption.[35]

He was deeply unpopular because he had no tangible improvements to show, particularly in terms of the Oblast's notoriously bad infrastructure; this became one of the main complaints of Tulyaki for many years, symbolizing the deterioration of public space and unworthiness of living conditions. Dmitriy Medvedev then installed the Muscovite supermarket entrepreneur and billionaire Vladimir Gruzdev. This marked a transition both in generation and in style: media-savvy forty-four-year-old Gruzdev traveled the Oblast' and met people, built new roads, and finished the highway to Moscow.

Aleksandr Tkachev, who was the governor of Krasnodar Kray from 2001 to 2015, fit a similar profile: "Tkachev's historical mission was to turn Krasnodar into an investment place for ambitious twenty-first-century projects," writes Svetlana Shishkova-Shipunova.[36] During his tenure, the regional budget increased from 13.5 to 200 billion rubles. Agricultural reforms multiplied yields, and he fostered an unprecedented real estate boom. Sochi regained its leading position in tourism, a development that culminated in the 2014 Winter Olympics.

The fact that both Putin and Medvedev used the mundane resort town as their summer residence ensured a close relationship to the Kremlin that was reminiscent of the days under Sergey Medunov. Other similarities included the absence of political competition in the Kray, the profound lack of transparency in political affairs, and the frequent corruption allegations against Tkachev's entourage.[37]

OVERCOMING SYMBOLIC POVERTY

Tkachev and Gruzdev, then, were two typical governors of the Putin era—pro-business, ideologically flexible, but statist—and loyal to Moscow. The Kremlin expects this type of modernizing technocrat to secure political stability, not least by providing the population with improvements in their quality of life. Although reassembled under conditions of a capitalist system, this ruling technique features elements familiar from Soviet times, including the selection and dispatch of cadres from Moscow, as well as a paternalist social contract.

Modernization and "Sovereign democracy," however, do not suffice to explain political stability under Vladimir Putin.[38] Miguel Vázquez Liñán points out that society needs a "place" to return to. "Thus, the narratives of modernization and historical memory become the two sides of hegemonic political discourse in Russia."[39]

Putin reestablished a heroic discourse on the Great Patriotic War. The years following the collapse of the Soviet Union were indeed marked by a poverty of symbols, as Boris Dubin has pointed out.[40] Boris Yeltsin abolished the Victory Day parade on May 9, hoping to create a less militaristic official culture for the country—not least because the army leadership had supported the coup in August 1991. However, his government did not succeed in creating a post-Soviet canon of holidays.[41] Alternative celebrations on Victory Day, such as a "peace parade" sponsored by corporations, did not gain traction either. In

1993, the government organized ceremonies at the newly opened monument at Poklonnaya Gora. The communist-nationalist opposition met at the Tomb of the Unknown Soldier near the Kremlin, holding a competing event that was particularly popular among veterans.

Yeltsin reintroduced the military parade in 1995, inviting a number of international leaders to the fiftieth anniversary of victory. At the request of Bill Clinton, who did not want to appear to endorse the Chechen War, the parade was divided into two parts, with the military hardware being shown only at Poklonnaya Gora and not at Red Square.[42] During his second term after 1996, Yeltsin would accentuate patriotic rhetoric and symbolism, without building consensus.[43] The post-Soviet crisis was too present still, and the ailing leader was ill-suited to inspire confidence and unity.

The chaos, political weakness, and ideological uncertainty has left a deep impression on Russian society. Most do not remember the 1990s as a time of democratization but as a "Time of Troubles," the historical analogy being the *smuta* in the early seventeenth century. My interviews consistently reflected this view. Respondents associate economic difficulties and cynicism with the 1990s. University professor Irina Sycheva calls the decade a "horrible" and "dirty" time, in which the names of Tula's heroes and the Hero City were besmirched as historians deconstructed the propaganda surrounding Soviet feats.[44]

Sycheva exemplifies a general tendency found particularly among older Russians: to associate the de-heroization of the war—which gave rise to a more sober investigation into its history—with the "decomposition" (*rassloenie*) of the state and society in which they were raised. Even Sergey Stepuzhin, the high school history teacher in Tula, whose father underwent dekulakization, blames the political crisis of the 1990s on the absence of the positive values that had been connected to war memory.[45]

Most Russians thus exhibit a low tolerance for alternative interpretations of history.[46] Tumarkin writes that "the loss of the war cult was another loss of something familiar, and to many citizens, comforting."[47] I would go even further in arguing that it meant the loss of the "bracket" that held Russia together. Communist ideology had already lost its integrative function in the late USSR. Now, official war memory had lost its social power as well. With the collapse of the state that had promoted the link between the heroic past and the socialist present, spiritual dislocation was complete, accompanied by the loss of wide swaths of the former empire and a downward economic spiral.

Vladimir Putin understood the need for a new state ideology. The creation of patriotic symbols was among his first priorities on assuming power. They included tsarist and Soviet elements, extending the transgenerational unity beyond 1917. Still, the Great Patriotic War played the most important role.[48] Putin moved his own inauguration to May 7, 2000, immediately before Victory Day, ritually linking the two dates.[49] In his speeches on war memory, the president began to reproduce Brezhnev-era discourse and symbolism—only leaving out the socialist signifiers.[50] The pompous military parade in honor of victory's sixtieth anniversary in 2005 was the first highpoint of the revived war cult.

The new Russian patriotism, which was expressed through official war memory, fulfilled a function similar to that of its Brezhnev-era predecessor: as in 1965, it sutured together a national identity that had been dislocated by controversy. The heroic and idealized history stood for pride in historical achievements, the power of the state, and the unity of generations and various sectors of society. That it referred back to the past of a different nation, the Soviet Union, added a certain inconsistency; on the other hand, it allowed for the projection of Russian "soft power" to Eurasian countries, where official war memory had also been widely disseminated during Soviet times.

Putin made use of the same link between increased popular welfare and the heroic past as Brezhnev; the 2000s saw a marked improvement in living conditions. The leader was again an important part of the war cult, albeit not as a veteran. Since 2004, Putin has talked regularly about his family's tragic war experience, thereby connecting his personal history with that of millions of Russians. In meetings with veterans, he presents himself as a dutiful son who provides for their needs. In reminding youth of their moral obligations through patriotic education, he occupies a paternal role.[51] In the parades, he becomes a strong commander in chief—elevating the symbolic status of the Russian military.

Contemporary official war memory may be strongly state sponsored, but it is not nearly as controlled by the center's ideological and societal institutions as in the Soviet Union. In spite of authoritarian traits, Russia is a much more open society. Critical discussions about all aspects of the war take place on the internet, in newspapers, and on television. A variety of websites collect uncensored histories of veterans and make them available to readers. Local historians, journalists, and organizations—among them Memorial in more than fifty Russian regions—document the past objectively and largely without false pathos.[52]

Their work has become more difficult in recent years, however. Some have moved on to other fields, frustrated by the increasing pressure and extreme difficulty of making a living in academia or as independent cultural actors, particularly in the provinces. Others are disillusioned by the fact that Vladimir Medinskiy, Russian minister of culture until January 2020, keeps his PhD title in history, even though an expert panel ruled that he had plagiarized his dissertation. He strongly promoted "patriotic" history and insists that feats such as the desperate last stand of twenty-eight Panfilov soldiers against an entire German division took place as described in Stalinist propaganda.[53] Two comedies on Stalin and the war, on the other hand, were banned because they were "insulting."[54]

Internationally renowned institutions such as the European University in Saint Petersburg struggle: the school only regained its teaching permission and accreditation recently, after the educational authorities at Rosobrnadsor had withdrawn it on the basis of bogus charges.[55] Critical nongovernmental organizations like Memorial have been labeled "foreign agents" because of their links abroad. Visa regulations for foreign researchers are much more strictly enforced than in 2012–13, when the bulk of the research for this book was conducted.

Russia under Putin is a country in which state institutions distrust independent, grassroots initiatives—especially in a cultural field that is as sensitive as official war memory. They seldom use overt censorship, but they set systematic disincentives for critical voices and appropriate others. This combination of embracement and repression appears familiar from the Brezhnev era.

RUSSIA'S MEMORY SUPERMARKET

The mourning ritual Immortal Regiment (*bessmertnyy polk*) illustrates the approach. In 2007 a veteran from Tyumen called upon his compatriots to carry portraits of people who had fought in the war through the city.[56] Journalists in Tomsk extended this grassroots initiative and founded a march to honor family members who had served in the Great Patriotic War. In 2012, six thousand people in various places, including Tula, gathered for a walk, without explicit political or commercial motives, carrying simple photographs of their relatives on small wooden poles.

Two years later, Putin's chief of staff Sergey Ivanov instructed the officials of the ruling party United Russia to join the marches across the whole country and created separate structures to organize them.[57] The original initiators were sidelined.[58] In 2018, ten million people marched through Russia's cities—with Vladimir Putin leading the main manifestation in Moscow.[59] In Tula, 150,000 people marched behind the new governor, Aleksey Dyumin; in Novorossiysk, there were 52,000 participants.

The state's appropriation of a private form of commemoration has led to considerable controversy. Mischa Gabowitsch considers such a manifestation as significant as a struggle for power because of war memory's towering political significance.[60] "Millions of Russians took to the streets declaring their right to history—this became the most powerful political declaration in all of Russia's post-Soviet history," writes Ivan Kurilla. State authorities recognized this and reacted with distrust and a desire for control. Whether they will succeed is, in Kurilla's opinion, as of yet undetermined, since family memory maintains a distance from state-imposed interpretations.[61]

The case studies in Tula and Novorossiysk showed that family recollections may shed light on some blank spots in official memory, but they seldom contradict them—in part because they could hardly be articulated outside of the heroic framework during the Soviet era. Nevertheless, Victory Day remains a highly significant day for today's generation, some of whom appropriate it in idiosyncratic ways, like the cyclists in Tula who organize a bike ride every year—honoring both war memory and the city's tradition in cycling sports (see fig. 7.2). There is most certainly room for individual expression in official war memory, but the important institutions of the country remain its driving forces.

Moreover, war memory has become a commercial commodity and pop culture phenomenon: hats and uniforms are available at every tourist shop, banks advertise with Victory Day deals, and supermarkets play wartime songs and sell victory cups. Stephen Norris adequately called current commemorative culture in Russia a "memory supermarket."[62]

Official war memory in today's Russia assumes an unideological guise, appearing depoliticized, as part of a societal fabric that Michael Billig called "banal nationalism."[63] The main message of national pride nevertheless remains the same—and largely unquestioned exactly because of its depoliticized form and apparent variety.

A crucial new actor among these post-Soviet "entrepreneurs of memory" is the Orthodox Church.[64] The powerful institution, which is closely aligned to the Russian state, has greatly expanded its role in commemoration. Patriarch Kirill first addressed Victory Day in 2010, ordering all churches to say special prayers in honor of the fallen and in gratitude for their sacrifice.[65] In his liturgy on May 9, Kirill called the war "punishment for our sins," a kind of Last Judgment for the godlessness of Bolshevism.[66]

This notion of a cleansing is reminiscent of postwar ideas about the conflict as the "Armageddon of the Revolution,"[67] albeit in an opposed ideological context. The church's adaptation of war memory makes explicit the quasi-religious

Figure 7.2. Cyclists gather in Tula's Victory Square to celebrate Victory Day in 2012. © Ivo Mijnssen

significance such memory had even during Soviet times. The eternal flame at war monuments, the language of martyrdom, and the ritualistic language formed an ersatz religion in an atheist state.

Today, the golden domes of Orthodox churches complement the sites of many war monuments, from Moscow to Volgograd. Putin regularly showcases his piety by attending church on high holidays. Regional leaders like Tula governor Dyumin follow this example: on Victory Day 2018, he integrated a church visit into his official program. Dressed in his parade uniform, his chest covered by awards, he lit a candle in Uspenskiy Cathedral, located in the immediate vicinity of the Tula Kremlin and its White House.[68] He thus combined Tula's military, historical, and religious traditions and reproduced official discourse on the regional level.

Similarly combining religion and war memory, Kirill put forward the idea of erecting a cathedral at Malaya Zemlya on a visit to Novorossiysk in 2011. The Russian Federation, the owner of the land, had no objections, and Kirill laid the keystone on the construction site in October 2014; the church collected 800 million rubles in donations from its members.

Shortly afterward, however, project posters showed not only a cathedral but a huge complex of sixteen buildings—including a hotel and a conference hall—that had not been part of the original plans. Hundreds of Novorossians gathered for demonstrations, and the church had to stop construction. Their motivations were twofold. Archaeologists and ecologists warned that the new buildings would destroy a highly sensitive local ecosystem and the ruins of a Turkish fort. They demanded that the government uphold its legal obligations to protect this space, especially since the construction permit was insufficient for the planned project.[69]

A more important factor of mobilization and division, however, was the struggle over the significance of war memory. Novorossians hold widely differing views of whether religion should be part of commemoration; 9,355 of them signed a petition against the cathedral, with 12,000 in favor of it. Interestingly enough, both claim to defend the sanctity of memory at Malaya Zemlya.

The author of the petition against the cathedral, Elena Moskvicheva, wrote: "The vast complex intrudes into the memorial zone of Malaya Zemlya, which is holy for us."[70] Orthodox activist Igor' Vereshchagin said: "It is very important that the church is built in such a special place. This eternalizes the memory of the defenders of the Fatherland from Novorossiysk who sacrificed themselves in the fight with the German-fascist occupiers."[71]

Conversely, Yuriy Cherniy, a local inhabitant interviewed by internet newspaper *gazeta.ru*, considers the construction of a church "on the remains of fallen heroes" to be a sacrilege (*koshchunstvo*).[72] The director of the memorial complex, Larisa Kolbasina, on the other hand, believes that the new cathedral would "adorn" the ensemble.[73] For her, Orthodoxy and official war memory are easily combined. However, the coordinator of the group "Let Us Save Malaya Zemlya," Anton Ryzhkov, disagrees: "The fighters who liberated Novorossiysk represented various confessions and were mostly atheists. They did not fight for their belief in God but for the Homeland. To put any religious building on this earth is an affront to the memory of the fallen soldiers."[74]

The question underlying this controversy concerns ownership of victory and the significance of reverence. Even if Vicky Davis is right in asserting that the content of the local war myth largely coincides with its national counterpart, some tension remains.[75] Unlike Kirill, many in Novorossiysk and elsewhere doubt whether the fight for the atheist Soviet state can be reinterpreted in a religious framework. Another disagreement, familiar from the Brezhnev era, arises over the appropriate usage of the battlefield: not only does the construction of apartments evoke mixed feelings, but so does that of a cathedral. In particular, the additional buildings, erected for economic purposes, were considered unworthy of such a place.

The struggle touches questions of democracy and power dynamics. The petitioners around Moskvicheva criticize the fact that the Orthodox Church did not take into account the opinion of local inhabitants when making their plans. This top-down, nontransparent decision-making is unfortunately as symptomatic for today's Russia as it was for the Soviet Union, and it does not bolster the legitimacy of decisions.

It rather contributes to a sense of powerlessness that is a significant factor for the passivity in Russian society. It also reflects the absence of a social contract that would regulate obligations and rewards—even if its ideal remained unfulfilled, as in the Soviet Union. Instead, Russians consider the distance between them and "power" (*vlast'*) to be unbridgeable.

The city authorities did make some efforts to resolve the cathedral controversy by convening a roundtable. Ultimately, however, the political will behind the project proved too strong. In November 2016, the regional parliament decided that there had been no violations in the permit and that the church's construction did not affect the environmental protection zone. It rejected all the opponents' arguments.[76]

THE HERO CITIES RETURN

The proponents advanced an additional argument for the construction of the church: Episcope Feognost of Novorossiysk and Gelendzhik, the local clergyman in charge of the project, explained that it would make Novorossiysk "the first Hero City with a cathedral."[77] This is only one example of how the honorary status, which had almost disappeared from public discourse in the 1990s, has reemerged in recent years. Its re-elevation began in 2000, when the Central Bank issued ten million commemorative coins for the seven Hero Cities that remained within the national borders of Russia after the collapse of the USSR.[78] Soviet-era discussions about adding new members were rekindled. In January 2003, the mayor of Voronezh expressed his great disappointment that Putin had not approved the city's fourth attempt at joining the "family."[79]

The controversies about places like Voronezh and Kursk led the Kremlin to institute a new category of Hero Cities. In 2006, Vladimir Putin signed a decree creating the Cities of Military Glory (*goroda voinskoy slavy*).[80] Unlike the award of Hero City, the decree conveyed no material privileges, reflecting the changed logic of resource allocation in a capitalist system.

The award ceremonies, however, were large political spectacles reminiscent of the 1970s. The cities received their own plaque next to those of the Hero Cities at the Tomb of the Unknown Soldier in Moscow—somewhat smaller but equally central. Moreover, they received the right to erect a monument in the city center containing the text of the presidential decree in their honor, embellished by their coat of arms instead of the Order of Lenin.

Many of the forty-five cities that were added rapidly between 2007 and 2015 played an important role in the war. Kursk and Voronezh are the most prominent; others, like Mozhaysk, are known in relation to the defense of Moscow or, like Bryansk, are seen as a hotbed of partisan activity. These cities received the recognition they deserved—if not quite on the highest level of the heroarchy.

In the years since the annexation of Crimea, the selection has become markedly more politicized: the Chechen capital Groznyy, a City of Military Glory since 2015, is known for the wartime deportation of Chechens in 1944 rather than for its contribution to victory. Presumably, the goal behind its inclusion is to tie it firmly to a mental map of Russia after the horrors of the two Chechen Wars in the post-Soviet era. Feodosiya on Crimea fulfills a similar purpose of connecting the annexed peninsula to the mainland.

Hero Cities naturalize current Russian borders in public discourse because of their high symbolic status. Putin justified the annexation of Crimea on March 18, 2014, by arguing that "in the people's heart and consciousness, Crimea always was and remains an inseparable part of Russia." He underlined his statement with historical arguments—the alleged baptism of Prince Vladimir the Great in Khersones and the many battles Russian armies had fought to include the peninsula in the empire: "Crimea is Sevastopol', the city of legends, the city of a great fate, the fortress city and the home of the Russian Black Sea Military Fleet. (*applause*) Crimea, this is Balaklava and Kerch', Malakhov Kurgan and Sapun-Gora. Each one of these places is holy for us, as a symbol of Russian military glory and singular heroism."[81]

The Russian president combines famous battles from the Crimean and the Great Patriotic Wars with the two Hero Cities of Kerch' and Sevastopol' to construct an organic historical narrative and transgenerational unity. He thereby excludes any doubts concerning the political legitimacy of the annexation, which took place in violation of international law and agreements the Russian state had signed after the collapse of the Soviet Union.

The historical borders Putin describes are independent of the current geopolitical situation; they circumscribe Russia's great power ambitions and point to a kind of imperial phantom pain that still ails it. Hero Cities, which were the symbols of Soviet identity, now highlight division: between 1991 and 2014, almost half of them—Odessa, Sevastopol', Kiev, Brest Fortress, Kerch', and Minsk—came to lie outside Russia's borders. Since then, Putin has brought two of them "home" by military force.

Both Tula and Novorossiysk played an important role in the annexation of Crimea, which attests to their renewed military significance. According to the newspaper *Novaya Gazeta*, paratroopers from Tula participated in the seizing of the capital city, Simferopol'.[82] Aleksandr Khramchikhin, the deputy director of the Institute for Political and Military Analysis, writes that many of the troops without insignia (colloquially called "little green men") were transported through the port of Novorossiysk, which hosts the second largest part of the Black Sea Fleet after Sevastopol'.[83]

Because of the tug of war between Kiev and Moscow over the Russian Navy's stationing in Sevastopol' before the takeover, the military had planned to expand the base in Novorossiysk. This was a big topic when I conducted my interviews in the city in 2013: Novorossians were concerned about the plans, since the bay is narrow and there is little room for additional ships. Some even worried that their city might be closed because of its military significance.

Today, a radical enlargement of the base appears to be off the table, but Defense Minister Sergey Shoygu made it clear in 2015 that he wanted to continue stationing additional units in Novorossiysk, particularly submarines. The growing role of Russia's Navy, not least in the war in Syria, also means that Novorossiysk's role as a supply port might increase further.[84]

Tula has benefited both politically and economically. The crisis of the defense industry is only a distant memory today. Russia's military expenditures have increased almost fourfold between 1999 and 2019—from 17.3 to 64.1 billion dollars.[85] Tula's large weapons producers, the KBP Instrument Design Bureau, the weapons factory, and Tulamashzavod, provide the military with advanced weapons, specializing in canons and guns.

In view of this strategic significance, Putin installed one of his most trusted lieutenants in the governor's seat in 2016: Alexey Dyumin, called "Putin's bodyguard" in Russian media. Dyumin, a classic example of a *silovik* (a powerful member of the security organs), had served in the Federal Protective Service charged with keeping the president safe for almost two decades. He also commanded the foreign military intelligence agency GRU's Special Forces during the annexation of Crimea and was awarded the title Hero of the Russian Federation—presumably for the extraction of Ukrainian president Viktor Yanukovich.[86] In 2017, a monument to the "little green men" was erected in Tula.[87]

Dyumin, who was a deputy minister of defense before his appointment in Tula, maintains close relations to key figures in Moscow. He has made it clear that he wants to further increase production in the defense sector, which has been the driving force behind Tula's industrial revival.[88] The militaristic tradition of the city, ranging back to the proto-industrial period, still determines its economic success.

The region remains dependent on state contracts—in spite of an increasingly diversified economy. As in Tula, where Rostec controls most defense enterprises, the Russian state owns a majority stake in Novorossiysk's harbor. The Federal Agency for State Property Management and the Ministry of Energy control Novorossiysk's Commercial Sea Port, in part through subsidiaries.[89] It is Russia's largest harbor by turnover and the third largest in Europe, processing 147.4 million tons in 2017, primarily oil, construction materials, and agricultural products.[90] According to investigative journalists, the sudden increase in trade volume in recent years is also due to its role as a circumvention port for sanctioned goods delivered to Crimea.[91]

RE-BREZHNEVIZATION

The annexation of Crimea marked a caesura in Russian politics and culture. Putin's return to the presidency in 2012, accompanied by mass protests over election fraud, was followed by a conservative and repressive turn, quashing hopes of liberalization.[92] Official war memory became more militaristic, not unlike in the early 1980s, after the end of détente. The Kremlin quickly ended a campaign that focused on the human costs of war under Putin's predecessor Dmitriy Medvedev.

Medvedev's decisive opposition to attempts at rehabilitating Stalin in connection with the sixty-fifth anniversary of victory in 2010 remained an interlude;[93] 2014 was the first year in which a majority of those surveyed by the Levada Center expressed a positive opinion about the dictator. The main reason is that his biggest achievement—victory in the Great Patriotic War—overshadows his crimes in popular perception.[94]

Stalin's position in official discourse has been inconsistent in the last two decades—ranging from tacit approval to condemnation. Thomas Sherlock rightly remarked that the Putin regime has treated the troublesome historical figure with a mix of "silence, praise, and criticism—in that order."[95] Putin never explicitly lauded Stalin, but he makes political use of the notion that Stalin laid the foundation for the Soviet Union's postwar power. As in 1965 under Leonid Brezhnev, this weak compromise serves to neutralize a politically divisive figure and cleanse victory of all associations with Stalin's dark side.

This idealization of victory and the imperial Stalinist state that emerged from the war is troublesome. Inevitably, it calls attention to the fact that Russia's mental border does not correspond to its national frontiers: the entire post-Soviet space remains the reference point of official war memory, even though it consists no longer of one but of fifteen states. War memory's usage as a guide for society and foreign policy thus creates considerable instability.[96] It tends to promote militarization and an antagonistic foreign policy, as it works with a strong sense of enmity and threat.

This causes troubles with neighbors. Ukraine is only the most prominent conflict. Others include the fraught relationship with Poland and the so-called memory war with Estonia in 2007 over the removal of a Soviet monument.[97] While Russia is far from the only country in Central and Eastern Europe that uses historical myths as a political weapon, it is the most powerful—and the only one that has used violence to resolve such conflicts in the post-Soviet era. If modernization and official war memory are indeed two sides of hegemonic discourse, as Liñán suggests, they often contradict each other, sidetracking and isolating Russia.[98]

Scholars like Dina Khapaeva[99] and Taras Kuzio[100] are right to worry about the Russian state's use of the past to promote authoritarian tendencies. Their conclusion that this amounts to a re-Stalinization of society is nevertheless imprecise. No one in the Russian leadership desires a return to the murderous repression and military carnage of the 1930s and 1940s. The period only evokes nostalgia through the lens of its Brezhnev-era representation—cleansed of death and violence, as an idealized time of unity and state power. The "golden era" under Brezhnev, with its socialist contract, stability, and international prestige is the real object of longing for millions of Russians.[101] In popular memory, the great power status, peaceful development, upward social mobility, and economic security of the first half of Brezhnev's rule overshadow the decline and ossification the aging general secretary embodied in later years.

The current regime seems to seek legitimacy in a kind of "re-Brezhnevization" under conditions of capitalism. State paternalism, great power rhetoric, and official war memory are its integrative elements. Surveys show that this nostalgia transcends generations—and that it is growing. Only among those under twenty-four years of age does a majority not yearn for a return to the USSR.[102] The deep post-Soviet crisis reinforced the turn to the past—and made paternalist ideas appear attractive even to young Russians.[103] Knowing little to nothing about the 1990s, except for a memory of chaos, and hardly influenced by democratic ideals, "current students are closer to statists than to libertarians," write Valeria Kasamara and Anna Sorokina.[104]

Figure 7.3. Young Novorossians dressed in wartime uniforms commemorate the city's liberation in 2013 in a manner very much reminiscent of Soviet practices. © Ivo Mijnssen

The downsides of re-Brezhnevization are formalism, a movement toward stagnation, corruption, and authoritarian reflexes. Younger Russians tend to accept older compatriots' view of history uncritically, having failed to develop their own "symbolic discourse," according to Levada Center sociologist Karina Pipiya.[105] Davis arrives at similar conclusions in Novorossiysk, where a young generation appears to reproduce official war memory without really appropriating it.[106] The Soviet-style ceremony on Hero Square pictured in figure 7.3 from 2013 is emblematic of this tendency.

While I did not analyze young Russians' opinions systematically, episodic evidence points in the same direction. In Tula as elsewhere, the rituals of the Brezhnev era are returning almost unchanged, aimed at raising youngsters with the same values of transgenerational unity and sacrifice for the nation. Since 2015, the honorary guard at Post Nomer 1 is once more active around the clock, after a hiatus of almost a quarter century. Its rhetoric, tasks, and goals remain virtually identical.

In her study on heroism and martyrdom, Yuliya Minkova concludes that their emphasis "becomes complicit in providing an ideological basis for political militarism that is responsible for the current enactment of the state of exception."[107] Minkova is certainly right, but the efficiency of patriotic education nevertheless remains questionable. The expansion of war memory within Russian society in politics, popular culture, and the economy is reminiscent of the late Brezhnev era—with its commercialization as a new aspect. The danger of banalization is as great today as it was then. The repetition of war memory without appropriation can transform it into a cliché, repeated for the sake of political correctness but not necessarily believed in. In the absence of a vision for the future, Russia's obsessive return to the past makes the country turn in circles.[108]

In Novorossiysk and Tula, where pride and reverence for the sacrifices of the Hero City remain significant, respondents were ambivalent about the new war cult. For Novorossian journalist Lyudmila Shalagina, the rebirth of official war memory mostly amounts to staged, inauthentic "kvas-patriotism."[109] In the new millennium, Novorossiysk has seen a flurry of monument construction by various actors of memory, commemorating such disparate historical episodes as the escape of the counterrevolutionary Armed Forces of South Russia in 1920 and the short-lived Novorossiysk Republic in 1905, complementing Soviet-era memorials of the Great Patriotic War.[110] Since 2004, the only Brezhnev statue in Russia depicts him in his younger years, with a jacket slung over his shoulder.[111]

This remarkable variety, also symptomatic of other historical cities in the post-Soviet space, is often sponsored by corporations in order to demonstrate their patriotism.[112] Lyudmila Shalagina, the writer and gallery owner who critically follows artistic developments, dismisses most of the monuments as *gadost'* (gunk, ugliness), not worthy of a Hero City.[113] Even though she explained the undemocratic nature of the Soviet system and its corruption under Brezhnev at length during the interview, she prefers it to the current regime, which is, in her opinion, similarly undemocratic but less embedded in a binding set of artistic and social standards.

What she finds lacking is responsibility and accountability for the city and the community as a whole.[114] This is an often-heard complaint in Russia, where urban decay is as visible as the spatial and social segregation of the elite from the rest of the population.

Viktor Shcheglov, a radio journalist in Tula, also considers today's official war memory to be rather "formal," as opposed to its "real" Brezhnev-era predecessor.[115] He doubts that younger Russians can relate to the "unity of generation" they felt in the 1960s and 1970s, when war heroes were still alive and active. The few who remain today are old and frail. These statements reflect the impossibility of simply reconstituting official war memory for a new generation in a political system without an ideological monopoly by the state.

THE PAST IS NO FUTURE

In order to bridge this gap in lifeworlds, the mayors and governors of Russia's most important and visible areas are increasingly active in the curation and beautification of urban space, attempting to combine historical traditions and modern leisure. Tula's and Novorossiysk's downtown areas have changed almost beyond recognition. Tula, ten years ago a drab, gray industrial city, has renovated numerous parks. It is in the process of revitalizing the banks of the River Upa and creating a large pedestrian zone downtown.

On the grounds of an abandoned factory, a creative zone hosts an art gallery, a store selling comic books, and a trendy coffee shop. These services are aimed at younger Tulyaki who work in well-paid jobs in the large service industry hubs between the Hero City and Moscow. In Novorossiysk, the new embankment is a similar lighthouse project—"the first thing to see" in the city, according to a large cruise operator.[116]

In the Soviet paternalist tradition, all these initiatives aimed at raising the quality of life are run by the state, which also prescribes their usage. They nevertheless remain subordinate to economic interests; the commodification of urban space signals a change in ideology, toward individual consumerism under authoritarian conditions.[117] It is no replacement for a participative system, in which civil society and the authorities have real stakes in determining their future. Whereas Putin took over the imbalance of power from the Soviet Union, his societal model lacks an ideological foundation and a sense of accountability by the state. This is another reason that re-Brezhnevization will fail to live up to its own standards.

The Russian brand of capitalism has led to a stark increase in social differentiation, making it one of the most unequal countries in the world.[118] This inequality manifests itself in the living conditions of millions of Russians: one of them is the Novorossian Mariya Inozemetseva, who still lives in her Brezhnev-era apartment in a poorly maintained building made of prefabricated concrete slabs.

The crises of the 1990s cost pensioners their meager savings. Most of them continue to work past their retirement age in order to cover the cost of living, which rose as a result of economic development. Conversely, young Russians struggle to get their own apartments if they are not lucky enough to inherit them, as the interest on mortgages is frequently prohibitively high. The inequality creates feelings of envy and resentment. Inozemetseva, for instance, complained about politicians who steal and businessmen of the "new Russia."[119] The COVID-19 pandemic will most likely further increase the social gap.

Putin's sharp drop in popularity in 2018 was largely due to the government's attempt to raise the retirement age, thus limiting pensioners' already meager benefits.[120] It has remained low because Russians see this attempt as an attack on the bare minimum of a social contract that the post-Soviet state has committed to. Pensions, as well as guaranteed services, such as medicine, provide a minimal safety net at a time of economic stagnation and declining real incomes since 2014.[121]

This is especially important to the rapidly growing group of pensioners in this aging society. The fact that social policy is so emotionally charged—in part because of the crisis experience of the 1990s—makes reforms that would show a way out of Russia's demographic and economic dead end almost impossible. A reform of the Constitution in 2020 now allows Putin to stay in power far beyond the year 2024.

The urban landscapes of Novorossiysk and many other cities reflect these stark contrasts. While the Soviet-era blocks still make up the bulk of the housing stock, elite apartment towers rise up in the most prestigious locations. The Sochi Olympics in 2014 and the port's growth led to a construction boom in Novorossiysk. Some respondents, like the marine lawyer Valeriy Sviderskiy and Georgiy Shcherbakov, who lives in a large, modern house on the outskirts of town, have been able to take advantage of the entrepreneurial opportunities in the post-Soviet era. The majority of Novorossians have not.

The most megalomaniac project, however, is only in its initial stages: the renowned Zaha Hadid Architects won a competition in June 2018 to build an entire new neighborhood on fourteen hectares with thousands of apartments, offices, and hotel rooms. A promotional video shows futuristic glass towers on Admiral Serebryakov Embankment, lush plazas, and a luxurious marina.[122] The goal, according to architects and promoters, is to "establish Novorossiysk on the world map" and to create a "Bilbao-effect," attracting tourists interested in architecture from all over the world.[123]

Like so many Russian prestige projects, it is more reminiscent of a UFO that has landed in Novorossiysk than something that would fit organically into urban space or serve the needs of the local population. Equally symptomatic is the fact that while it enjoys political backing, its finances are completely untransparent: *Kommersant"* reports that the main investor's company had a turnover of less than 80,000 dollars in 2016. He expressed hope, however, that he would receive at least some of the financing from the federal program to develop domestic tourism.[124] If the project should receive the backing of the Kremlin, investors close to the state could be found. At the moment, and in view of the federal government's tight finances, it appears highly unrealistic.

The Hero Cities of Tula and Novorossiysk, then, reflect the contradictory dynamics of development in contemporary Russia. The state-sponsored oligarchic economic model promotes the port and the defense industry, which pollutes the water and poisons the air—largely unaffected by regulation. At the same time, the paternalist state wants to demonstrate its concern for the population by improving quality of life and beautifying the cities. It actively promotes nostalgia for the socialist contract and transgenerational unity of the wartime and Brezhnev eras, while it supports elites that accentuate inequalities ever further. Under the surface of an officially proclaimed unity, the lifeworlds of Russians are drifting apart, leading to increased polarization between center and provinces, rich and poor, young and old.

To an extent, this is an expression of Russia's firm embedment in a globalized system, having overcome many of the economic legacies of socialism. Paradoxically, however, state propaganda increasingly projects the image of a traditional country firmly oriented in its heroic past. It appears to be a global phenomenon, considering the rise of right-wing populists in Europe and the United States. The philosopher Zygmunt Bauman described this phenomenon as "retrotopia."[125]

Russia is nevertheless unique because Putin recognized the force of an idealized past earlier than other politicians; the strategy has a long political tradition here. The contrast between past ideal and present reality is that much starker because the regime of Vladimir Putin has actively worked against a de-Sovietization of the population. As the Hero Cities show in exemplary fashion, the socialist contract is no longer valid under conditions of capitalism. People know this, as the coherent ideological system of the Soviet era is fortunately no longer in place. The wide gap between propaganda and reality leads to disillusionment and cynicism.

The unresolved traumata of the war and the Soviet collapse keep a simmering sense of fear alive. At its worst, this fear accentuates a sense of outside threat—especially since the values associated with victory in the Great Patriotic War serve as the main guideposts for society. The emphasis on foreign enemies threatening the nation becomes a convenient political tool to smooth over internal divisions.

In a milder form, the turn to the past prioritizes a precarious stability, as change can only bring a turn for the worse in the eyes of most Russians. The lingering, transgenerational fear forestalls renewal, a vision for the future, and a process of adaptation in the present. Whether Putin and his allies will realize this is doubtful. The lesson that the Brezhnev era and the twentieth century as a whole can teach is clear, however: without evolutionary change, there will be revolution—which in Russia always brought a change for the worse.

NOTES

1. Etkind, *Warped Mourning*, 17.
2. Zemtsov, *Chernenko, the Last Bolshevik*.
3. *Rossiyskiy Gosudarstvennyy Arkhiv Sotsial'no-Politicheskoy Istorii* (RGASPI), f. M-1, op. 145, d. 34, l. 2.
4. RGASPI, f. M-1, op. 145, d. 34, ll. 50–64.
5. Gorbatschow, "Sowjetische Heldentat bewies," accessed September 22, 2020.
6. Aleksey Ivanov, *Goroda-Geroi i Goroda Voinskoy Slavy Rossii*, 14–15.
7. Zaslavsky, "Čornobyl, Katyn und Gorbačev."
8. Tumarkin, "Story of a War Memorial," 127–33.
9. *Arkhiv Presidenta Rossiyskoy Federatsii* (APRF), f. 89, op. 5, d. 721, ll. 123–25, 161–63, quoted in Federal'noe Arkhivnoe Agenstvo and Rossiyskiy Gosudarstvennyy Arkhiv Noveyshey Istorii, *Pamyatnik Pobedy*, 365, 379.
10. Ganzenmüller, "Die siegreiche Rote Armee und ihre Führung," 24.
11. Estonian State Commission on Examination of the Policies of Repression, *White Book*.
12. Sokolow, "Von Mythen des Kriegs zu Mythen der Literatur."
13. "Victory Parade on May 9, 1990," YouTube, accessed October 6, 2018, https://www.youtube.com/watch?v=ndMkKdPiQOg.
14. Tumarkin, *Living and the Dead*, 214.
15. Paramonova, *Tula. XX Vek*, 215.
16. Sieca-Kozlowski, "Russian Military Patriotic Education," 77–78.
17. Paramonova, *Tula. XX Vek*, 223–24.
18. Paramonova, *Tula. XX Vek*, 229, 234, 236.
19. Izyumov et al., "Market Reforms and Regional Differentiation," 959–60.
20. Orttung, *Republics and Regions of the Russian Federation*, 562.
21. Baglione and Clark, "Tale of Two Metallurgical Enterprises," 176.

22. Chebankova, *Russia's Federal Relations*, 104.
23. Orttung, *Republics and Regions of the Russian Federation*, 278.
24. Shishkova-Shipunova, *10 Praviteley Kubani*, accessed September 21, 2020.
25. Artem'ev, "Kuda Ischez 'Krasnyy Poyas.'"
26. Orttung, *Republics and Regions of the Russian Federation*, 275.
27. Artem'ev, "Kuda Ischez 'Krasnyy Poyas.'"
28. Badovskii and Shutov, "Regional Elites in Post-Soviet Russia," 35–37.
29. On statists, see Casula, *Hegemonie und Populismus in Putins Russland*, 107–10.
30. Baglione and Clark, "Tale of Two Metallurgical Enterprises," 176–77.
31. International tensions over the NATO bombing campaign in Kosovo contributed to this increase. Izyumov et al., "Market Reforms and Regional Differentiation," 962.
32. Slider notes that only twenty-two of fifty-five governors elected in Russia enjoyed the Kremlin's support. Slider, "Putin and the Election of Regional Governors," 108.
33. Artem'ev, "Kuda Ischez 'Krasnyy Poyas.'"
34. Chebankova: *Russia's Federal Relations*, 143.
35. Vinokurova and Surnacheva, "Pritulilsya."
36. Shishkova-Shipunova, *10 Praviteley Kubani*.
37. Kustikov, "Zhizn'."
38. Vladislav Surkov, one of the most influential ideologues of the Putin regime, emphasizes state-run modernization as a central element of "Sovereign Democracy." Surkov, "Natsionalizatsiia Budushchego."
39. Vázquez Liñán, "Modernization and Historical Memory in Russia," 23.
40. Dubin, "Bremia Pobedy."
41. Kathleen Smith, *Mythmaking in the New Russia*, 86–87.
42. Wood, "Performing Memory," 191.
43. Kathleen Smith, *Mythmaking in the New Russia*, 181.
44. Irina Sycheva, interview with the author, Tula, May 17, 2012, 43.32 min.
45. Sergey Stepuzhin, interview with the author, Tula, May 28, 2012, 47.46 min.
46. Morozov, "Sovereignty and Democracy in Contemporary Russia," 160.
47. Tumarkin, *Living and the Dead*, 225.
48. Sakwa, *Russian Politics and Society*, 224.
49. Wood, "Performing Memory," 182.
50. For an extensive discussion of the similarities, see Mijnssen, *Back to Our Future!*, 42–47. The journals *Osteuropa* (4–6) and *Neprikosnovennyy Zapas* (40) published a joint issue about the war on the sixtieth anniversary of its end in 2005. See also Bomsford and Bordyugov, *60-letie Okonchaniya Vtoroy Mirovoy i Velikoy Otechestvennoy*.

51. Veterans were again expected to play a leading role in the new programs for patriotic education. Sieca-Kozlowski, "Russian Military Patriotic Education"; Wood, "Performing Memory," 175–76.
52. See, for instance, Gusev, *Tayny Tul'skikh Ulits*; Irina Shcherbakova: "Wenn Stumme mit Tauben Reden"; Yurina, *Novorossiyskoe Protivostoyanie*.
53. Poselyagin, Elimov, and Zakalsk, "State Ideology in Russia."
54. Luxmoore, "Legacy Issue."
55. Sommerbauer, "European University in Russland unter Druck."
56. Kurilla, "'Bessmertnyy Polk,'" 3.
57. Prokopeva, "Russia's Immortal Regiment."
58. Kurilla, "'Bessmertnyy Polk,'" 4.
59. Kramer, "River of Pictures of the Dead."
60. Gabowitsch, "Pamyatnik i Prazdnik."
61. Kurilla, "'Bessmertnyy Polk,'" 9.
62. Norris, "Memory for Sale," 229.
63. Billig, *Banal Nationalism*.
64. Norris, "Memory for Sale," 202.
65. Kirill: "Tsirkulyar Svyateyshego Patriarkha Kirilla Eparkhial'nym Preosvyashchennym, Namestnikam i Nastoyatel'nitsam Stavropigial'nykh Monastyrey Rossii o Liturgicheskom Pominovenii, Priurochennom k Prazdnovanii Dnya Pobedy v Velikoy Otechestvennoy Voyne."
66. Norris, "Memory for Sale," 214.
67. Weiner, *Making Sense of War*, 17.
68. "Aleksey Dyumin v Chest' Dnya Pobedy Postavil Svechu v Uspenskom Kafedral'nom Sobore Tuly."
69. Regnum, "Khram na Maloy Zemle v Novorossiyske Vozvodyat bez Razresheniya."
70. Moskvicheva, "Ne Dopustite Stroitel'stva v Memorial'noy Zone Maloy Zemli."
71. Quoted in Regnum, "Zastroyka Protiv Pamyatnika Prirody na Kubani: Kto Pobedit?"
72. Quoted in Maetnaya, "Novaya Bitva za Maluyu Zemlyu."
73. Quoted in Maetnaya, "Novaya Bitva za Maluyu Zemlyu."
74. Quoted in Toporkova, "Khram Razdora."
75. Davis, *Myth Making in the Soviet Union and Modern Russia*, 262.
76. Lapshin, "Deputaty Zaksobraniya Kubani ne Nashli Narusheniy v Proekte Stroitel'stva Kafedral'nogo Sobora na Maloy Zemle."
77. Quoted in Toporkova, "Khram Razdora."
78. Buylov, "TsB Vypustil Pamyatnye Monety."
79. The city's administration had already applied in 1975, 1995, and 2000. *Kommersant"* author Dmitriy Orishchenko writes that the reason the candidacy

failed was the destruction of the city's industrial base by the Soviet authorities during the war. Orishchenko, "Voronezh ne Stal Gorodom-Geroem." Other historians believe the reason to be the fact that the city changed hands multiple times and was the location of particularly costly battles for the Red Army.

80. Aleksey Ivanov, *Goroda-Geroi i Goroda Voinskoy Slavy Rossii*, 17.

81. Putin, "Poslanie Prezidenta Rossiyskoy Federatsii ot 18.03.2014 g. b/n," accessed September 23, 2020.

82. Shiryaev, "'Vezhlivye Lyudi v Krymu."

83. Khramchikhin, "Rossiya Ubrala Vtoroy Psevdoflot iz Chernogo Morya."

84. Safronov, "Chernomorskiy Flot Gotov Perevooruzhat'sya Osnovatel'no."

85. In constant (2018) US dollars. Stockholm International Peace Research Institute, "SIPRI Military Expenditure Database," accessed September 23, 2020.

86. Politiki, "Vot Tula Priletela."

87. Vernigorina, "V Tule Poyavilsya Pamyatnik 'Vezhlivym Lyudyam.'"

88. "Shoygu I Dyumin Obsudili Narashchivanie Tempa Vypolneniya Gosoboronzakaza v Tule i Perekhod k Dolgosrochnym Kontraktam v OPK."

89. Gruppa NMTP, "Aktsii I GDR."

90. "Gruzooborot Morskikh Portov Rossii v 2017 Godu Vyros na 9%."

91. Alikin, "Crimea."

92. Sakwa, *Putin Redux*, 193.

93. Norris, "Memory for Sale," 211–14.

94. Pipiya, "Stalin v Obshchestvennom Mnenii."

95. Sherlock, *Historical Narratives*, 183.

96. Morozov, "Sovereignty and Democracy in Contemporary Russia," 175.

97. See, for instance, the special issues of the journals *Osteuropa* 6/2008 and *Otechestvennye Zapiski* 5/2008 on the Hitler-Stalin Pact or Communist and Post-Communist Studies (1/2016) on the Putin regime. On the eve of the seventy-fifth anniversary of the war's end, Putin has added additional fuel to the conflict by assigning blame to Poland for the beginning of the conflict in 1939. See Putin, "The Real Lessons of the 75th Anniversary of World War II."

98. Makarychev, "Politics, the State, and De-Politicization."

99. Khapaeva, "Triumphant Memory of the Perpetrators."

100. Kuzio, "Soviet and Russian Anti-(Ukrainian) Nationalism and Re-Stalinization."

101. Dubin, "Goldene Zeiten des Krieges."

102. The main reasons for Soviet nostalgia, according to a recent survey by the Levada Center, are economic uncertainty in the present, the wish to belong to a great power, and the lack of trust. Levada Center, "Nostal'giya po SSSR."

103. Pipiya, "Kuda Propal Konflikt Ottsov i Detey."

104. Kasamara and Sorokina, "Post-Soviet Collective Memory," 144.

105. Pipiya, "Kuda Propal Konflikt Ottsov i Detey."

106. Davis, *Myth Making in the Soviet Union and Modern Russia*, 237.
107. Minkova, *Making Martyrs*, 20.
108. Etkind, *Warped Mourning*, 10.
109. Lyudmila Shalagina, interview with the author, Novorossiysk, September 27, 2013, 72.14 min.
110. Antipin, "Novorossiyskaya Evakuatsiya."
111. See Davis's extensive discussion of the monument's construction process and significance. Davis, *Myth Making in the Soviet Union and Modern Russia*, 114–40.
112. For instance, in Odessa, Gubar and Herlihy, "Persuasive Power of the Odessa Myth," 156.
113. Shalagina, interview, 13.20 min.
114. Shalagina, interview, 52.14 min.
115. Viktor Shcheglov, interview with the author, Tula, May 17, 2012, 12 min.
116. *Infoflot*, accessed October 18, 2018, https://www.черноморскиекруизы.рф.
117. Gelazis, Czaplicka, and Ruble, "What Time Is This Place?," 1.
118. Walker, "Unequal Russia."
119. Mariya Inozemetseva, interview with the author, Novorossiysk, September 26, 2013, 35.31 min.
120. Mijnssen, "Putin bringt es wenig, dass er Beliebtheitswerte hat, von denen andere Politiker nur träumen können."
121. Aris and Tkachev, "Long Read."
122. "Admiral Serebryakov I Zaha Hadid I," Vimeo, accessed October 18, 2018 https://vimeo.com/269224709.
123. Mikheenko, "Ot Novorossiyska Zhdut 'Effekta Bil'bao.'"
124. Mikheenko, "Ot Novorossiyska Zhdut 'Effekta Bil'bao.'"
125. Bauman, *Retrotopia*.

APPENDIX: ARCHIVES AND INTERVIEWS

GOSUDARSTVENNYY ARKHIV ROSSIYSKOY FEDERATSII / RUSSIAN STATE ARCHIVE (GARF)

f. R-5446 (*Upravleniya po Delam Soveta Ministrov SSSR*)

f. R-7021 (*Chrezvychaynaya Gosudarstvennaya Komissiya po Ustanovleniyu i Rassledovaniyu Zlodeyaniy Nemetsko-Fashistskikh Zakhvatchikov i ikh Soobshchnikov i Prichennogo imi Ushcherba Grazhdanam, Kollektivnym Khozyaystvam* (Kolkhozam), *Obshchestvennym Organizatsiyam, Gosudarstvennym Predpriyatiyam i Uchrezhdeniyam SSSR*)

f. R-7523 (*Verkhovnyy Sovet SSSR*)

f. A-150 (*Gosudarstvennyy Komitet Soveta Ministrov RSFSR po Delam Stroitel'stva i Arkhitektury*)

f. A-259 (*Sovet Ministrov RSFSR, Ministerstvo Kul'tury*)

f. A-374 (*Tsentral'noe Statisticheskoe Upravlenie RSFSR*)

f. A-411 (*Ministerstvo Finansov RSFSR, Otdel Byudzhetov ASSR, Kraev i Oblastey*)

f. A-501 (*Ministerstvo Kul'tury RSFSR*)

ROSSIYSKIY GOSUDARSTVENNYY ARKHIV SOTSIAL'NO-POLITICHESKOY ISTORII / RUSSIAN STATE ARCHIVE OF SOCIO-POLITICAL HISTORY (RGASPI)

f. M-1 (*Molodezhnye Organizatsii*)

ROSSIYSKIY GOSUDARSTVENNYY ARKHIV NOVEYSHEY ISTORII / RUSSIAN STATE ARCHIVE OF CONTEMPORARY HISTORY (RGANI)

f. 4 (*Sekretariat TsK KPSS*)
f. 5 (*Apparat TsK KPSS*)

ROSSIYSKIY GOSUDARSTVENNYY ARKHIV EKONOMIKI / RUSSIAN STATE ARCHIVE OF THE ECONOMY (RGAE)

f. 1562 (*TsSU SSSR*)

ROSSIYSKIY GOSUDARSTVENNYY ARCHIV LITERATURY I ISKUSSTVA /
RUSSIAN STATE ARCHIVE OF LITERATURE AND ART (RGALI)

f. 3151 (*Direktsiya Khudozhestvennykh Fondov i Proektirovaniya Pamyatnikov*)

TSENTR NOVEYSHEY ISTORII TUL'SKOY OBLASTI / CENTER OF
CONTEMPORARY HISTORY OF TULA OBLAST' (TSNITO)

f. P-3 (*Tul'skiy Gorodskoy Komitet KPSS*)
f. P-177 (*Tul'skiy Oblastnoy Komitet KPSS*)
f. P-188 (*Tul'skiy Oblastnoy Komitet VLKSM*)
f. P-1295 (*Tul'skiy Gorodskoy Komitet VLKSM*)

GOSUDARSTVENNYY ARKHIV TUL'SKOY OBLASTI /
STATE ARCHIVE OF TULA OBLAST' (GATO)

f. R-2640 (*Ispolnitel'nyy Komitet Tul'skogo Oblastnogo Soveta Trudyashchikhsya*)
f. R-3306 (*Tul'skiy Oblastnoy Ispolnitel'nyy Komitet*)

TSENTR DOKUMENTATSII NOVEYSHEY ISTORII KRASNODARSKOGO KRAYA /
DOCUMENTATION CENTER OF CONTEMPORARY HISTORY OF KRASNODAR
KRAY (TSDNIKK)

f. 2 (*Krasnodarskiy Sel'skiy Kraevoy Komitet KPSS*)
f. 3495 (*Novorossiyskiy Gorkom VLKSM*)

GOSUDARSTVENNYY ARKHIV KRASNODARSKOGO KRAYA /
STATE ARCHIVE OF KRASNODAR KRAY (GAKK)

f. R-1246 (*Krasnodarskoe Kraevoe Upravlenie Statistiki*)
f. R-1624 (*Krasnodarskiy Kraevoy Sovet po Turizmu i Ekskursiyami*)
f. R-1792 (*Soyuz Arkhitektorov SSSR Krasnodarskaya Organizatsiya*)

INTERVIEWS

TULA

Bozhenko, Elena. Interview with the author. Tula, May 17, 2012. Length: 212.39 min.
Kotenev, Vasiliy. Interview with the author. Tula, May 21, 2012. Length: 172.50 min.
Molchanova, Raisa. Interview with the author. Tula, April 18, 2013. Length: 73.48 min.
Neizvestnaya, Marina (pseudonym). Interview with the author. Tula, April 17, 2013. Length: 57.10 min.
Romanov, Vladimir. Interview with the author. Tula, April 17, 2013. Length: 108.54 min.
Shcheglov, Sergey. Interview with the author. Tula, May 16, 2012. Length: 117.09 min.

Shcheglov, Viktor. Interview with the author. Tula, May 17, 2012. Length: 76.28 min.
Stepunin, Evgeniy. Interview with the author. Tula, May 18, 2012. Length: 147.01 min.
Stepuzhin, Sergey. Interview with the author. Tula, May 28, 2012. Length: 93.21 min.
Sycheva, Irina. Interview with the author. Tula, May 17, 2012. Length: 59.38 min.
Yurchikov, Vladimir. Interview with the author. Tula, April 16, 2013. Length: 58.18 min.

NOVOROSSIYSK

Bozhok, Galina. Interview with the author. Novorossiysk, September 26, 2013. Length: 96.20 min.
Dorosh, Lyudmila. Interview with the author. Novorossiysk, September 21, 2013. Length: 145.17 min.
Grigor'eva, Natal'ya. Interview with the author. Novorossiysk, September 23, 2013. Length: 77.08 min.
Gusev, Vladimir (pseudonym). Interview with the author. Novorossiysk, September 25, 2013. Length: 83.52 min.
Inozemetseva, Mariya (pseudonym). Interview with the author. Novorossiysk, September 26, 2013. Length: 87.14 min.
Shalagina, Lyudmila. Interview with the author. Novorossiysk, September 27, 2013. Length: 76.17 min.
Shcherbakov, Georgiy. Interview with the author. Novorossiysk, September 20, 2013. Length: 69.05 min.
Sviderskiy, Valeriy. Interview with the author. Novorossiysk, September 23, 2013. Length: 31.23 min.
Tsymbal, Sergey. Interview with the author. Novorossiysk, September 23, 2013. Length: 53.23 min.
Yurina, Tamara. Interview with the author. Novorossiysk, September 18, 2013, and Krasnodar, October 9, 2013. Length: 193.38 min.

BIBLIOGRAPHY

PRINTED SOVIET SOURCES

Speeches, Books, Resolutions, Archival Material

Andronikov, N., et al., eds. *Istoriya Vtoroy Mirovoy Voyny 1939—1945 v Dvenadtsati Tomakh: Tom Chetvertyy, Fashistskaya Agressiya protiv SSSR. Krakh Strategii 'Molnienosnoy Voyny'*. Moskva: Voenizdat, 1975.

Andryushenko, V. *Novorossiysk: Ocherki o Gorode i Lyudyakh*. Novorossiysk: Krasnodarskoe Knizhnoe, 1968.

Apsit, Aleksandr. "Vrag Khochet Zakhvatit' Tulu." *RussianPoster.ru*. Accessed September 9, 2020. http://www.russianposter.ru/archive.php?sid=dIpxxL8EZV wpzK&rid=30120042200014.

Ashurkov, V., ed. *Tula: Pamyatniki Istorii i Kul'tury. Putevoditel'*. Tula: Priokskoe Knizhnoe, 1973.

Beevor, Anthony, and Vasily Grossman. *A Writer at War: Vasily Grossman with the Red Army 1941–1945*. Edited and translated by Anthony Beevor and Luba Vinogradova. London: Harvill, 2005.

Blatov, A., ed. *Vydayushchiysya Podvig Zashchitnikov Tuly. Prebyvanie General'nogo Sekretarya TsK KPSS Tovarishcha Brezhneva v Gorode-Geroe Tule na Torzhestvakh, Posvyashchennykh Vrucheniyu Gorodu Medali 'Zolotaya Zvezda', 17–19 Yanvarya 1977 Goda*. Moskva: Politizdat, 1977.

Brezhnev, Leonid. *The Great Victory of the Soviet People*. Translated from Russian. Moscow: Progress, 1965.

———. *Trilogy: Little Land, Rebirth, The Virgin Lands*. Translated by Pavel Shikman. New York: International, 1980.

Brezhnev, Leonid, and Andrey Grechko. "Prosim Rassmotret' Vopros." In *Vestnik Arkhiva Prezidenta. Spetsial'noe Izdanie: General'nyy Sekretar' L. I. Brezhnev, 1964–1982*, edited by Sergey Kudryashov, 150–54. Moskva: Arkhiv Prezidenta Rossiyskoy Federatsii, 2006.

Brudnyy, V. *Obryady Vchera i Segodnya*. Moskva: Nauka, 1968.
Chernyaev, Anatoliy. *Sovmestnyy Iskhod. Dnevnik Dvukh Epokh, 1972–1991 Gody*. Moskva: Rosspen, 2010.
Chernyakhovskiy, M., ed. *Al'bom-Vystavka po Knige Leonida Il'icha Brezhneva Malaya Zemlya*. Moskva: Plakat, 1980.
Durdevich-Dukich, Olga. *Narodni Heroji Jugoslavije*. Beograd: Mladost, 1975.
Eremenko, Aleksandr, and Konstantin Podyma. *Imenem Rossii Narechennyy*. Moskva: Sovetskaya Rossiya, 1988.
Finogenov, Viktor, ed. *Tula-Gorod Ordenonosnyy*. Tula: Priokskoe Knizhnoe, 1967.
Galitsan, Anatoliy, and Dado Muriev. *Tula: Gorod-Geroy*. Moskva: Voenizdat, 1981.
Garbuzov, I. "Tula's Military Feat." *Soviet Military Review* 11 (1977): 12–14.
Gessen, N. ed. *Goroda-Geroi. Sbornik*. Leningrad: Gospolitizdat, 1943.
Golikov, Viktor. "Na Segodnya v Novorossiyske vse Gotovo." In *Vestnik Arkhiva Prezidenta. Spetsial'noe Izdanie: General'nyy Sekretar' L. I. Brezhnev, 1964–1982*, edited by Sergey Kudryashov, 168. Moskva: Arkhiv Prezidenta Rossiyskoy Federatsii, 2006.
———. *Podvig Naroda: Pamyatniki Velikoy Otechestvennoy Voyny, 1941–1945*. Moskva: Politizdat, 1980.
Goncharuk, Vladimir. *Pamyatnye Znachki Gorodov-Geroev*. Moskva: Sovetskaya Rossiya, 1986.
Grechko, Andrey. *Bitva za Kavkaz*. Moskva: Voenizdat, 1967.
Grigor'evich, Yuriy. *Gorod-Geroy Novorossiysk*. Krasnodar: Krasnodarskoe Knizhnoe, 1983.
Gorbatschow, Mikhail. "Sowjetische Heldentat bewies: Sozialismus ist unbesiegbar! Rede zum 9. Mai 1985." *Zeitgeschichte-online.de*. Accessed September 22, 2020. http://www.zeitgeschichte-online.de/sites/default/files/media/gorbatschow85.pdf.
Grossman, Vasily. *Life and Fate*. 1980. Translated by Robert Chandler. New York: New York Review of Books, 2012.
Kadchenko, N., and V. Lamzin, eds. *Goroda-Geroi Velikoy Otechestvennoy Voyny. Gorod-Geroy Tula*. Moskva: Glavnoe Upravlenie Geodezii i Kartografii pri Sovete Ministrov SSSR, 1983.
Kampars, P., and N. Zakovich. *Sovetskaya Grazhdanskaya Obryadnost'*. Moskva: Mysl', 1967.
Karavaeva, A., ed. *Komplekt Otkrytok po knige L. I. Brezhneva 'Malaya Zemlya'*. Moskva: Plakat, 1980.
Kassin, E., and V. Vozbranniy, eds. *Tula: Iz Glubiny Vekov do Nashikh Dney*. Tula: Priokskoe Knizhnoe, 1988.
Khrushchev, Nikita. "The Cult of the Individual: Part 3." *Guardian*, April 26, 2007. http://www.theguardian.com/theguardian/2007/apr/26/greatspeeches3.

———. "The Cult of the Individual: Part 4." *Guardian*, April 26, 2007. http://www.theguardian.com/theguardian/2007/apr/26/greatspeeches5.

Kim, Maksim, ed. *Istoriya SSSR (1938–1978 gg.). Uchebnik dlya 10 Klassa*. Moskva: Prosveshchenie, 1980.

Kinelev, Konstantin, and Vitaliy Medvedev. *Goroda-geroi Chernomor'ya: Sevastopol', Odessa, Kerch', Novorossiysk. Fotoal'bom*. Simferopol': Tavriya, 1978.

Kirin, I. *Chernomorskiy Flot v Bitve za Kavkaz*. Moskva: Voenizdat, 1958.

Kolesnik, Aleksandr. *Narodnoe Opolchenie Gorodov-Geroev*. Moskva: Nauka, 1974.

Kolesnikov, Georgiy, and Aleksandr Rozhkov. *Ordena i Medali SSSR*. Moskva: Voenizdat, 1974.

Kolesov, Nikolay. *V Pamyati i v Serdtse—navsegda. Novorossiyskiy Reportazh*. Moskva: Politizdat, 1975.

Kutuzov, I., et al., eds. *Goroda-Geroi Velikoy Otechestvennoy Voyny*. Atlas. Moskva: Glavnoe Upravlenie Geodezii i Kartografii pri Sovete Ministrov SSSR, 1975.

Lepekhin, A., ed. *Srazhenie za Tulu*. Tula: Grif i K, 2012.

Mikhaylov, K. *Gorod-Geroy Novorossiysk*. Moskva: Stroyizdat, 1978.

Moskovskiy Gorodskoy Komitet VLKSM, et al. *Goroda-Geroi Velikoy Otechestvennoy Voyny*. Moskva: Iskra Revolyutsii, 1943.

Novorossiyskiy Gorodskoy Sovet Deputatov Trudyashchikhsya. *Kompleksnyy Plan Sotsial'no-Ekonomicheskogo Razvitiya g. Novorossiyska na 1976–1980 Gody*. Novorossiysk: Novorossiyskoe Proizvodstvennoe Ob"edinenie Upravleniya Izdatel'stv, 1977.

Pen'kov, V., and S. Stekunov. *Kray Nash Tul'skiy. Kraevedcheskoe Posobie dlya Uchashchikhsya IV Klassa*. Tula: Priokskoe Knizhnoe, 1966.

Pospelov, Petr, et al., eds. *Istoriya Velikoy Otechestvennoy Voyny Sovetskogo Soyuza 1941–1945—Tom 2: Otrazhenie Sovetskim Narodom Verolomnogo Napadeniya Fashistskoy Germanii na SSSR, Sozdanie Usloviy dlya Korennogo Pereloma v Voyne (Iyun' 1941 g.-Noyabr' 1942 g.)*. Moskva: Voenizdat, 1961.

Pospelov, Petr, et al., eds. *Velikaya Otechestvennaya Voyna Sovetskogo Soyuza 1941–1945. Kratkaya Istoriya*. Moskva: Voenizdat, 1965.

Prezidium Verkhovnogo Soveta SSSR. "Ukaz ot 6 Sentyabrya 1967 Goda: Ob Ustanovlenii Dopolnitel'nykh L'got Geroyam Sovetskogo Soyuza, Geroyam Sotsialisticheskogo Truda i Litsam, Nagrazhdennym Ordenami Slavy Trekh Stepeney." *Wikisource*. Accessed September 24, 2020. https://ru.wikisource.org/wiki/Указ_Президиума_ВС_СССР_от_6.09.1967_№_1863-VII.

Pridius, Petr, and Vladislav Filimonov, eds. *Bol'shaya Sud'ba Maloy Zemli*. Krasnodar: Krasnodarskoe Knizhnoe, 1978.

Prokof'ev, A. *Voenno-Patrioticheskoe Vospitanie v Vysshey Shkole*. Moskva: Vysshaya Shkola, 1973.

Rastrepin, Nikolay. *Podvig Novorossiyska*, Krasnodar: Krasnodarskoe Knizhnoe, 1978.

Savchenko, Vitaliy. *Gorod-Geroy Tula*. Moskva: Stroyizdat, 1979.
Shiyan, Ivan. *Novorossiysk—Gorod-Geroy*. Moskva: Voenizdat, 1982.
Shurin, Serafim. *Novorossiysk Stroitsya*. Krasnodar: Krasnodarskoe Knizhnoe, 1957.
Smirnov, N. *Atlas Istorii SSSR dlya 4ogo Klassa*. Moskva: Glavnoe Upravlenie Geodezii i Kartografii pri Sovete Ministrov SSSR, 1970.
Smirnov, Sergey. *Rasskazy o Neizvestnykh Geroyakh*. Moskva: Molodaya Gvardiya, 1963.
Sokolov, Georgiy. *U Yungi tozhe Serdtse Moryaka. Rasskazy*. Moskva: Detskaya Literatura, 1976.
Sorokin, Viktor. *They March Ahead (The Story of the Soviet Youth)*. Translated from Russian. Moscow: Novosti, 1971.
Sovet Narodnykh Komissarov. *O Meropriyatiyakh po Vosstanovleniyu Rasrushennykh Nemetskimi Zakhvatchikami Gorodov RSFSR: Smolenska, Vyaz'my, Rostova-na-Donu, Novorossiyska, Pskova, Sevastopolya, Voronezha, Novgoroda, Velikikh Luk, Kalinina, Bryanska, Orla, Kurska, Krasnodara i Murmanska*. Postanovlenie Sovnarkoma Soyuza SSR ot 1 Noyabrya 1945 g. No 2722.
Sovetskoe Informatsyonnoe Buro. *Fal'sifikatory Istorii: Istoricheskaya Spravka*. Moskva: Gospolitizdat, 1948.
———. "Operativnaya Svodka za 11 Sentyabrya." *Soldat.ru*. Accessed September 15, 2020. http://www.soldat.ru/doc/sovinfburo/1942/1942_09.html.
Stalin, Joseph. "Prikaz Narodnogo Komissara Oborony SSSR 7 Noyabrya 1942 Goda No 345." In *Sochineniya—tom 15*, 129–31. Moskva: Pisatel', 1997.
———. *Über den Grossen Vaterländischen Krieg der Sowjetunion*. Translated from Russian. Moskau: Verlag für fremdsprachige Literatur, 1946.
———. "Vystuplenie na Prieme v Kremle v Chest' Uchastnikov Parada Pobedy." In *Sochineniya—tom 15*, 129–31. Moskva: Pisatel', 1997.
S"ezd Narodnykh Deputatov SSSR. "Postanovlenie Snd SSSR ot 14.12.1989 n 979-1 o Politicheskoy i Pravovoy Ozsenke Sovetsko-Germanskogo Dogovora o Nenapadenii ot 1939 Goda." *Seychas.ru*. Accessed September 24, 2018. http://www.lawmix.ru/docs_cccp.php?id_1241.
Thompson, Llewelyn. *Conversation between N. S. Khrushchev and Governor Harriman, June 23, 1959*. Mount Holyoke College website. Accessed September 24, 2020. https://www.mtholyoke.edu/acad/intrel/harriman.htm.
Tsentr Dokumentatsii Noveyshey Istorii Krasnodarskogo Kraya (TsDNIKK), f. 2, op. 1, d. 252, l. 7, quoted in Upravlenie po Delam Arkhivov Krasnodarskogo Kraya, *Stranitsy Istorii v Dokumentakh Arkhivnogo Fonda Kubani*. Krasnodar: Megadom, 2002.
Tsentral'nyy Arkhiv Ministerstva Oborony RF (TsAMO): f. 208, op. 2511, d. 1034, l. 103. *Wikisource*. Accessed September 8, 2020. http://ru.wikisource.org/wiki/Доклад_командующему_50-й_армии_(ноябрь_1941).

Tsygikalo, F., ed. *Podvig Geroev Bessmerten: Vruchenie Ordena Lenina i Medali 'Zolotaya Zvezda' Gorodu-geroyu Novorossiysku*. Krasnodar: Krasnodarskoe Knizhnoe, 1974.
Voronov, Nikita. *Sovetskaya Monumental'naya Skul'ptura 1960–1980*. Moskva: Iskusstvo, 1984.
Vyrobov, I., ed. *Moskva—Gorod-Geroy*. Moskva: Voenizdat, 1978.
Yunak, Ivan. *Vernost' Geroicheskim Traditsiyam*. Moskva: Politizdat, 1984.
Yurchenko, V. *Atlas Istorii SSSR dlya 4ogo Klassa*. Moskva: Glavnoe Upravlenie Geodezii i Kartografii pri Sovete Ministrov SSSR, 1988.
Zav'yalov, A., and T. Kalyadin. *Bitva za Kavkaz, 1942–1943 gg*. Moskva: Voennoe, 1957.
Zaytsev, Aleksey. *Memorial'nye Ansambli v Gorodakh-Geroyakh*. Moskva: Stroyizdat, 1984.
Zhavoronkov, Vasiliy, and A. Marshani, eds. *Gorod-Geroy Tula*. Moskva: Plakat, 1978.
Zhukov, Georgiy. *Georgiy Zhukov: Stenogramma Oktyabr'skogo (1957 g.) Plenuma TsK KPSS i Drugie Dokumenty*. Moskva: Mezhdunarodnyy Fond "Demokratiya," 2001.
———. "V Bitve za Stolitsu." *Voenno-Istoricheskiy Zhurnal* 9 (1966): 55–65.
———. *Vospominaniya i Razmyshleniya*. Moskva: Novosti, 1974.
Zhurkin, Yuriy. *Gorod-Geroy Novorossiysk: Stranitsy Revolyutsionnoy, Trudovoy i Boevoy Slavy*. Moskva: Mysl', 1983.
Zinchenko, Oleg, A. Mamaev, and T. Khasmamedov. *Boevoy Otryad Leninskogo Komsomola*. Moskva: Voenizdat, 1968.

Newspaper Articles

Al'tshul', A. "Malaya Zemlya." *Za Kommunizm*, November 19, 1943.
Bednyy, Dem'yan. "Gorodu-Geroyu." *Pravda*, August 23, 1941, 3.
Brezhnev, Leonid. "Uchastnikam Torzhestvennogo Zasedaniya i vsem Trudyashchimsya Goroda Novorossiyska." *Novorossiyskiy Rabochiy*, September 16, 1973, 1.
Bukharin, Nikolai. "VII Vserossiyskiy i VII Vsesoyuznyy S''ezdy Sovetov." *Izvestiya*, November 24, 1934, 3.
El'kin, Aleksandr. "Geroyam Slavnogo Podviga." *Kommunar*, October 17, 1968, 1.
"Geroicheskiy Stalingrad." *Pravda*, October 5, 1942, 1.
"Interv'yu Tov. I. V. Stalina s Korrespondentom 'Pravdy' Otnositel'no Rechi g. Cherchillya." *Pravda*, March 14, 1946, 1.
Ivanov, P. "Polgoda Oborony Sevastopolya." *Izvestiya*, April 30, 1942, 3.
Ivanov, Vsevolod. "Zhitel' Otchizny." *Izvestiya*, July 26, 1941, 2.
Kalishevskiy, V., and K. Shcheglov. "Simvol Muzhestva i Otvagi." *Pravda*, September 17, 1982, 3.

Kislyakov, V. "Novorossiysku Posvyashchaetsya." *Novorossiyskiy Rabochiy*, September 15, 1973, 2.

Kommunar, December 10, 1976, 1.

Makhanov, Aleksandr. "Gorod-Krepost'." *Izvestiya*, June 16, 1939, 3.

"Muzhestvennye Zashchitniki Velikogo Goroda." *Izvestiya*, September 14, 1941, 1.

Nadykta, N. "Kunikovka." *Komsomolets Kubani*, September 15, 1973, 3.

"Nepristupna, kak Krepost'!" *Kommunar*, December 9, 1976, 1.

"Orden Lenina—na Znameni Leningrada." *Izvestiya*, January 28, 1945, 2.

Petrov, P. "Segodnya Otkrytie Muzeya Oborony Tsaritsyna im. Stalina." *Izvestiya*, January 3, 1937, 2.

Polevoy, Boris. "Stena Stalingrada." *Pravda*, October 23, 1942, 2.

———. "Za Volgu-Matushku." *Pravda*, October 12, 1942, 2.

Pravda and TASS. "Za Podvig Ratnyy i Trudovoy." *Pravda*, December 9, 1966, 1–2.

"Priumnozhat' Slavnye Revolyutsionnye, Boevye i Trudovye Traditsii." *Sovetskaya Kuban'*, September 17, 1982, 1–3.

Ryl'skiy, Maksim, and Yuriy Yanovskiy. "Salyut Gorodu-Geroyu!" *Izvestiya*, April 11, 1944, 3.

"Slavnaya Pobeda pod Leningradom." *Izvestiya*, January 19, 1943, 1.

Sobolev, Leonid. "Put' k Sevastopolyu." *Pravda*, April 23, 1944, 3.

Stalin, Joseph. "Prikaz Verkhovnogo Komanduyushchego No 20." *Pravda*, May 1, 1945, 1.

TASS. "Gorod-Geroy Privetstvuet Velikogo Vozhdya." *Pravda*, July 31, 1944, 1.

———. "Na Zemle Boevoy i Trudovoy Slavy." *Novorossiyskiy Rabochiy*, September 10, 1974, 1.

———. "Podvig Moskvy—Podvig Rodiny." *Pravda*, December 7, 1966, 1–2.

"Trudovoy Den' Stalingrada." *Izvestiya*, February 2, 1945, 3.

"Velikaya Pobeda pod Leningradom." *Pravda*, January 28, 1944, 1.

Viktorov, V., and Aleksandr El'kin. "Tula Salyutuet Prazdniku Pobedy." *Kommunar*, May 12, 1970, 1–2.

"Vysoko Nesti Zvanie Goroda-Geroya, Byt' v Pervykh Ryadakh Bortsov za Delo Nashey Partii." *Novorossiyskiy Rabochiy*, September 21, 1974, 1–4.

Zakiev, R., and N. Yartsev. "Vchera v Novorossiyske." *Sovetskaya Kuban'*, September 17, 1982, 1–2.

Zen'kov, A., and N. Yartsev. "Potomkam na Pamyat'." *Sovetskaya Kuban'*, August 19, 1982, 3.

Zimenkov, Ivan. "Stalingrad Segodnya." *Izvestiya*, November 19, 1943, 3.

MONOGRAPHS, ARTICLES, AND ONLINE PUBLICATIONS

Afanas'eva, Anna. "Tula Stala Gorodom-Geroem Blagodarya Yunaku." *Sloboda*, March 19, 2008. http://myslo.ru/news/arhiv/article-4085.

"Aleksey Dyumin v Chest' Dnya Pobedy Postavil Svechu v Uspenskom Kafedral'nom Sobore Tuly." Government of Tula Oblast'. May 9, 2018. https://tularegion.ru/presscenter/press-release/?ELEMENT_ID=129825.
Alexijewitsch, Swetlana. *Der Krieg hat kein weibliches Gesicht*. Berlin: Henschelverlag, 1987.
Alikin, Alexander. "Crimea: Circumventing Trade Sanctions via Novorossiysk." *Eurasianet*, June 29, 2017. https://eurasianet.org/crimea-circumventing-trade-sanctions-via-novorossiysk.
Almquist, Peter. *Red Forge: Soviet Military Industry Since 1965*. New York: Columbia University Press, 1990.
Al'tman, Il'ya. *Kholokost na Territorii SSSR: Entsiklopediya*. Moskva: Rosspen, 2009.
Andreev, Dmitriy, and Gennadiy Bordyugov. "Prostranstvo Pamyati: Velikaya Pobeda i Vlast'" In *60-letie Okonchaniya Vtoroy Mirovoy i Velikoy Otechestvennoy: Pobediteli i Pobezhdennye v Kontekste Politiki, Mifologii i Pamyati: Materialy k Mezhdunarodnomu Forumu (Moskva, Sentyabr' 2005)*, edited by Falk Bomsford and Gennadiy Bordyugov, 113–44. Moskva: Fond Fridrikha Naumanna, 2005.
Antipin, Yu. "Novorossiyskaya Evakuatsiya—Prolog Russkogo Iskhoda 1920 Goda." *Istoricheskie Zapiski* 7 (2011): 248–55.
Aparin, Yuriy. *Na Tul'skom Napravlenii*. Shchekino: Shchekinskaya Tipografiya, 2011.
Aris, Ben, and Ivan Tkachev. "Long Read: 20 Years of Russia's Economy under Putin, in Numbers." *Moscow Times*, August 19, 2019. https://www.themoscowtimes.com/2019/08/19/long-read-russias-economy-under-putin-in-numbers-a66924.
Arnold, Sabine. "Die Dankbarkeit der Heldenmasse: Jubiläumsfeiern in Volgograd." In *Politische Inszenierung im 20. Jahrhundert: Zur Sinnlichkeit der Macht*, edited by Sabine Arnold, 95–107. Wien: Böhlau, 1998.
———. *Stalingrad im sowjetischen Gedächtnis: Kriegserinnerung und Geschichtsbild im totalitären Staat*. Dortmund: Projekt, 1998.
Artem'ev, Maksim. "Kuda Ischez 'Krasnyy Poyas.'" *Forbes*, January 21, 2010. http://www.forbes.ru/ekonomika/vlast/36604-kuda-ischez-«krasnyi-poyas».
Ashplant, T. G., Graham Dawson, and Michael Roper. *The Politics of War Memory and Commemoration: Contexts, Structures and Dynamics*. London: Routledge, 2000.
Assmann, Jan. "Kollektives Gedächtnis und kulturelle Identität." In *Kultur und Gedächtnis*, edited by Jan Assmann and Tonio Hölscher, 9–19. Frankfurt am Main: Suhrkamp, 1988.
Bacon, Edwin. "Reconsidering Brezhnev" In *Brezhnev Reconsidered*, edited by Edwin Bacon and Marc Sandle, 1–21. Basingstoke, Hants: Palgrave, 2002.

Bacon, Edwin, and Marc Sandle. "Brezhnev Reconsidered." In *Brezhnev Reconsidered*, edited by Edwin Bacon and Marc Sandle, 203–17. Basingstoke, Hants: Palgrave 2002.

Badovskii, D., and A. Shutov. "Regional Elites in Post-Soviet Russia." *Russian Social Science Review* 38, no. 3 (1997): 32–55.

Baglione, Lisa, and Carol Clark. "A Tale of Two Metallurgical Enterprises: Marketization and the Social Contract in Russian Industry." *Communist and Post-Communist Studies* 30, no. 2 (1997): 153–80.

Bahry, Donna. "Politics, Generations, and Change in the USSR." In *Politics, Work and Daily Life in the USSR: A Survey of Former Soviet Citizens*, edited by James Millar, 61–99. Cambridge: Cambridge University Press, 1987.

Barmakov, Vladimir. "Ordena i Medali na Spichechnykh Etiketkakh." *Simvolika*. Accessed September 24, 2020. http://www.simvolika.org/mars_018.htm.

Barnes, Steven. *Death and Redemption: The Gulag and the Shaping of Soviet Society*. Princeton, NJ: Princeton University Press, 2011.

Bater, James H. *The Soviet City: Ideal and Reality*. London: Arnold, 1980.

Bauman, Zygmunt. *Retrotopia*. Oxford: Polity, 2017.

Baybakova, Ekaterina. "Yubiley Pobedy i Gastrol'nyy Bum." *Tula*, May 23, 2001, 7.

BBC. "Malta Gets George Cross for Bravery." BBC. April 15, 1942. http://news.bbc.co.uk/onthisday/hi/dates/stories/april/15/newsid_3530000/3530301.stm.

Beevor, Antony. *Stalingrad*. London: Viking, 1998.

Behrenbeck, Sabine. *Der Kult um die toten Helden: Nationalsozialistische Mythen, Riten und Symbole*. Vierow: SH, 1996.

Belge, Boris, and Martin Deuerlein. "Einführung: Ein goldenes Zeitalter der Stagnation?" In *Goldenes Zeitalter der Stagnation? Perspektiven auf die sowjetische Ordnung der Brežnev-Ära*, edited by Boris Belge and Martin Deuerlein, 1–33. Tübingen: Mohr Siebeck, 2014.

Beredin, O. *Malaya Zemlya: Kak Eto Bylo*. Novorossiysk: Novorossiyskaya Kinostudiya, 2009.

Bergman, Jay. "Soviet Dissidents on the Holocaust, Hitler and Nazism: A Study of the Preservation of Historical Memory." *Slavonic and East European Review* 70, no. 3 (1992): 477–504.

Biess, Frank, and Robert G. Moeller, eds. *Histories of the Aftermath: The Legacies of the Second World War in Europe*. New York: Berghahn, 2010.

Billig, Michael. *Banal Nationalism*. London: Sage, 1995.

Binns, Christopher. "The Changing Face of Power: Revolution and Accommodation in the Development of the Soviet Ceremonial System: Part II." *Man* 15, no. 1 (1980): 170–87.

Bittner, Stephen V. *The Many Lives of Khrushchev's Thaw: Experience and Memory in Moscow's Arbat*. Ithaca, NY: Cornell University Press, 2008.

Bohn, Thomas. *Minsk—Musterstadt des Sozialismus: Stadtplanung und Urbanisierung in der Sowjetunion nach 1945*. Köln: Böhlau, 2008.

Boog, Horst, et al. *Das Deutsche Reich und der Zweite Weltkrieg. Der Globale Krieg: Die Ausweitung zum Weltkrieg und der Wechsel der Initiative 1941–1943*. Stuttgart: Deutsche Verlags-Anstalt, 1990.

Bomsford, Falk, and Gennadiy Bordyugov, eds. *60-letie Okonchaniya Vtoroy Mirovoy i Velikoy Otechestvennoy: Pobediteli i Pobezhdennye v Kontekste Politiki, Mifologii i Pamyati: Materialy k Mezhdunarodnomu Forumu (Moskva, Sentyabr' 2005)*. Moskva: Fond Fridrikha Naumanna, 2005.

Bonwetsch, Bernd. "Der 'Grosse Vaterländische Krieg' und seine Geschichte." *Geschichte und Gesellschaft. Sonderheft* 14 (1991): 167–87.

———. "Der 'Grosse Vaterländische Krieg': Vom öffentlichen Schweigen unter Stalin zum Heldenkult unter Breschnew." In *'Wir sind die Herren dieses Landes': Ursachen, Verlauf und Folgen des deutschen Überfalls auf die Sowjetunion*, edited by Babette Quinkert, 166–87. Hamburg: VSA, 2002.

———. "War as a 'Breathing Space': Soviet Intellectuals and the 'Great Patriotic War.'" In *The People's War: Responses to World War II in the Soviet Union*, edited by Robert Thurston and Bernd Bonwetsch, 138–53. Urbana: University of Illinois Press, 2000.

Brandenberger, David. *National Bolshevism: Stalinist Mass Culture and the Formation of Modern Russian National Identity, 1931–1956*. Cambridge, MA: Harvard University Press, 2002.

Breslauer, George. *Khrushchev and Brezhnev as Leaders: Building Authority in Soviet Politics*. London: George Allen & Unwin, 1982.

Brudny, Yitzhak. *Reinventing Russia: Russian Nationalism and the Soviet State, 1953–1991*. Cambridge, MA: Harvard University Press, 1998.

Brunstedt, Jonathan. "Building a Pan-Soviet Past: The Soviet War Cult and the Turn Away from Ethnic Particularism." *Soviet and Post-Soviet Review* 38 (2011): 149–71.

———. "The Soviet Myth of the Great Fatherland War and the Limits of Inclusionary Politics under Brezhnev: The Case of Chalmaevist Literature." *Nationalities Papers* 41, no. 1 (2013): 146–65.

Burik, Elena. "Byvshie Sovetskie Plennye na Vosstanovlenii Novorossiyska." *Istoricheskie Zapiski* 5 (2007): 214–21.

Burkhardt, Benjamin: "Der Trifels und die nationalsozialistische Erinnerungskultur: Architektur als Medium des kollektiven Gedächtnisses." In *Medien des kollektiven Gedächtnisses: Konstruktivität—Historizität—Kulturspezifität*, edited by Astrid Erll and Ansgar Nünning, 237–54. Berlin: Walter de Gruyter, 2004.

Buylov, Maksim. "TsB Vypustil Pamyatnye Monety." *Kommersant"*, May 10, 2000. https://www.kommersant.ru/doc/24357.

Carlyle, Thomas. *On Heroes, Hero-Worship and the Heroic in History*. New Haven, CT: Yale University Press, 2013.
Casula, Philipp. *Hegemonie und Populismus in Putins Russland*. Bielefeld: Transcript, 2014.
Charisius, Hanno. "Traumatische Erlebnisse: Die Kinder des Krieges erinnern sich." *Spiegel*, November 1, 2008. http://www.spiegel.de/wissenschaft/mensch/traumatische-erlebnisse-die-kinder-des-krieges-erinnern-sich-a-585965.html.
Chebankova, Elena A. *Russia's Federal Relations: Putin's Reforms and Management of the Regions*. Oxon: Routledge, 2010.
Chernyshova, Natalya. *Soviet Consumer Culture in the Brezhnev Era*. Oxon: Routledge, 2013.
Chiari, Bernhard, and Robert Maier. "Volkskrieg und Heldenstädte: Zum Mythos des Großen Vaterländischen Krieges in Weißrußland." In *Mythen der Nationen: 1945—Arena der Erinnerungen. Band II*, edited by Monika Flacke and Rebekka Göpfert, 737–56. Mainz am Rhein: Philipp von Zabern, 2004.
Clark, Katerina. *The Soviet Novel: History as Ritual*. Chicago: University of Chicago Press, 1981.
Clark, William. *Crime and Punishment in Soviet Officialdom: Combating Corruption in the Soviet Elite, 1965–90*, London: Routledge, 1993.
Cook, Linda. *The Soviet Social Contract and Why It Failed: Welfare Policy and Workers' Politics from Brezhnev to Yeltsin*. Cambridge, MA: Harvard University Press, 1993.
Cooper, Julian. *The Soviet Defence Industry: Conversion and Reform*. London: Pinter, 1991.
Crump, Thomas. *Brezhnev and the Decline of the Soviet Union*. Oxon: Routledge, 2014.
Davies, Norman. *Rising '44: "The Battle for Warsaw."* London: Pan Books, 2003.
Davies, Sarah. "Stalin and the Making of the Leader Cult in the 1930s." In *The Leader Cult in Communist Dictatorships: Stalin and the Eastern Bloc*, edited by Balázs Apor et al., 29–46. Basingstoke: Palgrave Macmillan, 2004.
Davis, Vicky. *Myth Making in the Soviet Union and Modern Russia: Remembering World War II in Brezhnev's Hero City*. London: I. B. Tauris, 2018.
———. "Time and Tide: The Remembrance Ritual of 'Beskozyrka' in Novorossiisk." *Cahiers du Monde Russe* 54, no. 1 (2013): 103–29.
DeGraffenried, Julie. *Sacrificing Childhood: Children and the Soviet State in the Great Patriotic War*. Lawrence: University Press of Kansas, 2014.
DeHaan, Heather. *Stalinist City Planning: Professionals, Performance, and Power*. Toronto: University of Toronto Press, 2012.
Dobrenko, Evgeniy. "The Art of Social Navigation: The Cultural Topography of the Stalin Era." In *The Landscape of Stalinism: The Art and Ideology of Soviet*

Space, edited by Evgeniy Dobrenko and Eric Naiman, 163–200. Seattle: University of Washington Press, 2003.

Donavan, Victoria. "'How Well Do You Know Your Krai?' The *Kraevedenie* Revival and Patriotic Politics in Late Khrushchev-Era Russia." *Slavic Review* 74, no. 3 (2015): 464–83.

Dönninghaus, Victor, and Andrey Savin. "Leonid Brezhnev: Publichnost' protiv Sakral'nosti Vlasti." *Rossiyskaya Istoriya*, no. 4 (2012): 179–94.

Dornberg, John. *Breschnew: Profil des Herrschers im Kreml*. München: Praeger, 1973.

Dubin, Boris. "Bremia Pobedy." *Kriticheskaya Massa* 2 (2005). http://magazines.russ.ru/km/2005/2/du6.html.

———. "Gesellschaft der Angepassten: Die Brežnev-Ära und ihre Aktualität." *Osteuropa* 57, no. 12 (2007): 65–78.

———. "Goldene Zeiten des Krieges: Erinnerung als Sehnsucht nach der Brežnev-Ära." *Osteuropa* 55, no. 4–6 (2005): 219–33.

———. "Litso Epokhi: Brezhnevskiy Period v Stolknovenii Razlichnykh Otsenok." *Monitoring Obshchestvennogo Mneniya* 3, no. 65 (2003): 25–32.

Edele, Mark. *Soviet Veterans of the Second World War: A Popular Movement in an Authoritarian Society, 1941–1991*. Oxford: Oxford University Press, 2008.

Erll, Astrid. "Medium des kollektiven Gedächtnisses: Ein (erinnerungs-)kulturwissenschaftlicher Kompaktbegriff." In *Medien des kollektiven Gedächtnisses: Konstruktivität—Historizität—Kulturspezifität*, edited by Astrid Erll and Ansgar Nünning, 3–22. Berlin: Walter de Gruyter, 2004.

Erokhin, Mikhail. *Novorossiysk*. Krasnodar: AlVi-dizayn, 2012.

Estonian State Commission on Examination of the Policies of Repression. *The White Book: Losses Inflicted on the Estonian Nation by Occupation Regimes 1940–1991*. Tallinn: Estonian Encyclopedia Publishers, 2005.

Etkind, Alexander. *Warped Mourning: Stories of the Undead in the Land of the Unburied*. Stanford, CA: Stanford University Press, 2013.

Ewing, E. Thomas. *The Teachers of Stalinism: Policy, Practice, and Power in Soviet Schools of the 1930s*. New York: Peter Lang, 2002.

Fainberg, Dina, and Artemy M. Kalinovsky, eds. *Reconsidering Stagnation in the Brezhnev Era: Ideology and Change*. Lanham, MD: Lexington, 2016.

Federal'noe Arkhivnoe Agenstvo and Rossiyskiy Gosudarstvennyy Arkhiv Noveyshey Istorii. *Pamyatnik Pobedy: Istoriya Sooruzheniya Memorial'nogo Kompleksa Pobedy na Poklonnoy Gore v Moskve*. Moskva: Komitet po Telekommunikatsiyam i Sredstvam Massovoy Informatsii Pravitel'stva Moskvy, 2004.

Fieseler, Beate. "Arme Sieger: Die Invaliden des 'Grossen Vaterländischen Krieges.'" *Osteuropa* 55, no. 4–6 (2005): 207–17.

———. *Arme Sieger: Die Invaliden des 'Grossen Vaterländischen Krieges' der Sowjetunion 1941–1991*. Köln: Böhlau, 2013.

Filippov, Aleksandr. "Zhivopistsy 'Maloy Zemli': Kak Sozdavalis' Vospominaniya L. I. Brezhneva." *lenta.ru*, February 7, 2015. http://lenta.ru/articles/2015/02/07/brezhnev.

French, Richard Antony. *Plans, Pragmatism and People: The Legacy of Soviet Planning for Today's Cities*. Pittsburgh: University of Pittsburgh Press, 1995.

French, Richard Antony, and F. Hamilton. "Is There a Socialist City?" In *The Socialist City: Spatial Structure and Urban Policy*, edited by F. Hamilton and Richard Antony French, 1–21. Chichester: John Wiley, 1979.

Frey, Bruno, and Jana Gallus. "Awards Are a Special Kind of Signal." Working Paper 2014-04, Center for Research in Economics, Management and the Arts. Accessed September 13, 2020. http://www.crema-research.ch/papers/2014-04.pdf.

Furst, Juliane. "The Arrival of Spring? Changes and Continuities in Soviet Youth Culture and Policy between Stalin and Khrushchev." In *The Dilemmas of De-Stalinization: Negotiating Cultural and Social Change in the Khrushchev Era*, edited by Polly Jones, 135–53. London: Routledge, 2006.

———. *Stalin's Last Generation: Soviet Post-War Youth and the Emergence of Mature Socialism*. Oxford: Oxford University Press, 2010.

Gabowitsch, Mischa. "Pamyatnik i Prazdnik: Etnografiya Dnya Pobedy." *Neprikosnovennyy Zapas* 101, no. 3 (2015). https://magazines.gorky.media/nz/2015/3/pamyatnik-i-prazdnik-etnografiya-dnya-pobedy.html.

Ganzenmüller, Jörg. *Das belagerte Leningrad 1941–1944: die Stadt in den Strategien von Angreifern und Verteidigern*. Paderborn: Ferdinand Schöningh, 2005.

———. "Die siegreiche Rote Armee und ihre Führung: Konkurrierende Geschichtsbilder von den 'Vätern des Sieges.'" In *Kriegsbilder: mediale Repräsentationen des 'Grossen Vaterländischen Krieges'*, edited by Beate Fieseler and Jörg Ganzenmüller, 13–27. Essen: Klartext, 2010.

Gelazis, Nida, John Czaplicka, and Blair A. Ruble. "What Time Is This Place? Locating the Postsocialist City." In *Cities after the Fall of Communism: Reshaping Cultural Landscapes and European Identity*, edited by John Czaplicka, Nida Gelazis, and Blair A. Ruble, 1–13. Baltimore, MD: John Hopkins University Press, 2009.

Gorlizki, Yoram. "Too Much Trust: Regional Party Leaders and Local Political Networks under Brezhnev." *Slavic Review* 69, no. 3 (2010): 676–700.

Gorsuch, Anne. "'There's No Place Like Home': Soviet Tourism in Late Stalinism." *Slavic Review* 62, no. 4 (2003): 760–85.

———. "Time Travelers: Soviet Tourists to Eastern Europe." In *Turizm: The Russian and East European Tourist under Capitalism and Socialism*, edited by Anne Gorsuch and Diane Koenker, 205–26. Ithaca, NY: Cornell University Press, 2006.

Gorsuch, Anne, and Diane Koenker. Introduction to *Turizm: The Russian and East European Tourist under Capitalism and Socialism*, edited by Anne Gorsuch and Diane Koenker, 1–14. Ithaca: Cornell University Press, 2006.

Graham, Seth. *Resonant Dissonance: The Russian Joke in Cultural Context*. Evanston, IL: Northwestern University Press, 2009.

Gramsci, Antonio. *Selections from the Prison Notebooks*. Translated from Italian by Quintin Hoare and Geoffrey Nowell Smith. New York: International, 2003.

Grüner, Frank. "Die Tragödie von Babij Jar im sowjetischen Gedächtnis: Künstlerische Erinnerung versus offizielles Schweigen." In *Zerstörer des Schweigens': Formen künstlerischer Erinnerung an die nationalsozialistische Rassen- und Vernichtungspolitik in Osteuropa*, edited by Frank Grüner et al., 57–96. Köln: Böhlau, 2006.

Gruppa NMTP. "Aktsii I GDR." *NMTP*. Accessed October 18, 2018. http://www.nmtp.info/holding/investors/structure/.

"Gruzooborot Morskikh Portov Rossii v 2017 Godu Vyros na 9%." *Portnews*, January 12, 2018. http://portnews.ru/news/251806/.

Gubar, Oleg, and Patricia Herlihy. "The Persuasive Power of the Odessa Myth." In *Cities after the Fall of Communism: Reshaping Cultural Landscapes and European Identity*, edited by John Czaplicka, Nida Gelazis, and Blair A. Ruble, 137–66. Baltimore, MD: John Hopkins University Press, 2009.

Gubarenko, V. "Die Brester Festung: Geschichte und Bedeutung des Memorialkomplexes." In *Täter, Opfer, Helden: der Zweite Weltkrieg in der weißrussischen und deutschen Erinnerung*, edited by Olga Kurilo and Gerd-Ulrich Herrmann, 97–102. Berlin: Metropol, 2008.

Guderian, Heinz. *Erinnerungen eines Soldaten*. Stuttgart: Motorbuch, 1979.

Gudkov, Lev. "Die Fesseln des Sieges: Russlands Identität aus der Erinnerung an den Krieg." *Osteuropa* 55, no. 4–6 (2005): 56–73.

———. "Pobeda v Voyne: K Sotsiologii Odnogo Natsional'nogo Simvola." In *Negativnaya Identichnost': Stat'i 1997—2002*, 20–58. Moskva: Neprikosnovennyy Zapas, 2004.

Günther, Hans. *Der sozialistische Übermensch: M. Gor'kij und der sowjetische Heldenmythos*. Stuttgart: J. B. Metzler, 1993.

Gusev, Sergey. *Tayny Tul'skikh Ulits*. Tula: Dizayn-Kollegiya, 2011.

———. *Tayny Tul'skikh Ulits 2*. Tula: Dizaiyn-Kollegiya, 2012.

Hartmann, Christian. *Wehrmacht im Ostkrieg: Front und militärisches Hinterland 1941/42*. München: R. Oldenbourg, 2009.

Haumann, Heiko. "Die Verarbeitung von Gewalt im Stalinismus am Beispiel ausgewählter Selbstzeugnisse." In *Stalinistische Subjekte: Individuum und System in der Sowjetunion und der Komintern, 1929–1953*, edited by Brigitte Studer and Heiko Haumann, 379–96. Zürich: Chronos, 2006.

Hellbeck, Jochen. *Die Stalingrad Protokolle: Sowjetische Augenzeugen berichten aus der Schlacht*. Frankfurt am Main: Fischer, 2012.

Herman, Judith. *Trauma and Recovery: The Aftermath of Violence—from Domestic Abuse to Political Terror*. New York: Basic, 1992.

Hirsch, Marianne. *Family Frames: Photography, Narrative and Postmemory*. Cambridge, MA: Harvard University Press, 1997.

Holmes, Larry Eugene. *The Kremlin and the Schoolhouse: Reforming Education in Soviet Russia, 1917–1931*. Bloomington: Indiana University Press, 1991.

Hornsby, Robert. "Soviet Youth on the March: The All-Union Tours of Military Glory, 1965–87." *Journal of Contemporary History* 52, no. 2 (2017): 418–45.

Hösler, Joachim. *Die sowjetische Geschichtswissenschaft 1953 bis 1991: Studien zur Methodologie- und Organisationsgeschichte*. München: Otto Sagner, 1995.

Hurley, Christopher. *Russian Orders, Decorations, and Medals under the Monarchy*. London: Harrison & Sons, 1935.

Ignatieff, Michael. "Soviet War Memorials." *History Workshop* 17 (1984): 157–63.

Ivanov, Aleksey. *Goroda-Geroi i Goroda Voinskoy Slavy Rossii*. Moskva: Armpress, 2010.

Izyumov, Alexei, et al. "Market Reforms and Regional Differentiation of Russian Defence Industry Enterprises." *Europe-Asia Studies* 54, no. 6 (2002): 959–74.

Jones, Ellen. *Red Army and Society: A Sociology of the Soviet Military*. Boston: Allen & Unwin, 1985.

Jones, Jeffrey W. *Everyday Life and the 'Reconstruction' of Soviet Russia during and after the Great Patriotic War, 1943–1948*. Bloomington, IN: Slavica, 2008.

Jones, Polly. Introduction to *The Dilemmas of De-Stalinization: Negotiating Cultural and Social Change in the Khrushchev Era*, edited by Polly Jones, 1–18. London: Routledge, 2006.

———. *Myth, Memory, Trauma: Rethinking the Stalinist Past in the Soviet Union, 1953–70*. New Haven, CT: Yale University Press, 2013.

Kaltenegger, Roland. *Gebirgsjäger im Kaukasus: die "Operation Edelweiss" 1942/43*. Graz: Leopold Stocker, 1997.

Kasamara, Valeria, and Anna Sorokina. "Post-Soviet Collective Memory: Russian Youths about Soviet Past." *Communist and Post-Communist Studies* 48 (2015): 137–45.

Kelly, Catriona. *Children's World: Growing Up in Russia 1890–1991*. London: Yale University Press, 2007.

———. "The Retreat from Dogmatism: Populism under Khrushchev and Brezhnev." In *Russian Cultural Studies: An Introduction*, edited by Catriona Kelly and David Shepherd, 249–73. Oxford: Oxford University Press, 1998.

———. "The Shock of the Old: Architectural Preservation in Soviet Russia." *Nations and Nationalism* 24, no. 1 (2018): 88–109.

Kertzer, David. *Ritual, Politics and Power.* New Haven, CT: Yale University Press, 1988.
Khapaeva, Dina. "Triumphant Memory of the Perpetrators: Putin's Politics of Re-Stalinization." *Communist and Post-Communist Studies* 49 (2016): 61–73.
Kharkhordin, Oleg. *The Collective and the Individual in Russia: A Study of Practices.* Berkeley: University of California Press, 1999.
Kharlashkin, Viktor. "Byla li Bomba?" *Tul'skiy Kur'er* 3, no. 192 (2002): 10.
Khramchikhin, Aleksandr. "Rossiya Ubrala Vtoroy Psevdoflot iz Chernogo Morya." *Russkaya Planeta*, April 2, 2014. http://rusplt.ru/policy/Ukrainskogo-flota-net-9025.html.
King, Charles. *Odessa: Genius and Death in a City of Dreams.* New York: W.W. Norton, 2011.
Kirilenko, Yuriy. "Yanvar' 1977 Goda. Vizit L.I. Brezhneva v Tulu." *Tulainpast.ru*. February 18, 2013. http://www.tulainpast.ru/whatthreat/row1621.
Kirill. "Tsirkulyar Svyateyshego Patriarkha Kirilla Eparkhial'nym Preosvyashchennym, Namestnikam i Nastoyatel'nitsam Stavropigial'nykh Monastyrey Rossii o Liturgicheskom Pominovenii, Priurochennom k Prazdnovanii Dnya Pobedy v Velikoy Otechestvennoy Voyne." Moscow Patriarch. May 7, 2010. http://www.patriarchia.ru/db/text/1154886.html.
Kirschenbaum, Lisa. *The Legacy of the Siege of Leningrad, 1941–1995: Myth, Memories, and Monuments.* Cambridge: Cambridge University Press, 2006.
———. "Nothing Is Forgotten: Individual Memory and the Myth of the Great Patriotic War." In *Histories of the Aftermath: The Legacies of the Second World War in Europe*, edited by Frank Biess, 67–82. New York: Berghahn, 2010.
Klumbyte, Neringa, and Gulnaz Sharafutdinova. "What Was Late Socialism?" In *Soviet Society in the Era of Late Socialism, 1964–1985*, edited by Neringa Klumbyte and Gulnaz Sharafutdinova, 1–14. Lanham, MD: Lexington, 2013.
Konradova, Natal'ya, and Anna Ryleva. "Helden und Opfer: Denkmäler in Russland und Deutschland." *Osteuropa* 55, no. 4–6 (2005): 347–65.
Kotkin, Stephen. *Magnetic Mountain: Stalinism as a Civilization.* Berkeley: University of California Press, 1995.
Kramer, Andrew E. "A River of Pictures of the Dead from Russia's Sacred War." *New York Times*, May 10, 2018. https://www.nytimes.com/2018/05/10/world/europe/russia-immortal-regiment-parade-victory-day.html.
Krivosheev, Grigoriy, ed. *Soviet Casualties and Combat Losses.* London: Greenhill, 1997.
Krylova, Anna. *Soviet Women in Combat: A History of Violence on the Eastern Front.* Cambridge: Cambridge University Press, 2010.
Kudryashov, Sergey. "Erinnerung und Erforschung des Krieges: Sowjetische und russische Erfahrung." In *Der Zweite Weltkrieg in Europa: Erfahrung und*

Erinnerung, edited by Jörg Echternkamp and Stefan Martens, 113–41. Paderborn: Schöningh, 2007.

Kurilla, Ivan. "'Bessmertnyy Polk': 'Prazdnik so Slezami na Glazakh,' Parad Mertvetsov ili Massovyy Protest? Spory o Smysle i Perspektivakh Novogo Prazdnichnogo Rituala." *Kontrapunkt* 12 (2018): 1–11.

Kustikov, Alisa. "Zhizn'—v Konteynere, Protest—na Kladbishche." *Novaya Gazeta*, August 25, 2017. https://www.novayagazeta.ru/articles/2017/08/24/73576-zaplatili-zhivite-lesom-rodnye-ministra-tkacheva-zarabotali-sotni-millionov-sobrav-s-lyudey-dengi-za-doma-v-kottedzhnom-poselke-kotoryy-suschestvuet-tolko-na-bumage.

Kuzio, Taras. "Soviet and Russian Anti-(Ukrainian) Nationalism and Re-Stalinization." *Communist and Post-Communist Studies* 49 (2016): 87–99.

Laclau, Ernesto, and Chantal Mouffe. *Hegemony and Socialist Strategy: Towards a Radical Democratic Politics*. London: Verso, 2001.

Lane, Christel. *The Rites of Rulers: Ritual in Industrial Society—the Soviet Case*. Cambridge: Cambridge University Press, 1981.

Lapin, Evgeniy. "Byl li Predan Otchayannyy Desant?" *Novorossiyskiy Rabochiy*, February 3, 2001, 3.

———. "Malaya Zemlya Georgiya Sokolova." *Novorossiyskiy Rabochiy*, November 3, 2011. http://www.novorab.ru/ArticleSection/Details/4249 (link discontinued).

———. "Na Chertezhakh Iofana Novorossiysk Predstaval Grandioznym." *Novorossiyskiy Rabochiy*, February 20, 2012. http://novorab.ru/ArticleSection/Details/4993 (link discontinued).

Lapshin, Sergey. "Deputaty Zaksobraniya Kubani ne Nashli Narusheniy v Proekte Stroitel'stva Kafedral'nogo Sobora na Maloy Zemle." *Kommersant''*, November 10, 2016. https://www.kommersant.ru/doc/3138090.

Lazarev, Lazar. "Russian Literature on the War and Historical Truth." In *World War 2 and the Soviet People: Selected Papers from the Fourth World Congress for Soviet and East European Studies, Harrogate, 1990*, edited by John Garrard and Carol Garrard, 28–37. New York: St. Martin's, 1993.

Ledeneva, Alena. *Russia's Economy of Favours: Blat, Networking and Informal Exchange*. Cambridge: Cambridge University Press, 1998.

Levada Center. "Nostal'giya po SSSR." December 19, 2018. http://www.levada.ru/2018/12/19/nostalgiya-po-sssr-2/.

Levada, Yuriy. "'Rupture de Générations' en Russie." *Tocqueville Review* 23, no. 2 (2002): 15–35.

Ligachev, Egor. *Kto Predal SSSR*. Moskva: Eksimo, 2009.

Lincoln, Bruce. *Red Victory: A History of the Russian Civil War, 1918–1921*. New York: Da Capo, 1999.

Lovell, Stephen. *The Shadow of War: Russia and the USSR, 1941 to the Present*. Malden, MA: Wiley-Blackwell, 2010.

Löw, Martina. *Soziologie der Städte*. Frankfurt am Main: Suhrkamp, 2008.
Luxmoore, Matthew. "Legacy Issue: Comedy on Siege of Leningrad Attracts the Spotlight." *Radio Free Europe / Radio Liberty*, October 20, 2018. https://www.rferl.org/a/legacy-issue-comedy-on-siege-of-leningrad-attracts-the-spotlight/29554769.html.
Maddox, Steven. *Saving Stalin's Imperial City: Historic Preservation in Leningrad, 1930–1950*. Bloomington: Indiana University Press, 2015.
Maetnaya, Elizaveta. "Novaya Bitva za Maluyu Zemlyu." *Gazeta.ru*. May 7, 2016. https://www.gazeta.ru/politics/2016/05/07_a_8216867.shtml?updated.
Makarychev, Andrey. "Politics, the State, and De-Politicization: Putin's Project Reassessed." *Problems of Post-Communism* 55, no. 5 (2008): 62–71.
Malinichev, Vasiliy. *Na Puti k Krakhu*. Tula: Grif i K, 2004.
———. *Na Zakate. Istoriko-Ekonomicheskiy Ocherk o Zhizni Tul'skoy Oblasti v Poslednie Desyatiletiya Sovetskoy Vlasti*. Tula: Grif i K, 2009.
———. *V Romanticheskom Tumane*. Tula: Grif i K, 2007.
Mannheim, Karl. *Essays on the Sociology of Knowledge*. London: Routledge, 1997.
Markham, James. "Is Advertising Important in the Soviet Economy?" *Journal of Marketing* 28, no. 2 (1964): 31–37.
Markowitsch, Hans. *Dem Gedächtnis auf der Spur: vom Erinnern und Vergessen*. Darmstadt: Wiss. Buchgesellschaft, 2002.
Markwick, Roger, and Euridice Charon Cardona. *Soviet Women on the Frontline in the Second World War*. Houndmills, UK: Palgrave Macmillan, 2012.
Maslov, Valeriy. "Ozhivlenie v Zale." *Tul'skiy Kur'er* 2, no. 191 (2001): 10.
Massey, Doreen. *Space, Place and Gender*. Cambridge: Polity, 1994.
Medvedev, Roy. *Lichnost' Epokha: Politicheskiy Portret L.I. Brezhneva*. Moskva: Novosti, 1991.
Meier, Reinhard, and Kathrin Meier-Rust. *Sowjetrealität in der Ära Breschnew*. Stuttgart: Seewald, 1981.
Melikhova, Yuliya. "VLKSM—Organizator Poizkovokraevedcheskogo Dvizheniya Molodezhi v Seredine 1960-kh Godov." *Uchenye Zapiski Orlovskogo Gosudarstvennogo Universiteta* 1 (2011): 55–58.
Merridale, Catherine. *Ivan's War: Life and Death in the Red Army, 1939–1945*. New York: Metropolitan Books, 2006.
———. *Night of Stone: Death and Memory in Russia*. London: Granta, 2000.
Mijnssen, Ivo. *Back to Our Future! History, Modernity and Patriotism according to Nashi, 2005–2012*. Stuttgart: Ibidem, 2012.
———. "Putin bringt es wenig, dass er Beliebtheitswerte hat, von denen andere Politiker nur träumen können." *Neue Zürcher Zeitung*, February 1, 2019. https://www.nzz.ch/international/putin-wird-immer-unbeliebter-das-ist-fuer-den-kreml-ein-problem-ld.1456499.
Mikheenko, Dmitriy. "Ot Novorossiyska Zhdut 'Effekta Bil'bao.'" *Kommersant''*, June 1, 2018. https://www.kommersant.ru/doc/3645380.

Millar, James. "The Little Deal: Brezhnev's Contribution to Acquisitive Socialism." *Slavic Review* 44, no. 4 (1985): 694–706.

Minkova, Yuliya. *Making Martyrs: The Language of Sacrifice in Russian Culture from Stalin to Putin*. Rochester, NY: University of Rochester Press, 2018.

Mitrokhin, Nikolay. *Die "Russische Partei": Die Bewegung der russischen Nationalisten in der UdSSR 1953–1985*. Translated from Russian by Larisa Schippel et al. Stuttgart: Ibidem, 2014.

Moré, Angela. "Die unbewusste Weitergabe von Traumata und Schuldverstrickungen an nachfolgende Generationen." *Journal für Psychologie* 21, no. 2 (2013): 1–34.

Morozov, Viatcheslav. "Sovereignty and Democracy in Contemporary Russia: A Modern Subject Faces the Post-modern World." *Journal of International Relations and Development* 11, no. 2 (2008): 152–80.

Moskvicheva, Elena. "Ne Dopustite Stroitel'stva v Memorial'noy Zone Maloy Zemli." *Change.org*. Accessed September 24, 2020. https://www.change.org/p/патриарху-московскому-и-всея-руси-не-допустите-строительства-в-мемориальной-зоне-малой-земли.

Mühlhäuser, Regina. "'Mannestrieb' und 'Manneszucht': NS-Politiken im Umgang mit Vergewaltigung, Prostitution, hetero- und homosexuellen Verhältnissen deutscher Soldaten während des Kriegs in der Sowjetunion (1941–1945)." In *Männlichkeitskonstruktionen im Nationalsozialismus: Formen, Funktionen und Wirkungsmacht von Geschlechterkonstruktionen im Nationalsozialismus und ihre Reflexion in der pädagogischen Praxis*, edited by Anette Dietrich, 99–119. Frankfurt am Main: Peter Lang, 2013.

Neutatz, Dietmar. "Identifikation und Sinnstiftung: Integrative Elemente in der Sowjetunion." *Osteuropa* 57, no. 12 (2007): 49–63.

Noack, Christian. "Coping with the Tourist: Planned and 'Wild' Mass Tourism on the Soviet Black Sea Coast." In *Turizm: The Russian and East European Tourist under Capitalism and Socialism*, edited by Anne Gorsuch and Diane Koenker, 281–304. Ithaca, NY: Cornell University Press, 2006.

Norris, Stephen M. "Memory for Sale: Victory Day 2010 and Russian Remembrance." *Soviet and Post-Soviet Review* 38 (2011): 201–29.

Novikov, Sergey. "Bol'shaya Voda." *Novorosforum.ru*. Accessed March 9, 2015. http://novorosforum.ru/threads/antologija-gorodskoj-istorii-ot-sergeja-novikova.1421 (site discontinued).

———. "Kak 'Stolichnuyu' na 'Pepsi' Menyali." *Novorosforum.ru*. Accessed March 11, 2015. http://novorosforum.ru/threads/antologija-gorodskoj-istorii-ot-sergeja-novikova.1421 (site discontinued).

———. "K Voprosy ob Ostavlenii Novorossiyska v Sentyabre 1942 goda." In *Narod. Voyna. Pobeda*, edited by T. Lokhova and Sergey Novikov, 153–56. Penza: PGU, 2015.

———. "Podpol'e na Peredovoy: K Probleme Ob''ektivnogo Istoricheskogo Analiza Deyatel'nosti Podpol'noy Gruppy S. G. Ostroverkhova v Okkupirovannom Novorossiyske." In *Vklad Kubani v Velikuyu Pobedu: Materialy X Kraevoy Nauchno-Prakticheskoy Konferentsii Arkhivistov, Kraevedov, Istorikov*, 162–68. Krymsk: Kranodarskoe Kraevoe Otdelenie ROIA, 2015.

———. "Strategii Vyzhivaniya Naseleniya Osvobozhdennogo g. Novorossiyska: Sentyabr' 1943–1945 gg." In *Pamyat' i Vremya: Vliyanie Voyn i Vooruzhennykh Konfliktov XX v. na Rossiyskoe Obshchestvo*, edited by T. Lokhova and Sergey Novikov, 121–26. Penza: PGU, 2016.

Oberländer, Erwin. *Sowjetpatriotismus und Geschichte: Dokumentation*. Köln: Wissenschaft und Politik, 1967.

O'Flynn, Kevin. "Wanted: Matches." *Moscow Times*, April 7, 2011. https://www.themoscowtimes.com/2011/04/06/wanted-matches-a6166.

Oldenziel, Ruth, and Karin Zachmann, eds. *Cold War Kitchen: Americanization, Technology, and European Users*. Cambridge, MA: MIT Press, 2009.

Orishchenko, Dmitriy. "Voronezh ne Stal Gorodom-Geroem." *Kommersant'*, January 25, 2003. http://www.kommersant.ru/doc/413783.

Orttung, Robert W. *The Republics and Regions of the Russian Federation: A Guide to Politics, Policies, and Leaders*. Armonk: M.E. Sharpe, 2000.

Osipov, Yuriy, and Lyudmila Rostovtseva. *My Pomnim: Kniga Vospominanii i Rasmyshlenii Pokolenii*. Tula: Grif i K, 2010.

Osovik, Kirill. "Grigory Antonovich Ageev." *Geroi Strany*. Accessed September 8, 2020. http://www.warheroes.ru/hero/hero.asp?Hero_id=6007.

Otdel Politiki. "Vot Tula Priletela." *Kommersant'*, February 3, 2016. https://www.kommersant.ru/doc/2906839.

Overmans, Rüdiger. "Menschenverluste der Wehrmacht an der 'Ostfront.'" *Dokumentationsstelle Dresden, Stiftung Sächsische Gedenkstätten*. Accessed September 15, 2020. https://www.dokst.de/main/sites/default/files/dateien/texte/Overmans.pdf.

Palmer, Scott. *Dictatorship of the Air: Aviation Culture and the Fate of Modern Russia*. Cambridge: Cambridge University Press, 2006.

Paramonova, Irina. "Molodomu Kommunaru Otvechaet Sovmin." *Molodoy Kommunar*, September 14, 1999, 4.

———. "Nachal'nik GAI Sgorel na Rabote." *Molodoy Kommunar*, August 31, 1999, 4.

———. *Tula: Khronika XX Stoletiya*. Tula: Shar, 2003.

———. *Tula. XX Vek: Podrobnosti*. Tula: Dizaiyn-Kollegiya, 2008.

Pavlenko, Gavlina. "Brezhnev Privez v Tulu Apel'siny i Kol'basu." *Tul'skiy Kur'er* 5, no. 194 (2002): 10.

Pilkington, Hilary. *Russia's Youth and Its Culture: A Nation's Constructors and Constructed*. London: Routledge, 1994.

Pipiya, Karina. "Kuda Propal Konflikt Ottsov i Detey." *Vedomosti*, September 25, 2018. https://www.vedomosti.ru/opinion/articles/2018/09/25/782022-kuda-propal-konflikt-ottsov-i-detei.

———. "Stalin v Obshchestvennom Mnenii." Levada Center. April 10, 2018. https://www.levada.ru/2018/04/10/17896/.

Plaggenborg, Stefan. *Experiment Moderne: Der sowjetische Weg*. Frankfurt am Main: Campus, 2006.

Plokhy, Serhii. "The City of Glory: Sevastopol in Russian Historical Mythology." *Journal of Contemporary History* 35, no. 3 (2000): 369–83.

Podyma, Konstantin. "Viktor Golikov: 'Ya Veryu i Nadeyus . . .' Poslednee Interv'yu." *Novorossiyskie Izvestiya*, May 3, 2012. http://novodar.ru/index.php/novohistory-punkt/5683-vgpi-05-2012.

Poselyagin, Nikolay, Artem Elimov, and Yaryna Zakalsk. "State Ideology in Russia as a Generator of International Conflicts." In *Non-Objective Conflicts: Political Practices of Sharing the Common Past; Russia, Ukraine, Moldova and Transnistria*, edited by Sergey Rumyantsev, 23–52. Berlin: CISR, 2017.

Presidenza della Repubblica: "Onorificenze." *Italian Presidency*. Accessed September 24, 2020. http://www.quirinale.it/elementi/Onorificenze.aspx.

Prokopeva, Svetlana. "Russia's Immortal Regiment: From Grassroots To 'Quasi-Religious Cult.'" *Radio Free Europe / Radio Liberty*, May 12, 2017. https://www.rferl.org/a/russia-immortal-regiment-grassroots-to-quasi-religious-cult/28482905.html.

Putin, Vladimir. "Poslanie Prezidenta Rossiyskoy Federatsii ot 18.03.2014 g. b/n." *Kremlin*. Accessed September 23, 2020. http://www.kremlin.ru/acts/bank/39444.

———. "The Real Lessons of the 75th Anniversary of World War II." *National Interest*, June 18, 2020. https://nationalinterest.org/print/feature/vladimir-putin-real-lessons-75th-anniversary-world-war-ii-162982.

Qualls, Karl. *From Ruins to Reconstruction: Urban Identity in Soviet Sevastopol after World War II*. Ithaca, NY: Cornell University Press, 2009.

Raleigh, Donald. *Russia's Sputnik Generation: Soviet Baby Boomers Talk about Their Lives*. Bloomington: Indiana University Press, 2006.

Rauh, Manfred. *Geschichte des Zweiten Weltkriegs. Dritter Teil: Der Weltkrieg 1941–1945*. Berlin: Duncker und Humblot, 1998.

Reemtsma, Jan Philipp. "Der Held, das Ich und das Wir." *Eurozine*, 2009, 1–19.

Regnum. "Khram na Maloy Zemle v Novorossiyske Vozvodyat bez Razresheniya." *Regnum*, March 21, 2016. https://regnum.ru/news/society/2101746.html.

———. "Zastroyka Protiv Pamyatnika Prirody na Kubani: Kto Pobedit?" *Regnum*, September 12, 2018. https://regnum.ru/news/2480522.html.

Reid, Susan. "'Our Kitchen Is Just as Good': Soviet Responses to the American Kitchen." In *Cold War Kitchen: Americanization, Technology, and European Users*, edited by Ruth Oldenziel and Karin Zachmann, 83–112. Cambridge, MA: MIT Press, 2009.

Roeder, Philip. "Dialectics of Doctrine: Politics of Resource Allocation and the Development of Soviet Military Thought." In *Beyond the Soviet Threat: Rethinking American Security Policy in a New Era*, edited by William Zimmermann, 71–104. Ann Arbor: University of Michigan Press, 1992.

Roesler, Jörg. "Reaktionen der politischen Eliten der realsozialistischen Länder auf den 'Prager Frühling': Ein wirtschaftshistorischer Überblick." In *Die letzte Chance? 1968 in Osteuropa*, edited by Angelika Ebbinghaus, 196–207. Hamburg: VSA, 2008.

Rolf, Malte. *Das sowjetische Massenfest*. Hamburg: Hamburger, 2006.

Romanov, E. "Krovotochashchie Rany Voyny: Iz Opyta Razminirovaniya i Likvidatsii Vzryvoopasnykh Predmetov Vremen Velikoy Otechestvennoy Voyny v g. Novorossiyske." In *Novorossiysk: Pamyat' i Pravda o Velikoy Otechestvennoy Voyne. K Istoricheskoy Istine Cherez Istochnik*, edited by Departament Kul'tury Krasnodarskogo Kraya, 158–61. Novorossiysk: Tipografiya Variant, 2005.

Rosenthal, Gabriele. *Erlebte und erzählte Lebensgeschichte: Gestalt und Struktur biographischer Selbstbeschreibungen*. Frankfurt am Main: Campus, 1995.

Ruble, Blair A. *Leningrad: Shaping a Soviet City*. Berkeley: University of California Press, 1990.

Ruffley, David. *Children of Victory: Young Specialists and the Evolution of Soviet Society*. Westport: Praeger, 2003.

Rumyantsev, Vyacheslav. "Smirnov Sergey Sergeevich: Biograficheskiy Ukazatel'." *Khronos*. Accessed September 24, 2020. http://www.hrono.ru/biograf/bio_s/smirnov_ss.php.

Ryabikova, Elena. "Gensek i Tula." *Sloboda* November 29–December 6, 2006, 16.

Safronov, Ivan. "Chernomorskiy Flot Gotov Perevooruzhat'sya Osnovatel'no." *Kommersant''*, July 9, 2015. https://www.kommersant.ru/doc/2764141.

Sakwa, Richard. *Putin Redux: Power and Contradiction in Contemporary Russia*. London: Routledge, 2014.

———. *Russian Politics and Society*. London: Routledge, 2008.

Saneev, S. "Golubaya Liniya." In *Novorossiysk: Pamyat' i Pravda o Velikoy Otechestvennoy Voyne. K Istoricheskoy Istine Cherez Istochnik*, edited by Departament Kul'tury Krasnodarskogo Kraya, 65–70. Novorossiysk: Tipografiya Variant, 2005.

Sarasin, Philipp. *Geschichtswissenschaft und Diskursanalyse*. Frankfurt am Main: Suhrkamp, 2003.

Sarkisova, Oksana, and Olga Shevchenko. "'They Came, Shot Everyone, and That's the End of It': Local Memory, Amateur Photography, and the Legacy of State Violence in Novocherkassk." *Slavonica* 17, no. 2 (2011): 85–102.

Satjukow, Silke, and Rainer Gries. "Zur Konstruktion des 'sozialistischen Helden': Geschichte und Bedeutung." In *Sozialistische Helden: Eine Kulturgeschichte von Propagandafiguren in Osteuropa und der DDR*, edited by Silke Satjukow and Rainer Gries, 15–34. Berlin: Links, 2002.

Schäfer, Thomas, and Bettina Völter. "Subjekt-Positionen: Michel Foucault und die Biographieforschung." In *Biographieforschung im Diskurs*, edited by Bettina Völter et al., 161–85. Wiesbaden: VS Verlag für Sozialwissenschaften, 2005.

Schattenberg, Susanne. *Leonid Breschnew: Staatsmann und Schauspieler im Schatten Stalins*. Köln: Böhlau, 2017.

Scheide, Carmen. "Bild und Gedächtnis: Identitätskonstruktionen sowjetischer Fliegerinnen als Angehörige der Roten Armee im Zweiten Weltkrieg." In *Kriegsbilder: mediale Repräsentationen des 'Grossen Vaterländischen Krieges,'* edited by Beate Fieseler and Jörg Ganzenmüller, 29–46. Essen: Klartext, 2010.

Schenk, Frithjof Benjamin. "Mental Maps: Die Konstruktion von geographischen Räumen in Europa seit der Aufklärung." *Geschichte und Gesellschaft* 28 (2002): 493–514.

Scherrer, Jutta. "Siegermythos versus Vergangenheitsaufarbeitung." In *Mythen der Nationen: 1945—Arena der Erinnerungen. Band II*, edited by Monika Flacke and Rebekka Göpfert, 619–70. Mainz am Rhein: Philipp von Zabern, 2004.

Schmid, Hans-Dieter. "Helden des Proletariats? Kollektive Heroisierung und Heroenkult am Beispiel der Opfer des Kapp-Putsches in Leipzig." In *Die Helden in der Geschichte und der Historiographie*, edited by Jerzy Strzelczyk, 125–44. Poznan: Instytut Historii UAM, 1997.

Schneider, Kurt. "100 Jahre nach Napoleon: Rußlands gefeierte Kriegserfahrung." *Jahrbücher für Geschichte Osteuropas* 49, no. 1 (2001): 45–66.

Schönherr, Klaus. "IV. Der Rückzug der Heeresgruppe A über die Krim bis Rumänien." In *Das Deutsche Reich und der Zweite Weltkrieg. Die Ostfront 1943/44: der Krieg im Osten und an den Nebenfronten*, edited by Karl-Heinz Frieser, 451–90. München: Deutsche Verlags-Anstalt, 2007.

See, Klaus von. "Held und Kollektiv." *Zeitschrift für deutsches Altertum und deutsche Literatur* 122. no. 1 (1993): 1–35.

Semenov, Yuriy. "Nam Svetila Zvezda Udachi." *Novorossiyskiy Rabochiy*, December 17, 1999, 5.

Senyavskaya, Elena. *Psikhologiya Voyny v XX Veke: Istoricheskiy Opyt Rossii*. Moskva: Rosspen, 1999.

Senyavskiy, Aleksandr. *Rossiyskiy Gorod v 1960-e—80-e Gody*. Moskva: Logos, 1994.

Shalagina, Lyudmila. "Granitnyy Dozor Novorossiyska." *Novorossiyskiy Rabochiy*, May 10, 2012. http://novorab.ru/ArticleSection/Details/5589 (link discontinued).

Shapoval, Kseniya. "Bol'shaya Lozh' o 'Maloy Zemle.'" *Argumenty i Fakty*, no. 8 (February 2004): 8.

Shcherbakova, Irina. "Wenn Stumme mit Tauben Reden: Generationendialog und Geschichtspolitik in Russland." *Osteuropa* 60, no. 5 (2010): 17–25.

Sherlock, Thomas. *Historical Narratives in the Soviet Union and Post-Soviet Russia.* New York: Palgrave MacMillan, 2007.

Sheudzhen, Fatima. "Vzlety i Krakh Sergeya Medunova. Lichnaya Voyna Pervogo Sekretary." *Argumenty i Fakty Kuban*, September 22, 2015. http://www.kuban.aif.ru/society/details/vzlety_i_krah_sergeya_medunova_lichnaya_voyna_pervogo_sekretarya.

Shirokorad, Aleksandr. *Bitva za Chernoe More.* Moskva: Transzitkniga, 2005.

Shiryaev, Valeriy. "'Vezhlivye Lyudi v Krymu: Kak Eto Bylo." *Novaya Gazeta*, April 17, 2014. https://www.novayagazeta.ru/articles/2014/04/17/59255-171-vezhlivye-lyudi-187-v-krymu-kak-eto-bylo.

Shishkova-Shipunova, Svetlana. *10 Praviteley Kubani ot Medunova do Tkacheva. Ofitsial'nyy Sayt.* 2016. http://www.svu.ru/images/fm/shishkova/10_praviteli.PDF.

Shlapentokh, Vladimir. *A Normal Totalitarian Society: How the Soviet Union Functioned and How It Collapsed.* New York: Sharpe, 2001.

"Shoygu I Dyumin Obsudili Narashchivanie Tempa Vypolneniya Gosoboronzakaza v Tule i Perekhod k Dolgosrochnym Kontraktam v OPK." *Tulactive*, February 3, 2017. http://tulactive.ru/news/59959.

Sieca-Kozlowski, Elisabeth. "Russian Military Patriotic Education: A Control Tool against the Arbitrariness of Veterans." *Nationalities Papers* 38, no. 1 (2010): 73–85.

Simonov, Nikolay. *Voenno-Promyshlennyy Kompleks SSSR v 1920–1950-e Gody.* Moskva: Rosspen, 1996.

Sivkov, Sergey. "Novorossiysko-Tamanskaya Nastupatel'naya Operatsiya Krasnoy Armii: Novyy Vzglyad." In *Problemy Istorii Massovykh Politicheskikh Repressiy v SSSR*, edited by Sergey Kropachev, 219–24. Krasnodar: Ekoinvest, 2006.

Slider, Darrell. "Putin and the Election of Regional Governors." In *Federalism and Local Politics in Russia*, edited by Cameron Ross, 106–19. London: Routledge, 2009.

Smith, Kathleen. *Mythmaking in the New Russia: Politics and Memory during the Yeltsin Era.* Ithaca, NY: Cornell University Press, 2002.

Smith, Mark. *Property of Communists: The Urban Housing Program from Stalin to Khrushchev.* DeKalb: Northern Illinois University Press, 2010.

Snyder, Timothy. *Bloodlands: Europe between Hitler and Stalin.* New York: Basic, 2010.

Sokolova, Raisa. *Beskozyrka.* Novorossiysk: Variant, 2008.

Sokolow, Boris. "Von Mythen des Kriegs zu Mythen der Literatur: Russische und sowjetische Heldentaten im Ersten und Zweiten Weltkrieg." In *Verführungen der Gewalt: Russen und Deutsche im Ersten und Zweiten Weltkrieg*, edited by Karl Eimermacher, 709–56. Paderborn: Wilhelm Fink, 2005.

Sommerbauer, Jutta. "European University in Russland unter Druck." *Tagesspiegel*, November 9, 2018. https://www.tagesspiegel.de/wissen/st-petersburg-european-university-in-russland-unter-druck/23596564.html.

Sovtime. "Anekdoty pro Brezhneva." *Vremya SSSR–Sovtime.ru*. Accessed September 22, 2020. https://sovtime.ru/anekdot/brezhnev.

Stahel, David. *Operation Typhoon: Hitler's March on Moscow, October 1941*. New York: Cambridge University Press, 2013.

Stephan, Anke. "Erinnertes Leben: Autobiographien, Memoiren und *Oral-History*-Interviews als historische Quellen." *Virtuelle Fachbibliothek Osteuropa: Digitales Handbuch zur Geschichte und Kultur Russlands und Osteuropas* 10 (2004). Universitätsbibliothek München. Accessed September 24, 2020. http://epub.ub.uni-muenchen.de/627/1/Stephan-Selbstzeugnisse.pdf.

Stockholm International Peace Research Institute. "SIPRI Military Expenditure Database." SIPRI. Accessed September 23, 2020. https://www.sipri.org/databases/milex.

Stronski, Paul. *Tashkent: Forging a Soviet City 1930–1966*. Pittsburgh: University of Pittsburgh Press, 2010.

Studio Galakon. *Malaya Zemlya Leonida Brezhneva*. 2010.

Surkov, Vladislav. "Natsionalizatsiia Budushchego." *Surkov.info*. Accessed September 24, 2020. http://surkov.info/nacionalizaciya-budushhego-polnaya-versiya/.

Sviderskiy, Valentin. "Divizii Vermakhta v Novorossiyske." In *Novorossiysk: Pamyat' i Pravda o Velikoy Otechestvennoy Voyne. K Istoricheskoy Istine Cherez Istochnik*, edited by Departament Kul'tury Krasnodarskogo Kraya, 139–43. Novorossiysk: Tipografiya Variant, 2005.

Taldykin, Roman. "Iskupit' Vinu Krov''yu." *Khranitel'* 1, no. 2 (April 22, 2010): 7.

Taubman, William. *Khrushchev: The Man and His Era*. New York: W.W. Norton, 2003.

Terekhova, V. "Naselenie Novorossiyska v 40-e—60-e Gody XX Veka." *Istoricheskie Zapiski* 7 (2011): 273–86.

Tieke, Wilhelm. *The Caucasus and the Oil: The German-Soviet War in the Caucasus 1942/43*. Translated from German by Joseph Welsh. Winnipeg: J.J. Federowicz, 1995.

Toporkova, Yana. "Khram Razdora." *Argumenty i Fakty*, February 4, 2016. http://www.aif.ru/society/people/hram_razdora_v_novorossiyske_protestuyut_protiv_sobora_na_maloy_zemle.

Torfing, Jacob. *New Theories of Discourse: Laclau, Mouffe and Žižek*. Oxford: Blackwell, 1999.

Tromly, Benjamin. "Soviet Patriotism and Its Discontents among Higher Education Students in Khrushchev-Era Russia and Ukraine." *Nationalities Papers* 37, no. 3 (2009): 299–326.

Tsipursky, Gleb. *Socialist Fun: Youth, Consumption, and State-Sponsored Popular Culture in the Cold War Soviet Union, 1945–1970*. Pittsburgh: University of Pittsburgh Press, 2016.

Tumarkin, Nina. *The Living and the Dead: The Rise and Fall of the Cult of World War II in Russia*. New York: Basic, 1994.

———. "Story of a War Memorial." In *World War 2 and the Soviet People: Selected Papers from the Fourth World Congress for Soviet and East European Studies, Harrogate, 1990*, edited by John Garrard and Carol Garrard, 125–46. New York: St. Martin's, 1993.

Turchin, N. "O Zverstvakh Nemetsko-Fashistskikh Zakhvatchikov i ikh Soobshchnikov v Okkupirovannom Novorossiyske." In *Novorossiysk: Pamyat' i Pravda o Velikoy Otechestvennoy Voyne. K Istoricheskoy Istine Cherez Istochnik*, edited by Departament Kul'tury Krasnodarskogo Kraya, 144–46. Novorossiysk: Tipografiya Variant, 2005.

Turner, Victor "Betwixt and Between: The Liminal Period in Rites of Passage." In *Betwixt and Between: Patterns of Masculine and Feminine Initiation*, edited by Louise Carus Mahdi, Steven Foster, and Meredith Little, 3–19. LaSalle, IL: Open Court, 1987.

Usyskin, Grigoriy. "Istoriya Turizma v Rossii: Vsesoyuznyy Turistskiy Pokhod Molodezhi (1965–1987)." *Personal'nyy Sayt N. Kostereva*. Accessed September 24, 2020. http://nkosterev.narod.ru/met/ysuskin/ysus_13.html.

Vanyukov, Dmitriy. *Epokha Zastoya*. Moskva: Mir knigi, 2008.

Varga-Harris, Christine. "Forging Citizenship on the Home Front: Reviving the Socialist Contract and Constructing Soviet Identity during the Thaw." In *The Dilemmas of De-Stalinization: Negotiating Cultural and Social Change in the Khrushchev Era*, edited by Polly Jones, 101–16. London: Routledge, 2006.

———. *Stories of House and Home: Soviet Apartment Life during the Khrushchev Years*. Ithaca, NY: Cornell University Press, 2015.

Vayl', Petr, and Aleksandr Genis. *60-e: Mir Sovetskogo Cheloveka*. Moskva: Novoe Literaturnoe Obozrenie, 1998.

Vázquez Liñán, Miguel. "Modernization and Historical Memory in Russia." *Problems of Post-Communism* 59, no. 6 (2012): 15–26.

Vernigorina, Kristina. "V Tule Poyavilsya Pamyatnik 'Vezhlivym Lyudyam.'" *Myslo*, September 25, 2017. https://myslo.ru/news/tula/2017-09-25-v-tule-poyavilsya-pamyatnik-vezhlivym-lyudyam.

Vikhlyaeva, Marina. "Znachki o Novorossiyske." *Istoricheskie Zapiski* 5 (2007): 163–68.

Vinokurova, Ekaterina, and Elizaveta Surnacheva. "Pritulilsya." *Gazeta.ru*, June 3, 2011. https://www.gazeta.ru/politics/2011/06/03_a_3653545.shtml?updated.

Vishnevskiy, A., ed. *Naselenie Rossii 2006*. Moskva: Izdatel'skiy Dom GU VSHE, 2008.
Volkovskiy, N., ed. *Blokada Leningrada v Dokumentakh Rassekrechennykh Arkhivov*. Moskva: Poligon, 2004.
Von Saldern, Adelheid. "Einleitung: Herrschaft und Repräsentation in DDR-Städten." In *Inszenierte Einigkeit: Herrschaftsrepräsentationen in DDR-Städten*, edited by Adelheid von Saldern, 9–58. Stuttgart: Franz Steiner, 2003.
Walker, Shaun. "Unequal Russia: Is Anger Stirring in the Global Capital of Inequality?" *Guardian*, April 25, 2017. https://www.theguardian.com/inequality/2017/apr/25/unequal-russia-is-anger-stirring-in-the-global-capital-of-inequality.
Ward, Christopher. *Brezhnev's Folly: The Building of BAM and Late Soviet Socialism*. Pittsburgh: University of Pittsburgh Press, 2009.
Weiner, Amir. *Making Sense of War: The Second World War and the Fate of the Bolshevik Revolution*. Princeton, NJ: Princeton University Press, 2001.
Wette, Wolfram, ed. *Stalingrad: Mythos und Wirklichkeit einer Schlacht*. Frankfurt am Main: Fischer Taschenbuch, 2012.
Wood, Elizabeth A. "Performing Memory: Vladimir Putin and the Celebration of World War II in Russia." *Soviet and Post-Soviet Review* 38 (2011): 172–200.
Wulf, Christoph. "Performative Welten: Einführung in die historischen, systematischen und methodischen Dimensionen des Rituals." In *Die Kultur des Rituals: Inszenierungen—Kulturelle Praktiken—Symbole*, edited by Christoph Wulf and Jörg Zirfas, 7–45. München: Fink, 2004.
Yurchak, Alexei. *Everything Was Forever, until It Was No More: The Last Soviet Generation*. Princeton, NJ: Princeton University Press, 2006.
Yurina, Tamara. *Novorossiyskoe Protivostoyanie: 1942–1943 gg*. Krasnodar: Kniga, 2008.
Zaslavsky, Victor. "Čornobyl, Katyn und Gorbačev." In *Das Revolutionsjahr 1989: Die demokratische Revolution in Osteuropa als transnationale Zäsur*, edited by Bernd Florath, 43–55. Göttingen: Vandenhoeck & Ruprecht, 2011.
———. *In geschlossener Gesellschaft: Gleichgewicht und Widerspruch im sowjetischen Alltag*. Berlin: Klaus Wagenbach, 1982.
Zdravomyslova, Elena, and Viktor Voronkov. "The Informal Public in Soviet Society: Double Morality at Work." *Social Research* 69, no. 1 (2002): 49–69.
Zemtsov, Ilya. *Chernenko, the Last Bolshevik: The Soviet Union on the Eve of Perestroika*. New Brunswick: Transaction, 1989.
Zhirnov, Evgeniy. "Komanduyushchego Armiey Predat Sudu." *Vlast'-Kommersant'*, May 9, 2000. http://kommersant.ru/doc/16873.
Zhuk, Sergey. "Religion, 'Westernization,' and Youth in the 'Closed City' of Soviet Ukraine, 1964–84." *Russian Review* 67, no. 4 (2008): 661–79.

Ziemke, Earl, and Magna Bauer. *Moscow to Stalingrad: Decision in the East.* Washington, D.C.: Center of Military History, 1987.

Zubkova, Elena, and Hugh Ragsdale. *Russia after the War: Hopes, Illusions, and Disappointments, 1945–1957.* Armonk: M. E. Sharpe, 1998.

Zubok, Vladislav. *A Failed Empire: The Soviet Union in the Cold War from Stalin to Gorbachev.* Chapel Hill: University of North Carolina Press, 2007.

INDEX

Adzhimushkay Quarry, defense of, 28–29
Ageev, Grigoriy, 61
agricultural industry, in Tula, 101
alcoholism, in USSR, 131, 140n176
All-Union Tours to the Sites of Revolutionary, Military, and Labor Glory: Komsomol at, 1–2, 36, 37, 59; Malaya Zemlya sailor's hat ritual, 166; *pokhody* competitions at, 37; Tula 1985 celebration, 233–35, *234*
Al'tman, Il'ya, 148
Andropov, Yuriy, 118–19, 174, 233
Armageddon of the Revolution, 3, 10n8, 244
Arnold, Sabine, 19
Artem'ev, Maksim, 238
Assmann, Jan, 3, 10n12
atlas: on Great Patriotic War, *38*, 38–39; Tula publication of, 60–61
authoritative discourse, Soviet, 47, 192

Basistyy, Nikolay, 144
Bater, James, 60
Battle of Moscow, 231; Granin on, 105; loss of, 142; Tula in, 104–5, 134n40
Battle of the Caucasus, The (Grechko), 187–88
Battle of Tula anniversary, 103–8
Bednyy, Dem'yan, 17
Beevor, Anthony, 76

Beskozyrka. *See* sailor's hat ritual, at Malaya Zemlya
Billig, Michael, 244
black market trading, 217
blat system: Novorossiysk and, 216–21, 231; in Tula, 77
bombing, of Novorossiysk, 142–43, 177n17
Bonwetsch, Bernd, 23
Borshch', N., 153
Borzenko, Sergey, 201
Bozhenko, Elena: on Hero City, 127–29; in Komsomol, *114*; on official war memory discrepancy, 73–74; on Tula improvements, 131, 139n157; on Victory Day, 71, 73
Bozhok, Galina, 166, 182n100; on Hero City award worthiness, 222; on Malaya Zemlya, 156, 220; on Malaya Zemlya reconstruction, 207; on Novorossiysk poverty, 205
Brandenberger, David, 16, 35
Brandt, Willy, 216
Brest Fortress: Germans' attack of, xviii, 27; Gold Star of, xviii; as Hero Fortress in 1965, 29, *130*; Senyavskaya on Stalin's mistakes in, 27–28; Smirnov on, 28; tourism center at, xviii
Brest Fortress (Smirnov), 28

Brezhnev, Leonid Il'ich, xviii–xix, xix, xx, 2, 131, 184n168, 192; Brunstedt on Stalin reference by, 31, 54n164; censorship by, 32, 53n135; commemorations by, 3, 32, 35; de-Stalinization and, 31; embracing leadership of, 32, 47, 224n36; Gold Star Medal for, 52n119, 108, 232–33; Hero Cities standardization by, 29; on imperialism, 35, 53n123; on Malaya Zemlya commemoration, 159, 171–76; in Malaya Zemlya fighting, 3, 6, 187, 190, 199–201, *200*, 224n47; Malaya Zemlya role exaggeration, 199–201, *200*; memoirs of, 171–72, 185n170; Minsk visit by, 52n118; Murmansk and, xx; Novorossiysk visit by, 193–99, *196*, 221, 223n25; official war memory of, 30–31; sleeping tablets addiction, 54n157, 194; socialist contract of, 4, 45, 199–201, 232; on socialist values, 33–34; Tula visit by, 98–99, 121–25, *124*, 130, 138n122, 138n134; on USSR nuclear first-strike policy, 122; war impact on, 3, 35; on youth patriotism, 33–34; Yunak and, 107–8, 119

Brezhnev era, 7; improved living standards in, 45–46; official war memory simplicity in, 230; population mobilization in, 46; reformism in, 57n216; ritual politics during, 5, 6; Yurchak authoritative discourse in, 47

Brunstedt, Jonathan, 31, 35, 54n164

Bulgakov, Mikhail, 74

Cardona, Euridice Charon, 63
Carlyle, Thomas, 16
Carter, Jimmy, 122
casualties, military underreporting of, 50n63, 90n29
Caucasus, 141, 144, 180n73, 187–88
censorship, by Brezhnev, 32, 53n135
Chernenko, Konstantin, 233
Cherniy, Yuriy, 246
Chernobyl nuclear disaster, 235, 237
Chernyaev, Anatoliy, 122–23

children, in war: deGraffenried on, 62, 92n51, 142; postwar games of, 64–65, 155–58; PTSD of, 142; unexploded ammunition warnings, 100–101; veterans' care by, 76–79, 95n127

Cities of Military Glory, 247–48
Clark, Katerina, 16, 21
class equality, in USSR, 19
Clinton, Bill, 241
collective memory, 10n12
commemorations: by Brezhnev, 3, 32, 35; of Malaya Zemlya, 158–65, 174–76; Stalin and, 3

Commemorative Badges of the Hero-Cities (Goncharuk), 42

commemorative pins, 42–43, *43*
communicative memory, 10n12
communism: Khrushchev promise of, 24; post-Soviet Russian state and, 238–39
Communist Party of the Soviet Union (CPSU), 3–4, 90n10; Khrushchev on war victory by, 25; official war memory of, 23; Stalin and, 31; Tula's defense oath of, 68; utopian future abandonment, 46

consumer items, Hero Cities featured in, 56n189; commemorative pins, 42–43, *43*; matchbox images, 40–42, *41*

CPSU. *See* Communist Party of the Soviet Union

Crimea: Hitler on evacuation of, 150–51; Kerch' in, xix, 28–29, 187–89, 193; Novorossiysk deportation to, 145; Putin on annexation of, 248–49; Sevastopol' in, xvii, 15, 19–21, 28, 58, 142, 248; Tula and Novorossiysk role in, 249

Crimean War, xvii, 15, 20
cultural memory, 10n10, 10n12; of Three Bayonets, 66

Daniel, Yuliy, 97n156
Davis, Vicky, 11n26, 183n132, 246; on Brezhnev's Novorossiysk visit, 193, 198; on Hero Square eternal flame, 151; on Jews in Novorossiysk, 148, 179n56; on

Novorossiysk, 6, 149; on Soviet Pepsi, 215; on youth official war memory, 252
defense industry, in Tula, xix, 66–67, 104, 122–23, 134nn50–52, 238; Dyumin and, 249–50; Ustinov on, 106–7
defitsit, in meat and milk, 113–16, 123, 138n135
deGraffenried, Julie, 62, 92n51, 142
deportation, from Novorossiysk, 146–49, 230; of Grigor'eva, 146; of Gusev, 145; Shcherbakov and, 146
design competition, for memorial construction, 26–27, 62–63, 168–69, 184n154
de-Stalinization: Brezhnev and, 31; of official war memory, 24–25, 51n87
Dnepr-Mafia, Dornberg on, 107–8
Dornberg, John, 107–9
Dorosh, Lyudmila, 180n59; on black market trading, 217; on Brezhnev's Novorossiysk visit, 195–96, 198; on Hero City award worthiness, 221–22; on Malaya Zemlya postwar findings, 156–57; on Novorossiysk mine-clearing, 202–3; on Novorossiysk partisans, 148; on tourism, 219
DOSAAF. *See* Volunteer Society for Cooperation with the Army, Aviation, and Fleet
Dubin, Boris, 70, 240
Dubinin, Timofey, 118
Dudintsev, Vladimir, 51n87
Dudka, Vyacheslav, 239
Dunyasha, Matushka Evdokiya, 65
Dyumin, Alexey, 249–50
Dyuzhev, Boris, 62–63, 66

economy: Great Patriotic War cost in, 2–3, 10n7; heroarchy questions for, 188; heroism link with, 21; Molchanova and Stepuzhin on postwar crisis in, 99–100; Novorossiysk development in, 208, 231; official war memory and, 231–32; reforms in, 101, 102–3; USSR problems in, 131–32
education: patriotic, 36, 38, 55n168, 59, 93n86, 236; of postwar generation, 44–45

Egorov, A., 84
El'kin, Aleksandr, 69
embracing leadership, of Brezhnev, 32, 47
Epishev, Aleksey, 32
Eremenko, Aleksandr, 180n62, 202
Ermakov, Arkadiy, 68
eternal flame, at Novorossiysk Hero Square, 151
Etkind, Alexander, 231
Ewing, E. Thomas, 16

family allegory, for Moscow, 40
family histories, 9; repression in, 74
Five-Year Plans: eighth, 57n217, 98, 113, 136n85; ninth, 108–9, 117, 135n68; tenth, 125, 136n76, 211
forced laborers, in Novorossiysk, 146–47
Ford, Gerald, 215
"Fortress City" (Makhanov), 15
Foucault, Michel, 10n11
freedom of speech, 3
Frey, Bruno, 46

Gabowitsch, Mischa, 50n68, 244
Gallus, Jana, 46
Ganzenmüller, Jörg, 32
Geller, I., 84–85
German Wehrmacht, 142; Brest Fortress attack, xviii, 27; Murmansk siege failure by, xx; official war memory resistance of, 29; Operation Neptune of, 145, 199–200; Tula attack by, 58, 90n21, 132n4
Gladkov, Fedor, 175
Gold Star medal, 30, 56n197; for Brest Fortress, xviii; for Brezhnev, 52n119, 108, 232–33; for Odessa, 29; for Tula, 61, 118
Golikov, Viktor, 6, 208–9, 216, 227n138; on Brezhnev's Novorossiysk visit, 190, 192–94
Goncharuk, Vladimir, 42
Gorbachev, Mikhail, 175, 194; failed coup of, 236; Hero Cities praise by, 235; imperialism criticism by, 235; official war memory reproduction by, 233
Gramsci, Antonio, 54n150, 80

Granin, Mikhail, 105
Great Patriotic War (1941–1945): atlas pages on, *38*, 38–39; Brezhnev impacted by, 3, 35; deaths in, 2, 22, 27, 52n101, 91n49, 99, 134n41, 145, 180, 228n165; economic cost of, 2–3, 10n7; Moscow and first phase of, xviii; national identity as symbol of, 25; Weiner on, 3
Great Victory of the Soviet People (Brezhnev), 53n120, 53n123
Grechko, Andrey, 118, 150; as historian, 187–88; on Novorossiysk Hero City, 188
Grigor'eva, Natal'ya, 153–54, 177n16; deportation of, 146; on Novorossiysk bombing, 142–43; on Novorossiysk reconstruction, 204
Grigor'evich, Yuriy, 184n153
Grossman, Vasily, 22, 76
Groznyy, as City of Military Glory, 248
Gruzdev. Vladimir, 239–40
Guderian, Heinz, 59
Gudkov, Lev, 94n92
Günther, Hans, 15, 219; on heroarchy, 16; on labor heroism, 55n175
Gusev, Sergey, 242
Gusev, Vladimir, 156; on Brezhnev's Novorossiysk visit, 195, 221; deportation of, 145; on Novorossiysk bombing, 142; on Novorossiysk poverty, 205; on Novorossiysk reconstruction, 204; on PTSD of father, 204; on suspicion of prisoners of war, 147

Haumann, Heiko, 55n167
hegemony, Gramsci on, 54n150, 80–81
Hellbeck, Jochen, 48n30
Helsinki Accords, 215
heroarchy, 5, 48n13; economic questions for, 188; Günther on, 16; of individuals and places, 29; material privileges in, 15–16, 104; of Tula and Novorossiysk, 232; Tula Hero City application and, 117
Hero Cities: map of, *xv*. See also *specific Hero City*
Hero-Cities of the Black Sea (Kinelev and Medvedev, V.), 141, 213, 214

Hero Fortress, Brest Fortress as 1965, 29, *130*
heroism: economy linked with, 21; Günther on labor, 55n175; Minkova on, 253; Pospelov on, 26; value and, 221–22
Hero of the Soviet Union, Ageev as, 61
Hero Square, at Novorossiysk, 141; eternal flame at, 151; Post Nomer 1 in, 152–54, *153*; Shostakovich's chimes at, 151; transgenerational unity in, 149–54
hidden inflation, in USSR, 113
Hirsch, Marianne, 8
History of the Great Patriotic War of the Soviet Union 1941–1945, 25–26; Grechko as historian for, 187–88
Hitler, Adolf, 144, 150–51
hooliganism: at Tula Victory Square, 84–85, 93n82, 96n140; of youth, 84–85
housing: campaigns, of Khrushchev era, 50n76, 135n65; of Kotenev, 110–11; of Molchanova, 110, 112; of Neizvestnaya, 112; Novorossiysk problems in, 201–2; Semenov on Novorossiysk shortage in, 210–11; of Stepuzhin, 112; Tula construction of, 108–10, *109*, 135n65, 135n68, 135n73, 135nn75–76, 136n81, 136n83; for veterans, 77; Yunak and Kamaev on Tula's needs for, 108, 136n83

Ideological Commission, rituals of, 36
Immortal Regiment ritual, 243–44
imperialism: Brezhnev on, 35, 53n123; Gorbachev criticism of, 235
infrastructure funding, Tula Obkom on, 103–4, 133n31
Inozemetseva, Mariya, 210, 226n110
Institute of Marxism-Leninism, 26; official war memory support by, 32
interviews: benefits of, 12n35; in Novorossiysk, 8; questions in, 13n41; in Tula, 8. See also *specific respondents*

Jews: Al'tman on, 148; Novorossiysk and murder of, 148, 179n56; Odessa and murder of, xviii; Sevastopol' extinction of, 20
Jones, Jeffrey, 49n39
Jones, Polly, 24

INDEX

Kalinin, Mikhail, 22
Kaltenegger, Roland, 150
Kamaev, Gerontiy, 133n26; on Moscow Railroads, 115; on Tula anniversary rewards, 103; on Tula housing needs, 108, 136n83
Kasamara, Valeria, 251
Kendall, Donald, 215–16
Kerch', xix, 248; Adzhimushkay Quarry defense near, 28–29; as Hero City in 1973, 29, 187–89, 193
Khapaeva, Dina, 251
Kholostyakov, Georgiy: Hero Square eternal flame lighting by, 151; on Malaya Zemlya commemoration, 158–59; on Novorossiysk Hero City, 188, 190
Khramchikhin, Aleksandr, 249
Khrushchev, Nikita, 108, 214; communism promise of, 24; local history promotion by, 28; Secret Speech of, 24–26; socialist contract promotion, 24, 45, 232; Stalin blamed by, 24–25; Tula Order of Lenin award by, 101; Zhukov as ally to, 26
Khrushchev era: housing campaigns of, 50n76, 135n65; Jones, P., on, 24; Thaw in, 24, 27, 105, 235
Kiev: Order of Lenin in 1954 and 1961, 27; prisoners of war, xviii; Red Army River Dnepr crossing, 56n197; Zhukov's retreat from, 27, 52n101
Kinelev, Konstantin, 141, 213, 214
Kirilenko, Yuriy, 118
Kirill, Osovik, 245–46
Kirschenbaum, Lisa, 34
Kolesnik, Aleksandr, 19
Kolesov, Nikolay, 194, 199; on Malaya Zemlya reconstruction, 206; on Novorossiysk destruction, 202
Komsomol youth organization, 85; All-Union Tours of, 1–2, 36, 37, 59; Bozhenko in, *114*; membership decline, 33; oath of, 1–2; patriotic education, 36, 55n168; Tula work brigades hero naming, 126, 139n149
Kondratenko, Nikolay, 238–39
Kosygin, Aleksey, 46, 57n215, 102; Soviet Pepsi and, 215

Kotenev, Vasiliy, 70, *111*; housing of, 110–11; in military preparation camp, *88*, 86–89; reconstruction criticism by, 101; on Tula as Hero City, 107, 128; on Tula improvements, 131; on veterans' benefits, 77; on Victory Square wedding rituals, 79
Kotkin, Stephen, 16
Kotov, Grigoriy, 188
Kudryashov, Sergey, 25
Kunikov, Tsezar': Malaya Zemlya war hero, 154–55, 207; sailor's hat ritual and, 166
Kurilla, Ivan, 244
Kuzio, Taras, 251

labor heroism, Günther on, 55n175
Lenin, Vladimir, 1; monument of, 175, 233; praise of Tula by, 118. *See also* Order of Lenin
Leningrad (Ruble), 5
Leningrad (Saint Petersburg), 14, 187; Bednyy poem on, 17; liberation of, 17; Makhanov on, 15; Order of Lenin in 1957, 27; Popkov speech on, 21–22; resurrection of, 21; Stalin's salute to, xvii
Leningrad Affair, 50n72
Levada, Yuriy, 44
Liberman, Evsey, 102
Life and Fate (Grossman), 22
Little Land. *See* Malaya Zemlya beachhead
living standards, in Brezhnev era, 45–46
local history, Khrushchev promotion of, 28

Maddox, Steve, 21
Makhanov, Aleksandr, 15
Malaya Zemlya (Sokolov), 154–55, 171–72, 199
Malaya Zemlya beachhead, xviii–xix, 7, 28, 178n36, 228n165; Basistyy at, 144; Bozhok on, 156, 220; Brezhnev fighting at, 3, 6, 187, 190, 199–201, *200*, 224n47; Brezhnev on commemoration of, 159, 171–76; Brezhnev's role exaggeration, 199–201, *200*; children playing dangerous games at, 155–58; commemoration of, 158–65; Dorosh on, 156–57; Kholostyakov, Oktyabr'skiy, and Sokolov on commemoration of, 158–59; Kunikov

Malaya Zemlya beachhead (*Cont.*)
  as war hero at, 154–55, 207; monument artistic competition, 168–69, 184n154; sailor's hat ritual at, 165–68, 183n133; Taldykin on penal battalions at, 155, 177n20; Tsigal' monument at, 158–61, *160*, 168–70, *170*, *171*, *173*, *174*
Malinichev, Vasiliy, 101; on meat and milk *defitsit*, 115
Malozemeltsy dream, of Malaya Zemlya, 205–8; Bozhok on, 207; Mikhaylov on, 206–7; Nadykta on, 207; reconstruction fund, 205; Shcherbakov on, 207; Sokolov and Kolesov on, 206
Markowitsch, Hans-Joachim, 94n106
Markwick, Roger, 63
Marridale, Catherina, 22
Martin, Olga, 40
martyrdom, Minkova on, 253
Master and Margarita (Bulgakov), 74
matchbox images, of Hero Cities, 40–41, *41*
material privileges, in heroarchy, 15–16, 104
Matveev, Oleg, 126–27
May 9. *See* Victory Day
Medinskiy, Vladimir, 243
Medunov, Sergey, 174–75, 185n188, 194, 195
Medvedev, Dmitriy, 250
Medvedev, Roy, 172
Medvedev, Vitaliy, 141, 213, *214*
memoirs, of Brezhnev, 171–72, 185n170
memorials: design competition for, 26–27, 62–63, 168–69, 184n154; Novorossiysk landscape of, 175–76; Shelepin's support for, 26; Zhukov's support for, 26. *See also* monuments
memories: collective, 10n12; cultural, 10n10, 10n12, 66; PTSD resurfacing of, 75, 94nn105–6; regional, 23. *See also* official war memory; postmemories
Merridale, Catherine, 22, 23
Mikhaylov, K., 206–7, 211–12
military: casualties underreporting by, 50n63, 90n29; Kotenev in preparation camp of, *88*, 86–89; national budget for, 35; official war memory support by, 32, 216; respect for, 35; response, to Brezhnev's Stalin reference, 31–32; Stalin's purging of leaders, 23; Yeltsin's parade reintroduction, 241
mine-clearing, in Novorossiysk, 202–3, 224n59
Minkova, Yuliya, 253
Minsk: Brezhnev's visit to, 52n118; Order of Lenin, 29–30; partisan activity in, xix
Molchanova, Raisa, 63–64, 91n47, 94n105; housing of, 110, 112; on postwar economic crisis, 99–100; on Tula improvements, 131, 139n167; on Tula Order of Lenin, 107
Molotov-Ribbentrop Pact, 27
monuments, xvii, 52n99; disrepair of, 84, 96n143; Gabowitsch on construction of, 50n68; of Lenin, 175, 233; Moscow construction of, 26, 167, 235; at Novorossiysk, 141; plan for Tula construction of, 91n34; postcards of Novorossiysk, 172; Sevastopol' Crimean War, 15; Shalagina on, 253; Stalin monuments replaced by, 8; Tsigal' Malaya Zemlya, 158–61, *160*, 168–70, *170*, *171*, *174*; Tula Obkom funds for, 62
Moré, Angela, 143
Morozov, Pavlik, 16
Moscow: family allegory for, 40; as Hero Cities patriarch, 43, 235; monument construction in, 26, 167, 235; in Patriotic War against Napoleon, 14; Red Army defense of, 1, 104–5; Russian navy stationing and, 249; as tourist center, 81; war first phase and, xviii. *See also* Battle of Moscow
Moscow Railroads, 114; Yunak and Kamaev on, 115
Moskvicheva, Elena, 246–47
Munich Agreement (1938), 31
Murmansk: Brezhnev and, xx; German siege failure in, xx; Order of the Patriotic War of, 30, 235

Nakykta, N., 207
national identity, as Great Patriotic War symbol, 25

Neizvestnaya, Marina, 63–64, 91n44; on housing, 112; on meat and milk *defitsit*, 113; on Tula improvements, 128; on Tula war destruction, 100–101
Nekrich, Aleksandr, 53n135
Nietzsche, Friedrich, 15
Nixon, Richard, 216
NKVD. *See* People's Commissariat for Internal Affairs
Not by Bread Alone (Dudintsev), 51n87
Novikov, Pyotr, 22
Novikov, Sergey, 154, 242; on Soviet Pepsi, 215
Novorossiysk, 7; blat system and, 216–21, 231; bombing of, 142–43, 177n17; Bozhok on poverty in, 205; Crimea role by, 249; Davis on, 6, 149; deportation in, 145–49, 230; disorganization and mass murder in, 231; economic development of, 208; export port of, 6; forced laborers in, 146–47; half-victory in, 144; Hitlerites in, 145; interviews in, 11n26; liberation of, 150, 252; memorial landscape in, 175–76; monuments at, 141; 1973 Hero City award, 5, 141, 187, 188; occupation in, 145–49, 179n56, 230; Order of the Patriotic War of, 167–68, 187; Ozereyka disaster, 144; partisans in, 145, 148–49, 179n56, 202; patriotic excursions to, 162–65, *163*, *164*; postwar dangerous games in, 155–58; prisoners of war and, 142, 144, 147, 178n33; under Putin regime, 254–57; Russian Navy stationing in, 249; Shiyan on defense of, 143; shortages in, 168–71; Stalingrad compared to, 220; strategic significance of, 5; tourism at, 161–65, 182n123; urban beautification in, 254; war destruction of, 230; Yurina on defense of, 143. *See also* Malaya Zemlya beachhead
Novorossiysk, Brezhnev's love of, 171–75, 186–222; black market trading, 217; Brezhnev statue in, 196–98, *197*; Brezhnev's visit to, 193–99, *196*, 221, 223n25; cement factories in, 199; economic investment program in, 231; future of, 208–12; Hero City celebrations in, 189–93, *191*; Hero City decision, 187–89; heroism value and, 221–22; housing development in, 210; jokes about, 219–20; Malozemeltsy dream, 205–8; port in, 199, 208; postwar wounds, 201–5; socialist contract and, 199–201; Soviet Pepsi and, 212–16, 228n142; special development programs in, 193; water supply development, 209

occupation, in Novorossiysk, 145–46, 230; enemy collaboration in, 149; Germans' relations in, 147–48; Jews and partisans target of, 148, 179n56; Ostroverkhov and, 149; of Shtirts, 147; starvation in, 148
October Revolution, 1, 29, 36
Odessa, 6, 162, 213, 222, 249; Gold Star medal of, 29; Jews murdered at, xviii; Sevastopol' link with, 20; Stalin salute to, xvii; tourism center at, xviii, 81
official war memory, 7–9, 10n9, 35–36; Bozhenko on discrepancy in, 73–74; Brezhnev's death impact on, 233; Brezhnev on, 30–31, 34; commercial commodity of, 244; of CPSU, 23; de-Stalinization of, 24–25, 51n87; dissolution of, 232–36; economization of, 231–32; generational conflict and, 4; Gorbachev's reproduction of, 233; Grossman's contradiction of, 76; Institute of Marxism-Leninism support of, 32; life experiences disconnect, 43–44; as military expenditures justification, 216; military support of, 32; pluralism of, 23; under Putin regime, 243–47; Russia and idealization of, 251; Shalagina on rebirth of, 253; Shcheglov on rebirth of, 253–54; Stalin's centralization of, 23; transgression punishment for, 80; Tula media on, 81; Wehrmacht resistance in, 29; women marginal position in, 63; Zhukov and Smirnov's influence on, 29
Oktyabr'skiy, Filipp, 158–59
Operation Barbarossa, xviii
Operation Neptune, of German Wehrmacht, 145, 199–200
Operation Typhoon, in Tula, 58, 105, 134n40

Order of Lenin, 56n197; Khrushchev Tula award of, 101; Kiev 1954 and 1961, 27; Leningrad 1957, 27; Minsk, 29–30; for Murmansk, 235; for Smolensk, 235; for Tula, 61, 104, 105, 106, 107, 108; for Volnyanskiy, 61

Order of the Patriotic War: of Murmansk, 30, 235; of Novorossiysk, 167–68, 187; of Ostroverkhov, 149; of Smolensk, 30, 104, 235

Order of Victory, of Brezhnev, 172, 233

Orthodox Church, post-Soviet Russian state and, 65, 244–45

Ostapenko, Elena, 166

Ostroverkhov, Stepan, 149

Ozereyka, Yuzhnaya, 144

Paramonova, Irina, 66, 131, 242; on post-Soviet Russian state impact on Tula, 237

partisans, 29, 39, 47n6, 52n101, 248; Minsk activity by, xix; in Novorossiysk, 145, 148–49, 179n56, 202; in Tula, 58, 64, 91n49

Pasternak, Boris, 22

Pastukhov, Viktor, 118

patriotic education, 38, 93n86; of Komsomol, 36, 55n168; official war memory collapse and, 236; rituals of, 36; in Tula, 59

patriotic tourism, 37, 40, 55n174

Patriotic War against Napoleon (1812): Moscow fight in, 14

penal battalions, at Malaya Zemlya, 155, 177n20

pensioners: post-Soviet Russian state and benefits for, 254–55; Tula Hero City application and, 117

People's Commissariat for Internal Affairs (NKVD), soldiers execution by, 18

Pilkington, Hilary, 33

Pipiya, Karina, 252

pluralism, of official war memory, 23

Podyma, Konstantin: on Novorossiysk reconstruction, 202; Yurina on, 165–66, 183n132

pokhody competitions, patriotic tourism and, 37, 40, 55n174

Poland, 251, 260n97

Polyakov, Eduard, 195

Popkov, Petr, 21–22

population: Brezhnev-era mobilization in, 46; Novorossiysk growth in, 204, 210; in Tula 1926–2019, *102*

Pospelov, Petr: on heroism, 26; Secret Speech preparation by, 26; on Zhukov and Kiev, 27, 52n101

postcards: of Brezhnev's Tula visit, *124*; of Novorossiysk monuments, 172; in Tula, 81–84, *82*, *83*; Victory Square on, 83–84, *83*

postmemories: Hirsch on, 8; resurfacing of, 75, 94nn105–6

Post Nomer 1: in Novorossiysk, 152–54, *153*; Russians' reengagement of, 252; in Tula, 85–89, *86*, *87*, 96n148, 97n152

post-Soviet Russian state: chaos of, 236–40; communism and, 238–39; defense budget reduction, 238; Orthodox Church and, 65, 244–45; prestige projects of, 255–56; social differentiation in, 254–55; socialist contract disbanding, 238; tourism reduction in, 238; victory idealization and, 251; Yeltsin and, 236–41; youth official war memory and, 252, 252–54

post-traumatic stress disorder (PTSD): of children of war, 142; of Gusev's father, 204; memories resurfacing in, 75, 94nn105–6; Senyavskaya on, 50n70

postwar generation: children's games of, 64–65, 155–58; education of, 44–45; social mobility and, 47; on Victory Day, 70–71; youth fear, 44

postwar wounds, in Novorossiysk: cement factories reconstruction, 203; housing problem, 201–2; lack of workers in, 203–4; mine-clearing, 202–3, 224n59; population, 204; poverty, 204–5; reconstruction efforts, 204

poverty: Novorossiysk postwar wounds of, 204–5; overcoming symbolic, 240–43

Presidium of the Supreme Soviet, 56n197; defenders medals by, 20

prisoners of war, 27, 52n101, 203; in Kiev and Smolensk, xix; Novorossiysk and, 142, 144, 147, 178n33; Stalin suspicion of, 147
priyaniki, in Tula, 115–16, 137n98, 139n167
PTSD. *See* post-traumatic stress disorder
public suppression, of veterans, 76–77
Putin, Vladimir: on Crimea annexation, 248–49; on de-Sovietization, 256; patriotic symbols creation by, 242–43; power recentralization by, 239; Sevastopol' annexation of, xvii; social integration under, 9; on Stalin, 250; on veterans, 242
Putin regime: Hero Cities return under, 247–50; modernization in, 240; new Hero Cities category, 247; official war memory under, 243–47; re-Brezhnevization and, 250–54; Tula and Novorossiysk under, 254–57

Qualls, Karl, 21, 59, 205

Razumovskiy, Georgiy, 174–75
re-Brezhnevization, Putin regime and, 250–54
reconstruction: Hero cities as symbols of, 21; Kotenev's criticism of, 101; in Malaya Zemlya, 206–8; in Novorossiysk, 202–4; Tula economic, 99; veterans' pension removal and, 23–24, 50n74
Red Army: Kiev River Dnepr crossing by, 56n196; Kolesnik's description of, 19; Moscow defended by, 1, 104–5; Odessa retaking by, xviii; Smolensk retaking by, xix; in Stalingrad, 18–19; tanks loss, 142
reformism, in Brezhnev era, 57n216
regional memories, 23
re-heroization, Epishev on youth and, 32
rituals, xviii, 11n17; awarding orders in, 30; Brezhnev-era politics, 5, 6; Haumann on, 55n167; of Ideological Commission, 36; Immortal Regiment, 243–44; interviewees on, 8; Kertzer and Wulf on, 55n178; Malaya Zemlya sailor's hat, 165–68, 183n133; of patriotic education, 36; transgenerational unity from, 36–37; Tula wedding, 79–81

Romanov, Vladimir, 70, 96n130, 114, 126–27; on Tula improvements, 128, 130–31
Ruble, Blair A., 5
Ruffley, David, 45
Russian Navy stationing, 249

sailor's hat ritual, at Malaya Zemlya, 165–68, 183n133
Saint Petersburg. *See* Leningrad
SALT I and SALT II treaties, 215
Sarasin, Philipp, 10n11
sausage train, Tula and, 113–15, 128, 137n92
Schooner of Peers. See *Shkhuna Rovesnikov*
Second Panzer Army, Guderian of, 59
Secret Speech, of Khrushchev, 24–26
Semenov, Yuriy: on Novorossiysk housing shortage, 210–11; on Soviet Pepsi, 215
Semichastnyy, Vladimir, 31–32
Senyavskaya, Elena: on PTSD, 50n70; on Stalin's mistakes at Brest Fortress, 27–28; on veterans, 22
Sevastopol', 248; Crimean War monument in, 15; defense length in, 19–20; fall of, 28, 142; Jews' extinction in, 20; Odessa's link with, 20; Putin annexation of, xvii; Qualls study of, 21, 58
Seventh All-Russian Congress of Soviets, Workers, Peasants, Cossacks, and Red Army Deputies, 14
Shalagina, Lyudmila, 169, 184n156, 253
Shapoval, Kseniya, 155
Shcheglov, Viktor, 94n97, 94n99; on Brezhnev's Tula visit, 121; on official war memory rebirth, 253–54; on veterans' disappointments, 100
Shcherbakov, Georgiy, 156, 166–67, 179n43, 219, 220–21, 255; on Malaya Zemlya reconstruction, 207; Novorossiysk deportation of, 146
Shelepin, Aleksandr, 31, 187; memorials support by, 26
Shiyan, Ivan, 148, 149; on Novorossiysk defense, 143; on Novorossiysk liberation, 150
Shkhuna Rovesnikov (Schooner of Peers) literary club, 165

Shlapentokh, Vladimir, 44
Shostakovich, Dmitriy, 151
Shoygu, Sergey, 249
Shtirts, Klotilda: occupation of, 147
Sinyavskiy, Andrei, 97n156
Smirnov, Sergey, 28, 158
Smolensk: monument in 1812, 15; Order of the Patriotic War of, 30, 104, 235; prisoners in, xix; Red Army retaking of, xix
Sobolev, Leonid, 20
social differentiation, in post-Soviet Russian state, 254–55
socialism: individual reward and, 16; Khrushchev's return to, 24; Stalinist cult and, 25
socialist contract, 7; of Brezhnev, 4, 45, 199–201, 232; disbanding of, 238; of Khrushchev, 24, 45, 232; Novorossiysk and, 199–201; Tula and, 117, 125–27; veterans and, 77
socialist Übermensch, Günther on, 15
socialist values, 16; Brezhnev on, 33–34
social mobility, postwar generation and, 47
Society for the Promotion of Defense, Aviation, and Chemical Industry: Novorossiysk mine-clearing effort by, 202
Sokolov, Georgiy, 154–55, 171–72; on Malaya Zemlya commemoration, 158–59; on Malaya Zemlya reconstruction, 206
Sorokin, Viktor, 44
Sorokina, Anna, 251
Soviet Pepsi, in Novorossiysk, 212–16, 228n142
Stalin, Joseph, xvii; commemoration and, 3; death and realignments, 24; dominant war narrative of, 23–24; Hero Cities pronouncement from, 20–21; Hero Cities ties to, 22; Khrushchev's blame of, 24–25; Medvedev, D., on, 250; mistakes, discussion on, 27; purging of military leaders by, 23; Putin on, 250; war heroes' pensions and privileges withdrawal, 23; war memory centralization by, 23; war monuments replacement of, 8; war weakness of, 22

Stalingrad (Volgograd), xvii, 15, 187; attack on, 142; fighting idealization in, 18–19; Hellbeck on executions in, 48n30; hero depiction of, 17–18; Novorossiysk compared to, 220; resurrection of, 21; Stalin salute to, xvii, 21
Stalinist cult: Gunther on, 15; socialism and, 25
Stalinist heroes, 15; Clark on, 16, 21
Starodubtsev, Vasiliy, 238–39
state-sponsored values, 3, 21
Stepunin, Evgeniy, 63, 74, 80, 91n46, 181n76; on Brezhnev's Tula visit, 121; on Tula Hero City, 129; on Tula war destruction, 100; on wedding rituals, 79
Stepuzhin, Sergey, 74, 80–81, 93n81, 241; housing of, 112; on postwar economic crisis, 99–100; on Tula breadlines, 102
Stories of Untold Heroes (Smirnov), 28
strategic significance, of Tula and Novorossiysk, 5
suffering and death metaphors, 17
Sviderskiy, Valentin, 146–47, 148, 188; on Hero City award worthiness, 222
Sviderskiy, Valeriy, 146–47, 179n45, 188, 255
Sycheva, Irina: on decade of 1990s, 241; on Dunyasha, 65; on postwar children's games, 64; on Tula breadlines, 102; on Tula Hero City, 129

Taldykin, Roman, 155
teaching: atlas map, 38, 38–39; patriotic education, 36, 38, 55n168, 59, 93n86, 236
Thaw, in Khrushchev era, 24, 27, 105, 235
Three Bayonets landmark, at Tula Victory Square, 58, 91n35; Dyuzhev as sculptor of, 62–63, 66; funds for, 62; mystery of, 66–69; Paramonova on design changes to, 66; Qualls on, 59; woman's removal from, 62–63; Zaytsev on, 59, 60
Tieke, Wilhelm, 150
Timurov movement, for veterans' care, 78
Tkachev, Aleksandr, 240
tourism: Dorosh on, 219; Moscow as center for, 81; patriotic, *pokhody* competitions

and, 37, 40, 55n174; post-Soviet Russian state reduction in, 238
tourism center: of Brest Fortress, xviii; at Novorossiysk, 161–65, 182n123; of Odessa, xviii, 81
transgenerational unity, 4, 32–35; in Novorossiysk Hero Square, 149–54; re-Brezhnevization and, 252; from rituals, 36–37; veterans and, 77
Trotsky, Leo, 15
Tsaritsyn. *See* Stalingrad
Tsement (Gladkov), 175
Tsigal', Vladimir, 158–61, 168–70, 173, 175, 184n158; pictures of, *160, 170, 171, 174*
Tsymbal, Sergey, 182n105, 205, 218–19; on Hero City award worthiness, 222
Tula: agricultural industry in, 101; All-Union Tours in 1985, 233–35, *234*; atlas publication on, 60–61; in Battle of Moscow, 104–5, 134n40; in blat system, 77; Bozhenko on improvements in, 131, 139n157; Brezhnev's visit to, 98–99, 121–25, *124*, 130, 138n122, 138n134; children's care of veterans, 76–79, 95n127; Communists' defense oath, 68; Crimea role by, 249; defense industry in, xix, 66–67, 104, 106–7, 122–23, 134nn50–52, 238, 249–50; El'kin on, 69; Ermakov's defense of, 68; German Wehrmacht attack on, 58, 90n21, 132n4; for Gold Star medal, 61, 118; Grossman on, 76; Hero City application, 116–21, *119, 120*; housing needs, 108–10, *109*, 135n65, 135n68, 135n73, 135nn75–76, 136n81, 136n83; Khrushchev's reforms and, 101; Lenin's praise of, 118; looting and chaos in, 231; meat and milk *defitsit* in, 113–16, 123, 138n135; media on official war memory, 81; memorial competition in, 62–63; 1976 award, 5; Operation Typhoon in, 58, 105, 134n40; Order of Lenin for, 61, 104, 105, 106, 107, 108; partisans in, 58, 64, 91n49; patriotic education in, 59; population 1926–2019, 102; postcards in, 81–84, *82, 83*; Post Nomer 1 in, 85–90, *86, 87*, 96n148, 97n152; post-Soviet state impact on, 237–38; postwar economic crisis, 99;

priyaniki, 115–16, 137n98, 139n167; under Putin regime, 254–57; sausage train, 113–15, 128, 137n92; socialist contract negotiation in, 117, 125–27; strategic significance of, 5; urban beautification in, 254; veterans' narratives on, 73–76; Victory Day in, 69–73; Volnyanskiy and Ageev war heroes, 61; war limited damage in, 230; war turning point in, 5; weapon production in, 5–6; wedding rituals in, 79–81; women in sculptures in, 63; work brigades hero naming, 126; workers' readiness in, *119*, 119–21, *120*; workers' regiment at, 61–62, 90n26; Yunak and Hero City application, 117–18; Yunak on anniversary rewards in, 103, 104; Zhavoronkov's defense of, 68. *See also* Victory Square, at Tula
Tula Obkom: on anniversary rewards, 103; on economic reforms, 102; on infrastructure funding, 103–4, 133n31; on monument disrepair, 84; on monument funds, 62; Order of Lenin lobbying, 108; Victory Day preparation by, 59–60; on water supply, 110
Tumarkin, Nina, 34, 93n84, 241
Tyshenko, V., 180n62

Ukraine, 251; Novorossiysk deportation to, 145
unexploded ammunition warnings, to children, 100–101
Union of Soviet Socialist Republic (USSR), 1, 3, 226n109; agricultural failures, 101; alcoholism in, 131, 140n176; Brezhnev on nuclear first-strike policy of, 122; class equality in, 19; hidden inflation in, 113; social and economic problems in, 131–32; Zaslavsky's opinion polls in, 13n40
Ustinov, Dmitriy, 105, 106–7, 118
utopian future, CPSU abandonment of, 46

values: socialist, 16, 33–34; state-sponsored, 3, 21; of war cult, 9
Varga-Harris, Christine, 4, 46, 117

veterans, 28, 95n116; children's care of, 76–79, 95n127; housing for, 77; Kotenev on benefits of, 77; living conditions and medical situations of, 77–78, 100; public suppression of, 76–77; Putin and, 242; reconstruction and pension removal for, 23–24, 50n74; Senyavskaya on, 22; Shcheglov on disappointment of, 100; socialist contract and, 77; transgenerational unity and, 77; Tula narratives of, 73–76; Victory Day participation, 71–72; Weiner on, 22–23; Zhukov on pensions to, 26

Victory Day (May 9), xviii, 20, 23, 36; Bozhenko on, 71, 73; Brezhnev on official war memory, 34; celebration activities of, 70–71; Dubin on, 70, 240; Kotenev and Romanov on, 70; postwar generation on, 70–71; in Tula, 69–73, 245; Tula Obkom preparation for, 59; veterans' participation in, 71–72

Victory Square, at Tula, 7, 58–90; Bater and von Saldern on, 60; disrepair and hooliganism at, 84–85, 93n82, 96n140; financing of, 67; Geller on disrepair of, 84–85; Great Patriotic War, Revolution of 1917, and Kremlin in, 61; groundwork for, 67; hero recognition at, 61; opening ceremony of, 68–69; on postcards, 81–84, *83*; Three Bayonets landmark at, 58, 59, 62–69, 91n35; wedding rituals and, 79–81

Volgograd. *See* Stalingrad

Volnyanskiy, Grigoriy, 61

Volunteer Society for Cooperation with the Army, Aviation, and Fleet (DOSAAF), 36

von Saldern, Adelheid, 60

Vorob'ev, Georgiy, 159

Vorotnikov, Vitaliy, 176, 185n188

war cult: climax after 1965, 2; decline after Brezhnev's death, 9; Putin's revival of, 242; Russia's new, 253; values of, 9

war memory. *See* official war memory

water supply, Tula Obkom on, 110

wedding rituals, in Tula, 79–81

Weiner, Amir, 3, 22–23

Western influences, on youth, 33

women: Dunyasha's Tula prophecy, 64–65; marginal position in official war memory of, 63; sexual violence against, 64; Three Bayonets removal of, 62–63; Tula sculptures of, 63

workers: Novorossiysk lack of, 203–4; readiness, in Tula, *119*, 119–21, *120*; regiment, at Tula, 61–62, 90n26

worthiness, of Hero Cities, 7, 221–22

Yanukovich, Viktor, 249

Yeltsin, Boris: military parade reintroduction by, 241; post-Soviet Russian state and, 236–41; Victory Day parade abolished by, 240

youth: Brezhnev on patriotism of, 33–34; Davis on official war memory of, 252; Epishev on re-heroization and, 32; hooliganism of, 84–85; *pokhody* tourism and competition for, 37, 55n174; postwar generation fear of, 44; Russia official war memory, 252, 252–54; *Shkhuna Rovesnikov* newspaper production, 165; Tula Hero City application and, 117; Western influences on, 33; Zinchenko on disorientation of, 33. *See also* Komsomol youth organization

Yunak, Ivan, 62, 99, 101, 129; Andropov's connection to, 118–19; Brezhnev and, 107–8, 119; economic reforms and, 102–3; on housing needs, 108, 136n83; on Moscow Railroads, 115; on Tula anniversary rewards, 103, 104; Tula Hero City application and, 117–18

Yurchak, Alexei, 5, 47, 192

Yurchikov, Vladimir, 74–75, 94n103, 128, 134n52

Yurina, Tamara, 151, 181n80, 221, 242; on Hero City award worthiness, 222; on Malaya Zemlya reconstruction, 207–8; on Novorossiysk defense, 143; on Novorossiysk Hero City celebration, 189–90; on Podyma, 165–66, 183n132; on Soviet Pepsi, 216

Zaslavsky, Viktor, 13n40
Zaytsev, Aleksey, 59, 60
Zhavoronkov, Vasiliy, 68, 82, 92n67, 118–19
Zhukov, Georgiy, 23; as Khrushchev's ally, 26; Kiev retreat and, 27, 52n101; memorial support by, 26; official war memory influenced by, 29; Tula Hero City application and, 118; on veterans' pensions, 26
Zhurkin, Yuriy, 149, 203
Zimenkov, Ivan, 21
Zinchenko, Oleg, 33

IVO MIJNSSEN is the Central and Eastern Europe correspondent of the German language newspaper *Neue Zürcher Zeitung* in Vienna. He holds a PhD from the University of Basel and has studied at Brown as well as Stanford. He is author of *Back to Our Future! History, Modernity, and Patriotism according to Nashi, 2005–2013*.

www.ingramcontent.com/pod-product-compliance
Lightning Source LLC
Chambersburg PA
CBHW030434300426
44112CB00009B/993